I0752983

HISTORIC PHOTOS OF AUSTIN

TEXT AND CAPTIONS BY MARSIA HART REESE

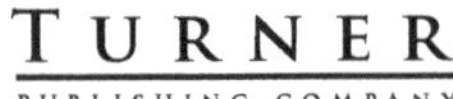

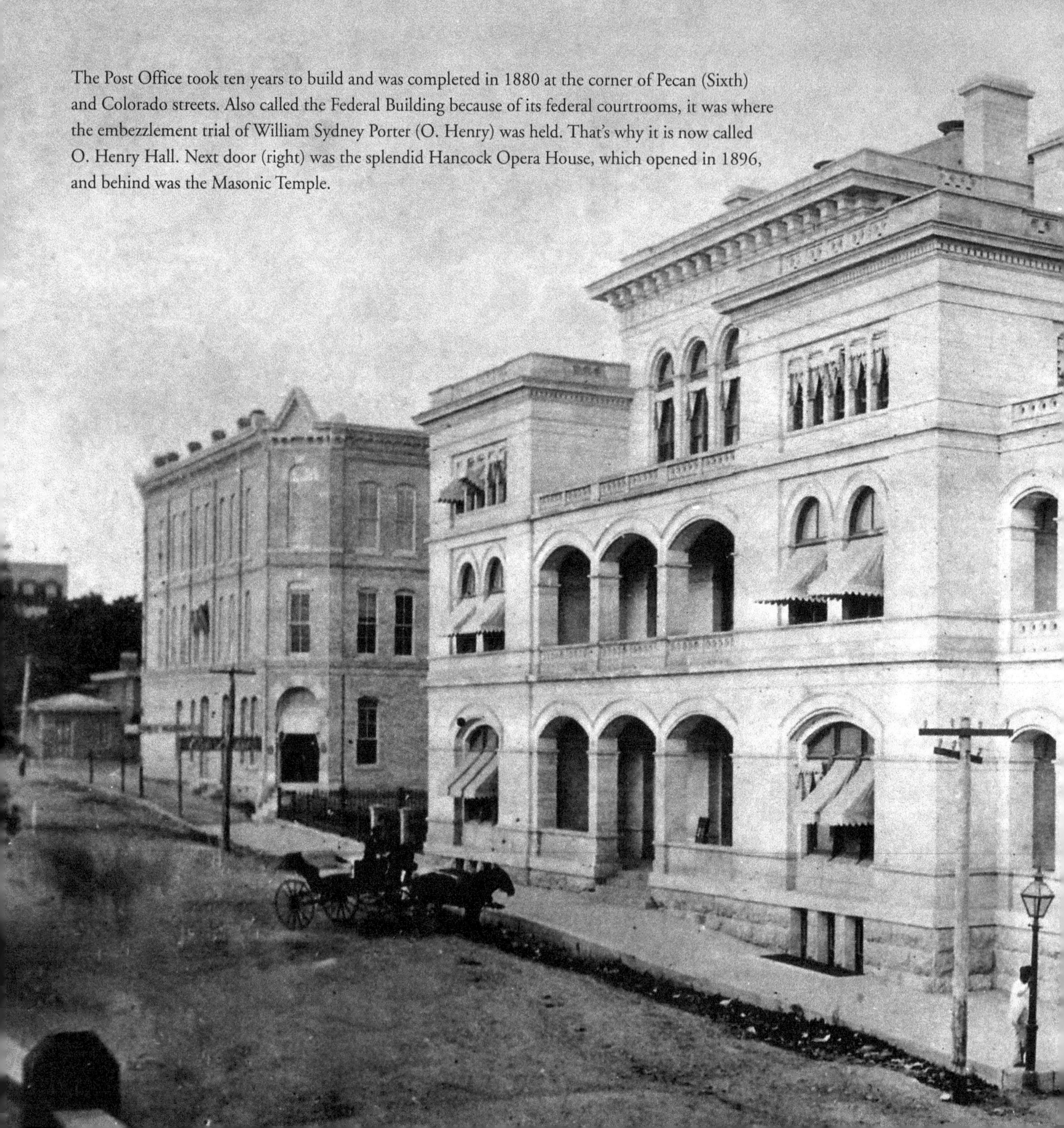

The Post Office took ten years to build and was completed in 1880 at the corner of Pecan (Sixth) and Colorado streets. Also called the Federal Building because of its federal courtrooms, it was where the embezzlement trial of William Sydney Porter (O. Henry) was held. That's why it is now called O. Henry Hall. Next door (right) was the splendid Hancock Opera House, which opened in 1896, and behind was the Masonic Temple.

HISTORIC PHOTOS OF AUSTIN

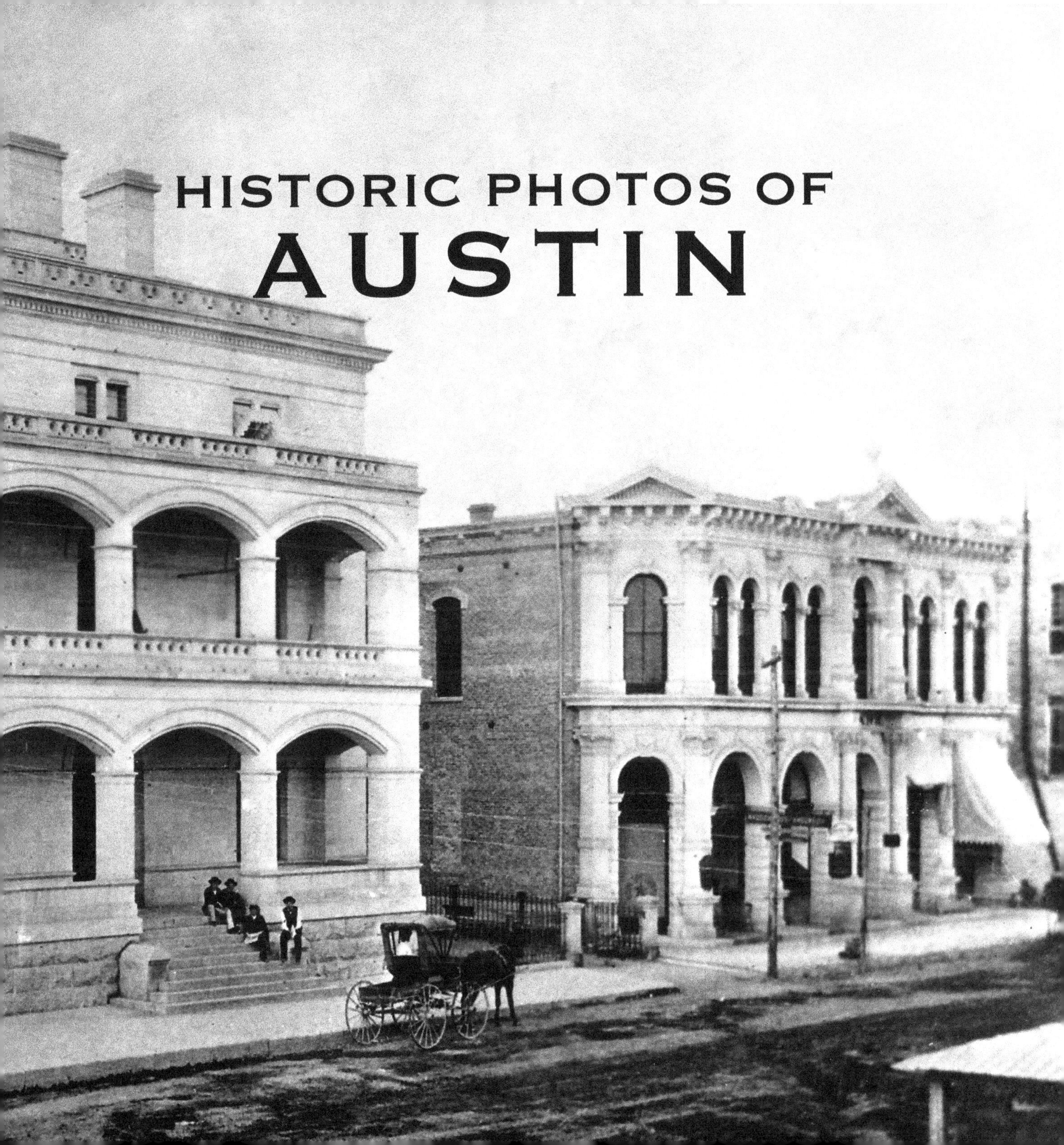

Turner Publishing Company
www.turnerpublishing.com

Historic Photos of Austin

Library of Congress Control Number: 2006929280

ISBN-13: 978-1-59652-295-4

ISBN 978-1-68336-921-9 (hc)

Contents

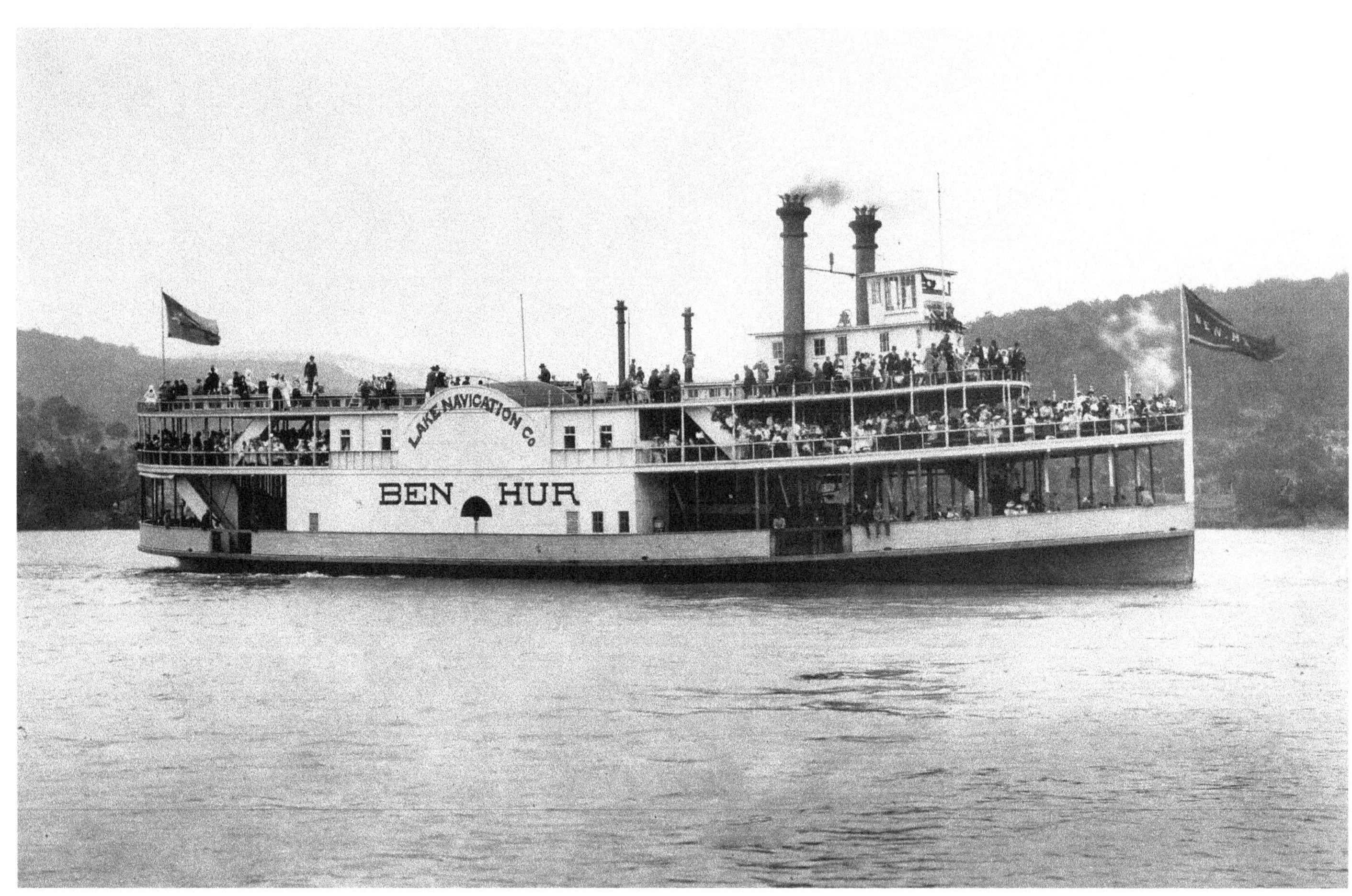

After the Austin Dam was built, creating Lake McDonald, Austinites and visitors enjoyed many a ride on the lake aboard the *Ben Hur*, a pleasure-cruise steamboat. For 50¢, one could take a tour that lasted more than three hours, and dances were frequently held on the decks after sundown. The *Ben Hur* was literally grounded during the flood of 1900.

ACKNOWLEDGMENTS

This volume, *Historic Photos of Austin*, is the result of the cooperation and efforts of many individuals, organizations, institutions, and corporations. It is with great thanks that we acknowledge the valuable contribution of the following for their generous support:

Austin History Center
Library of Congress
Lyndon Baines Johnson Library and Museum
Texas State Library and Archives Commission

We would also like to thank the following individuals for their valuable contributions and assistance in making this work possible:

Marsia Hart Reese, Writer and Editor
John Anderson, Archives and Information Services, Texas State Library

Preface

Austin has thousands of historic photographs that reside in archives, both locally and nationally. This book began with the observation that, while those photographs are of great interest to many, they are not easily accessible. During a time when Austin is looking ahead and evaluating its future course, many people are asking, How do we treat the past? These decisions affect every aspect of the city—architecture, public spaces, commerce, and infrastructure—and these, in turn, affect the way that people live their lives. This book seeks to provide easy access to a valuable, objective look into the history of Austin.

The power of photographs is that they are less subjective than words in their treatment of history. Although the photographer can make decisions regarding subject matter and how to capture and present it, photographs do not provide the breadth of interpretation that text does. For this reason, they offer an original, untainted perspective that allows the viewer to interpret and observe.

This project represents countless hours of review and research. The researchers and writer have reviewed thousands of photographs in numerous archives. We greatly appreciate the generous assistance of the individuals and organizations listed in the acknowledgments of this work, without whom this project could not have been completed.

The goal in publishing this work is to provide broader access to this set of extraordinary photographs that seek to inspire, provide perspective, and evoke insight that might assist people who are responsible for determining Austin's future. In addition, the book seeks to preserve the past with adequate respect and reverence.

With the exception of touching up imperfections that have accrued with the passage of time and cropping where necessary, no other changes have been made. The focus and clarity of many images is limited to the technology and the ability of the photographer at the time they were taken.

The work is divided into eras. Beginning with some of the earliest known photographs of Austin, the first section records photographs from before the Civil War through the end of the nineteenth century. The second section spans the beginning of the twentieth century through World War I. Section three moves from World War I to World War II. The last section covers from World War II to the 1970s.

In each of these sections we have made an effort to capture various aspects of life through our selection of photographs. People, commerce, transportation, infrastructure, religious institutions, and educational institutions have been included to provide a broad perspective.

We encourage readers to reflect as they go walking in Austin, strolling through the city, its parks, and its neighborhoods. It is the publisher's hope that in utilizing this work, longtime residents will learn something new and that new residents will gain a perspective on where Austin has been, so that each can contribute to its future.

—Todd Bottorff, Publisher

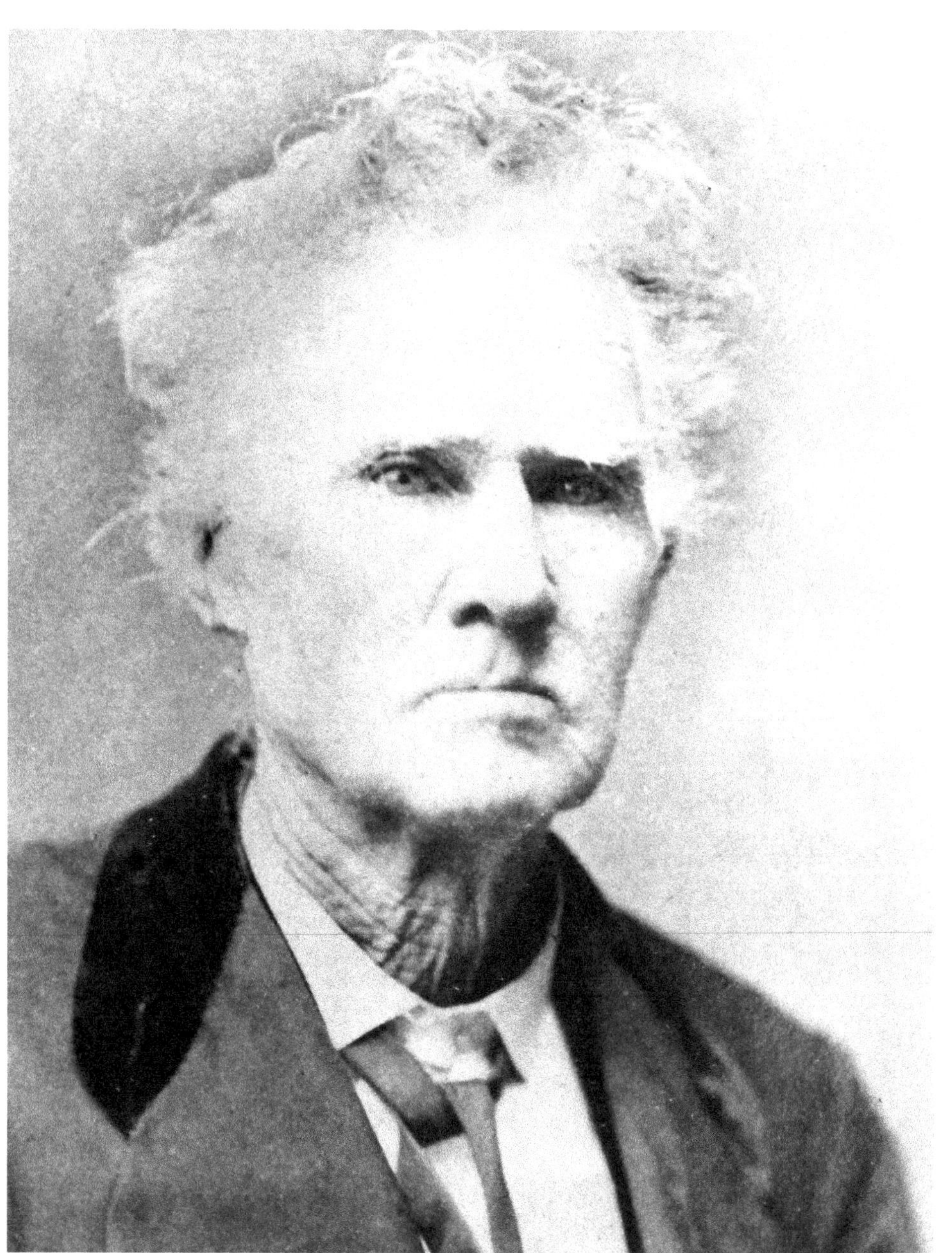

Judge Edwin Waller planned the layout of Austin in 1839, at the request of his friend Mirabeau B. Lamar, president of the Republic of Texas. Waller had signed the Texas Declaration of Independence and became Austin's first mayor. He named north-south streets for Texas rivers and east-west streets for Texas trees.

An Auspicious Location

(1838–1899)

The land that would become Austin was nestled among slopes of the Central Texas Hill Country on the banks of Texas' Colorado River. Mirabeau B. Lamar, president of the new Republic of Texas, encountered the area in 1838 while buffalo hunting. On the riverbank was the tiny settlement of Waterloo, soon renamed Austin to honor Stephen F. Austin, who had brought the first settlers to Texas in the 1820s. In 1839, Lamar's friend Edwin Waller laid out the city and began construction, naming north-south streets for Texas rivers and east-west streets for Texas trees.

After struggles over the capital's location (Sam Houston called the area "the most unfortunate site upon earth for the Seat of Government"), Austin became the temporary capital in 1845 when Texas joined the United States. In 1872, another statewide election established Austin as the permanent capital.

Although most Austinites opposed secession from the Union, the majority of Texas voters supported it. The Austin Light Infantry Company was formed in 1861, as was the Ladies' Needle Battalion (which sewed uniforms for Confederate volunteers). In 1864, hundreds of Austinites assembled for the funeral of General Tom Green, and the next year, news of the Emancipation Proclamation finally reached town. Union troops occupied Austin in 1865. Freed African Americans opened the Freedmen's Bureau School in 1868, the first school for black children. A pontoon bridge across the Colorado was completed in 1869 but washed away within a year. The *Democratic Statesman,* forerunner of today's major local newspaper, published its first issue in 1871, and on Christmas Day the Houston and Texas Central Railroad completed the first railway to the capital city, igniting an economic boom.

The 1880s saw many signs of growth: the opening of the University of Texas, the first telephone, a public hospital, a permanent bridge across the Colorado, the Driskill Hotel. The capitol building burned in 1881, but by 1888 a splendid pink granite capitol had replaced it. During the bustling 1890s Austin enjoyed its first dam and electric utility system, national banks, electric streetcars, the first residential subdivision (Hyde Park), the Hancock Opera House, and 31 "moonlight towers" to illuminate streets. Austinite William Sydney Porter (O. Henry) published a newspaper called *The Rolling Stone,* and football became a competitive sport at the university.

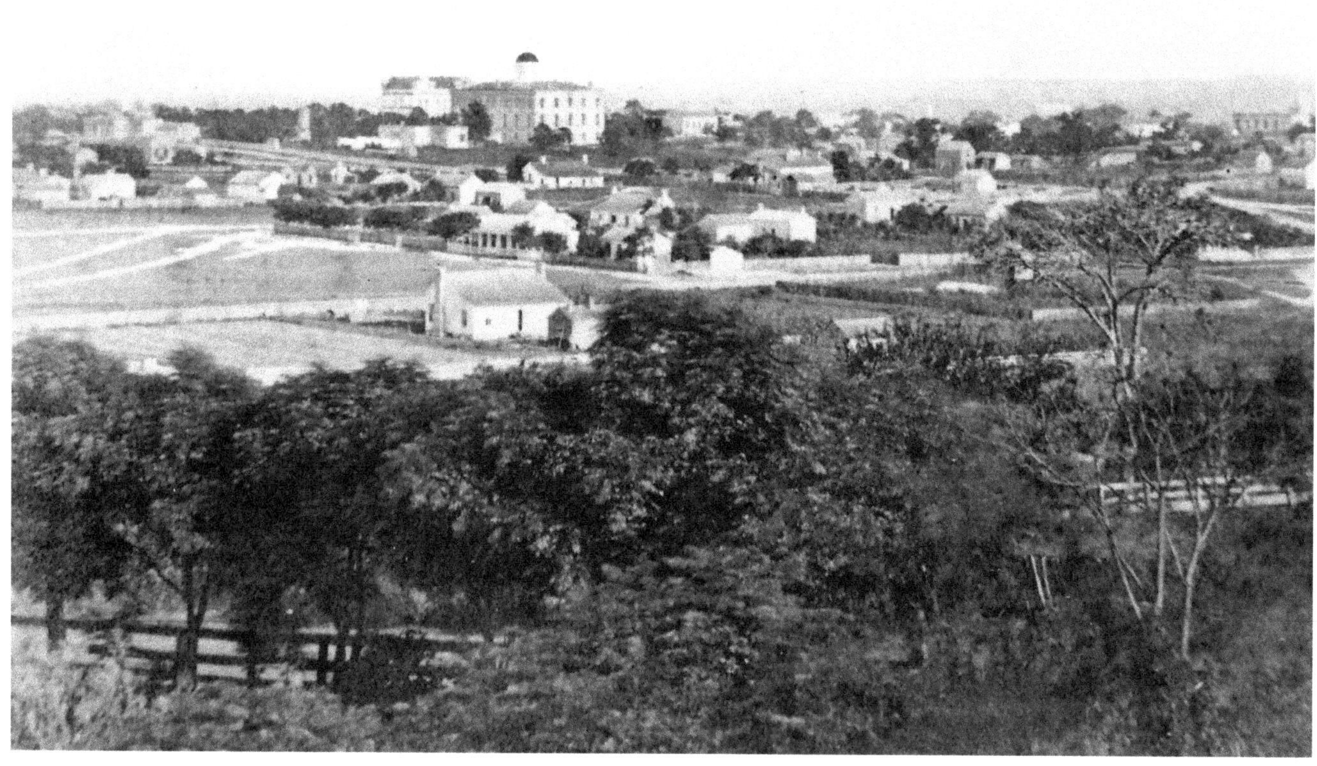

This view of Austin from the east shows the first "permanent" capitol building, completed in 1853, its height and dome setting it apart. The building's architectural style was a variation of Greek Revival. Previous capitols had been first a log cabin and then a simple frame structure. The photograph was taken by H. B. Hillyer, a professional photographer.

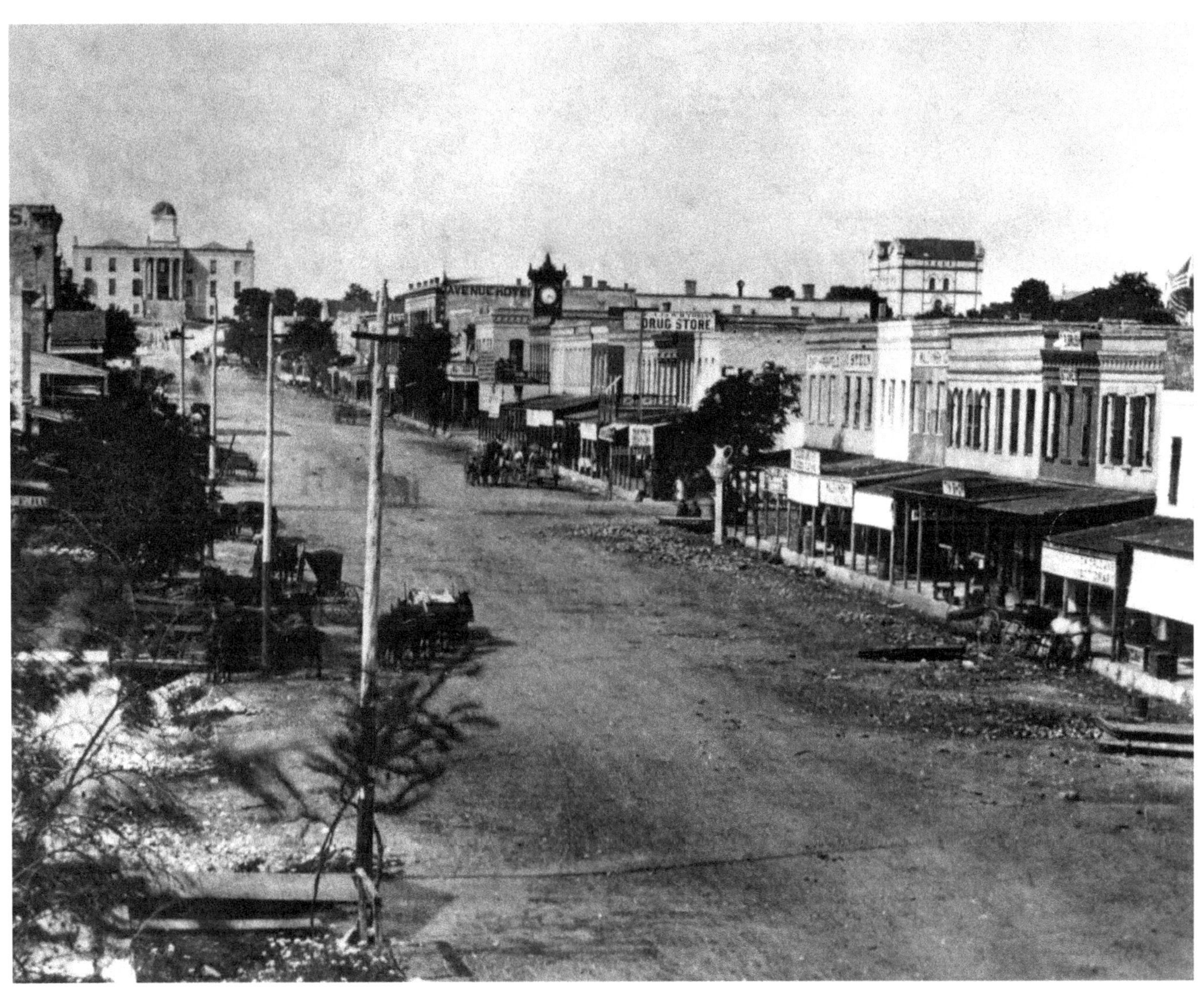

This view shows the 1853 Texas Capitol at the head of Congress Avenue in the early 1870s. By this time, some people were criticizing the statehouse as lacking distinction. Private businesses and government buildings with limestone and brick facades lined "the Avenue," along with saloons such as the Iron Front. This capitol burned in 1881, and plans soon began for building a bigger and better one.

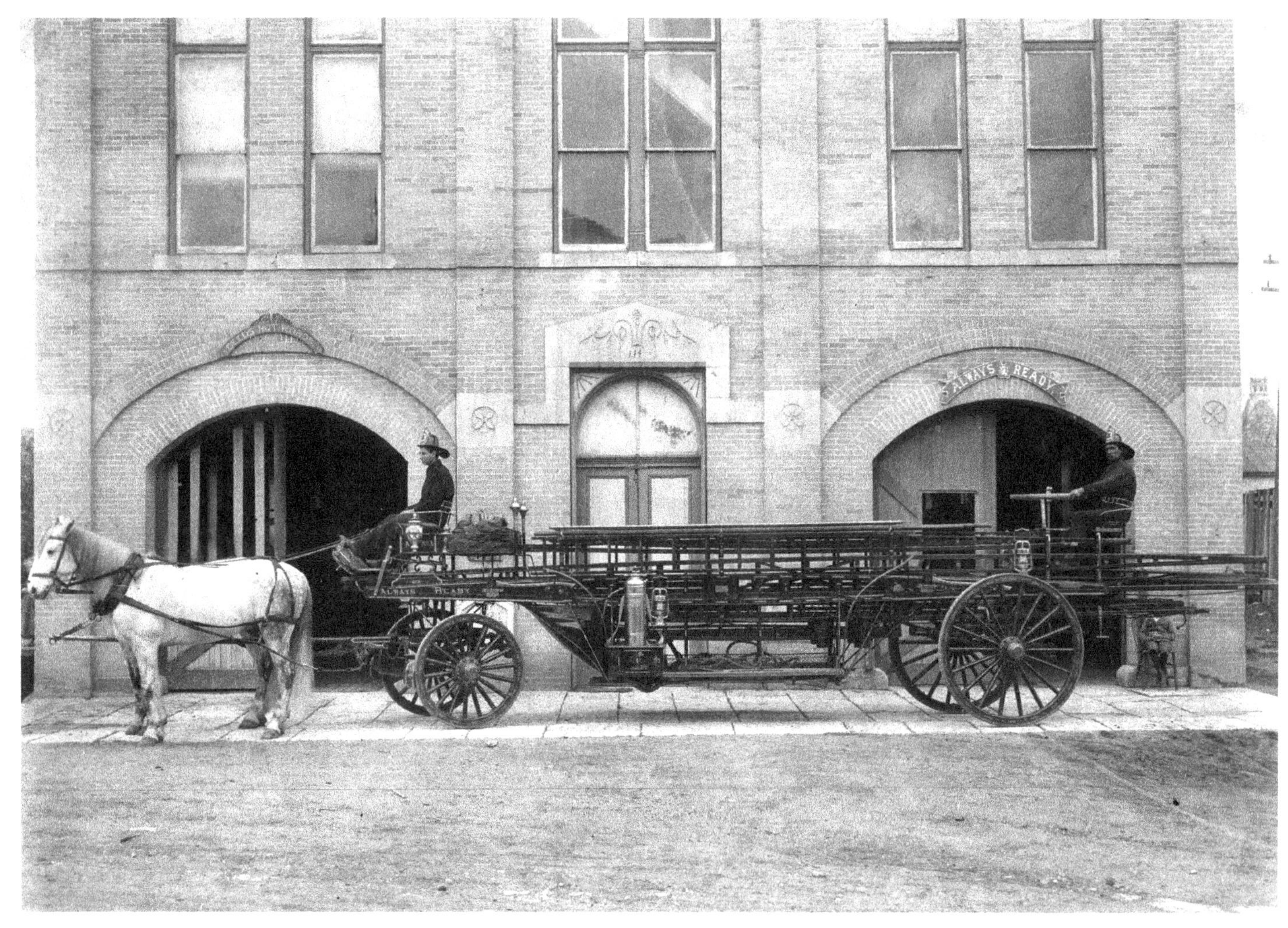

Austin's volunteer fire department was organized by John Bremond and William Walsh in the summer of 1858 as Hook and Ladder Company Number One. The fire station pictured here, built later, was on Hickory (Eighth Street) next to City Hall. A local newspaper noted in 1881, "The most prominent bankers, merchants, and professional men in Austin are firemen."

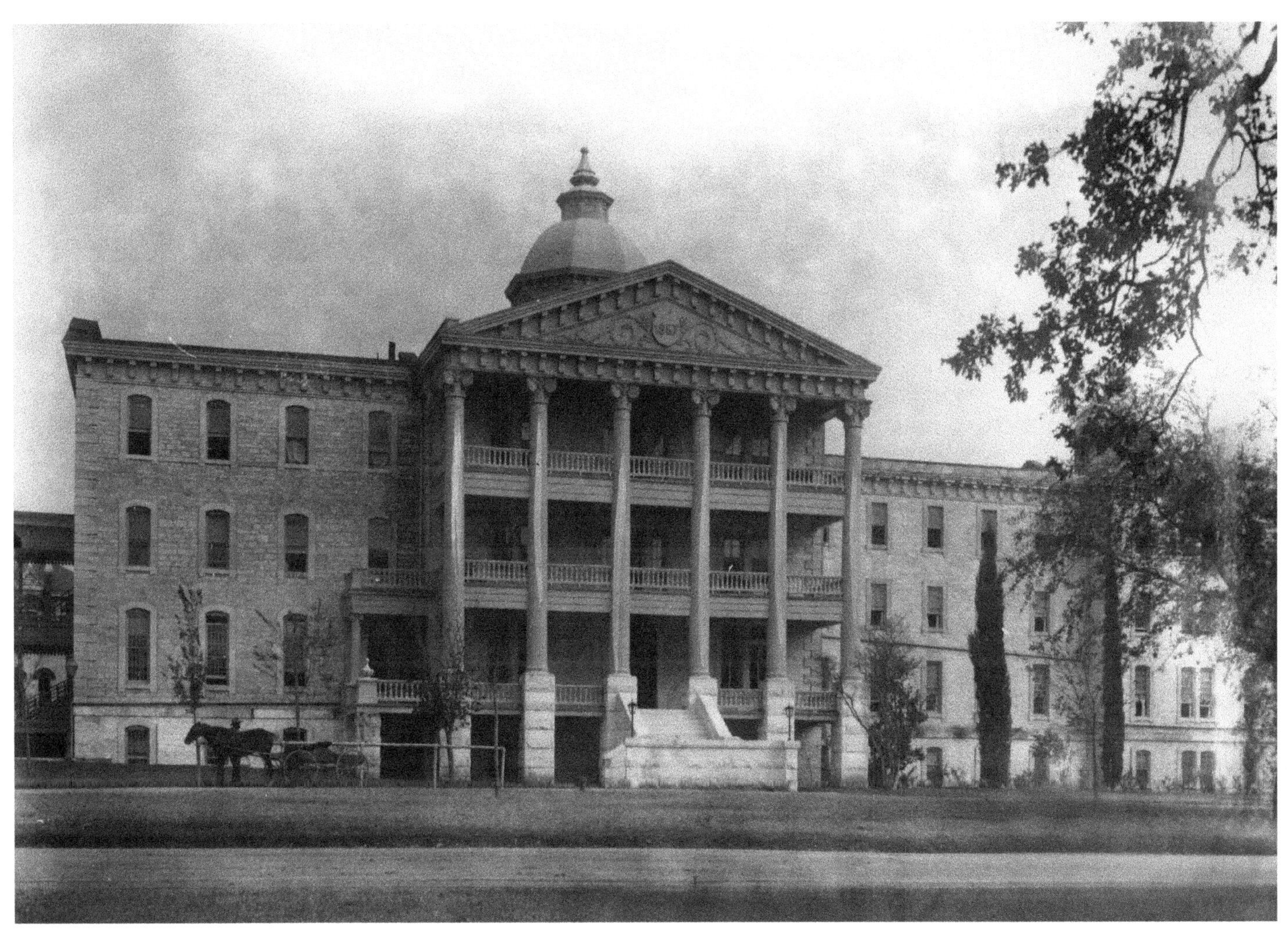

This imposing three-story structure with raised basement opened in March 1861 at what was then the northern outskirts of town. Texas's oldest hospital for the mentally ill, it was originally called the State Lunatic Asylum, but later the name was changed to the more humane Austin State Hospital. On opening day there were approximately 12 resident patients.

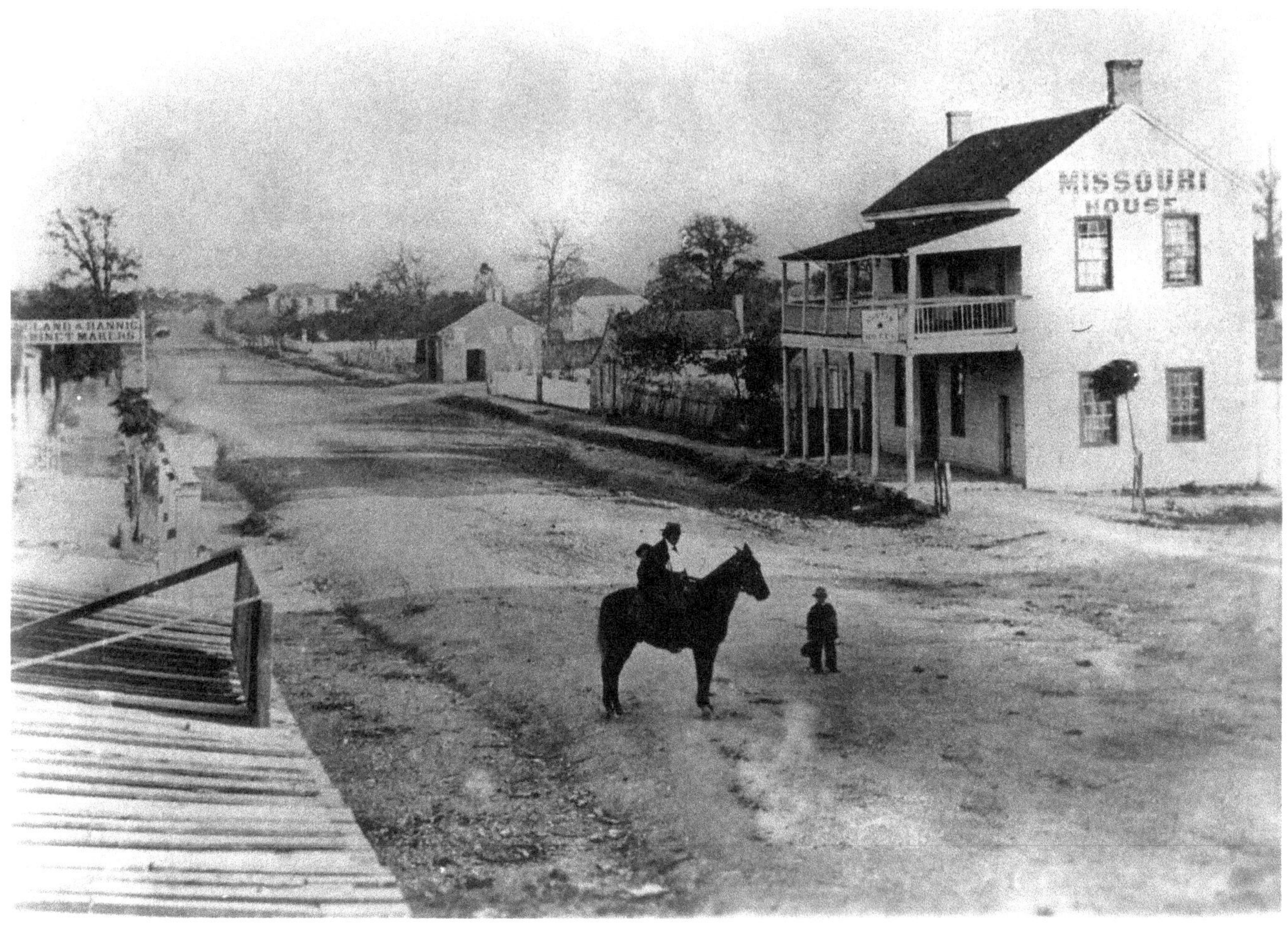

This 1866 photograph of Pecan Street (later Sixth Street) makes it difficult to imagine that it would become Austin's major east-west thoroughfare. The photographer, W. J. Oliphant, took the picture from his upstairs studio at the corner of Pecan and Brazos streets, where the Driskill Hotel now stands. The flat, wide street made it easy for wagons from farms in the surrounding countryside to bring produce to sell in Austin.

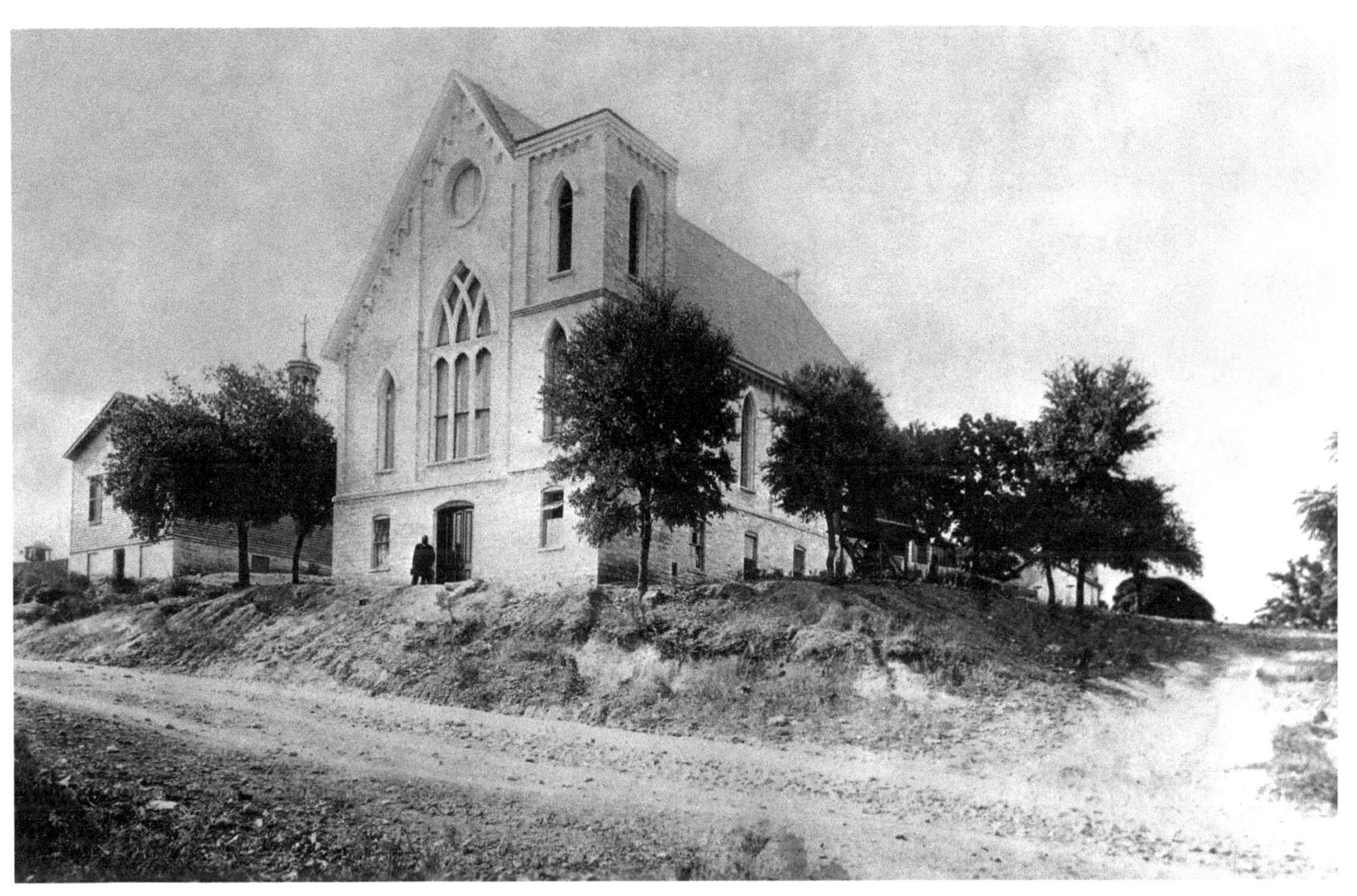

After the Civil War, freed African Americans quickly set about organizing schools and churches. The Wesley Chapel Methodist Episcopal Church was founded in March 1865, the first formally organized African American church in Austin. The permanent sanctuary pictured was later constructed at the southeast corner of San Antonio and Ninth streets.

A large crowd of Austin residents turned out on May 10, 1867, to see French tightrope performer Jean Devier take a death-defying walk across Congress Avenue without a net. The rope was suspended between the roof of the Avenue Hotel and the top of William Rust's building. Governor Pease has been identified as a spectator in the carriage at left.

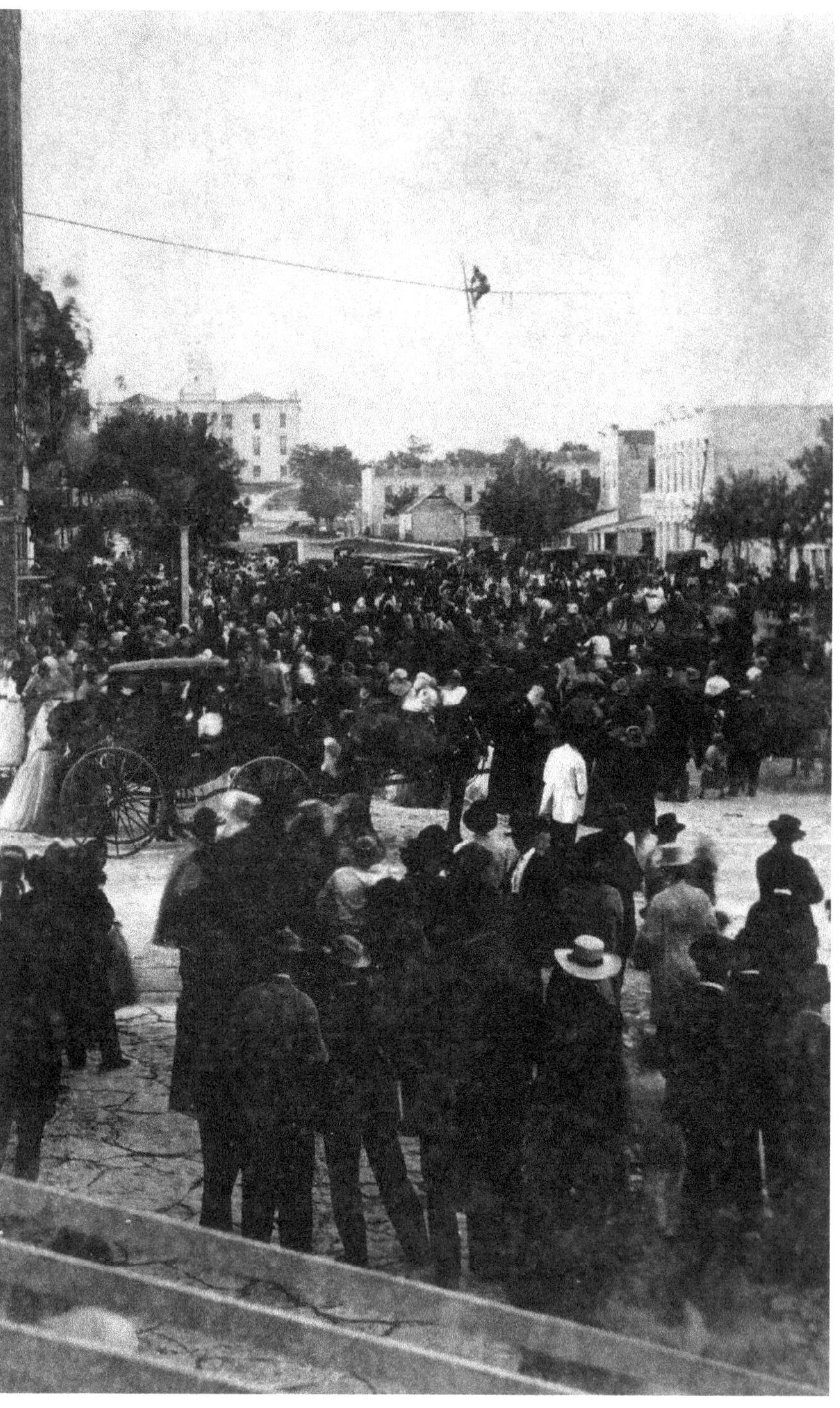

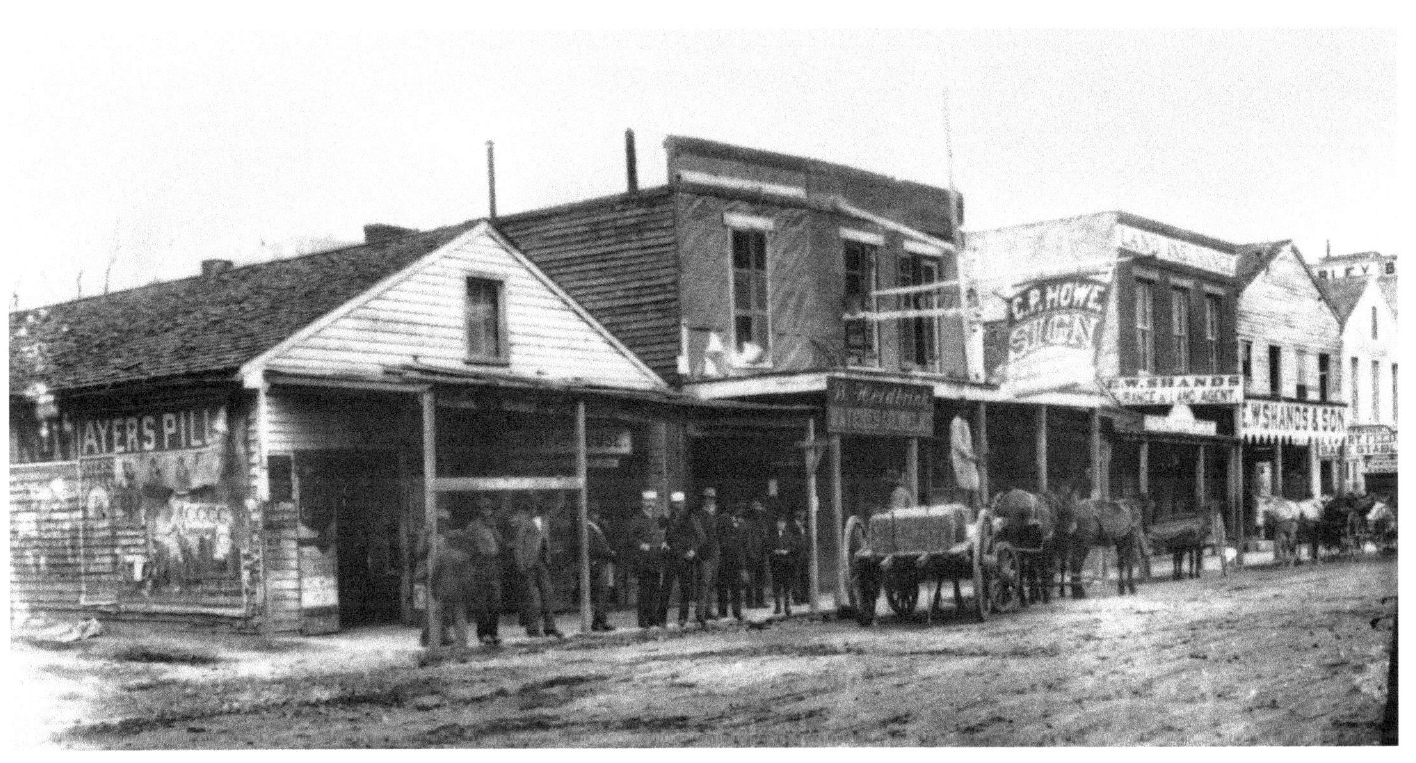

In its early years, Pecan Street sported a variety of businesses in simple frame buildings of one or two stories.

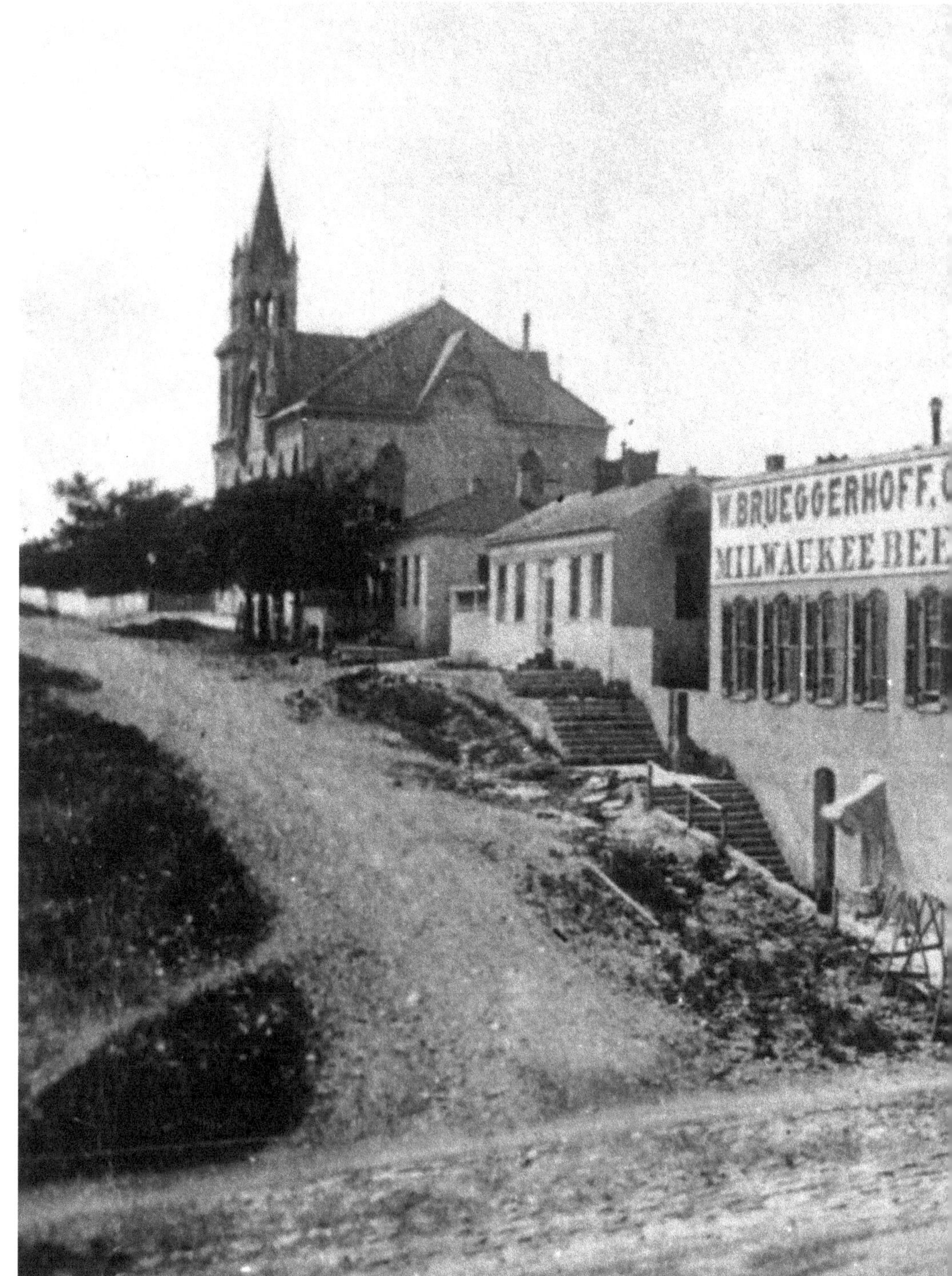

Many newspapers came and went since Austin's beginning, but July 26, 1871, marked the first issue of the one that is still the city's major daily. Now named the *Austin American-Statesman,* it has had many different names over the years, including the *Democratic Statesman* and the *Austin Farmer.* Pictured is its spacious office on Congress Avenue, conveniently situated above Brueggerhoff's grocery and beer dispensary.

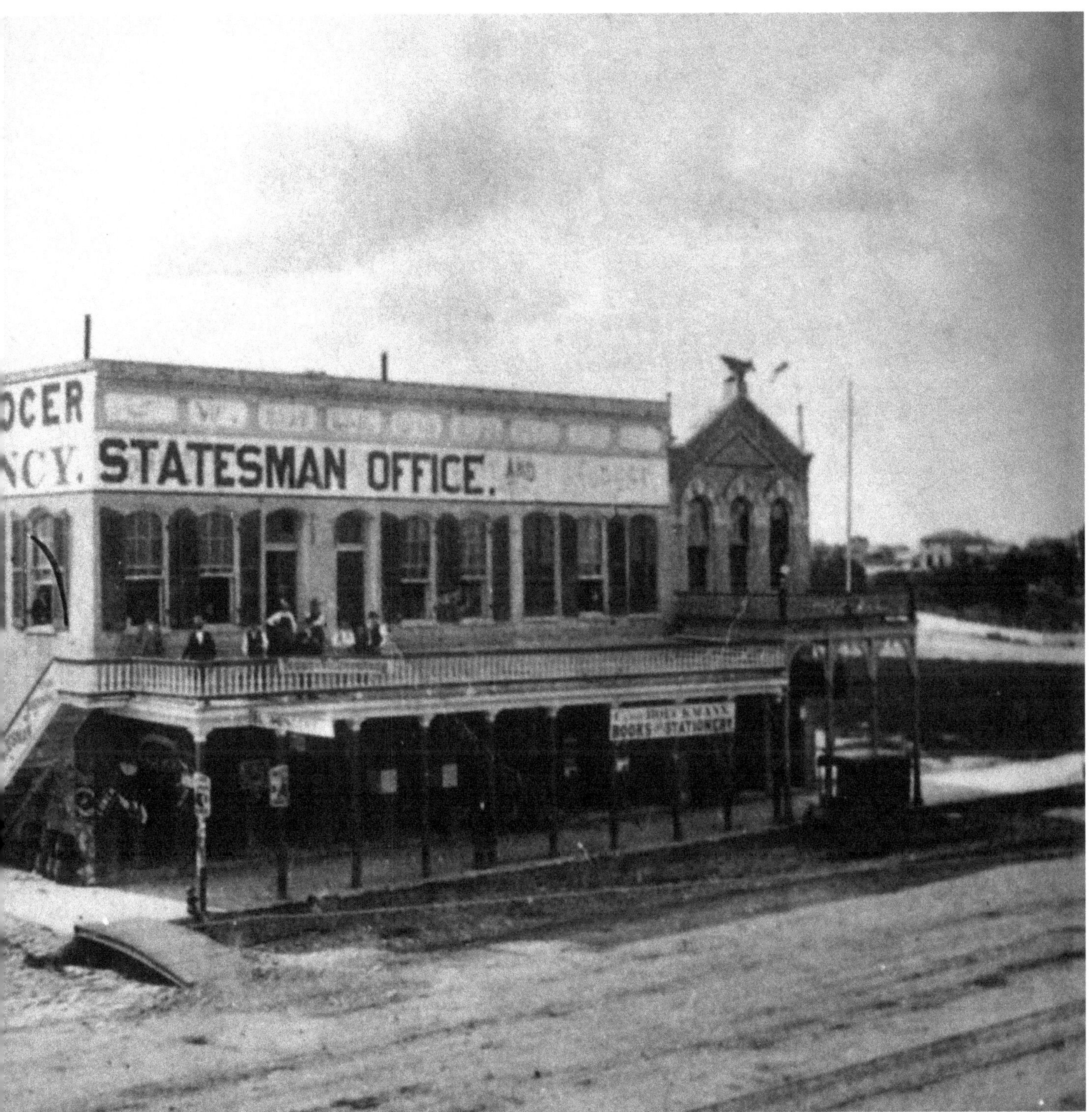
OCER
NCY.
STATESMAN OFFICE.

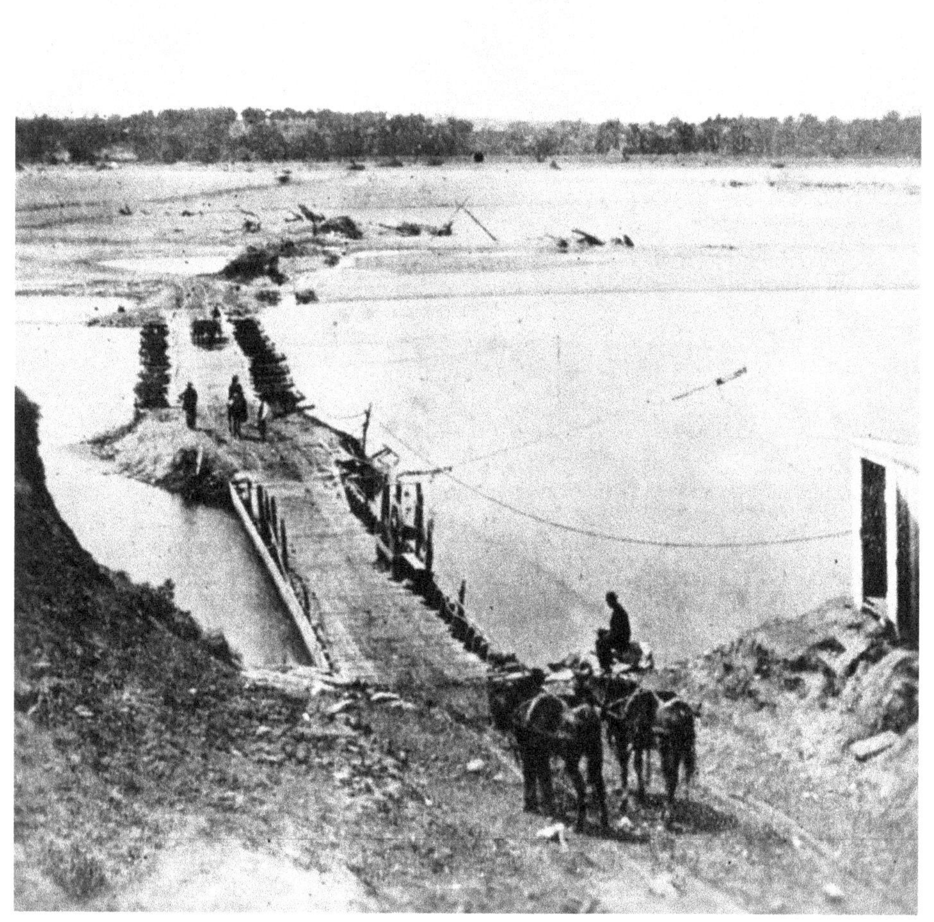

Austin's first attempt at spanning the Colorado River was the "pontoon bridge," completed in November 1869 at the end of Brazos Street and composed of 21 oaken boats spaced at regular intervals. Within a year, however, it was washed away by 36 hours of continuous rainfall. A more substantial bridge constructed later spurred city growth south of the river.

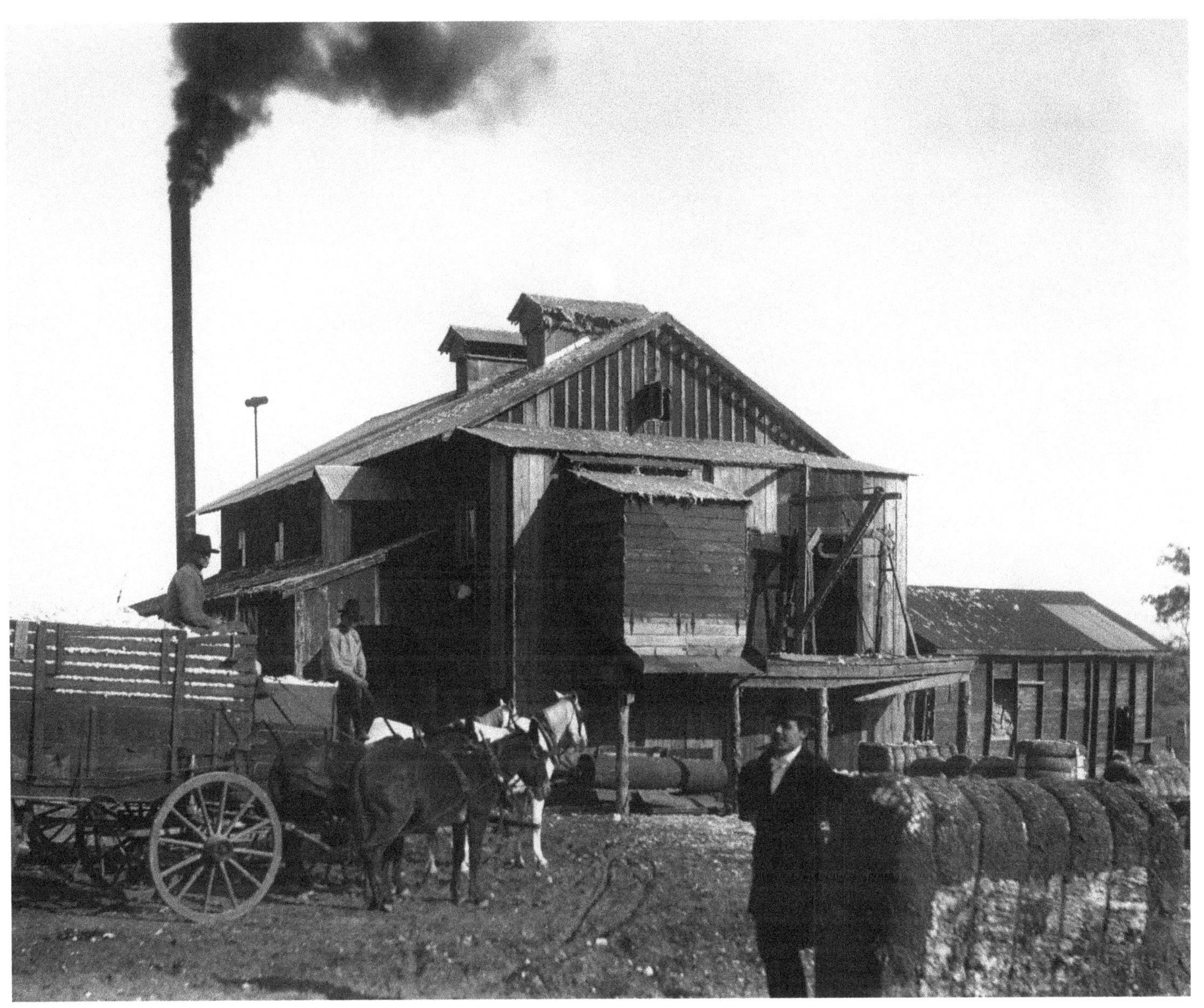

On January 2, 1872, the first bale of cotton was shipped out of Austin by rail, just a week after the first train arrived. Cotton was a major cash crop, and the railroad's appearance ensured a burgeoning market for products of the fertile soil of Central Texas. This photograph shows a cotton gin on a farm outside of Austin.

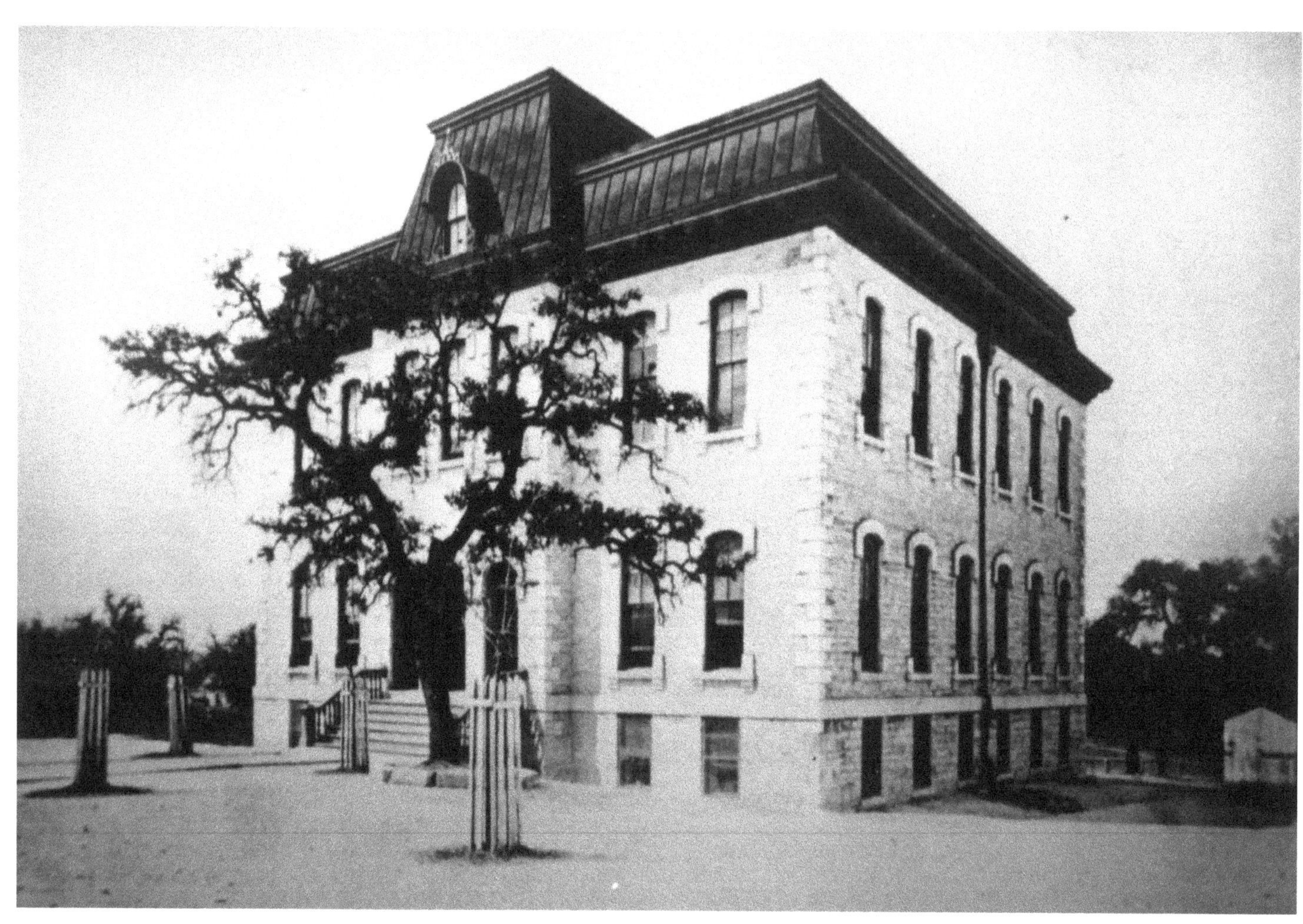

The Austin Graded School, opened in 1876, was the first Texas school built with public funds. It was later renamed Pease School in honor of Governor Elisha M. Pease.

The previous Travis County Courthouse, completed in 1876, stood quite grandly at the east corner of Congress Avenue and Eleventh (Mesquite) Street. The Capitol would be completed 12 years later across Eleventh Street (to the left) facing Congress. A new courthouse was built in the 1930s several blocks west on Guadalupe Street and is still in use today.

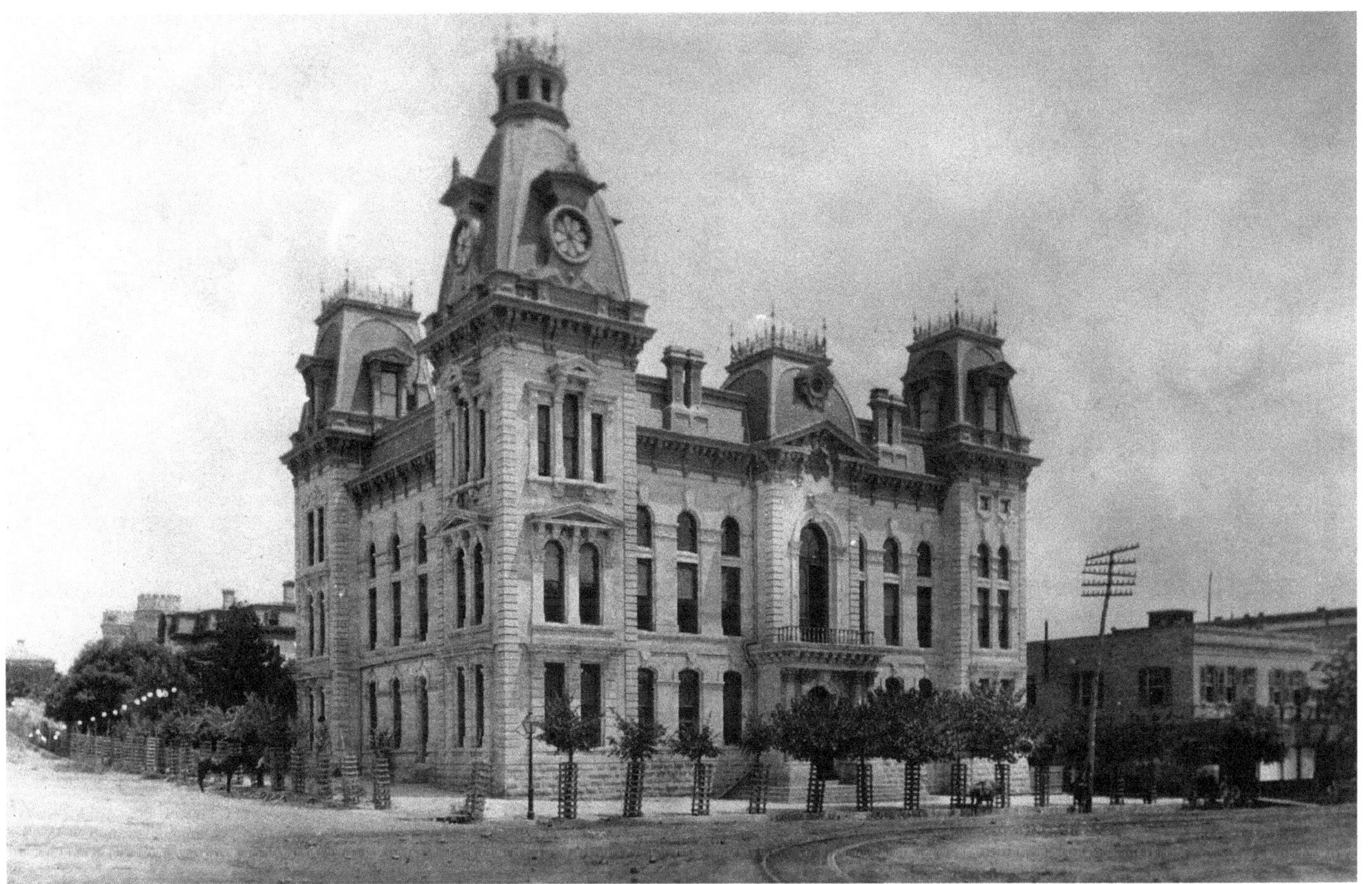

In the 1870s, William Kluge operated his popular restaurant and saloon on Congress Avenue between Pecan (Sixth) and Bois d'Arc (Seventh) streets. As Austin is located almost 300 miles inland from the Gulf Coast, it must have been quite a feat to obtain fresh oysters, but fresh fish could be caught locally.

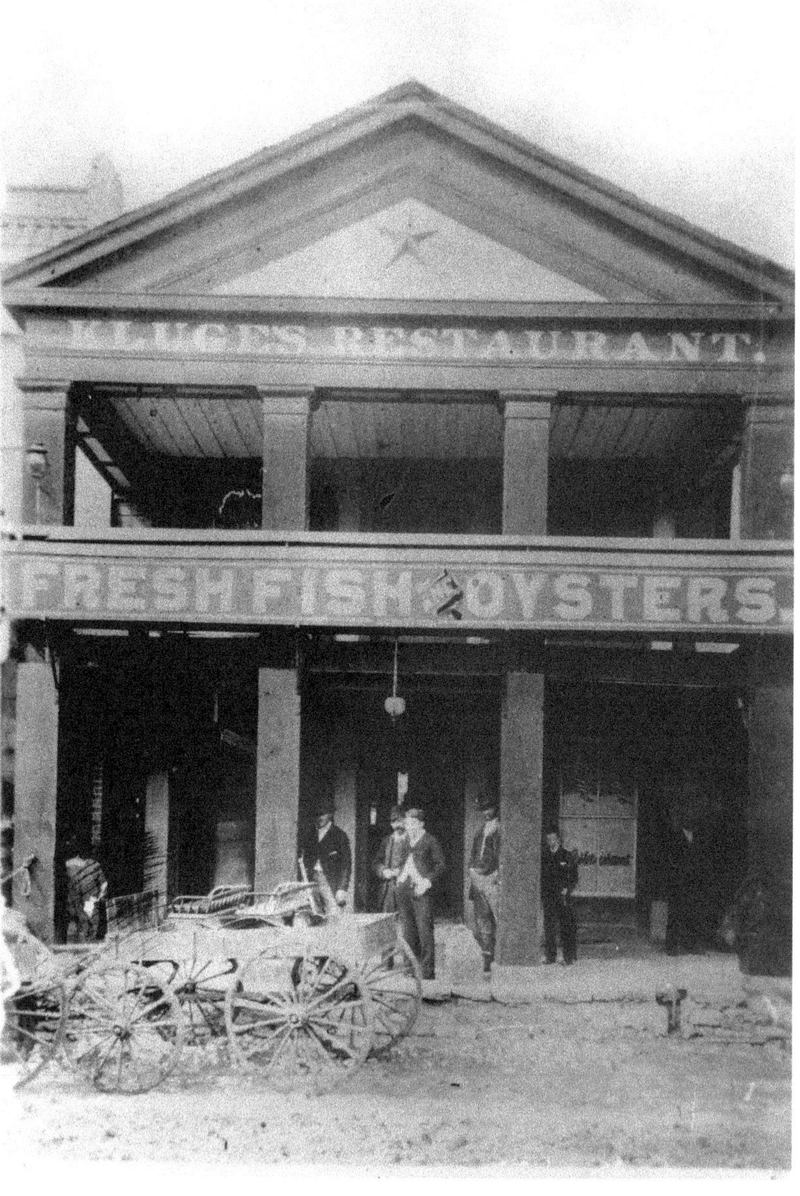

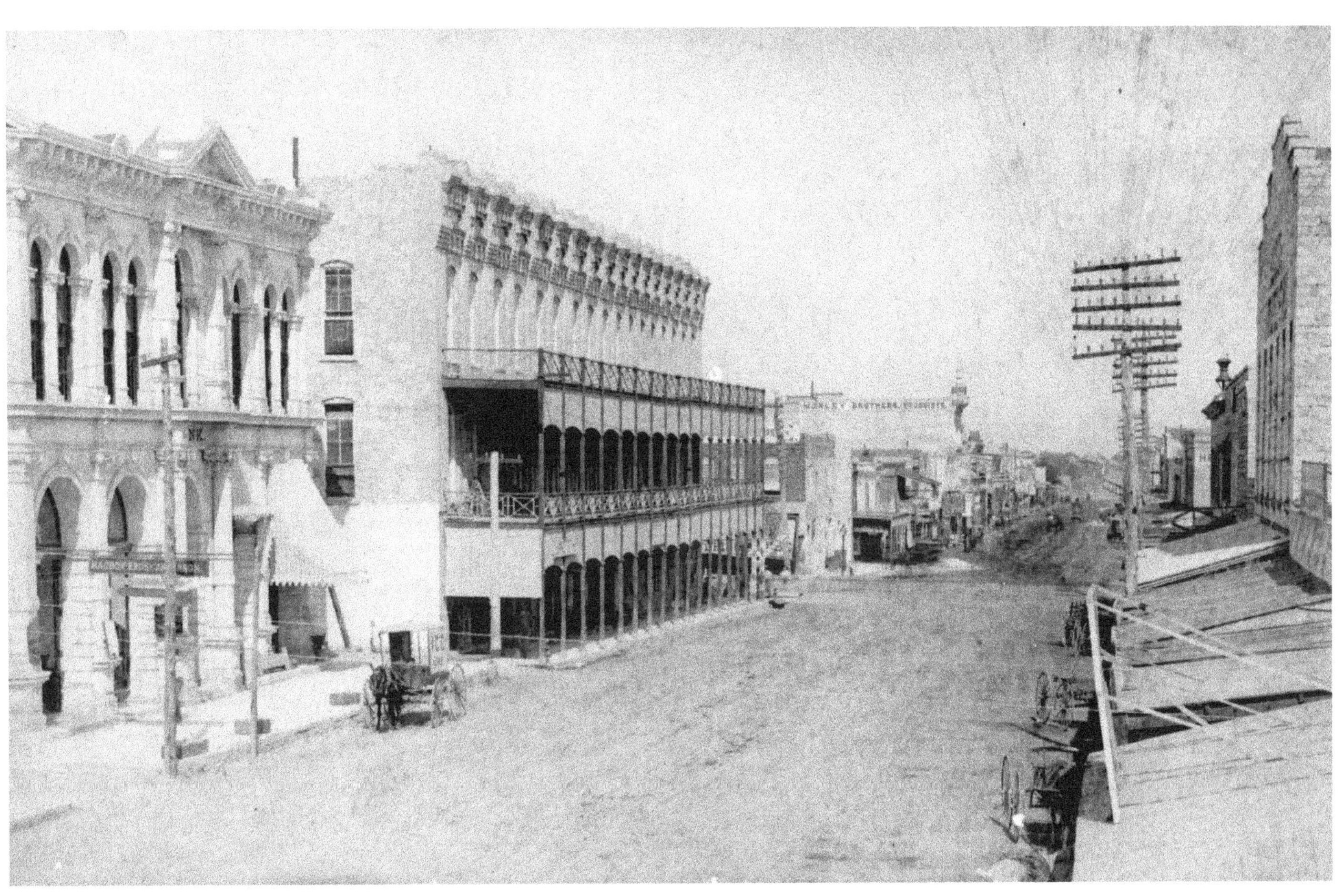

This 1879 view of Pecan (Sixth) Street looks east from Colorado Street. Eight years earlier, the arrival of the railroad had sparked a commercial boom. Victorian-style limestone business buildings proliferated, and a cluster of African American businesses began east of East Avenue, Austin's first eastern boundary street, which in later years would become Interstate 35, a busy highway.

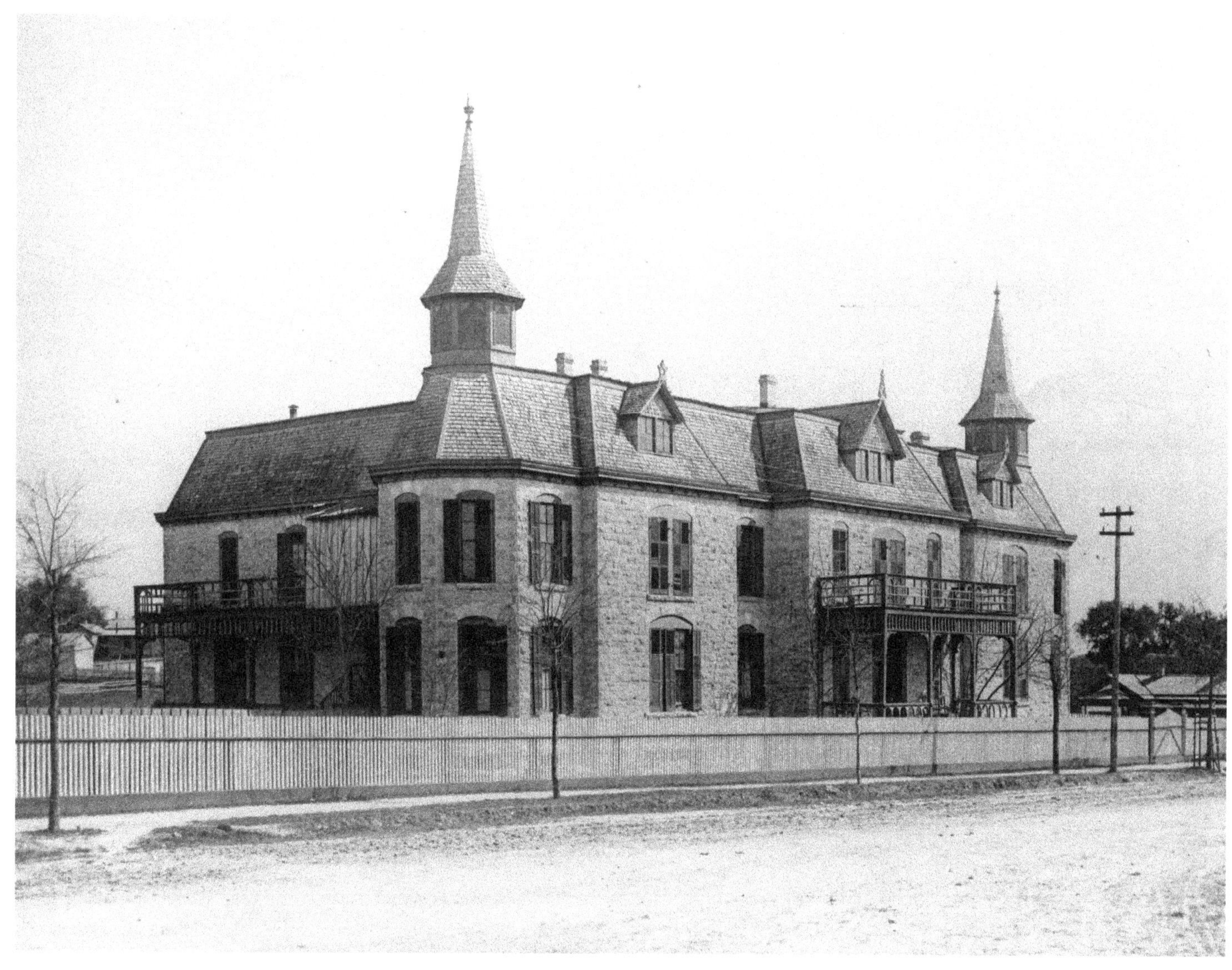

During Austin's first 45 years, citizens received medical care either at home, in private infirmaries, or in "pest camps" set aside for treating contagious diseases. In 1884, this public hospital was built on the farthest northeast lot of the original city's plan. The first public hospital in Texas, it could treat up to 40 patients, and a private room cost up to $2.50 per day. The city's Brackenridge Hospital occupies the same site today.

Workers prepare to place the formidable-looking *Goddess of Liberty* statue atop the Capitol's dome, where she would remain for almost a century. The newly completed building was dedicated in the spring of 1888, and in the mid-1980s, the statue was brought back down for reinforcement during the statehouse's major renovation.

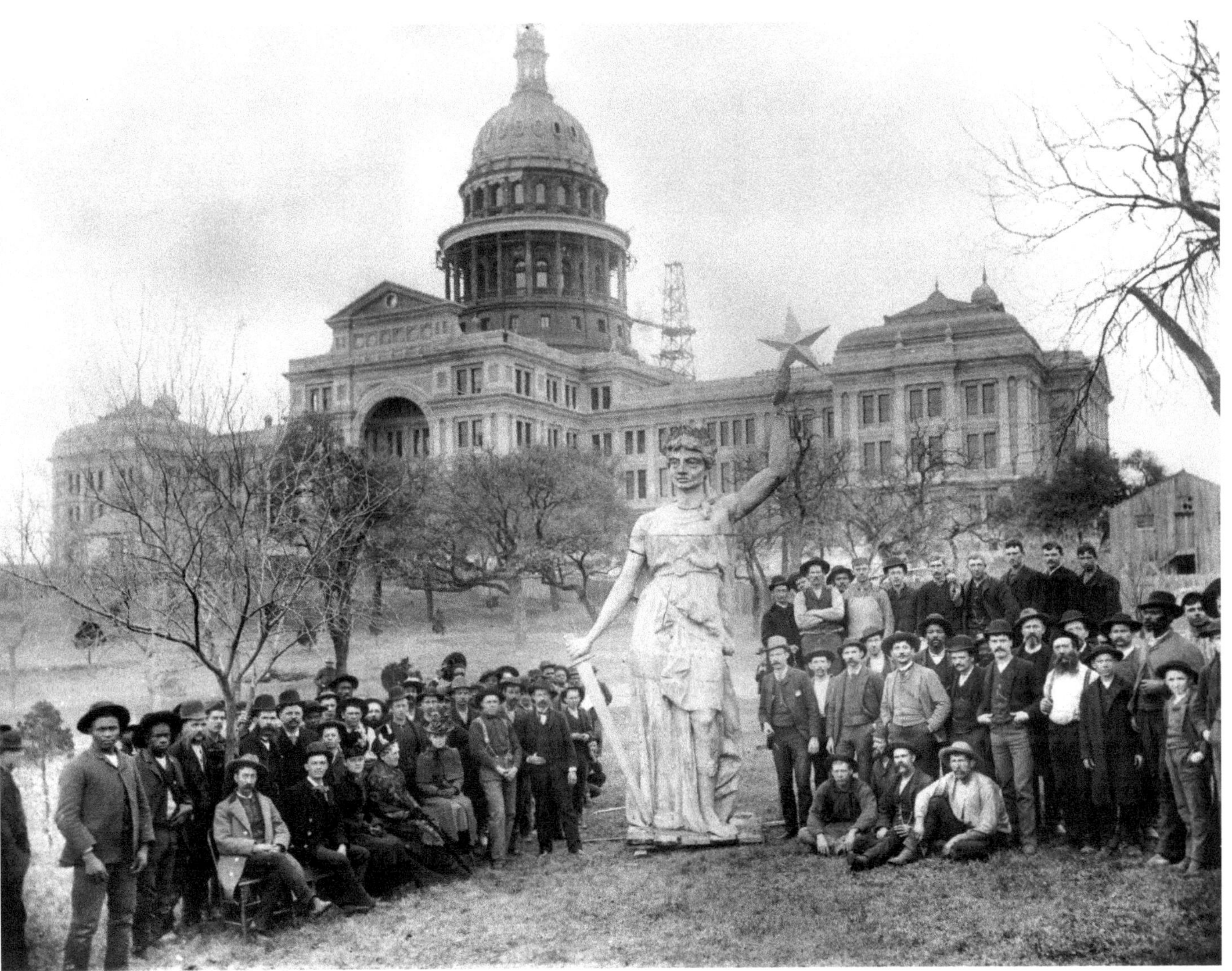

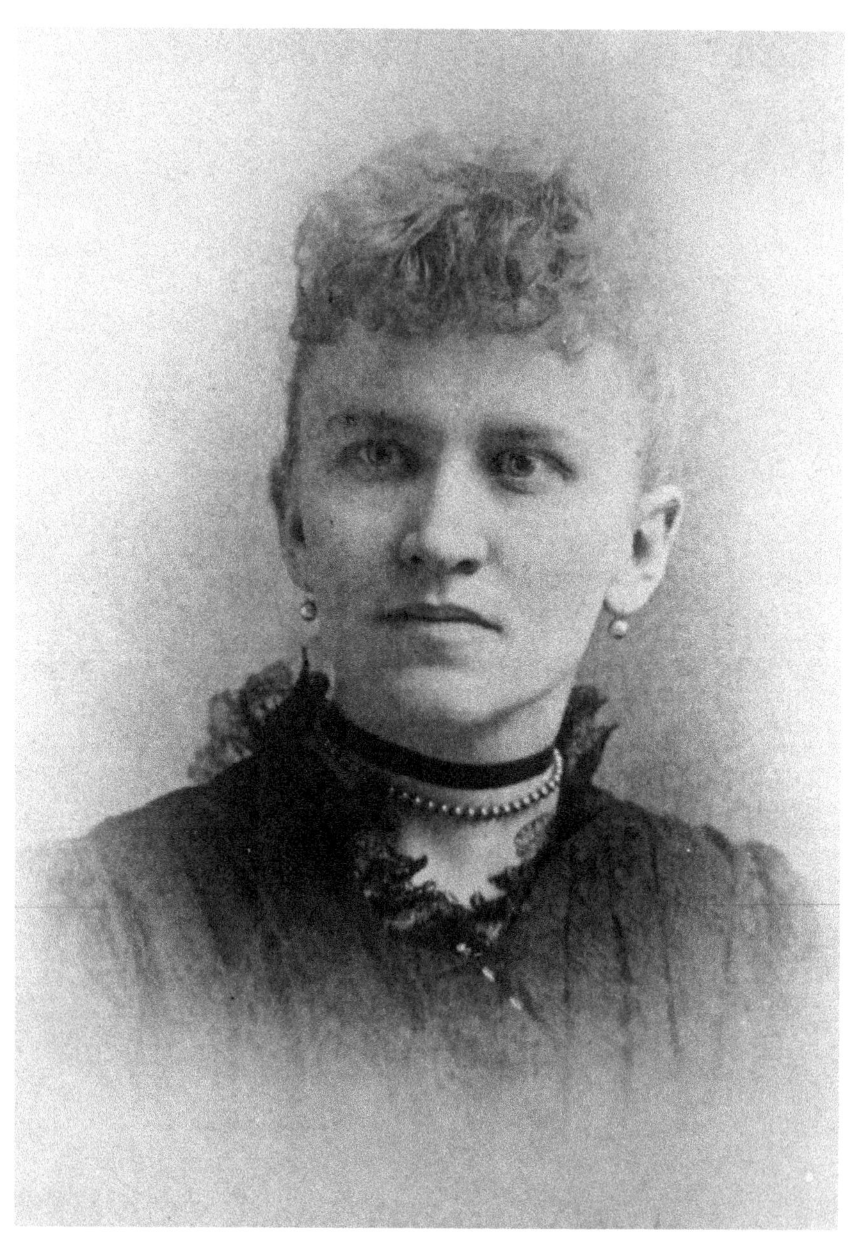

Fanny Margaret "Jessie" Andrews was the first woman to enroll at the University of Texas (in 1883, when she was 16), the first woman to graduate from the school, the first woman to be a member of its Alumni Association, and the first woman to teach there. She was an instructor in the German Department.

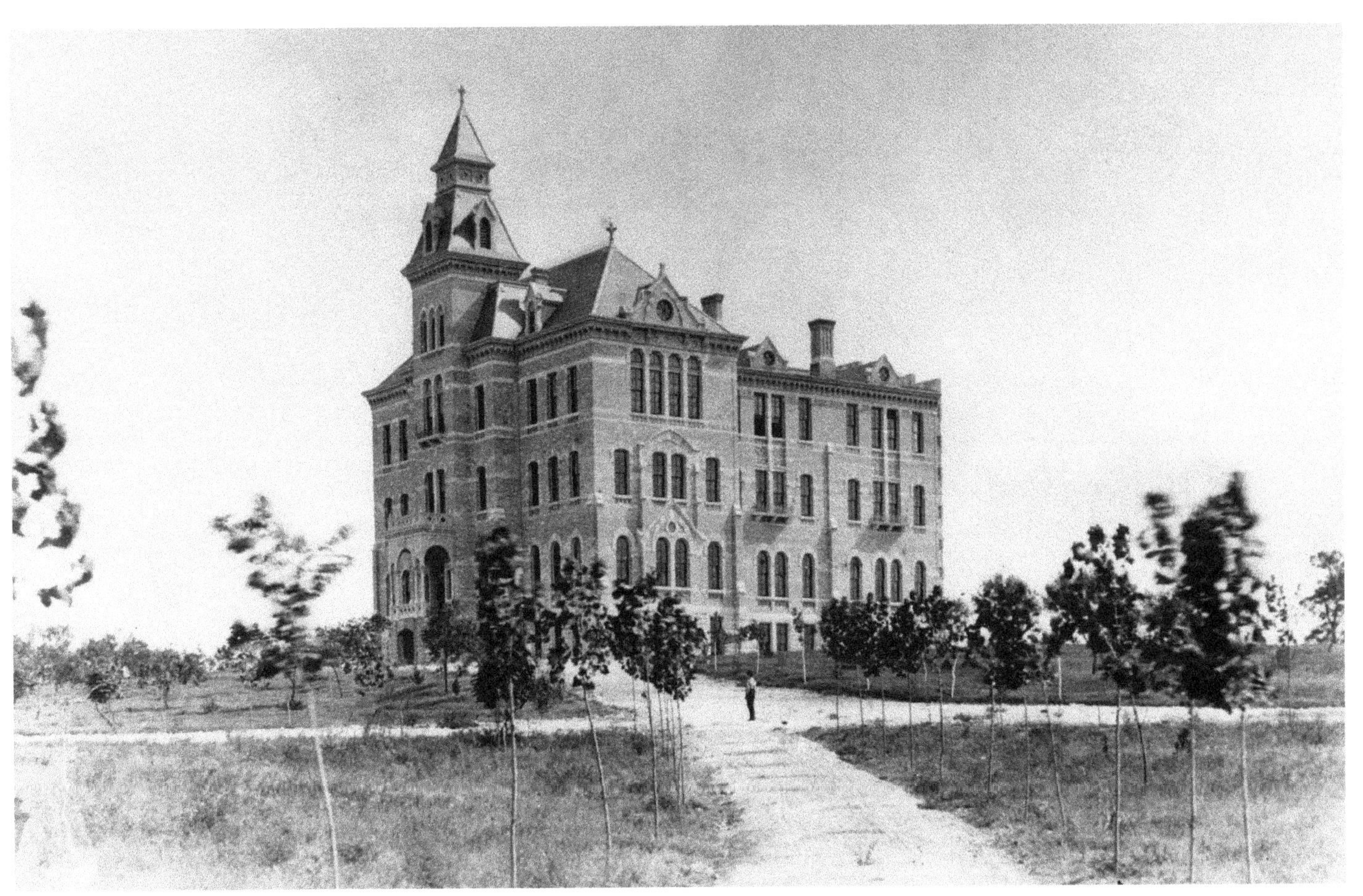

"Old Main" was the first building on the University of Texas campus. Before it was completed in the summer of 1884, classes were held in the temporary Capitol building, which was on the southeast corner of Congress Avenue at Eleventh (Mesquite) Street, across from the permanent Capitol's site, which faces Eleventh.

When it was established in 1876, Temple Beth Israel, Austin's first Jewish congregation, was about 30 families. Services were held at Mr. Sampson's Hall or the Odd Fellows Hall until this handsome stone synagogue was completed in 1884 at the corner of Mesquite (Eleventh) and San Jacinto streets.

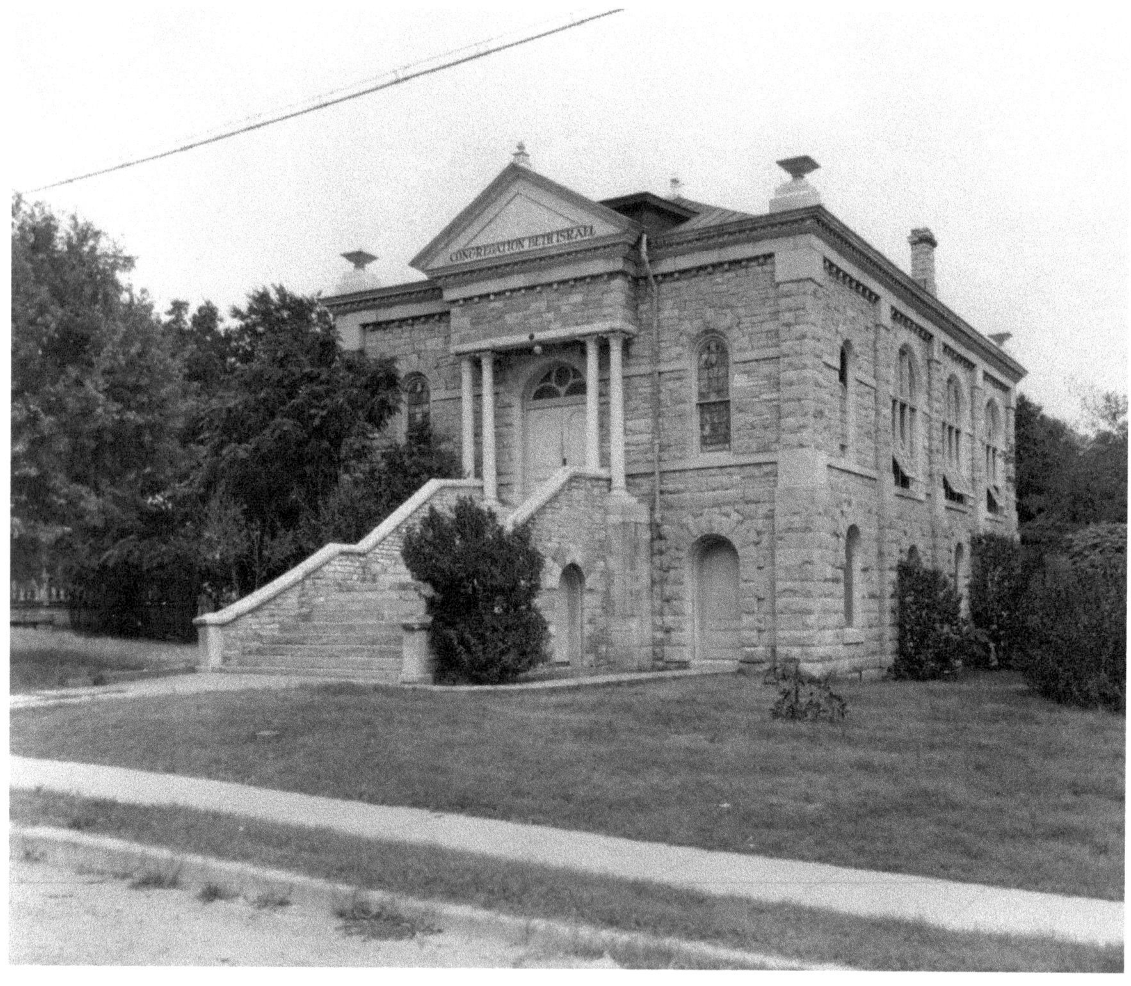

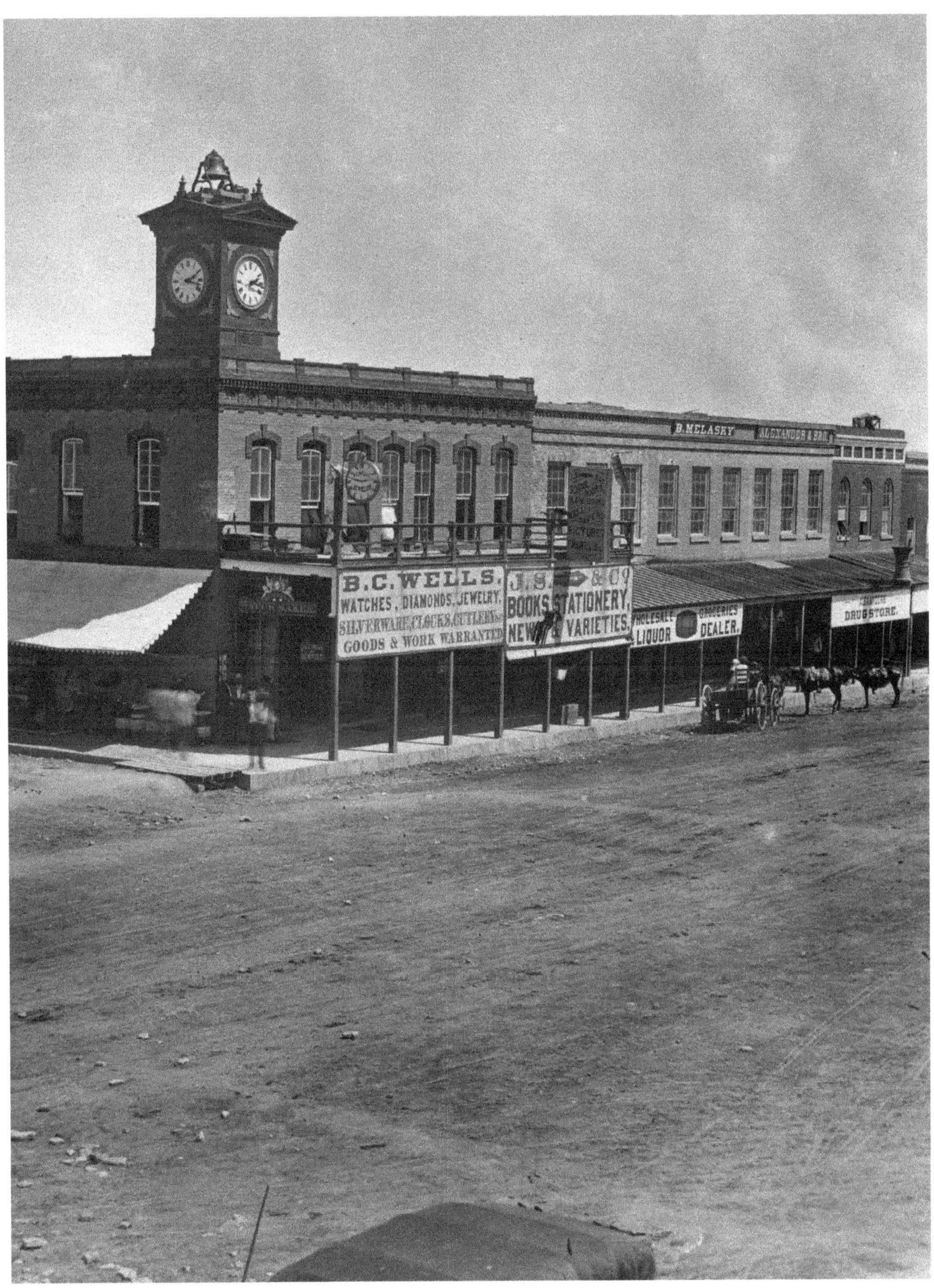

Early on, Pecan Street (Sixth Street) became a market center because of its location near the railroad and because it was wide and flat enough for a horse team and wagon to turn around in comfortably. This photograph shows a row of retail establishments on the street circa 1880, before the streetcar tracks were laid and before it was paved with bricks.

The house surrounded by a white fence near Colorado and Mulberry (Tenth) streets belonged to Swante Palm, promoter of Swedish immigration to Central Texas. Between 1850 and 1899, he held public offices including postmaster and city councilman, helped found the Gethsemane Lutheran Church, and in 1897 donated his library of 12,000 volumes to the University of Texas library, more than doubling its size.

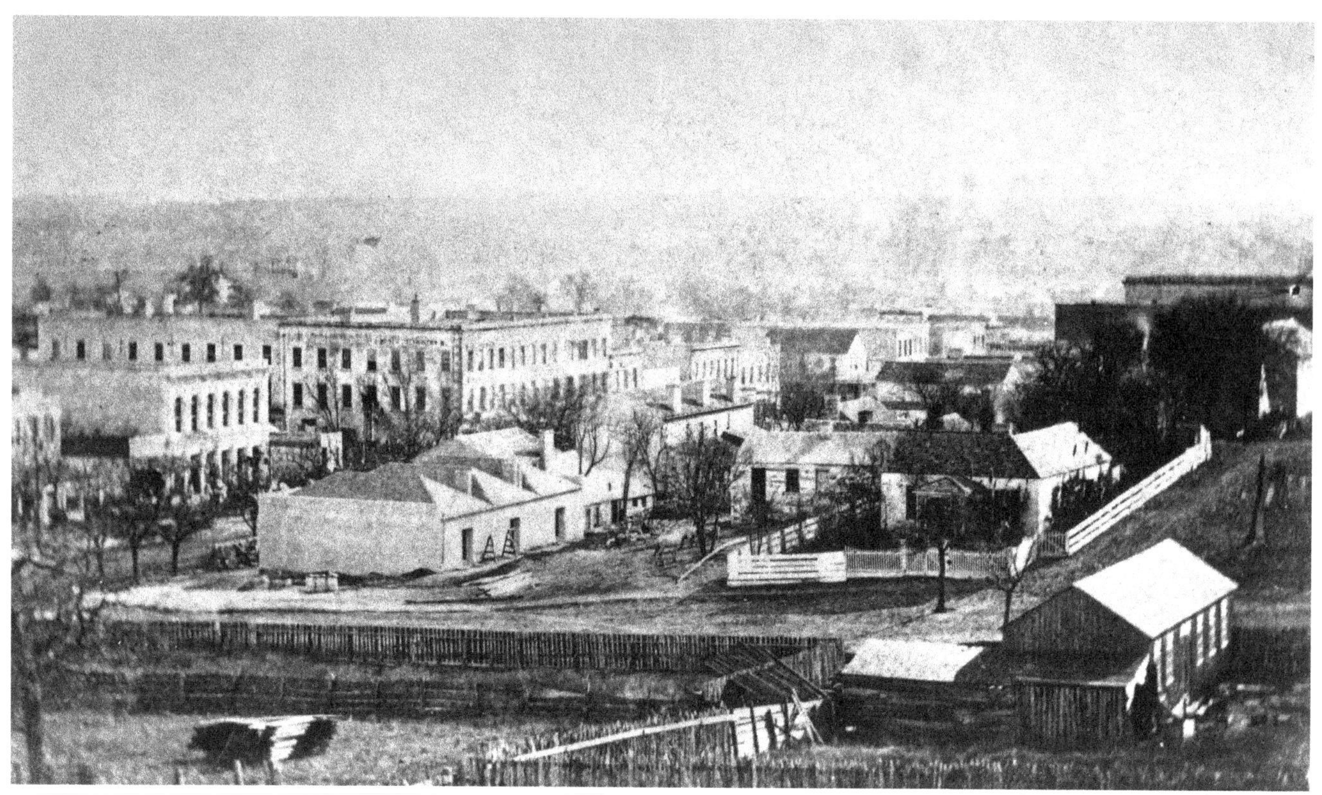

This iron bridge with stone supports, called the Corporation Bridge, spanned the Colorado River in 1884, replacing a wooden bridge that had collapsed in 1883. The iron bridge was replaced in 1910 by a concrete one, which still stands as the Congress Avenue Bridge. It is home to thousands of bats, which at sunset swarm out from under the bridge en masse, attracting tourists and local citizens alike.

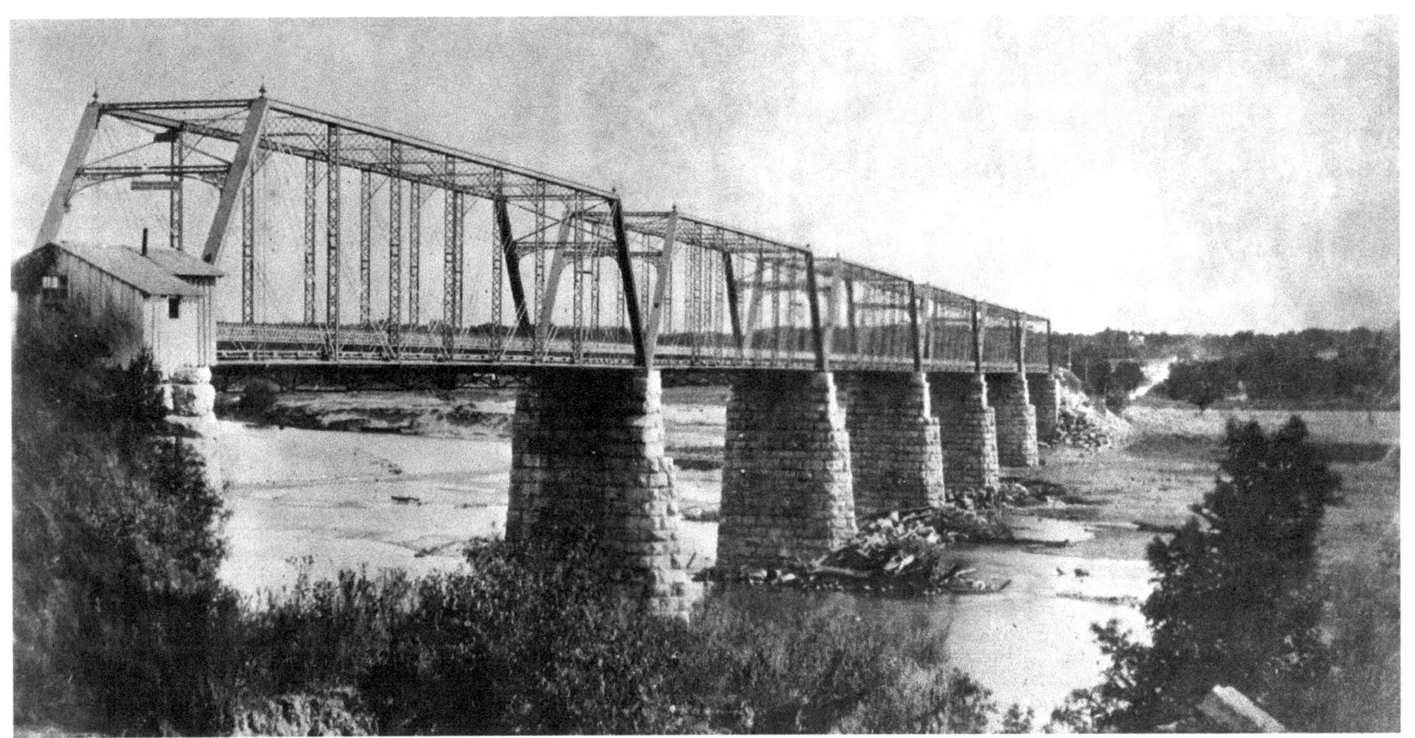

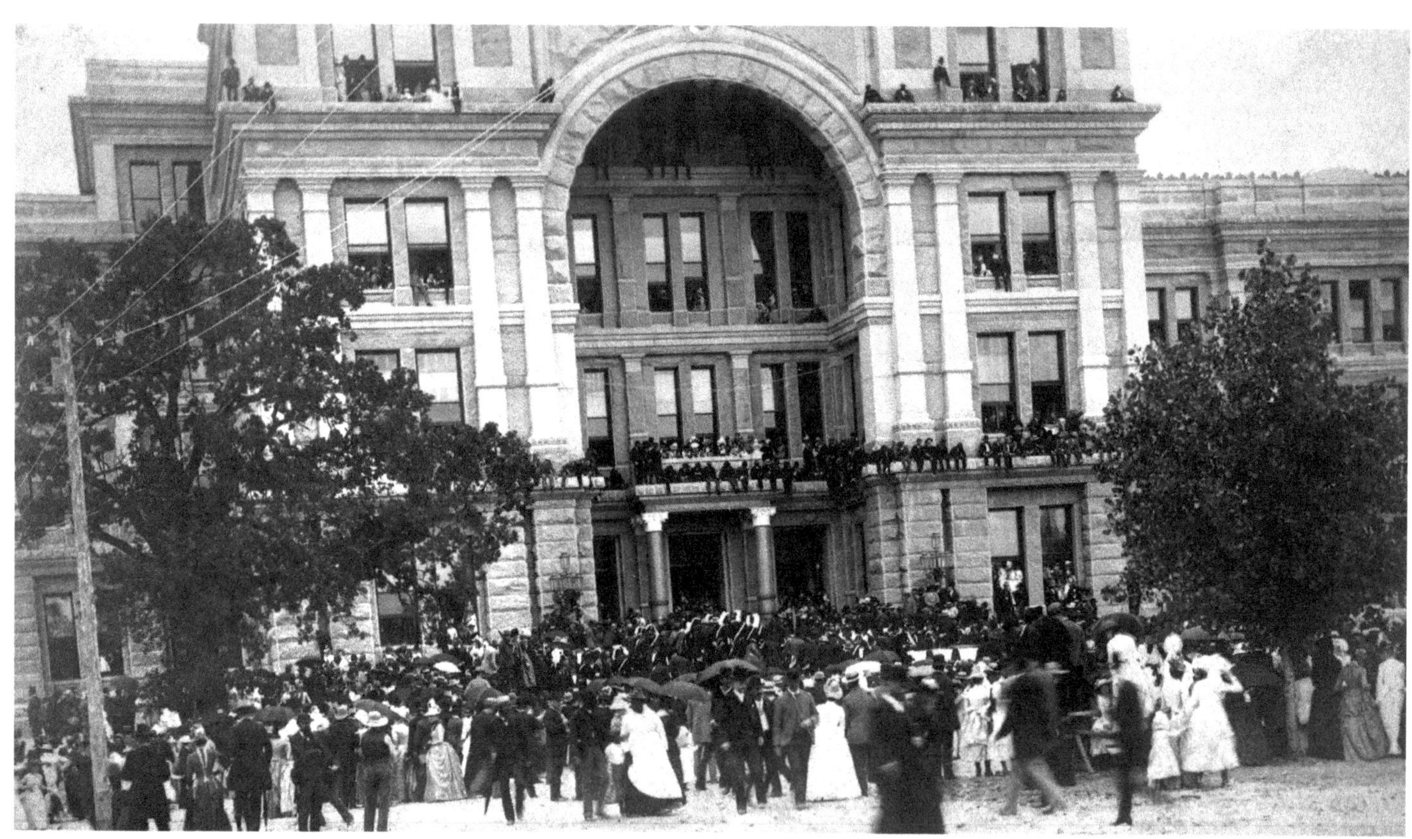

On the morning of May 16, 1888, the new Capitol's dedication day, crowds had gathered by 8:30. Early birds grabbed seats on the ledge of the second story, where they could watch the dedication ceremonies and the mile-long parade headed by the Masonic Grand Lodge of Texas. An entire week of planned festivities and entertainment included fireworks, bands, and displays by military drill teams from across the country.

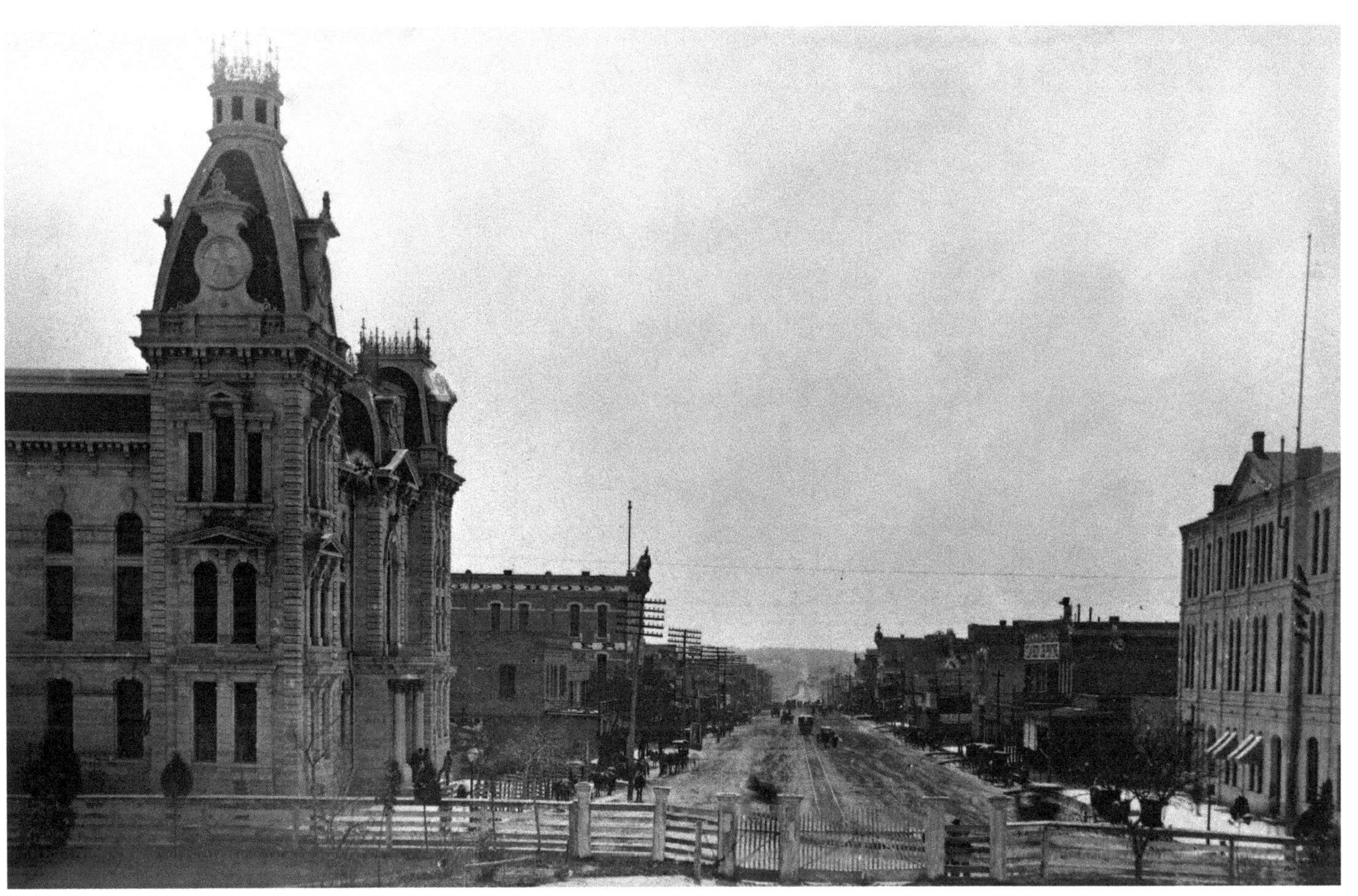

Photographer S. B. Hill took this photograph looking down Congress Avenue from the Capitol grounds circa 1888. The fence was a temporary structure while the new Capitol was under construction (in the foreground, parallel to Eleventh Street). The imposing building at left is the Travis County Courthouse. The Lundberg Bakery building is in the first block on the right.

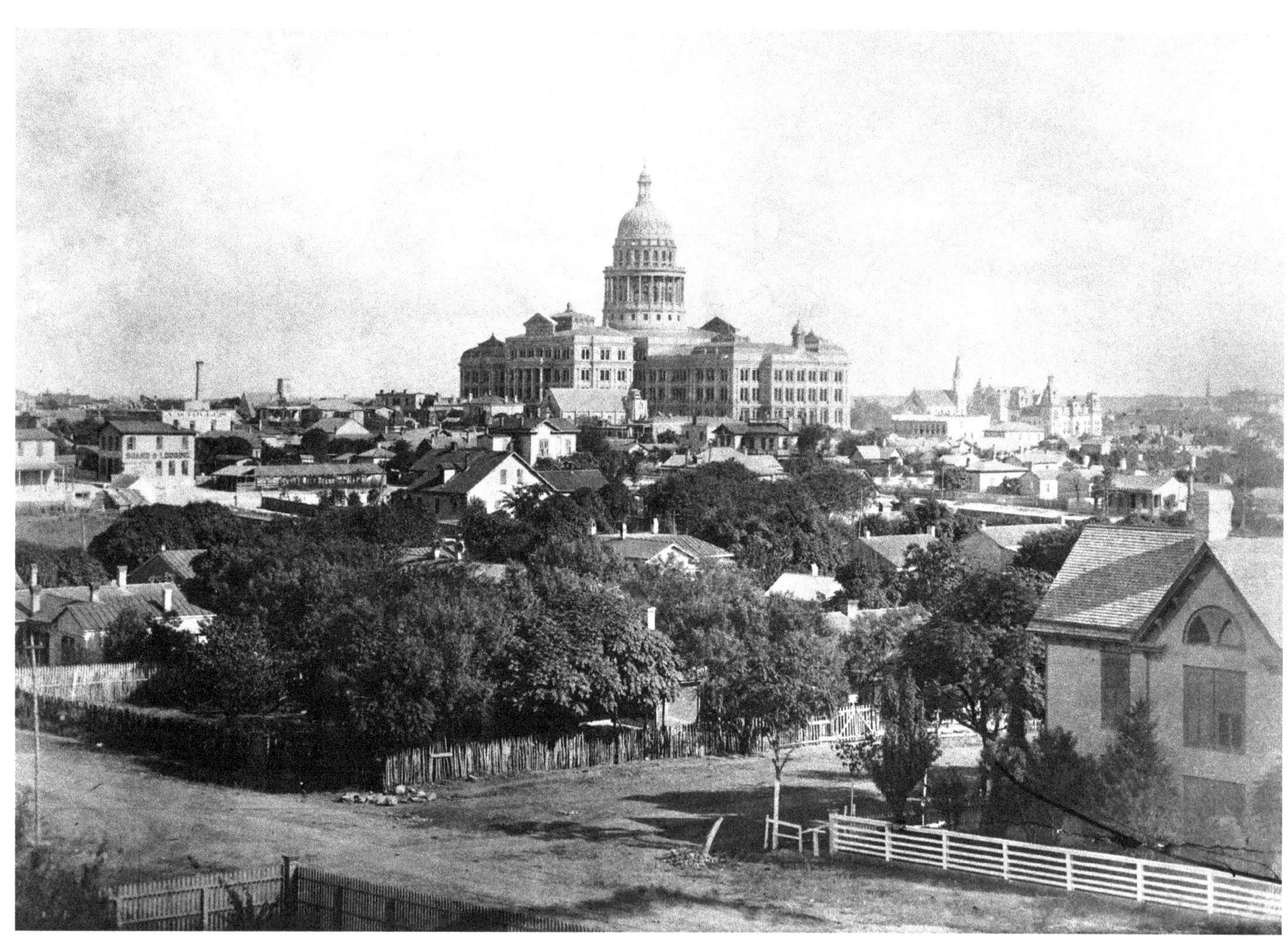

The Texas Capitol has been Austin's best-known landmark since its completion in 1888. For many years it towered above all other buildings in town, dominating the landscape.

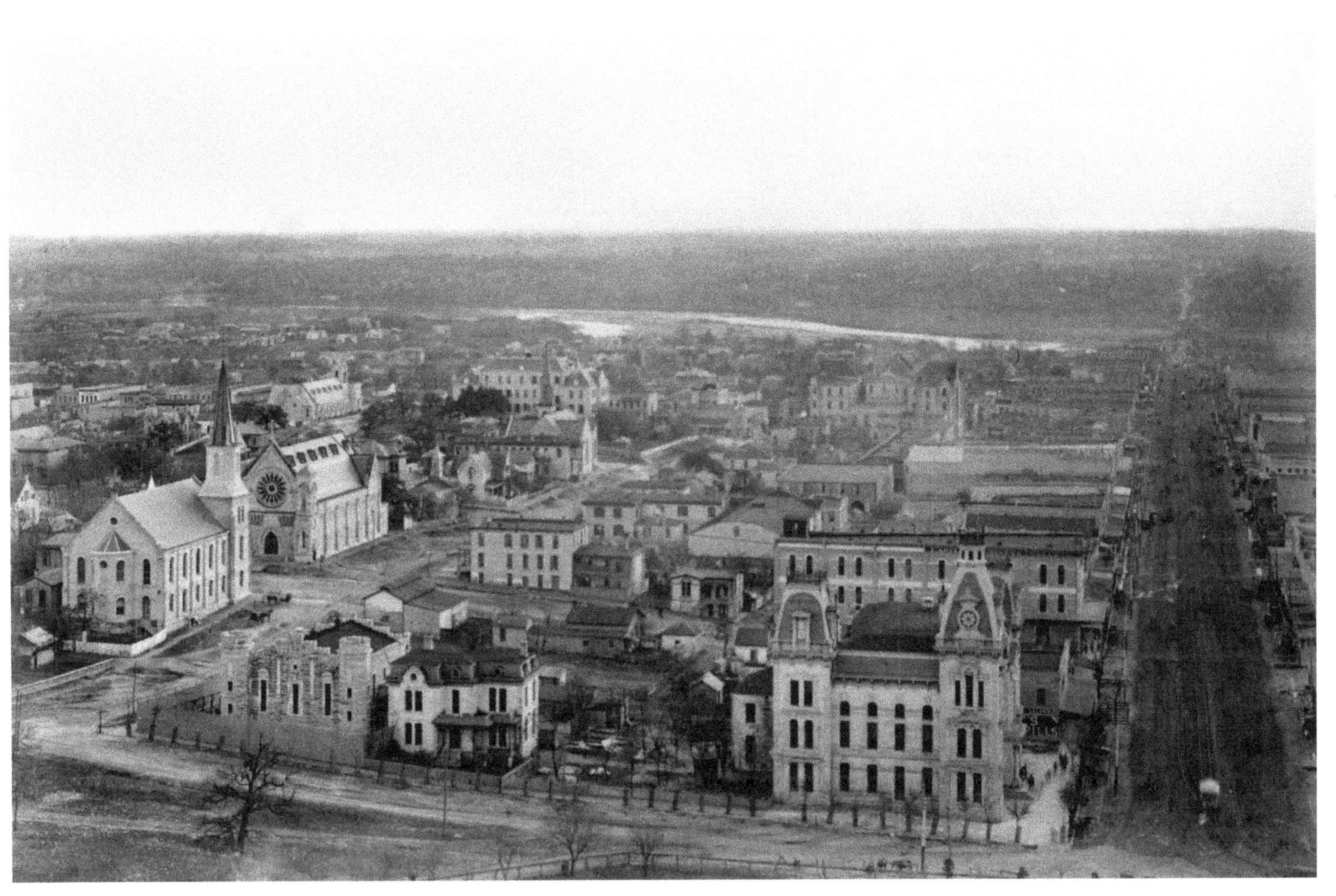

When the Capitol was completed, photographers took their cameras to its dome to capture the spectacular views. This shot looking south shows Congress Avenue, right, and Brazos Street, left. The Travis County Courthouse is at the corner of Congress and Eleventh. The Methodist Church and St. Mary's Cathedral face each other at the corner of Brazos and Tenth. Stone turrets identify the Travis County Jail.

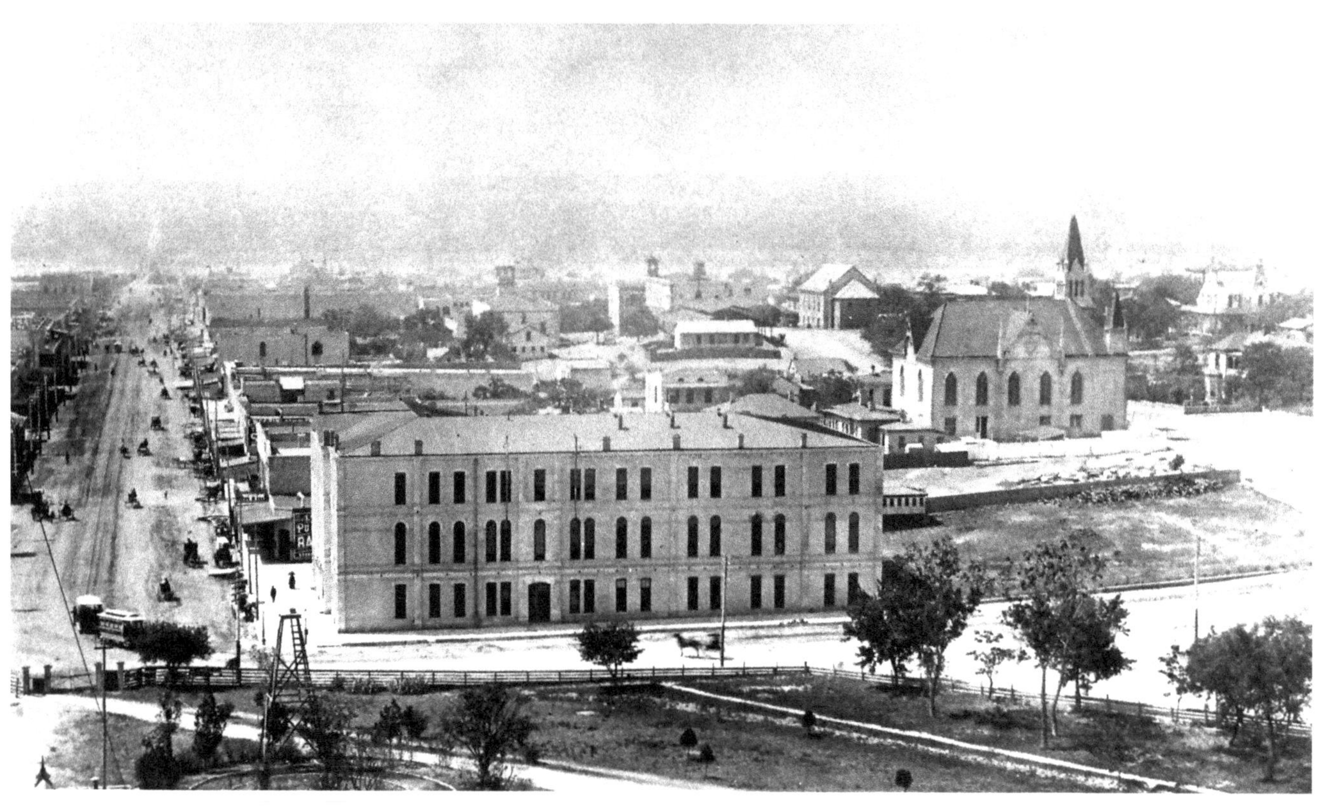

This view from the Capitol dome looks southwest of Congress Avenue. The large three-story building at center is the temporary Capitol, used while the 1888 Capitol was under construction. The steepled building at right is the Tenth Street Baptist Church.

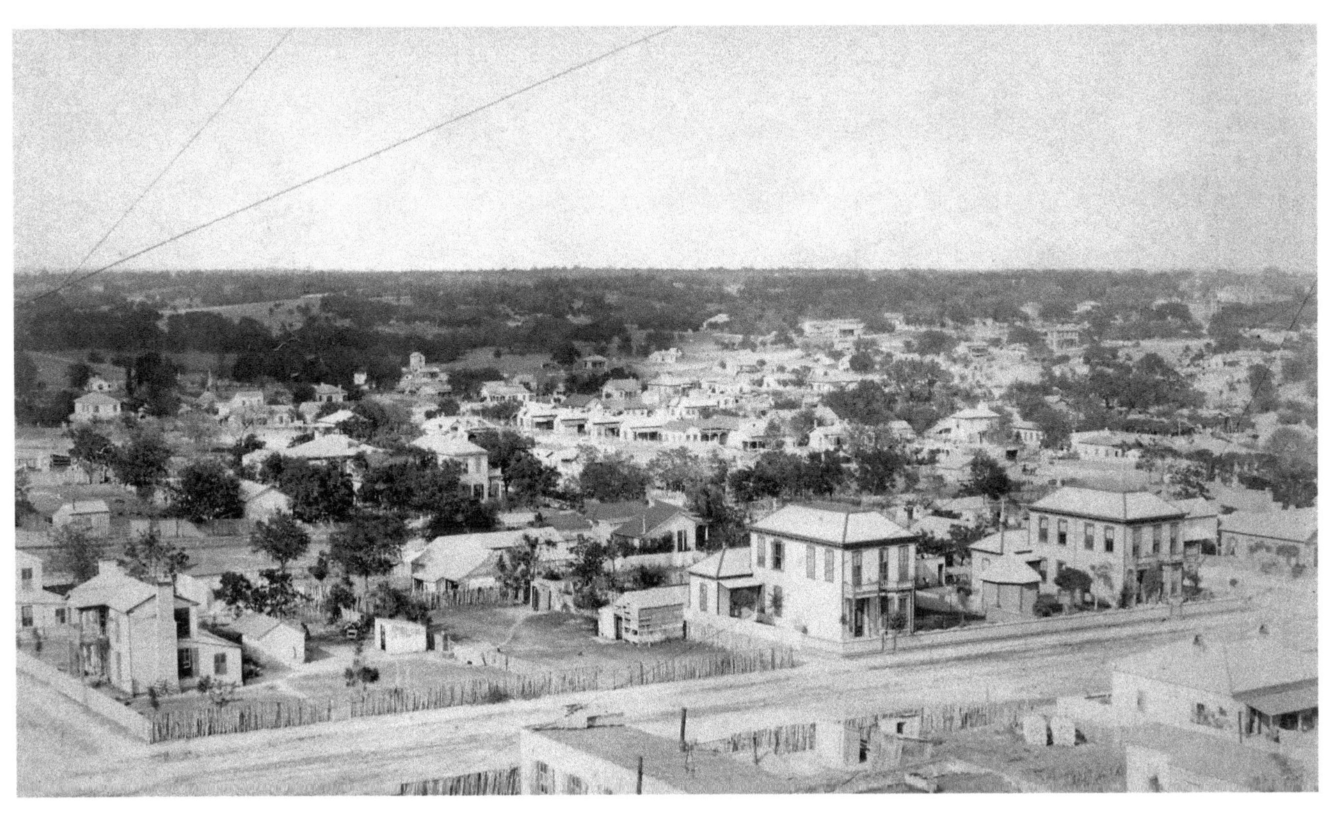

This view from the Capitol dome looking east shows the residential area that would become home to many of Austin's African American and Mexican American families in the twentieth century.

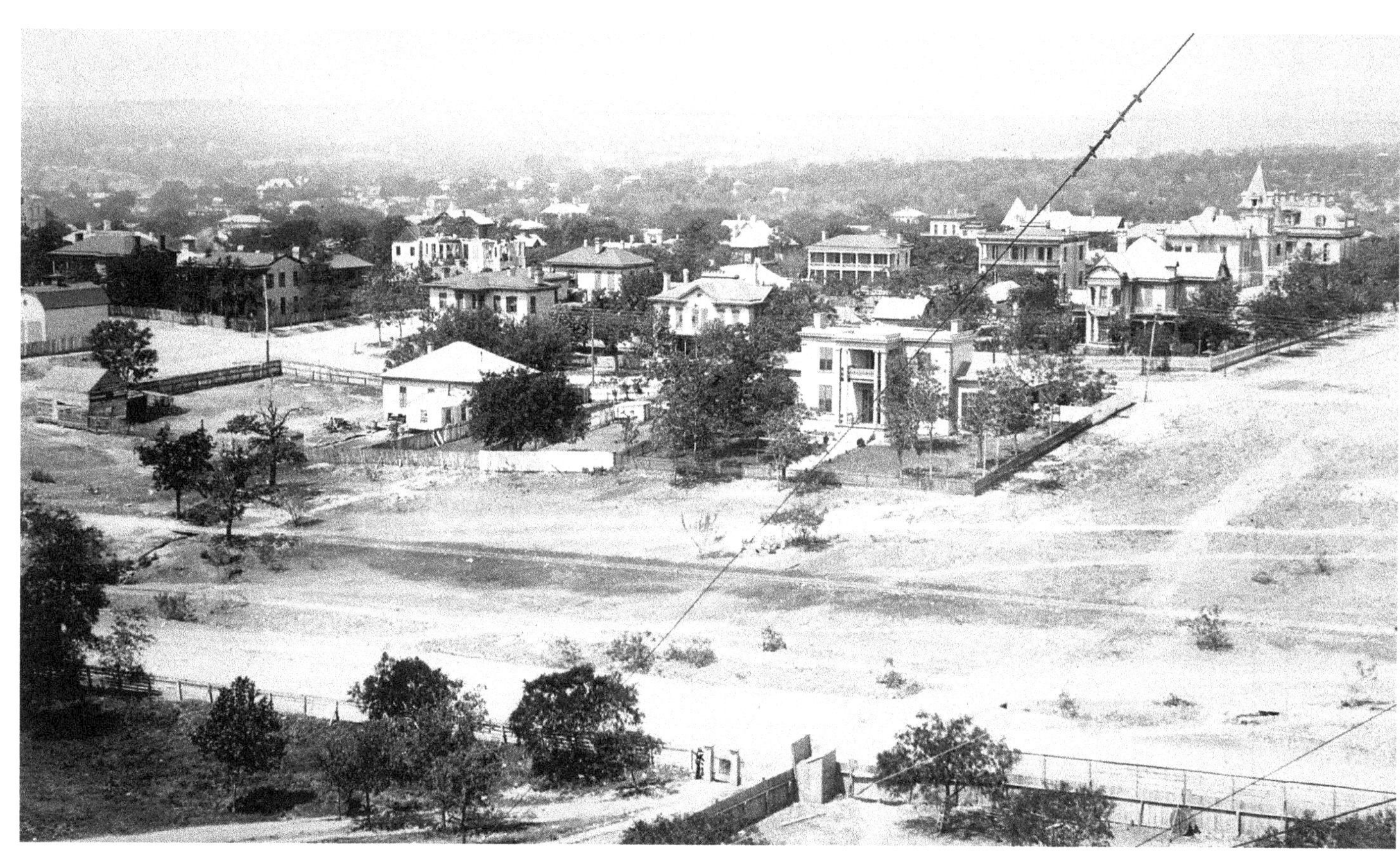

The view from the Capitol dome looking west shows many of the grand Victorian homes that would be torn down in the twentieth century to make room for businesses including parking garages.

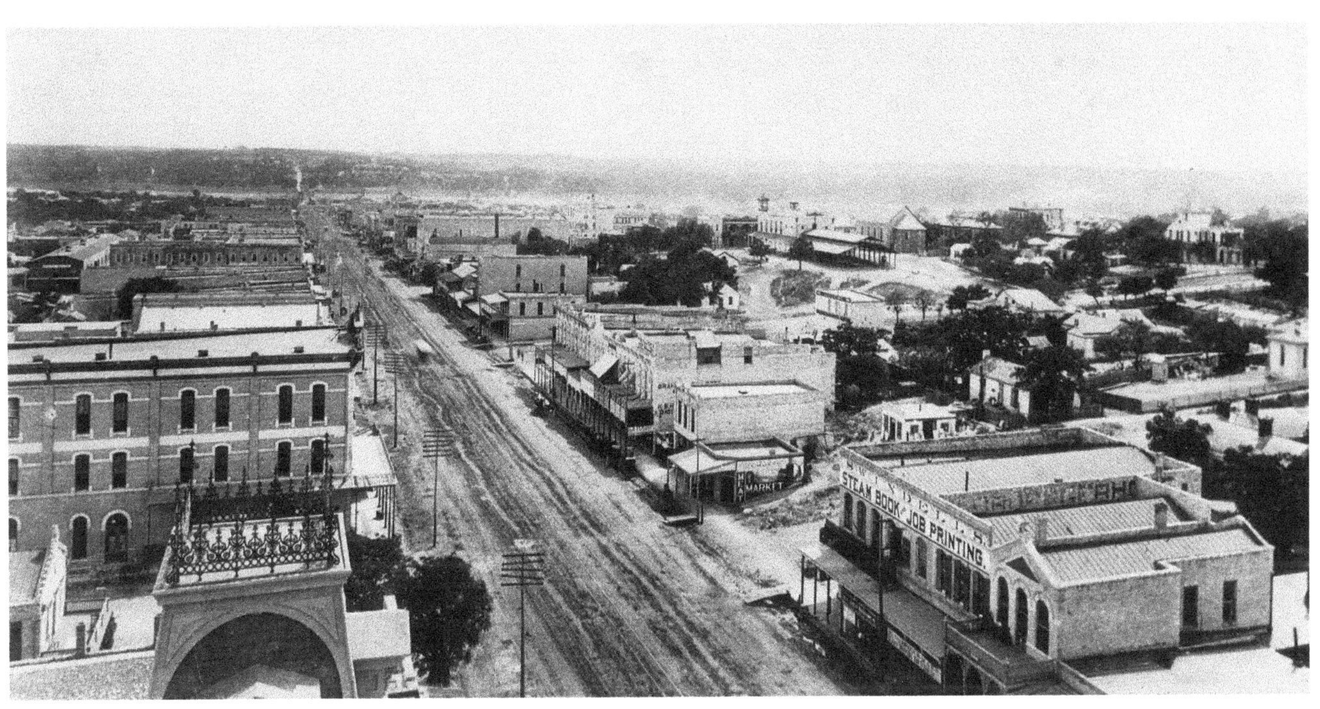

This view of Congress Avenue in the 1890s was taken from the roof of the Travis County Courthouse, which was across Eleventh (Mesquite) Street from the Capitol. The Colorado River is visible in the distance. The Lundberg Bakery building, lower right corner, is identifiable by its triple arches and the brass eagle atop its pediment.

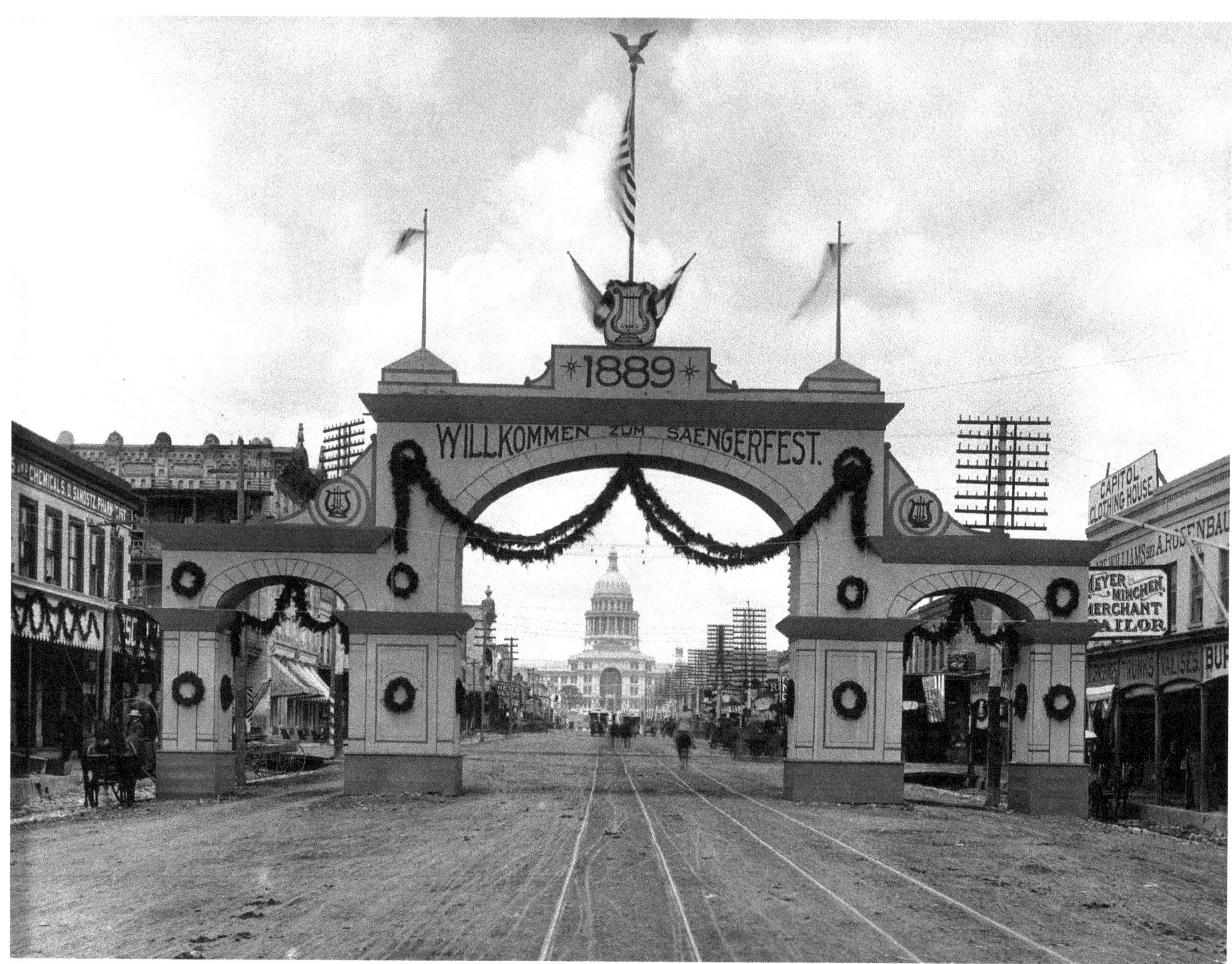

Austin has long been home to music festivals, thanks in no small part to its settlers of German descent. This temporary archway on Congress Avenue was erected in 1889 to welcome German singers from across Texas to a saengerfest, or songfest. The Saengerrunde, a German folk-singing society, had been founded a decade earlier. The club practiced at Scholz's beer garden, still home to this traditional style of singing.

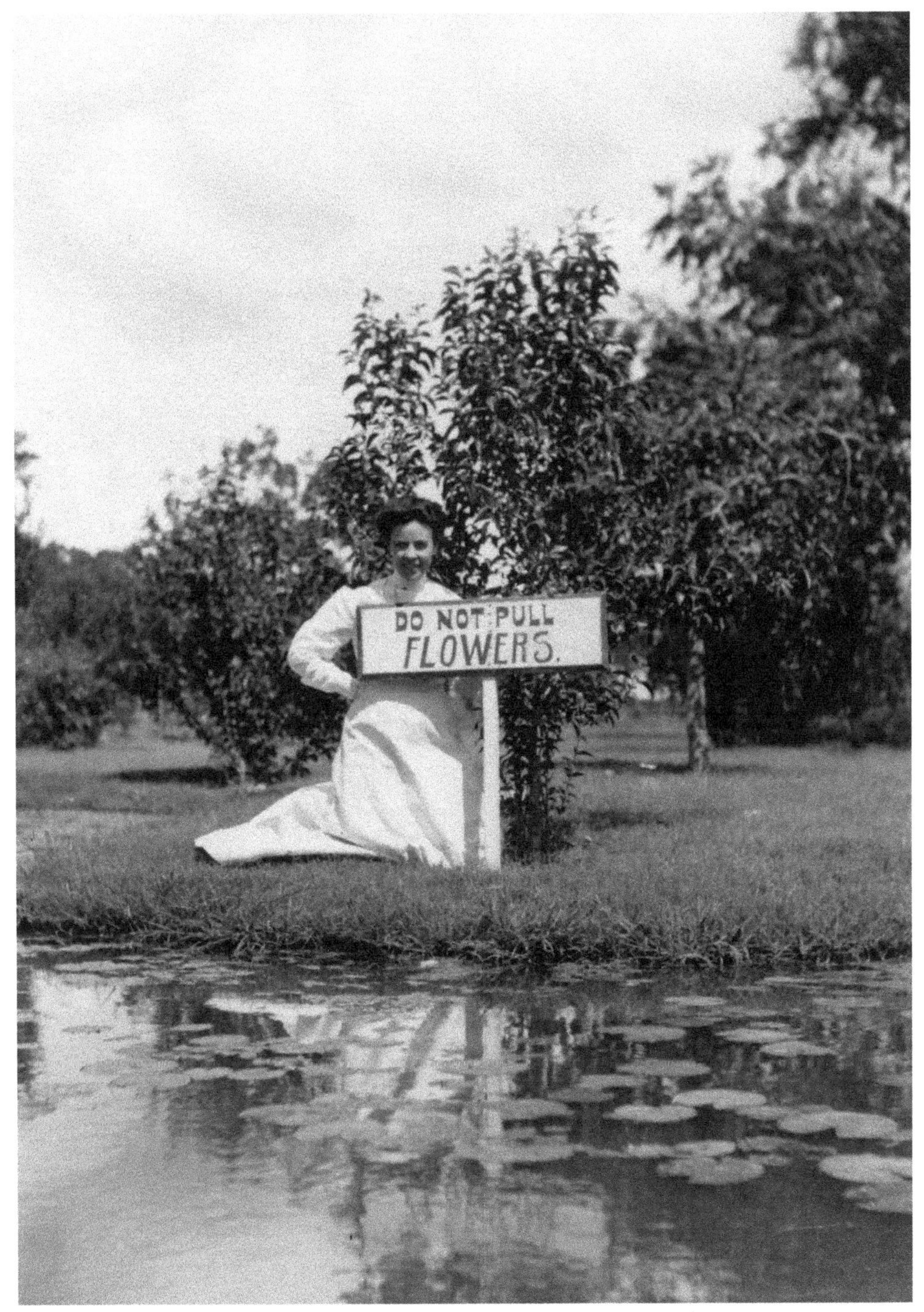

Hyde Park, Austin's first residential development, was sited on the old state fairgrounds, near the Lunatic Asylum (later renamed the State Hospital). Because strolls in the open air were thought to benefit inmates' health, its grounds were landscaped in the 1880s–1890s with driveways, lakes, and lily ponds. Hyde Park residents such as this young woman often attended afternoon social gatherings at the hospital gardens.

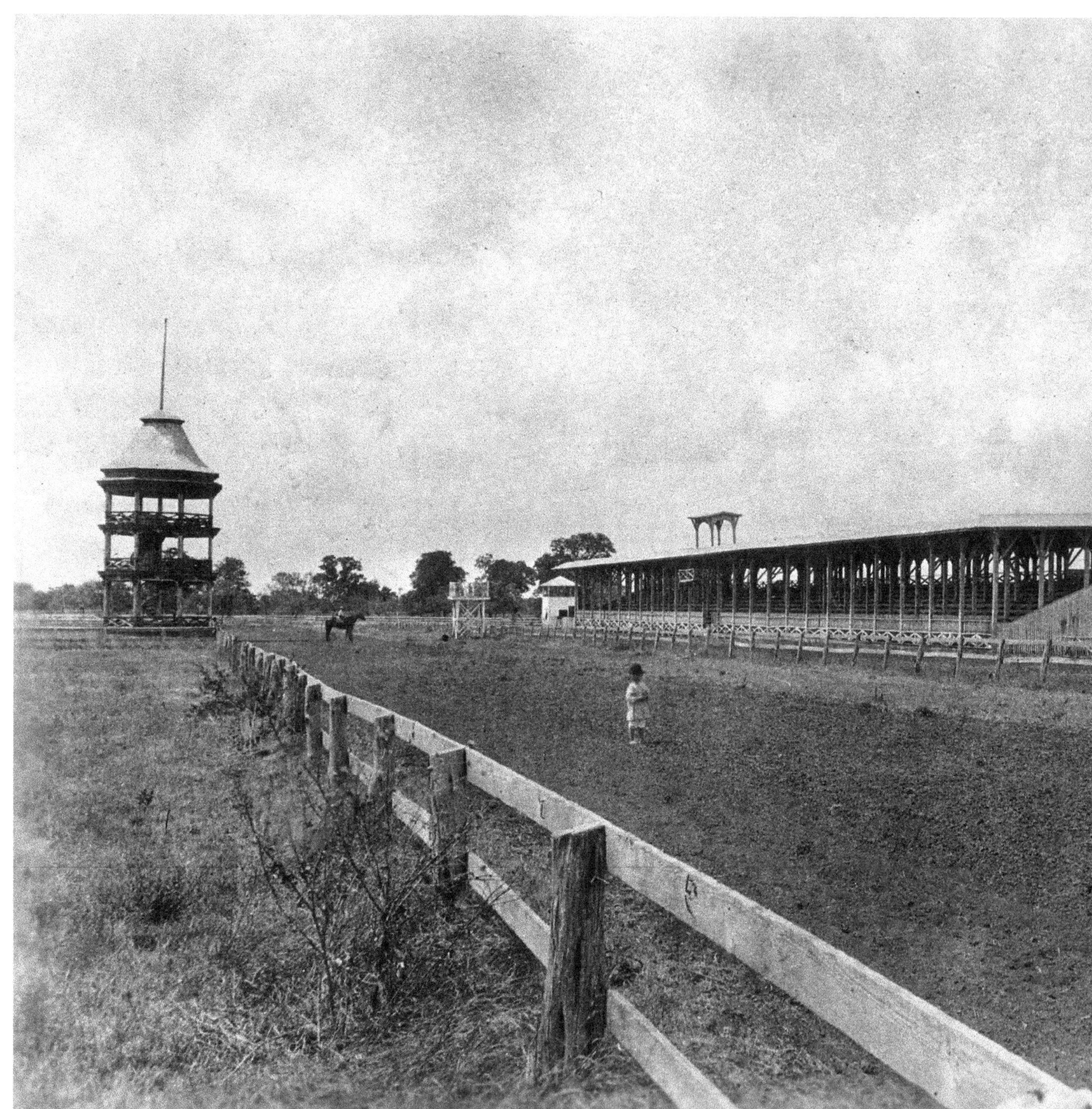

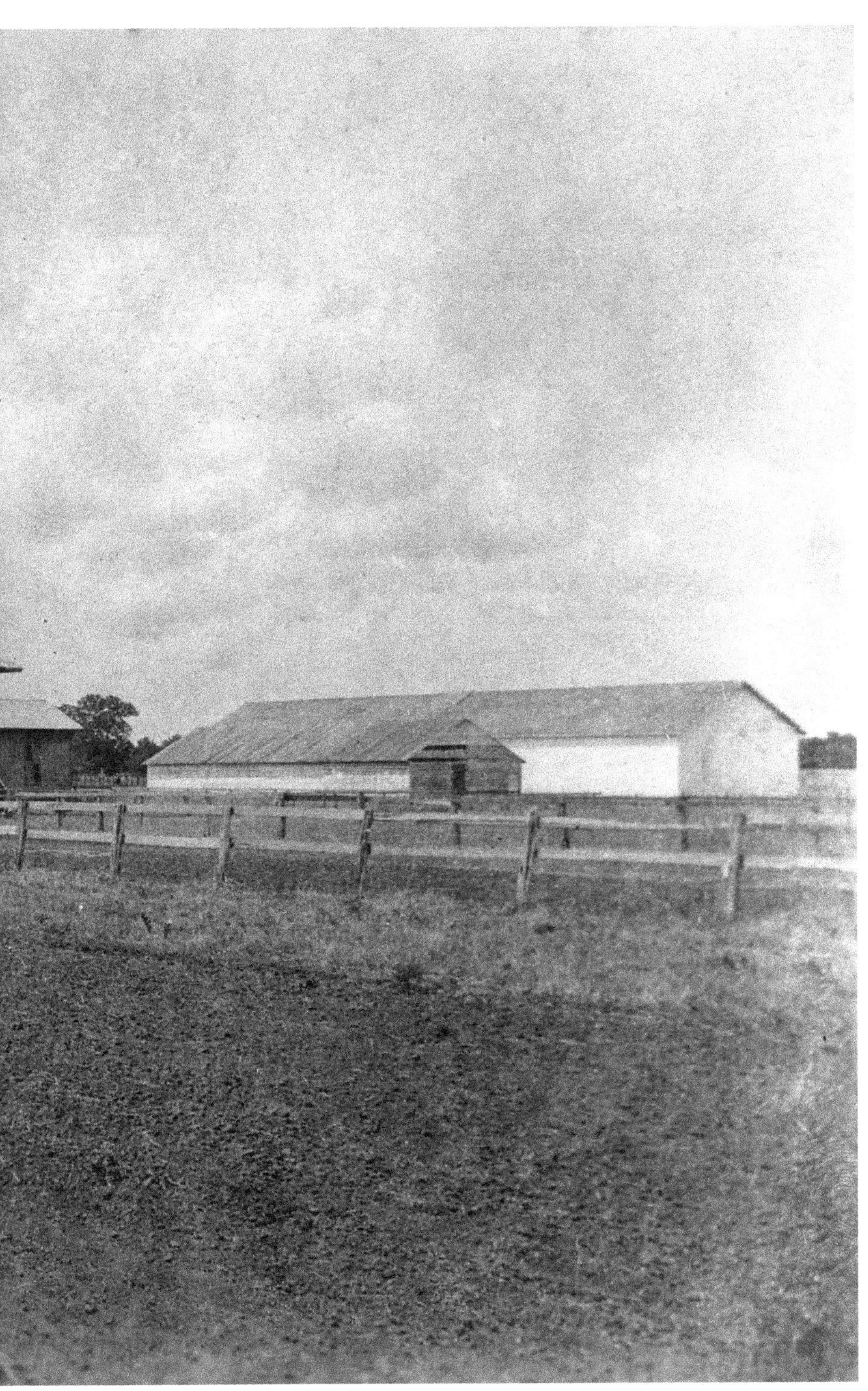

The racetrack, grandstands, and judging stand in Hyde Park had originally been part of the state fairgrounds, before Dallas became official host city of the Texas State Fair. When Hyde Park was developed in the early 1890s, the popular racetrack remained and continued to host horse races for several decades.

In the 1890s, young ladies could enjoy feeding the ducks near Gem Lake's landscaped central island on Sunday afternoon outings in Hyde Park, the residential community developed by Monroe Martin Shipe. Shipe had come to Austin from Kansas in 1889 to install the city's new streetcar railway system, and he stayed to develop his "elegant suburb," which was then more than a mile outside the city limits.

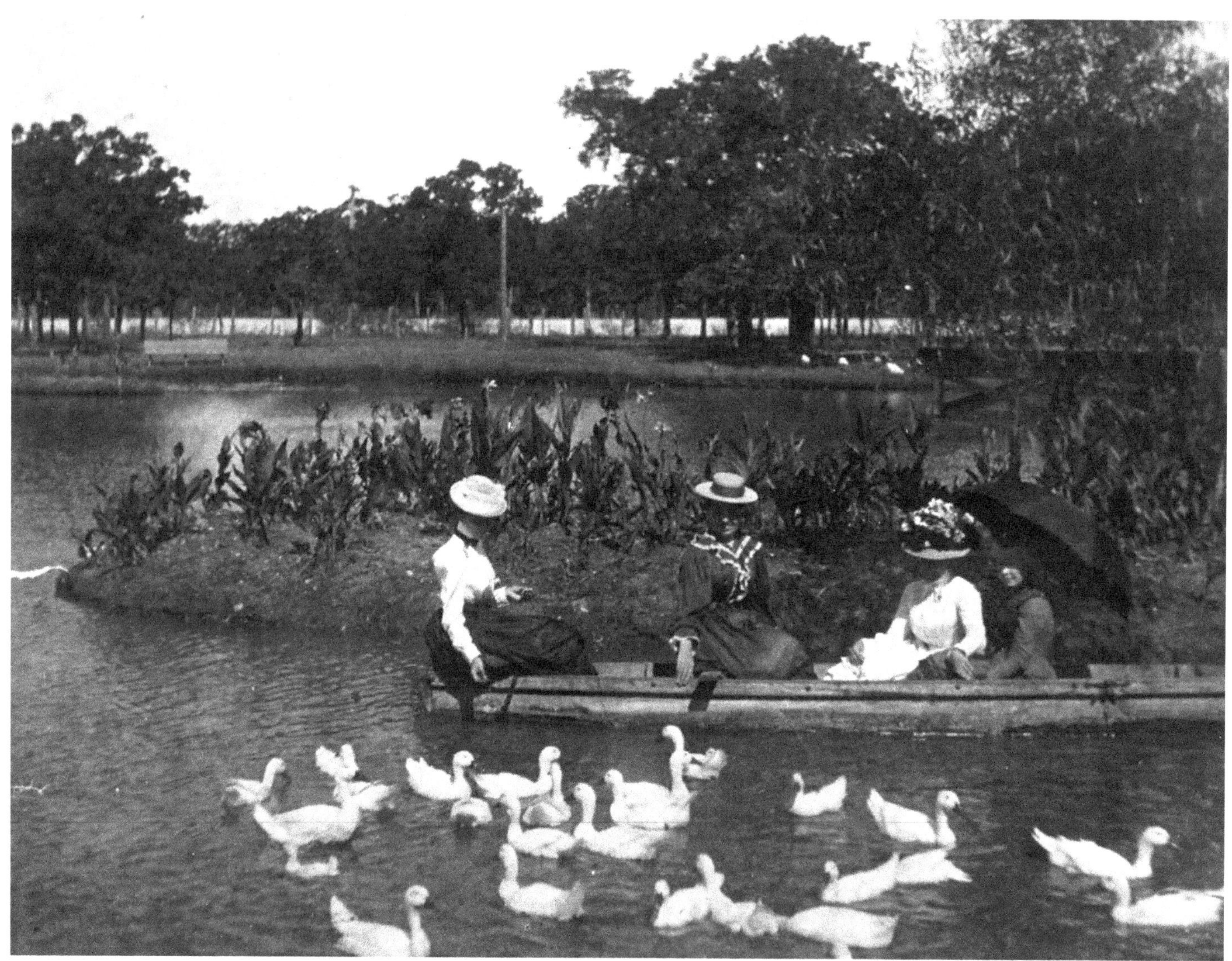

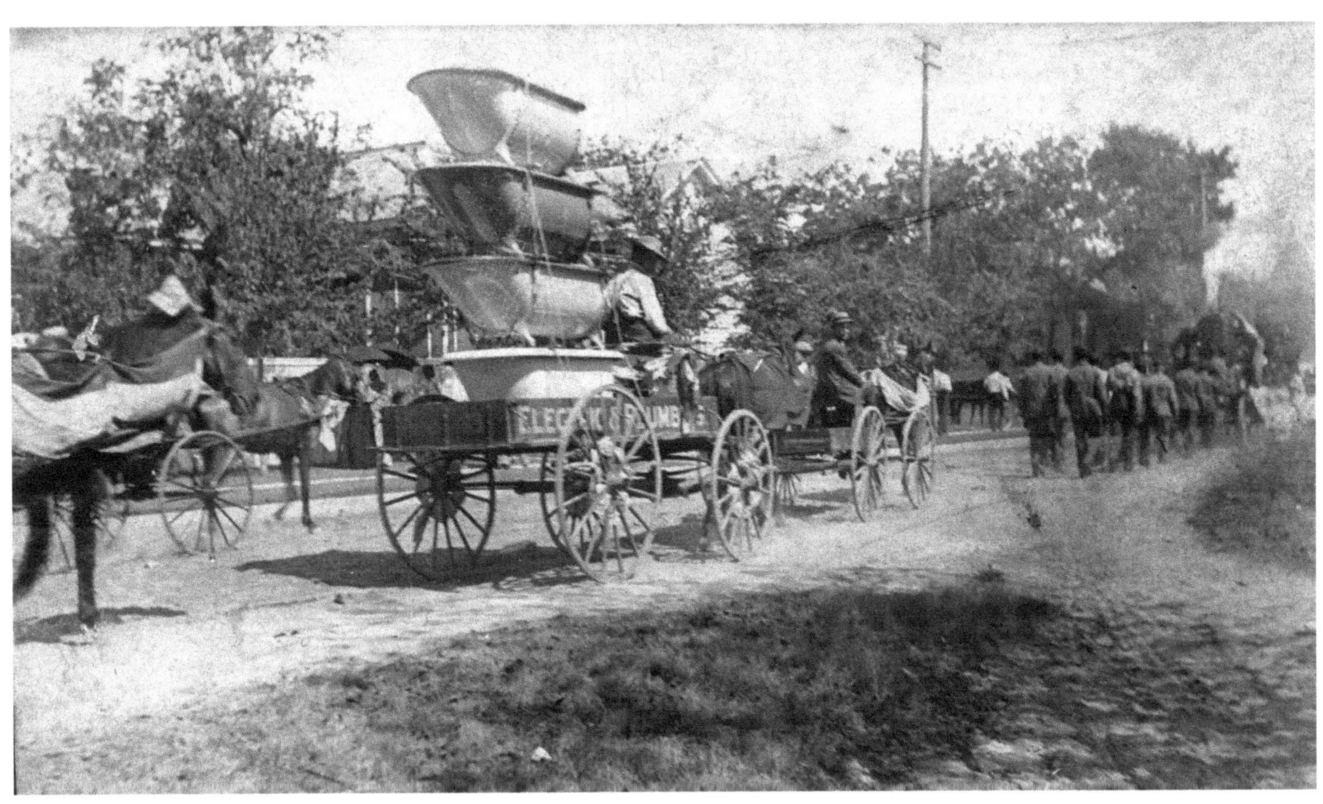

Local legend has it that Austin's first porcelain bathtub was installed in the home of lumberman Edgar Nalle on West Sixth Street. Nalle imported magnificent furnishings such as French crystal chandeliers for his elegant house and first saw the new porcelain tubs while visiting New York in the 1890s. When Nalle's house was demolished in the 1930s, it took ten men to carry the tub to the neighboring Smoot home.

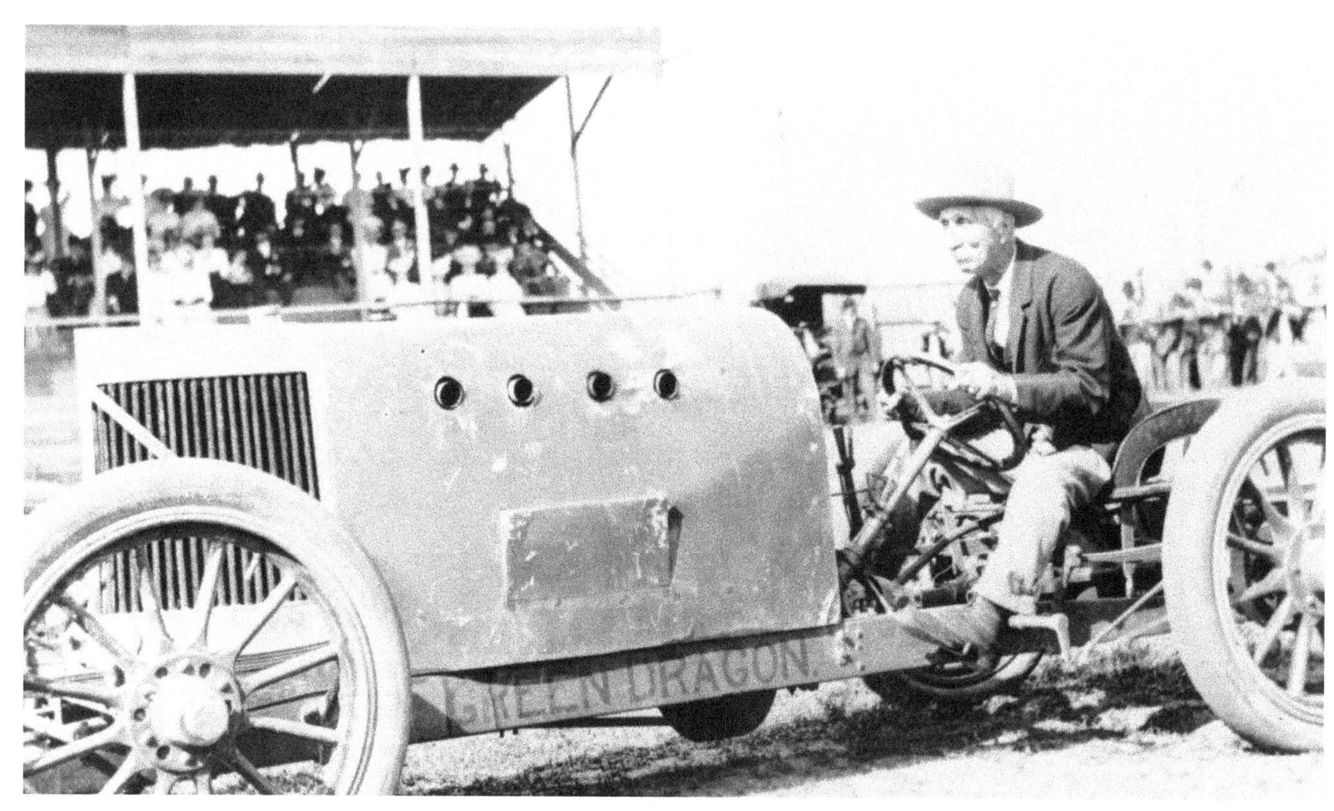

As this photograph attests, the races at Hyde Park's racetrack were not always limited to horses. This early version of a racecar, dubbed *Green Dragon,* looks like a potential winner.

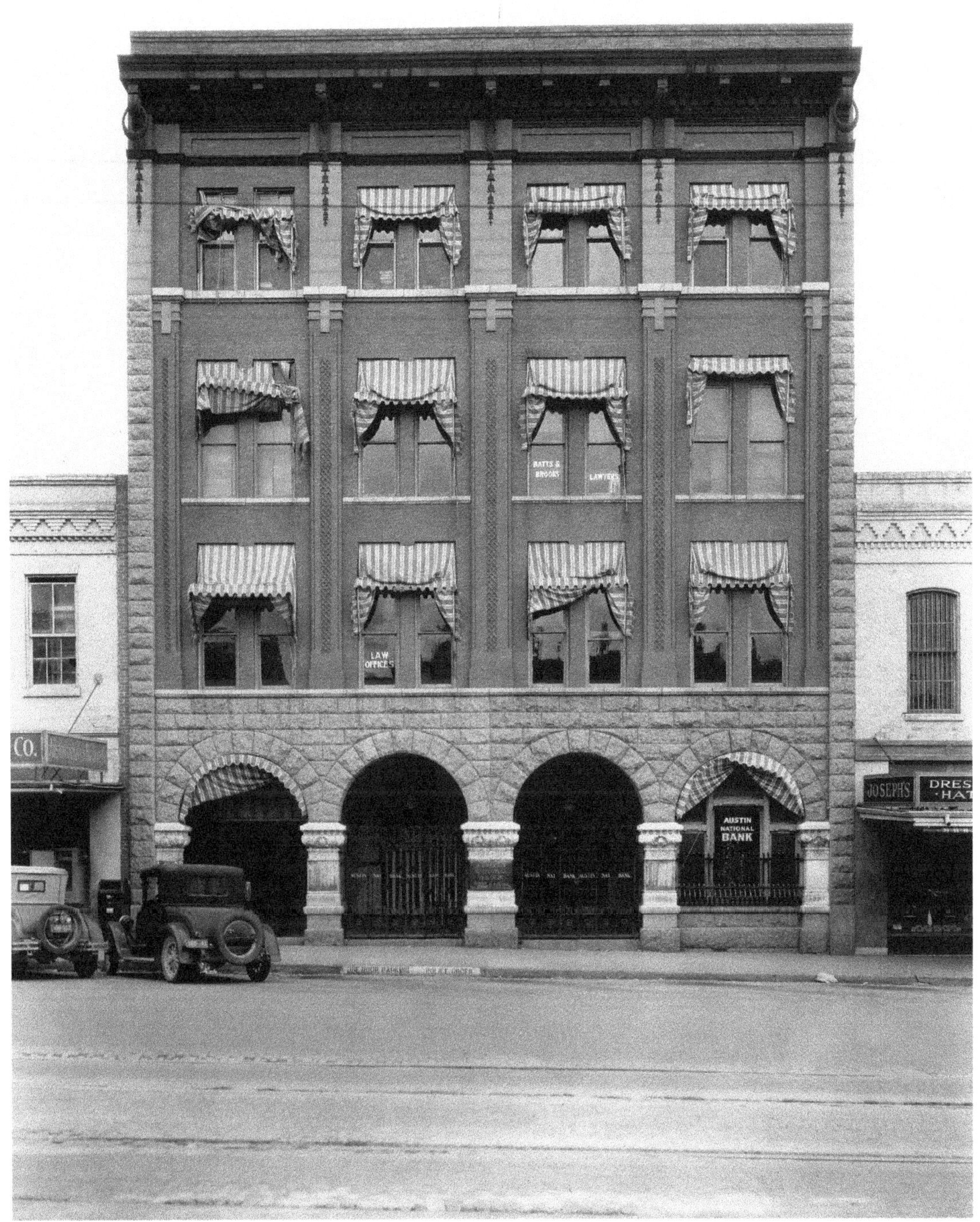

Austin National Bank opened its doors on June 16, 1890, in a leased space on the ground floor of the Hancock Building. Several law offices occupied spaces on upper floors. This building was in the 100 block of Pecan (now West Sixth) Street, which means it was just around the corner from Congress Avenue.

The First National Bank of Austin stood proudly at the northwest corner of Congress Avenue and Sixth (Pecan) Street.

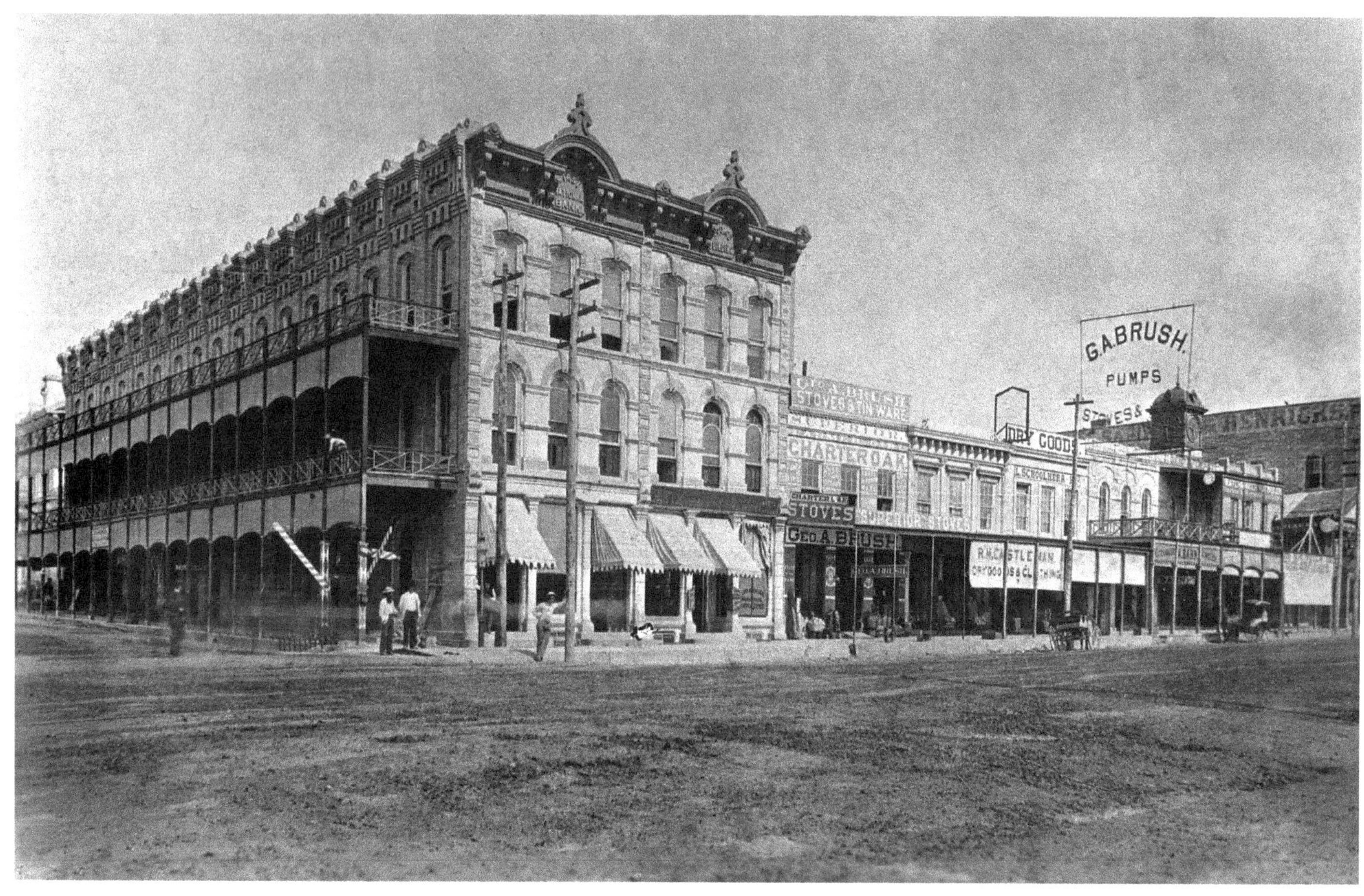

This photograph captured men hard at work laying track for the new electric streetcars at the corner of Sixth Street and Congress Avenue.

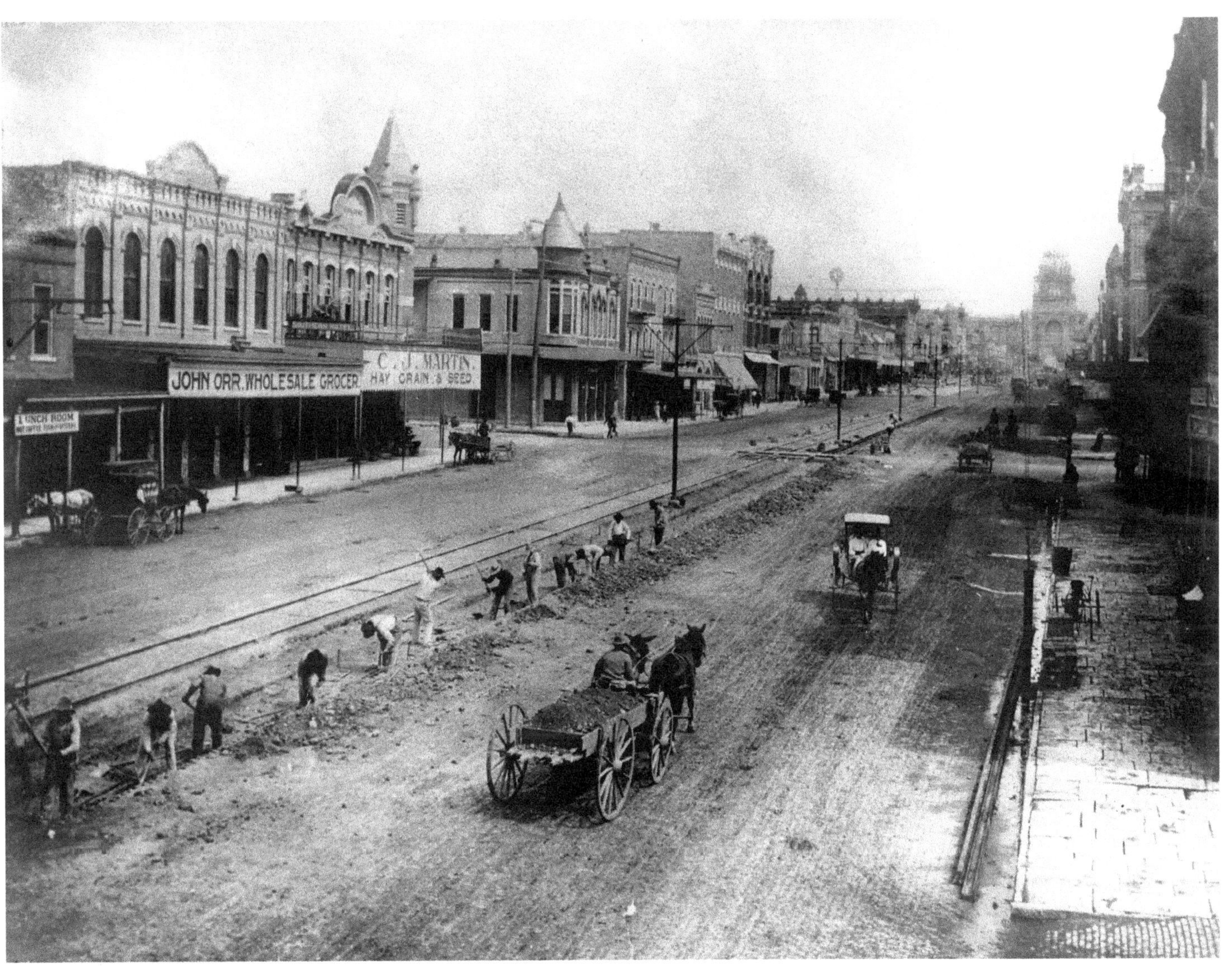

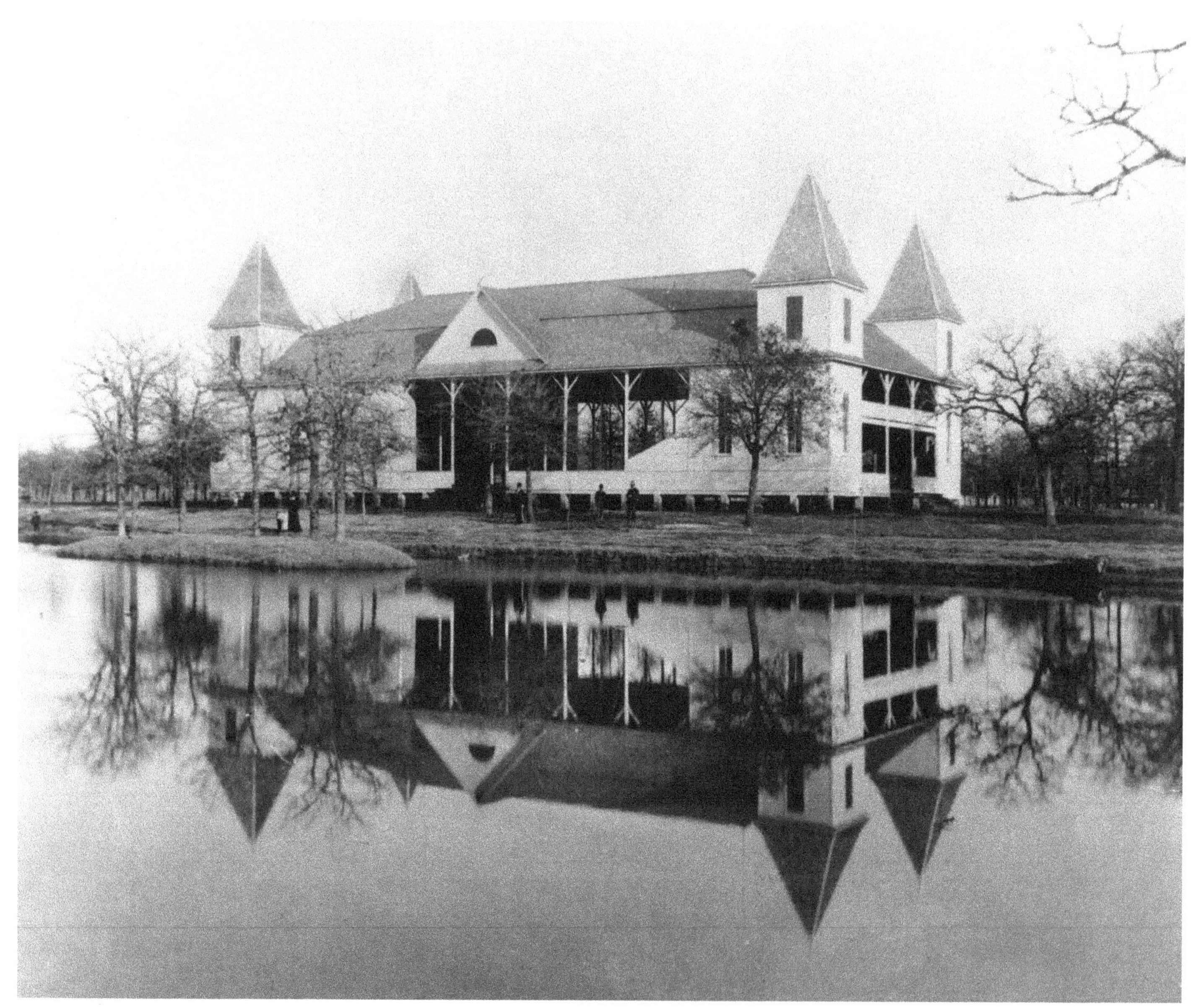

The Hyde Park Transit Pavilion, an open-air structure built in 1892, was owned by the street railway company whose streetcars regularly ran to it from town and back. The pavilion offered all kinds of entertainment: dances, puppet shows, plays, and musical performances such as Gilbert and Sullivan's *HMS Pinafore* by the Austin Musical Union.

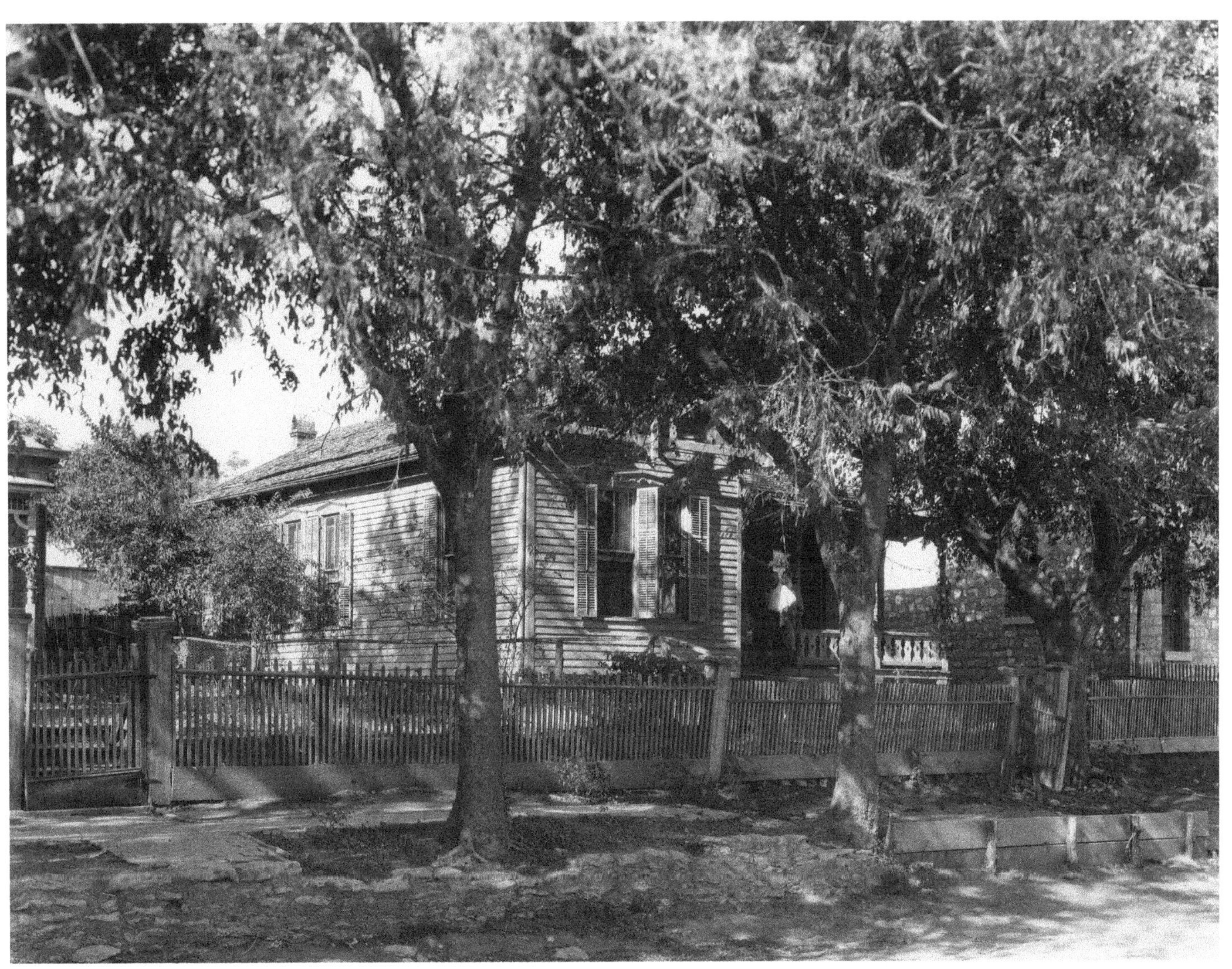

From 1893 to 1895, this Queen Anne–style cottage built in 1886 was home to William Sidney Porter, known also by his pen name O. Henry. Since this photograph was taken, the structure was moved to 409 East Fifth Street, restored, and made into the O. Henry Museum. It contains artifacts from the writer's 13 years in Austin. In a short story, O. Henry named Austin "The City of the Violet Crown" for its beautiful sunsets.

Construction is in progress on the first Austin Dam, completed in 1893. Its proponents envisioned that dam-generated electric power would transform Austin into a manufacturing center, but poor research before the dam's construction caused problems later. Electricity did not flow until 1895, a power shortfall in 1899 was so great that water and electric service had to be suspended, and in 1900 the dam burst, flooding the city.

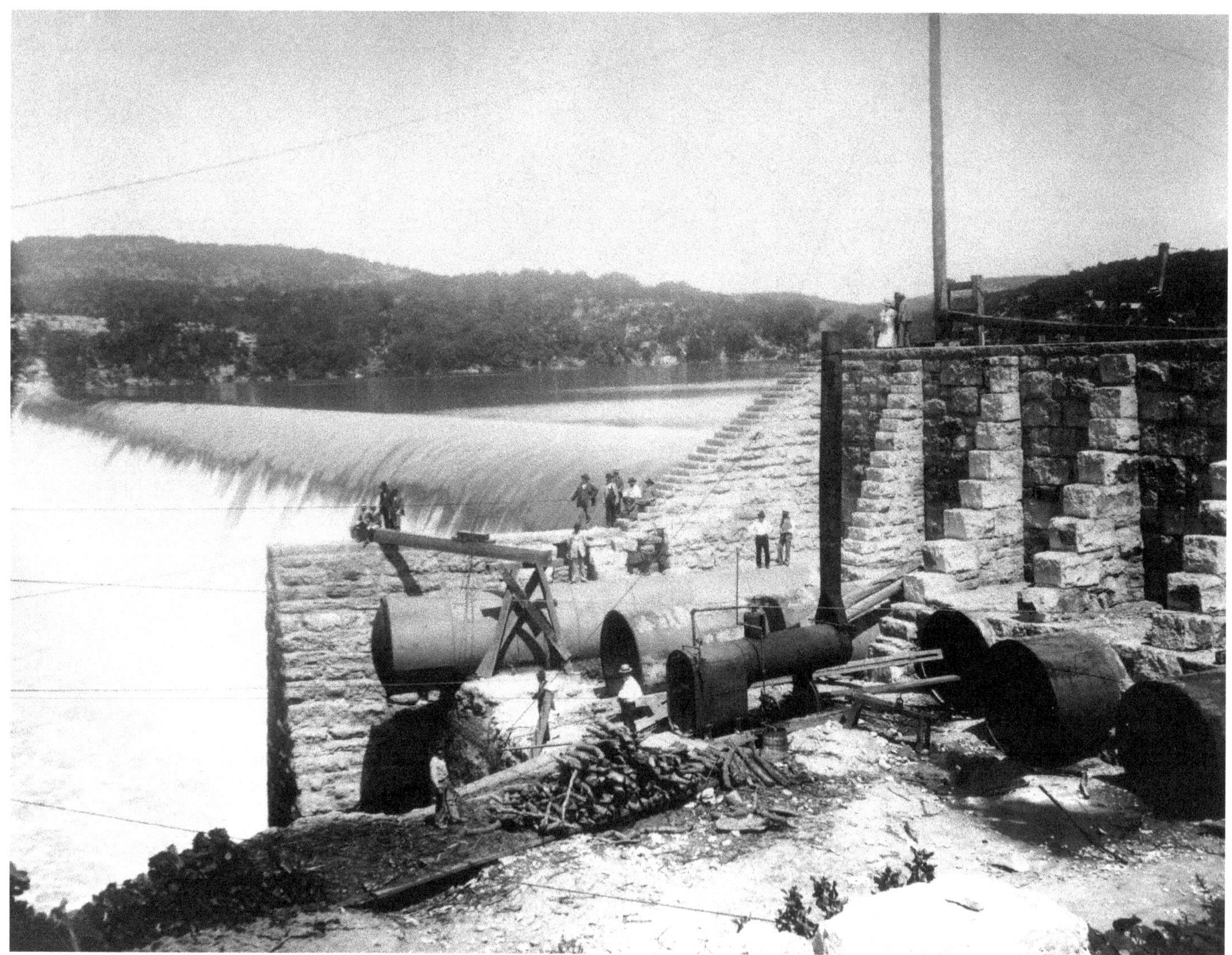

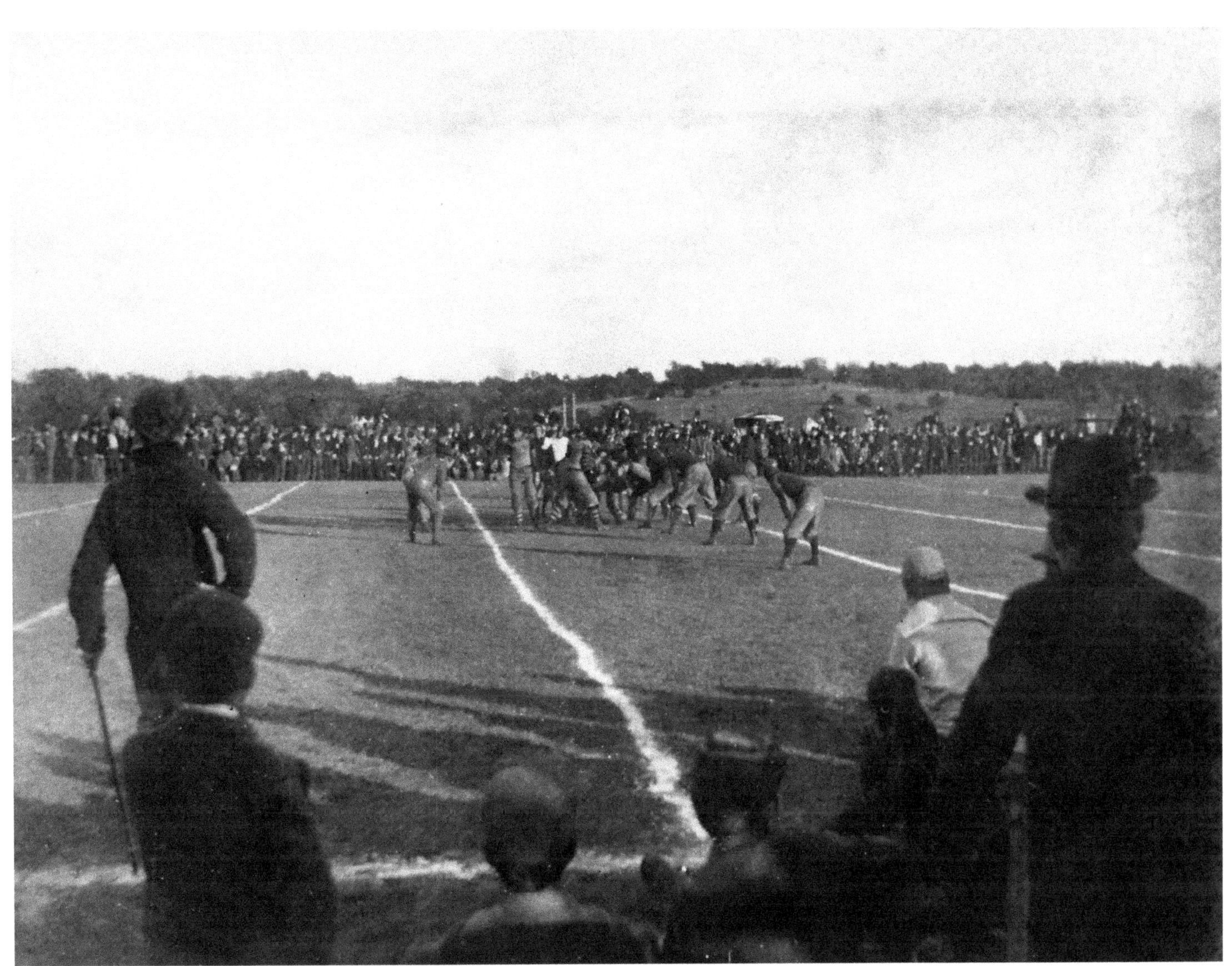

Young men at the University of Texas began playing football in 1893, whenever they could find an opposing team willing to meet for a game. The team played its first official intercollegiate game in October 1894 against Texas A&M University. The Austin team won 38 to 0, beginning a football rivalry that would continue for more than a century.

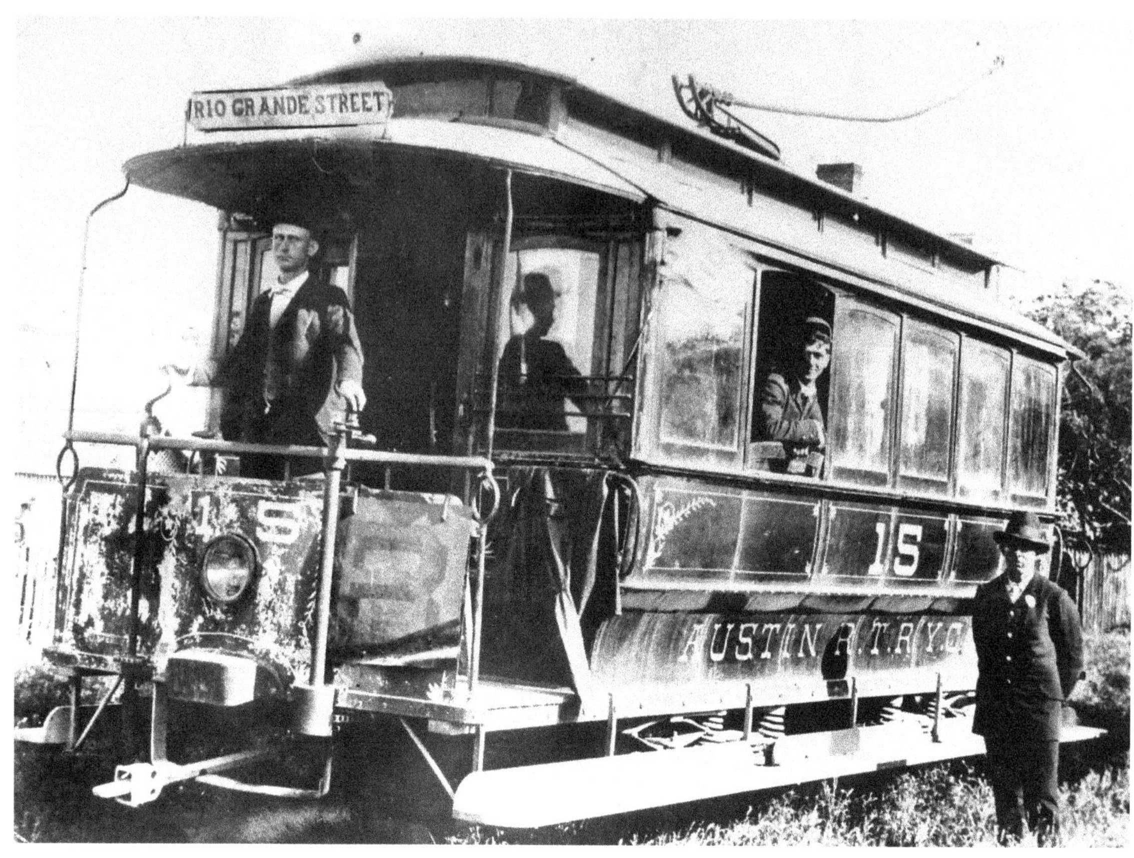

Streetcar Number 15, with its conductor and motormen, covered Rio Grande Street. The fare was 5¢ in 1891 and did not increase until 1920. Employee rules included: "Every employee must at all times give civil answers to all proper enquiries on the part of the public." Conductors and motormen used a system of bells to communicate. One clang from the conductor meant "Stop at next crossing." Two meant "Go ahead."

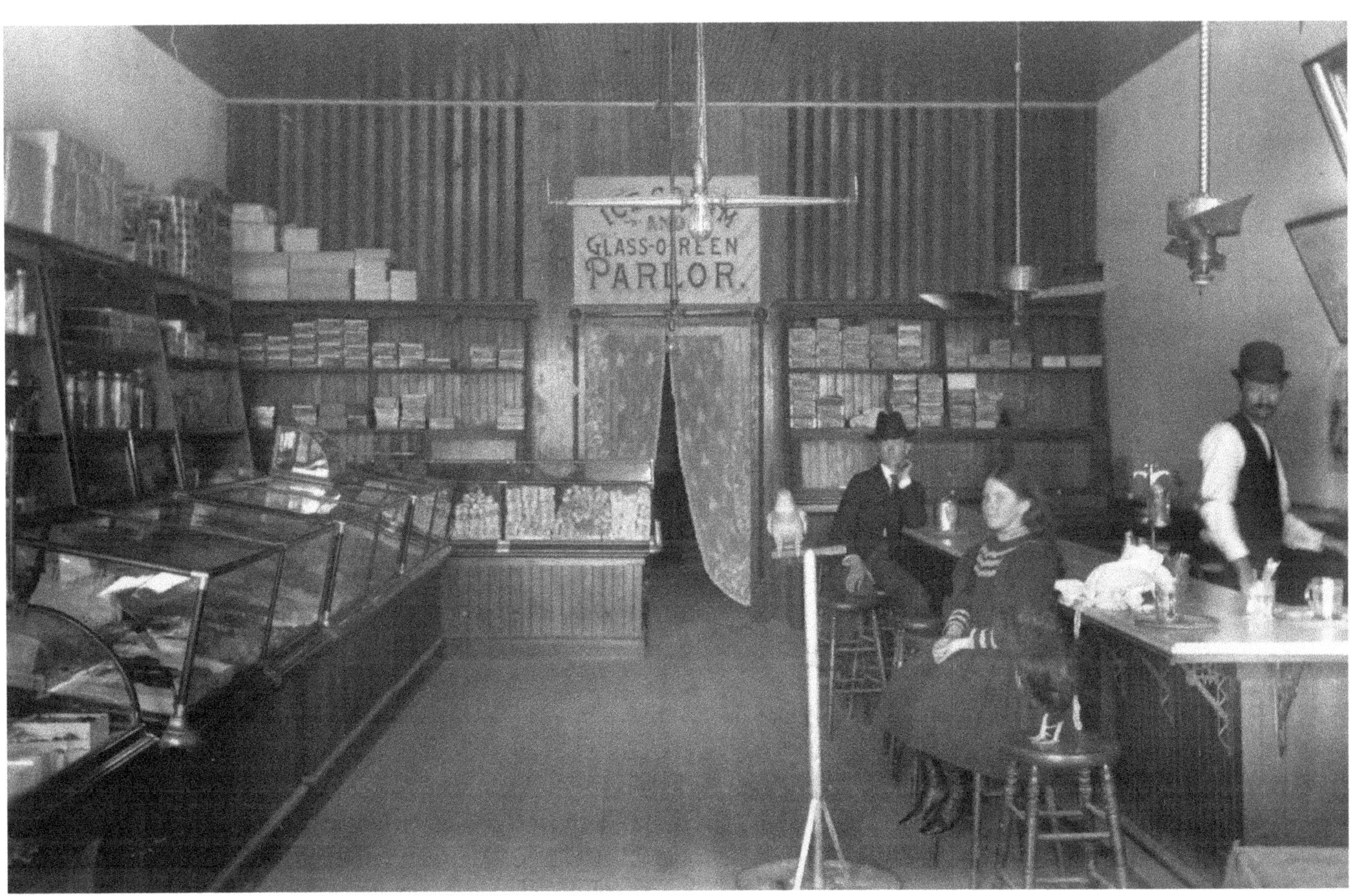

This photograph taken in 1897 shows Fulton's Ice Cream Parlor, 1608 Lavaca Street. Austinites were treated to their first taste of ice cream in the summer of 1869, at Charles W. Ohrndorf's Ice Cream Saloon. The cold dessert became available only after ice could be made. For many years, ice cream was a treat reserved for special occasions, so perhaps the little girl pictured is celebrating her birthday.

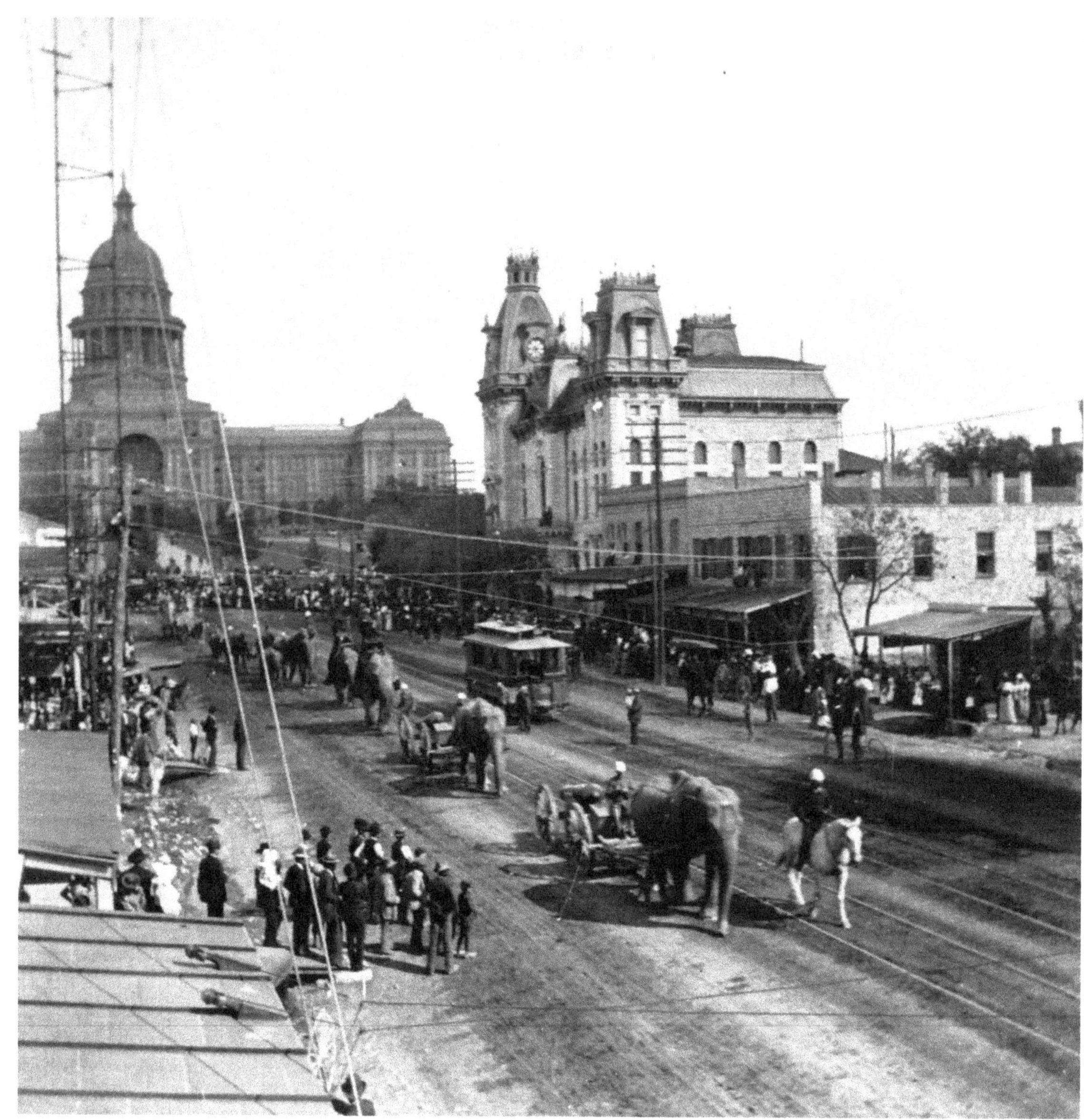

Austinites loved any kind of parade, but perhaps none was more thrilling than when the circus came to town. It was an amazing spectacle to see elephants lumbering down Congress Avenue alongside an electric trolley, circa 1897.

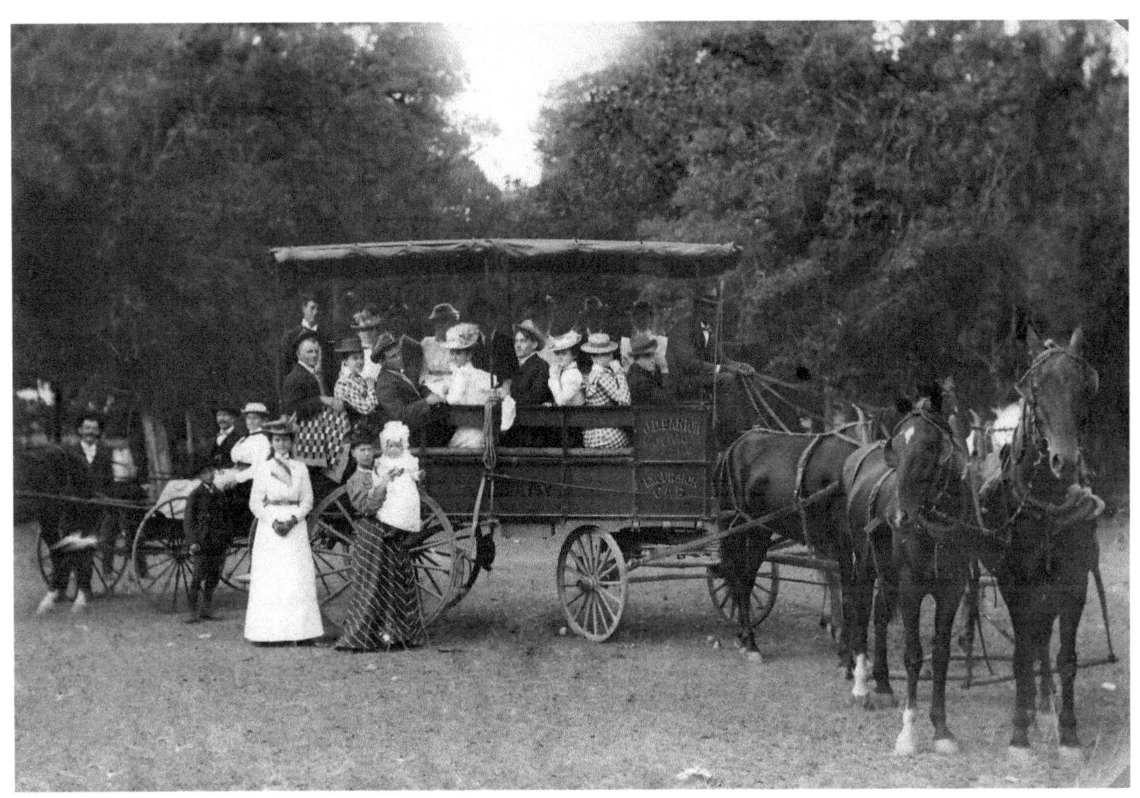

Before the Austin Street Railway brought electric streetcars to Austin, "mass" transportation took the form of mule-drawn streetcars similar to this horse-drawn conveyance, which was called an "excursion car" in 1899.

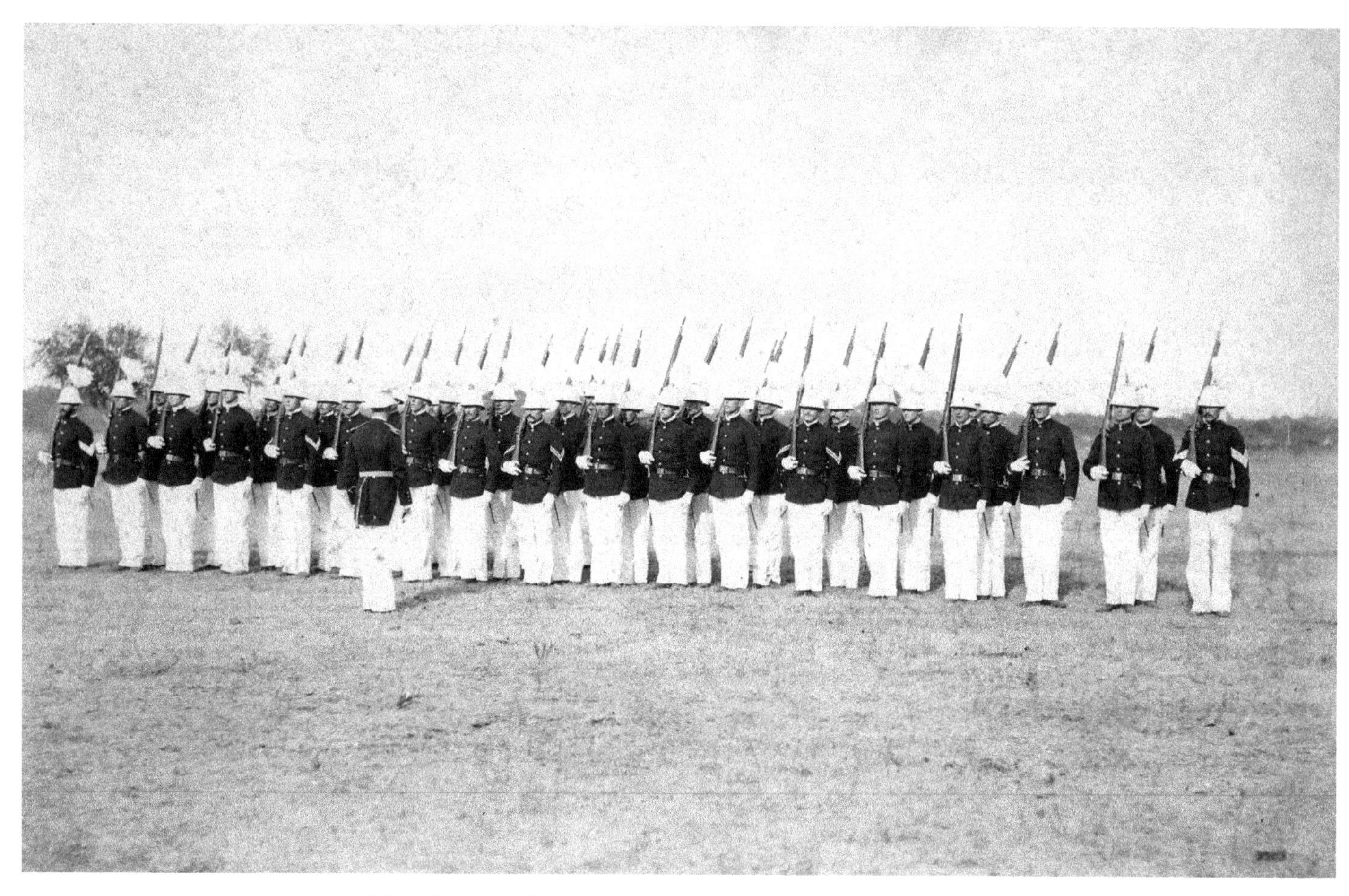

This elite group, known as the Governor's Guard or the Harper Kerby Rifles, is undergoing inspection, probably at Camp Mabry in the late 1890s. Originally 90 acres, Camp Mabry grew in size during the turn of the century. The federal government purchased additional acreage for training the National Guard, some land was donated, and by 1911 the camp had grown to encompass 400 acres.

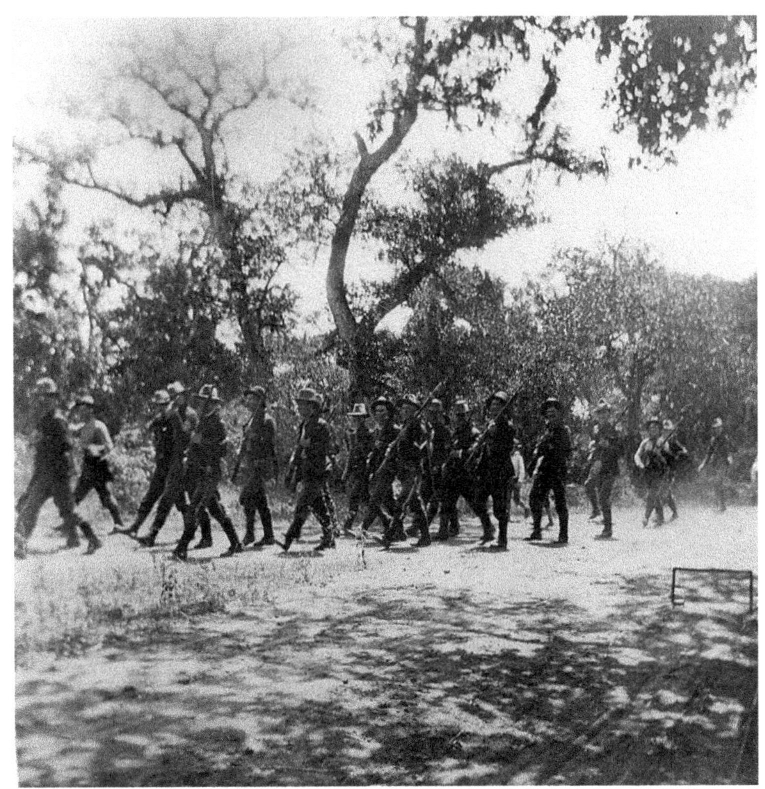

Texas Volunteer Guard troops (later the Texas National Guard) drill at Camp Mabry around 1898, preparing for action in the Spanish-American War. Camp Mabry had been founded in northwest Austin in 1892.

Austinites have long enjoyed outdoor sports. The city's first golfing club, later named the Austin Country Club, was organized on November 13, 1899. Golf is believed to have been introduced by Lewis Hancock, mayor from 1895 to 1897. He is said to have learned the game in New England while on summer vacations with his family.

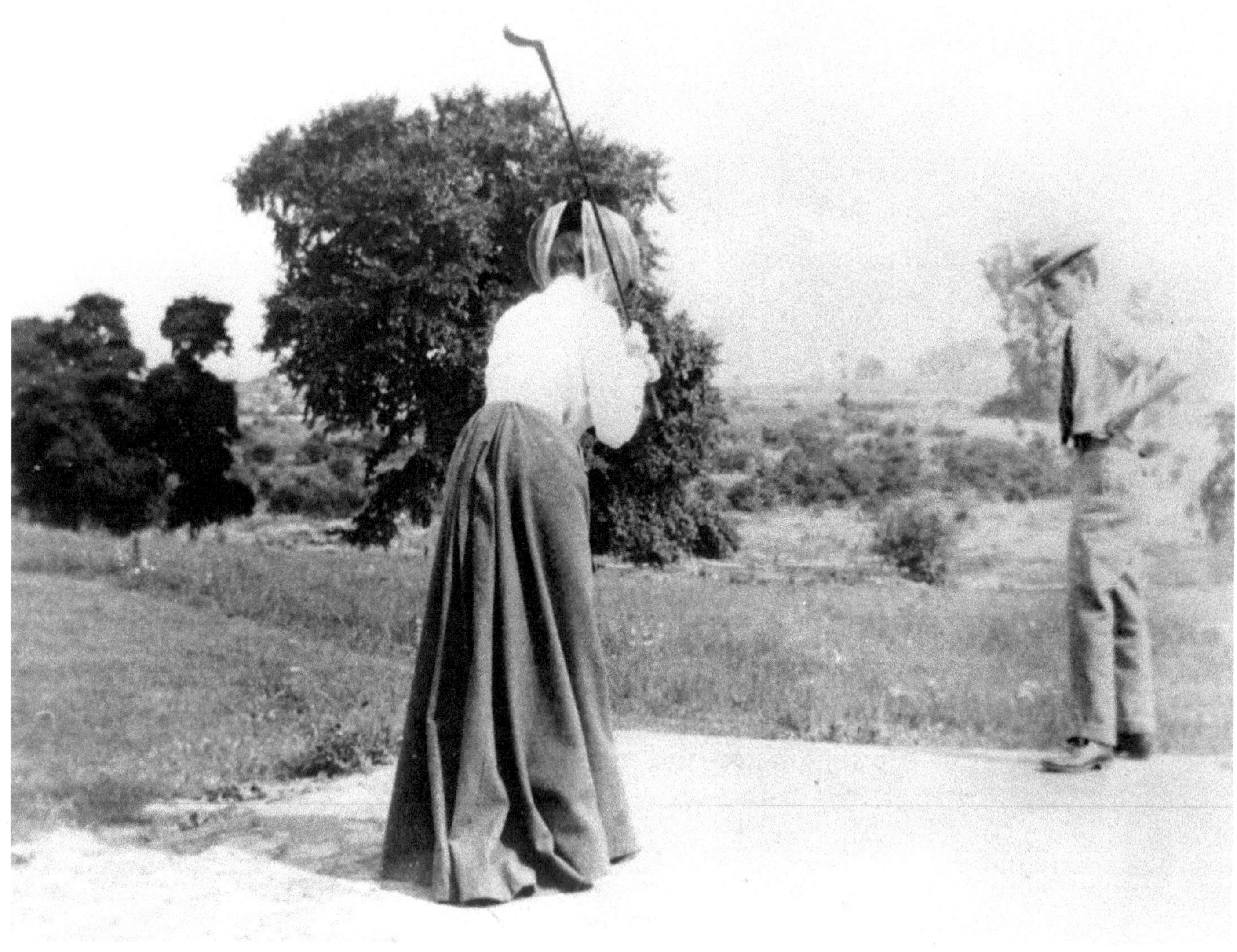

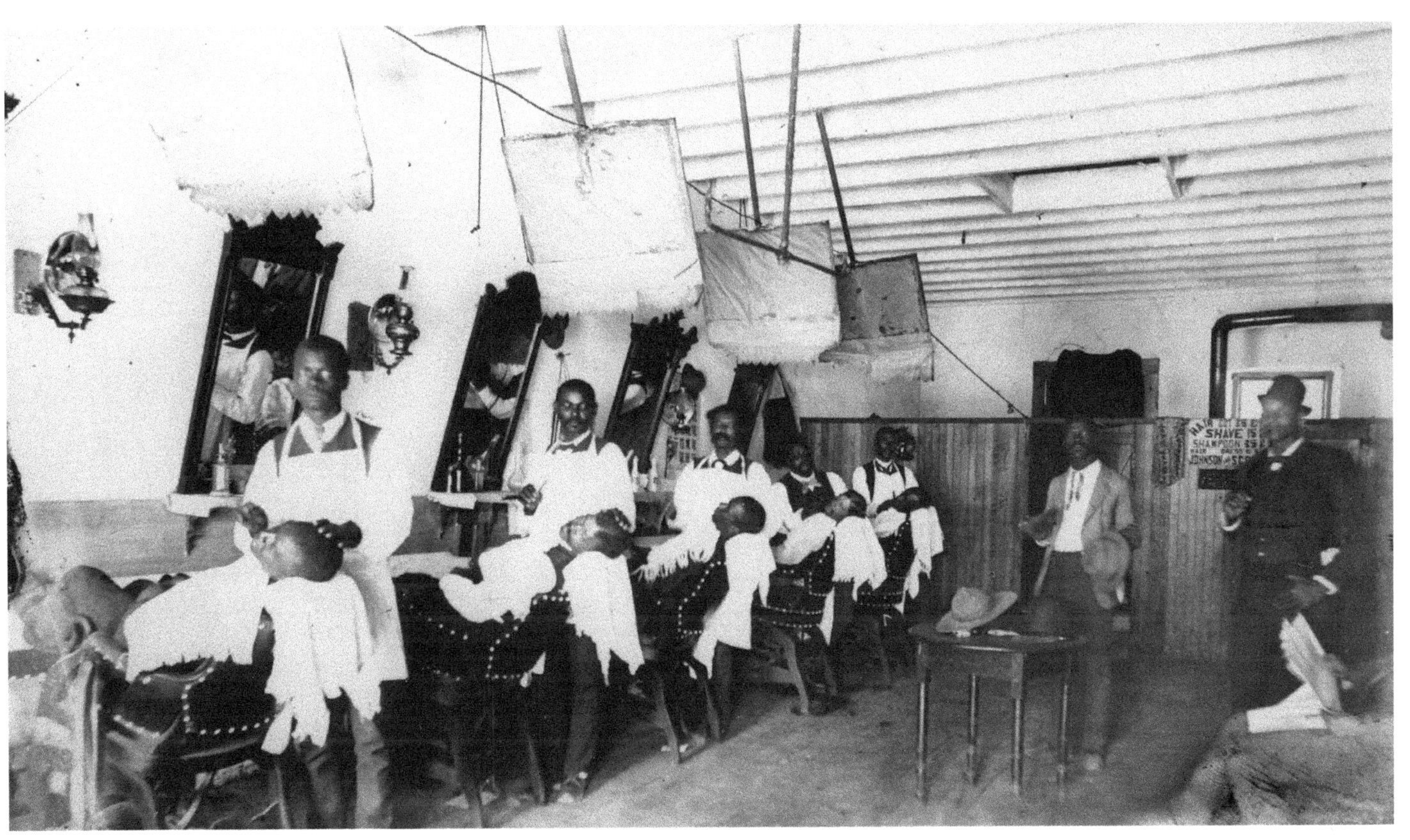

This busy barbershop in East Austin, owned and operated by and for African Americans, was photographed around 1895. It displays the latest conveniences, such as individual wall-mounted lamps and motorized ceiling fans, for the benefit of its customers.

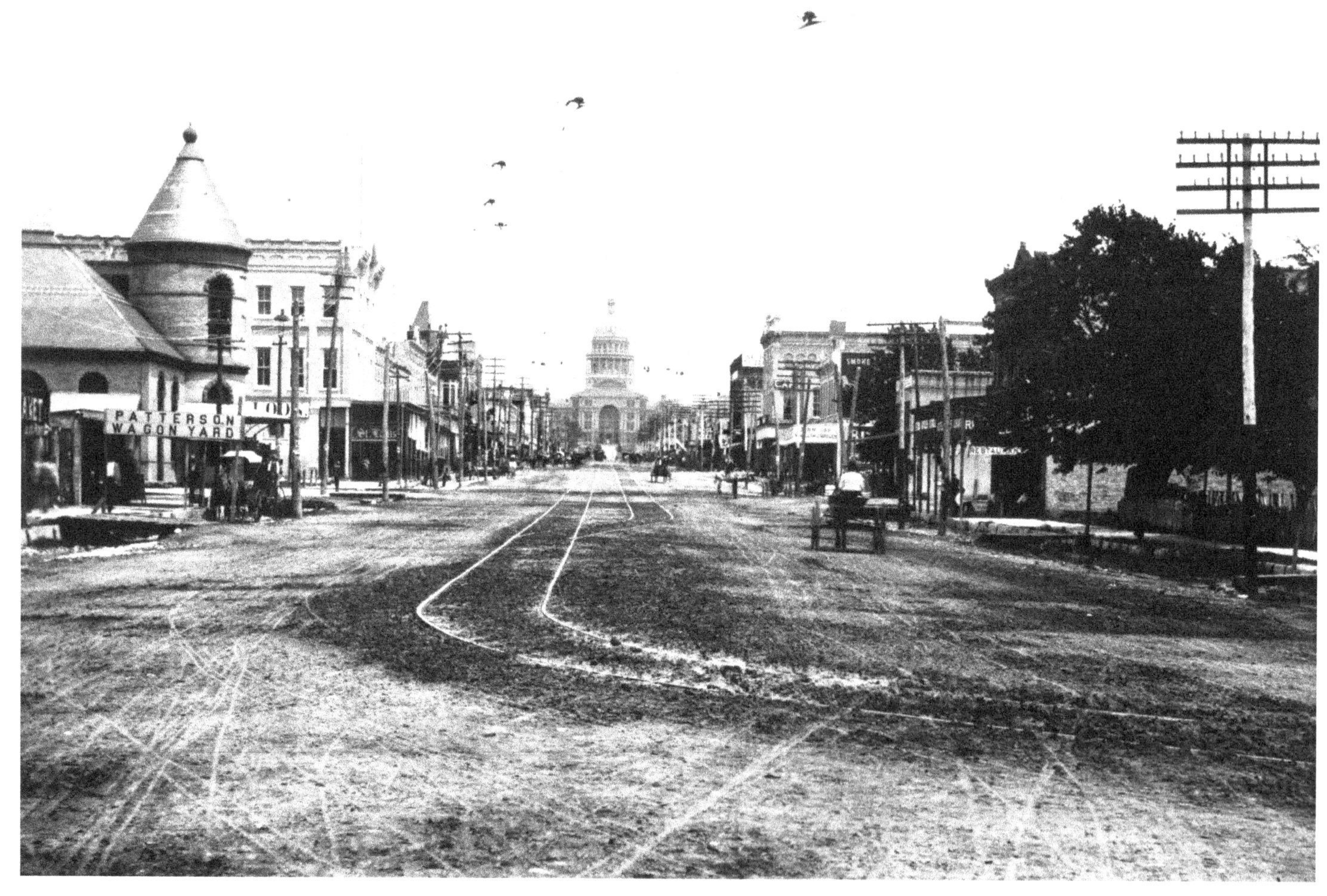

This view of Congress Avenue circa 1895 shows the Union Depot at the corner of Cypress (Third) Street with its recognizable rotunda (left), and the tracks for the electric streetcars, which began in 1891 running up and down the center of "The Avenue," powered by overhead cables connected to telegraph poles.

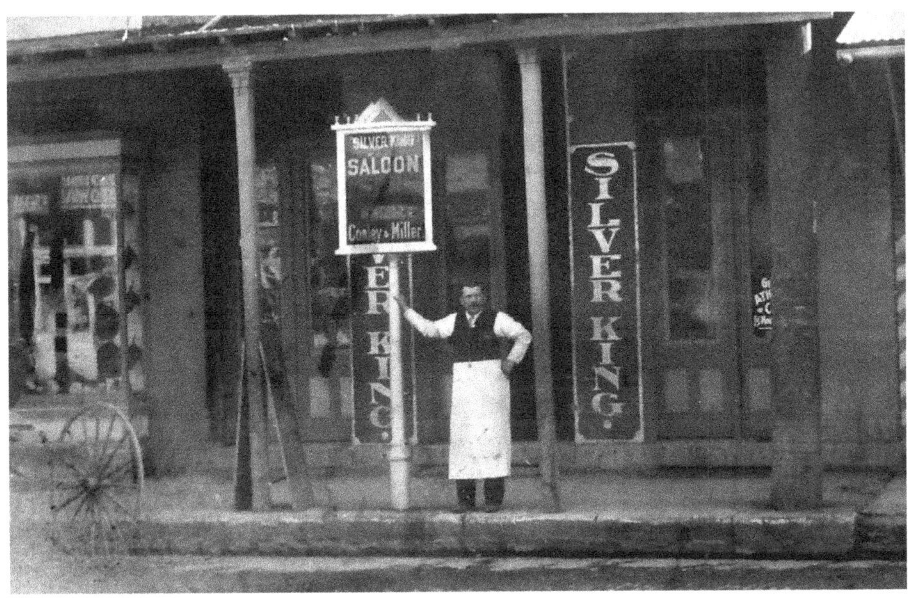

Proprietor Buck Miller takes a breath of fresh air outside the Silver King. Saloons of varying degrees of respectability were prevalent in Austin during the late 1800s, lending the town a somewhat unwholesome reputation among some Texans. It became the custom of proper ladies to avoid several blocks along Congress Avenue's east side because of the overflow of saloon patrons, some of whom also frequented the upstairs rooms for gambling.

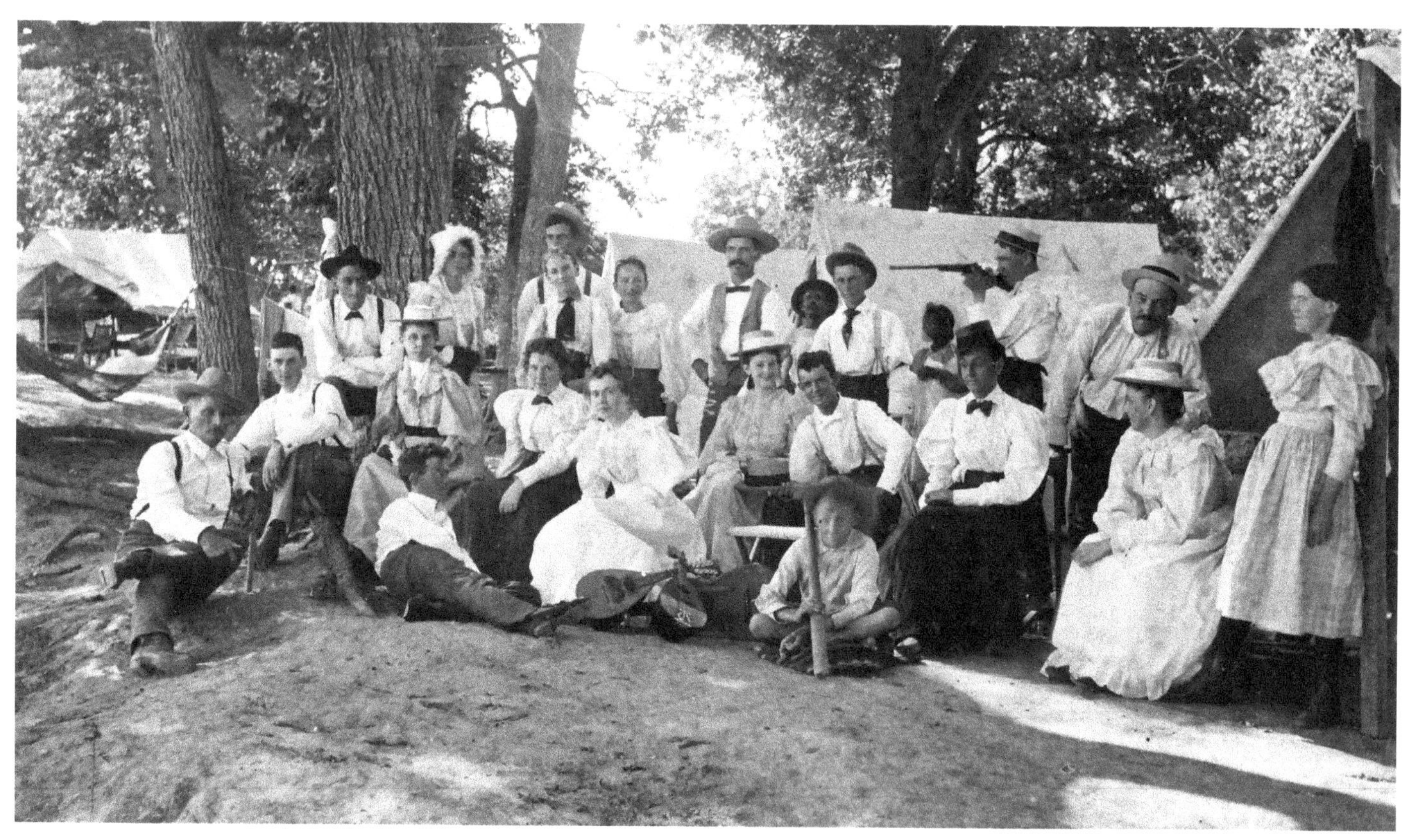

Families and friends loved to pitch their tents and camp out at Zilker Park around the turn of the century. It was an era when leisure was a rather new concept, and most adults wore hats (or sunbonnets) outdoors, even when relaxing.

An Era of Progress

(1900–1919)

In the new century Austin underwent improvements as its leadership reflected the nation's mood of progressivism. Disaster struck in the spring of 1900, however, as heavy rains caused the dam to collapse, flooding the city for miles and leaving Austinites without potable water or electricity. Mules pulled the city's streetcars until electricity was restored months later, and plans for an improved dam were approved. Austinites' spirits rose in 1901, when thousands turned out to welcome President McKinley's parade up Congress Avenue. A third major railroad—the Missouri, Kansas, and Texas (nicknamed "the Katy")—reached Austin in 1904, making the capital city even more accessible.

The following year Congress Avenue and Pecan Street were first paved. By this time, Pecan and other east-west streets had been renamed using numbers (Pecan became Sixth) to accommodate the city's growth.

Our Lady of Guadalupe Church was founded in 1907 to minister to the growing Catholic community. In 1908, citizens voted to change Austin's form of city government, and the Woman Suffrage Association was organized as the first and for several years to come the only active suffrage society in Texas. The first in what was to become a widely admired city park system was Wooldridge Park, dedicated in 1909. Austin's first skyscrapers, the Littlefield and Scarbrough buildings, were built on Congress Avenue, and the city's first fatal automobile accident occurred on East Sixteenth Street, one block north of Waller's original city borders.

The first airplane landed in a cow pasture north of Austin in 1911 (the pilot had been inspired by a land-developer's offer of $150), and in 1913 Mayor Wooldridge closed down Guy Town, the red-light district that had flourished since the 1870s. A progressive local government adorned Austin with a city hospital in 1915; a paid fire department in 1916; beginnings of a beautiful new residential area called Enfield, west of downtown on land that had been part of Governor Pease's estate; acquisition of Barton Springs; the very close Prohibition election of 1918 that closed some 70 saloons; and the introduction of supermarkets. Life in Austin was good and seemed to grow progressively better every day.

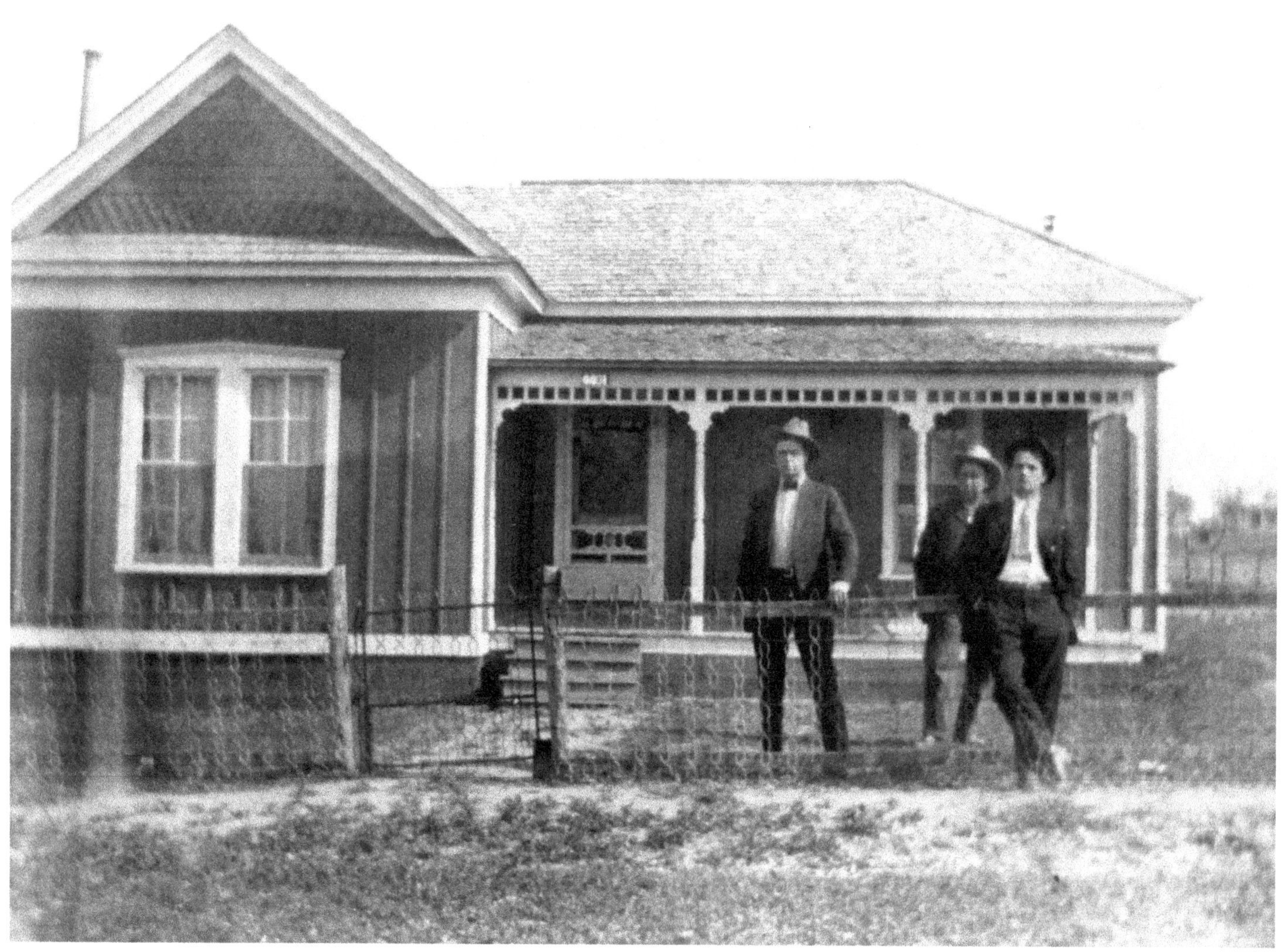

With its wide front porch and modest ornamentation, the Thorp house (pictured) was fairly typical of small one-story frame homes built in Austin around the turn of the century.

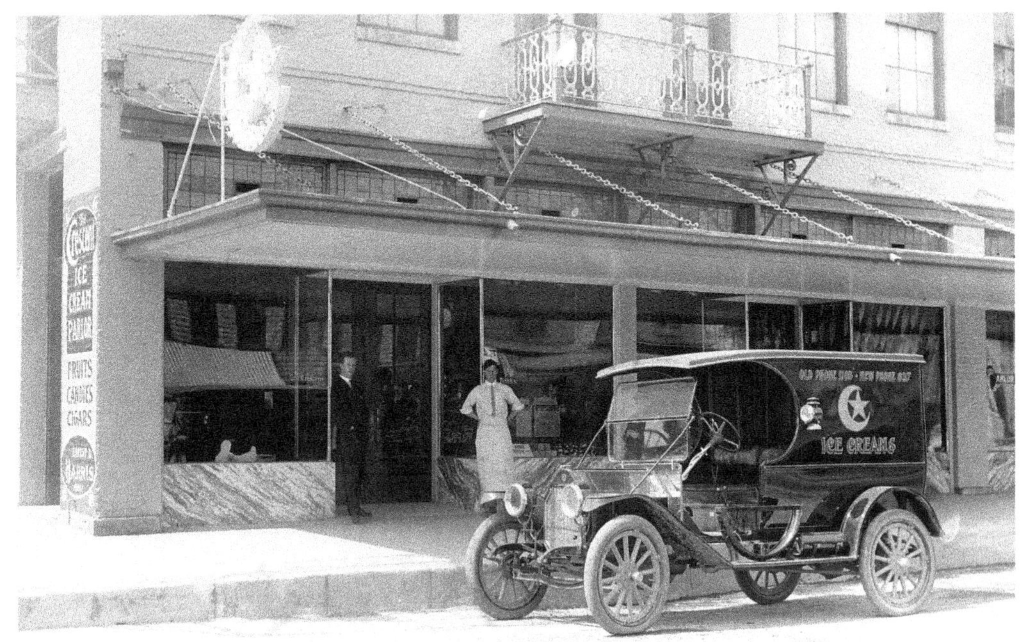

The Crescent, in the 1000 block of Congress Avenue, was one of several Austin ice cream parlors that flourished around the turn of the century. The Crescent was apparently so successful that the proprietors had their own company van, complete with advertising signage that featured their logo—a crescent moon and star.

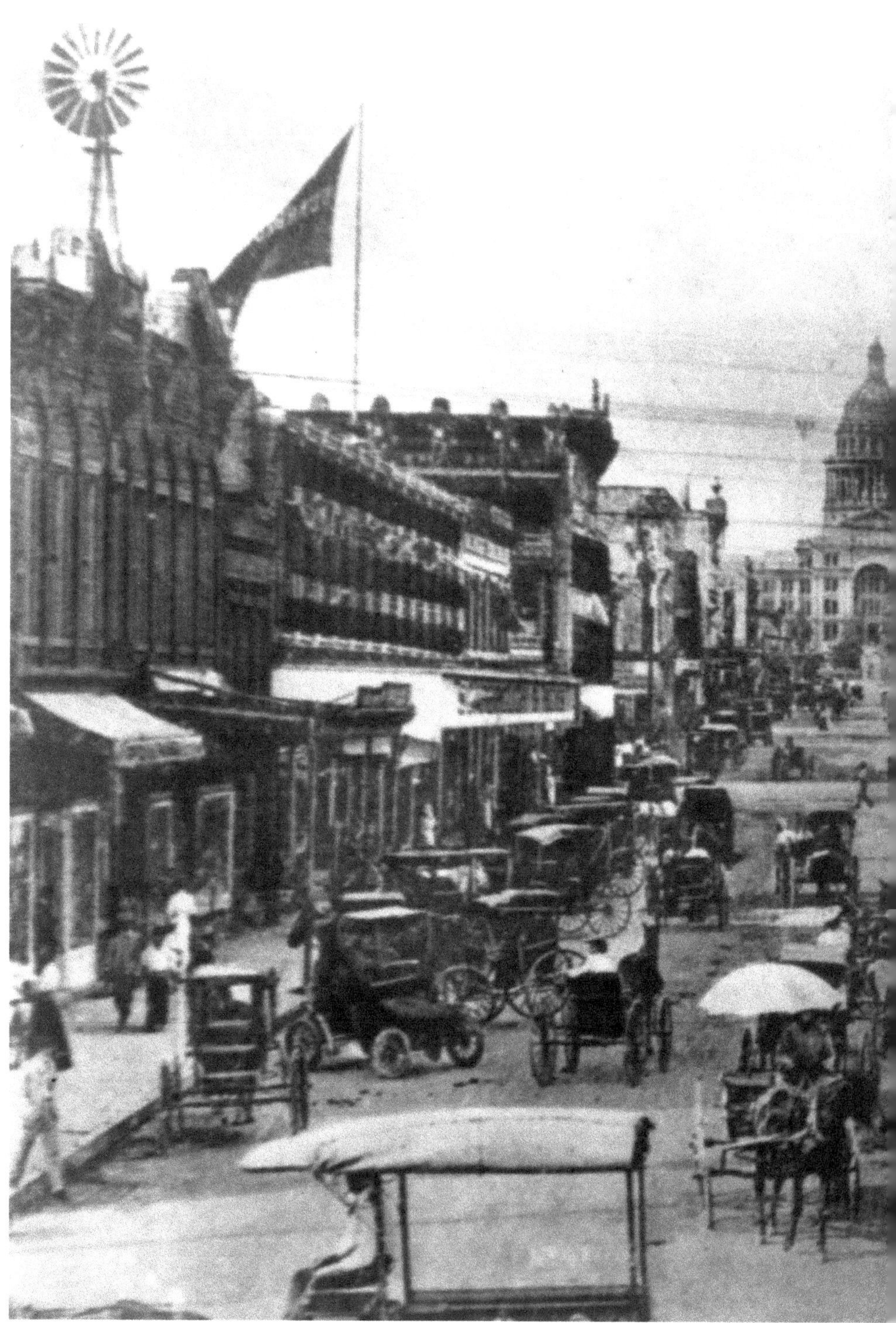

In the early 1900s, busy Congress Avenue was frequently the scene of traffic congestion, with electric streetcars, horse-drawn carriages, pedestrians, supply wagons, and even a few motorcars vying for room to move. Windmills like the one atop a roof at left were common on Texas farms but seldom seen in cities.

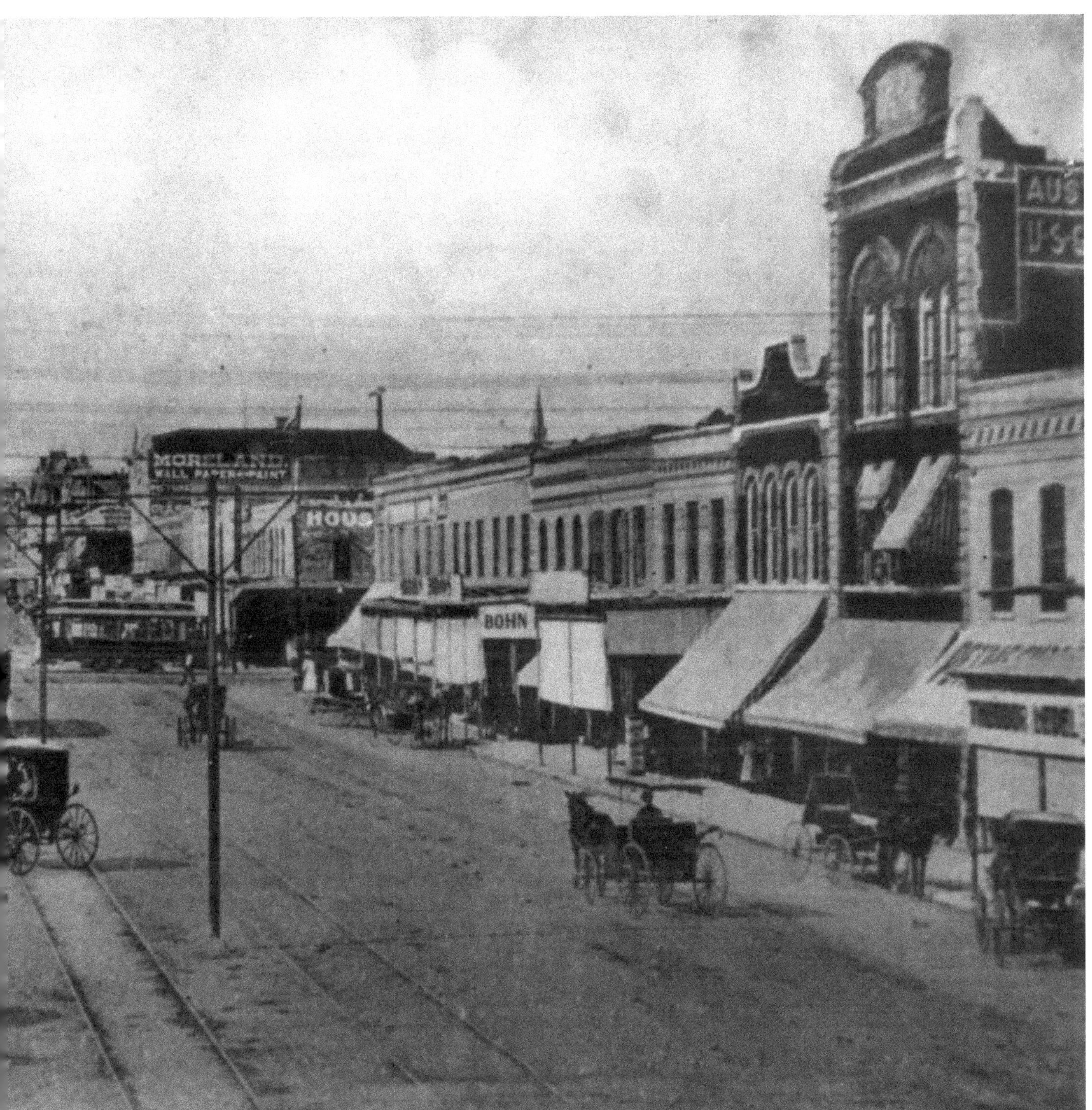
MORELAND
WALL PAPER & PAINT
HOUS
BOHN

Members of this Austin family gather to celebrate Emancipation Day in East Woods Park on June 19, 1900. After the Civil War, word of the Emancipation Proclamation did not reach Texas until June 19, 1865. Since then, African Americans in Texas have traditionally celebrated the date, nicknamed "Juneteenth," each year.

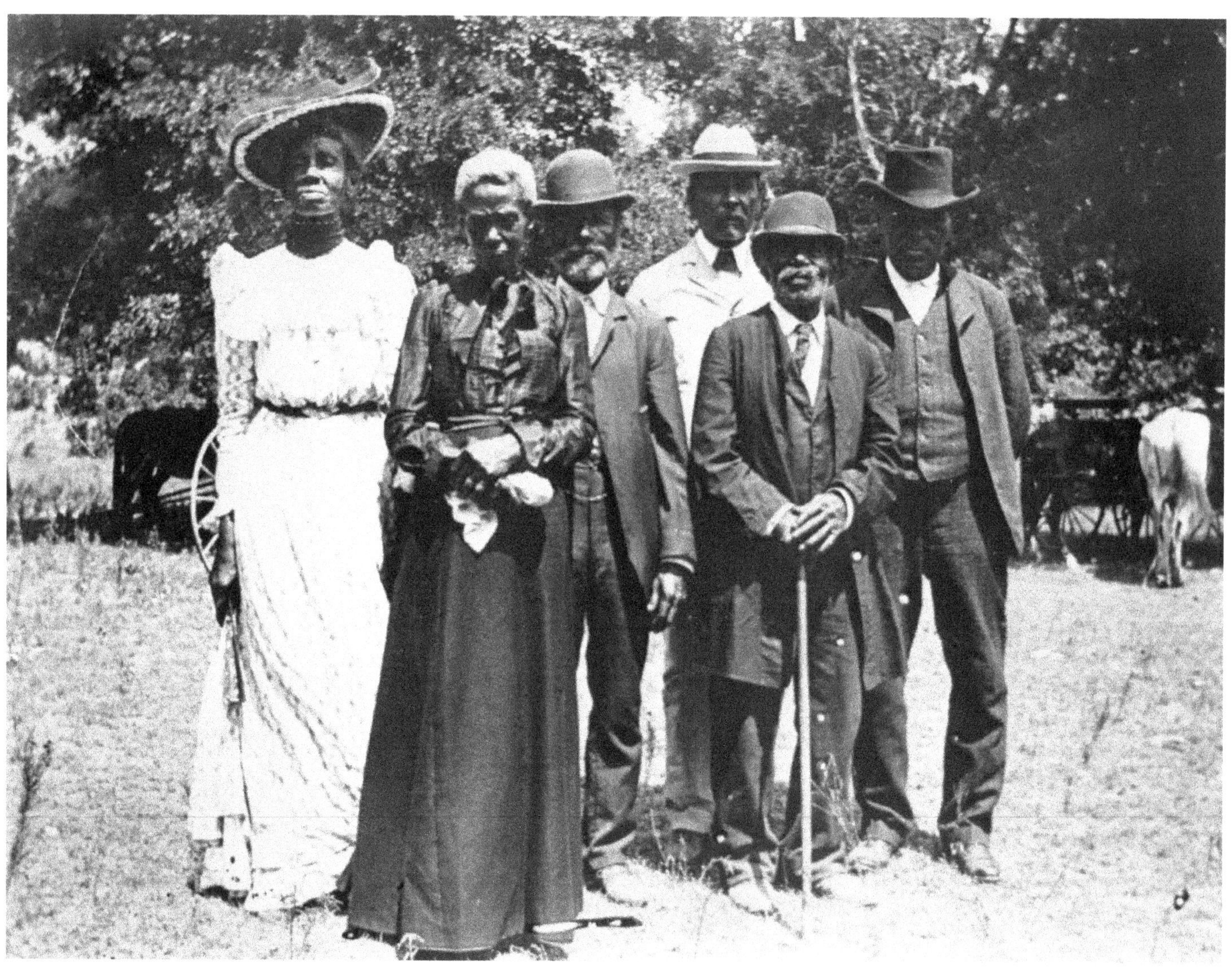

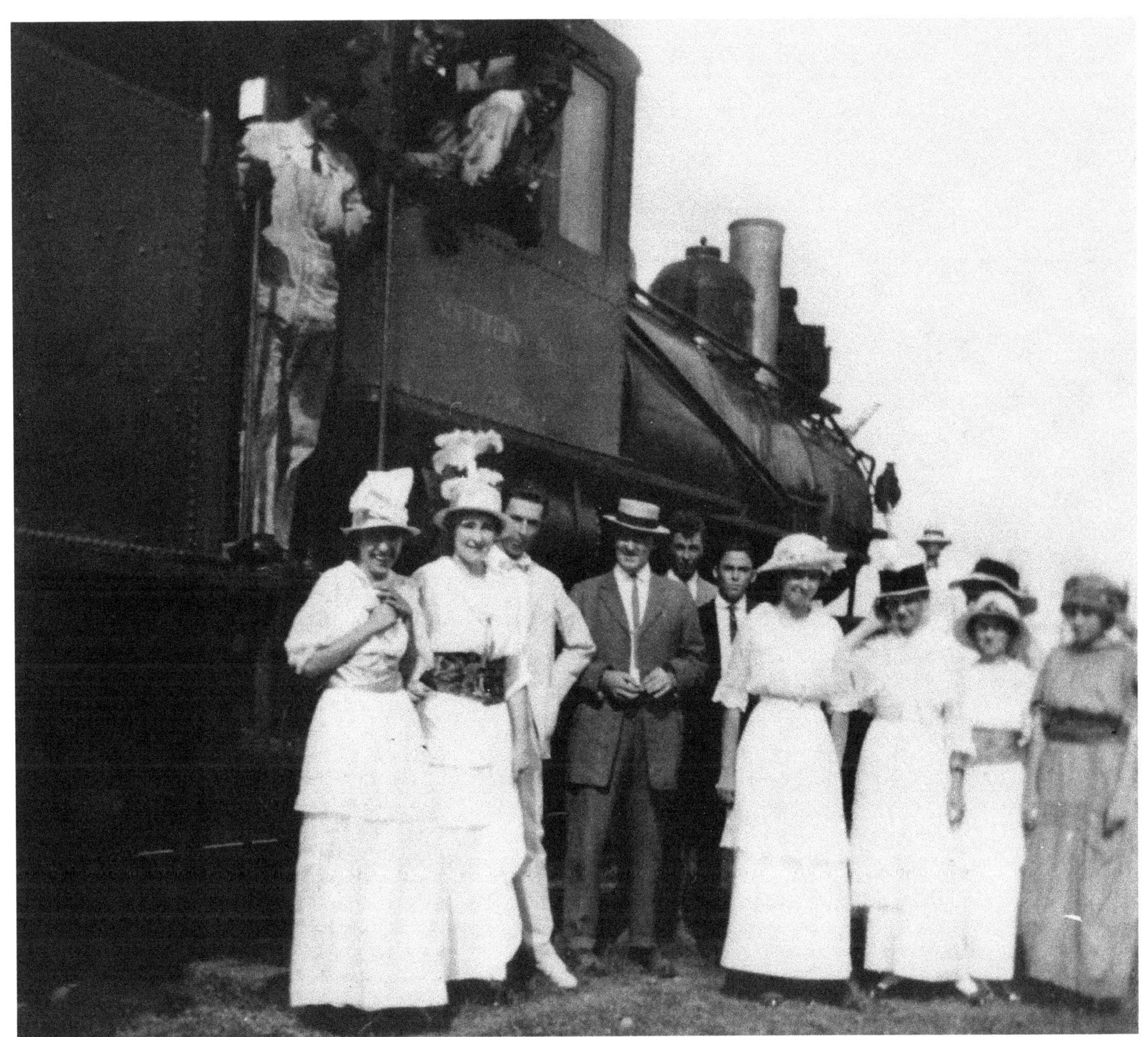

Dressed-up young Austinites pose after meeting the train to welcome friends in the early 1900s. The railroads made Austin a trading center for a large area of Texas, contributing to the city's economic growth.

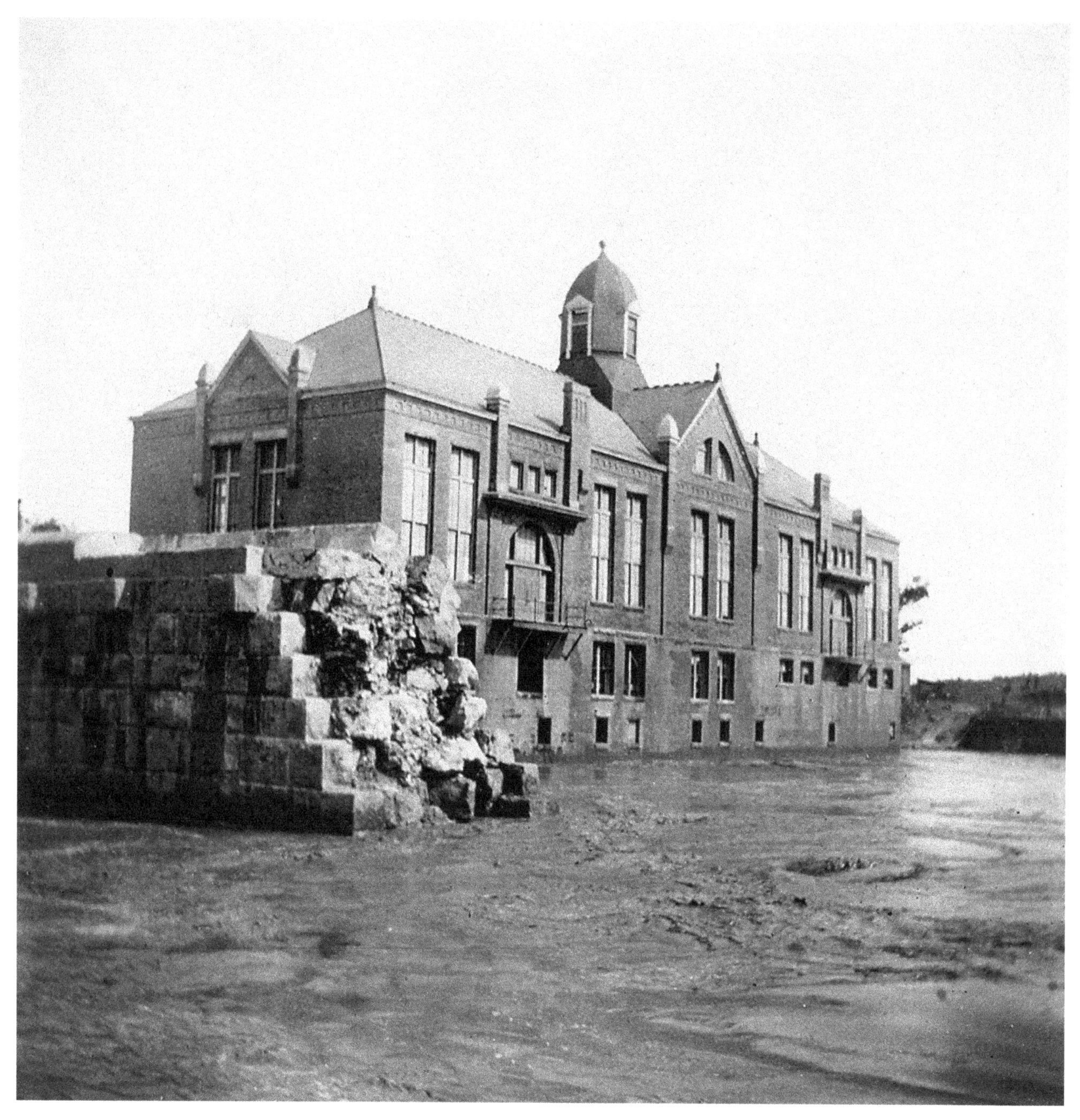

When the first dam collapsed in 1900, the waters of the Colorado River flooded the city for miles downstream, causing untold damage and loss of electrical power for months.

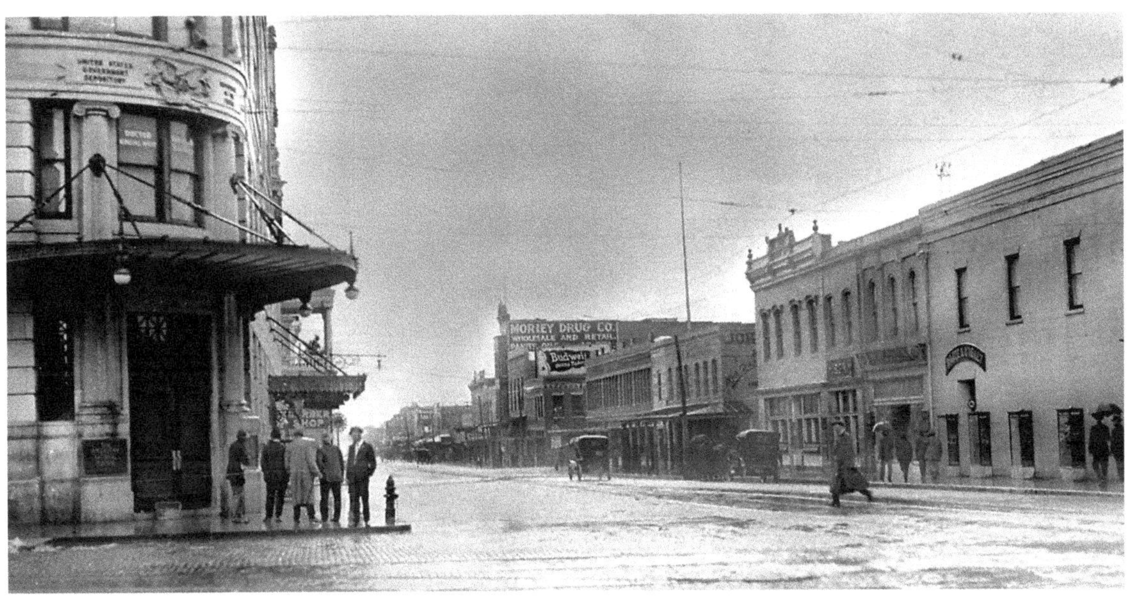

This photograph shows the aftermath of the 1900 flood on West Sixth Street.

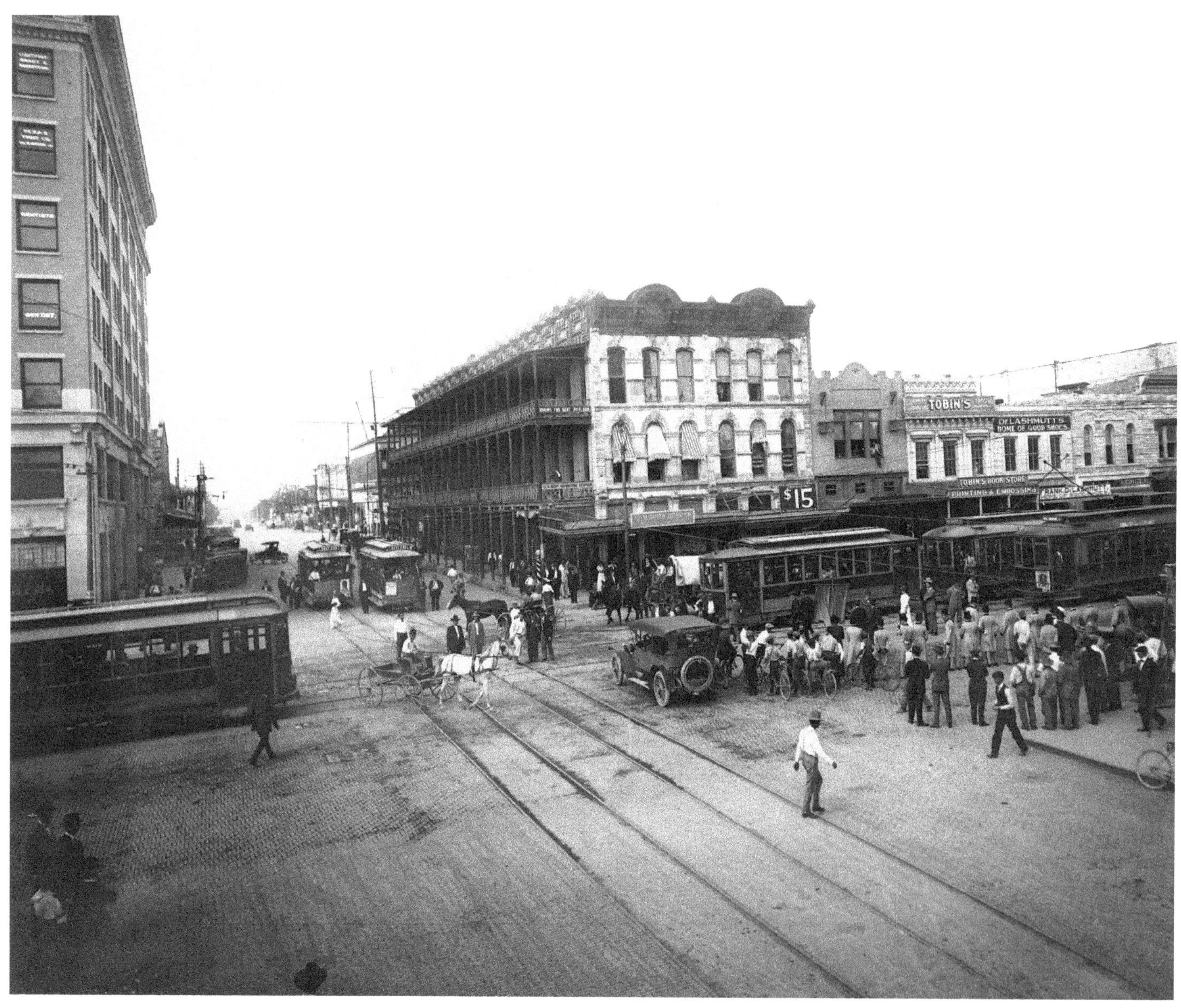

This view of Sixth Street (formerly Pecan Street) after the turn of the century illustrates the transition period of transportation: automobiles and electric streetcars compete for space with pedestrians, bicycles, and horse-drawn wagons.

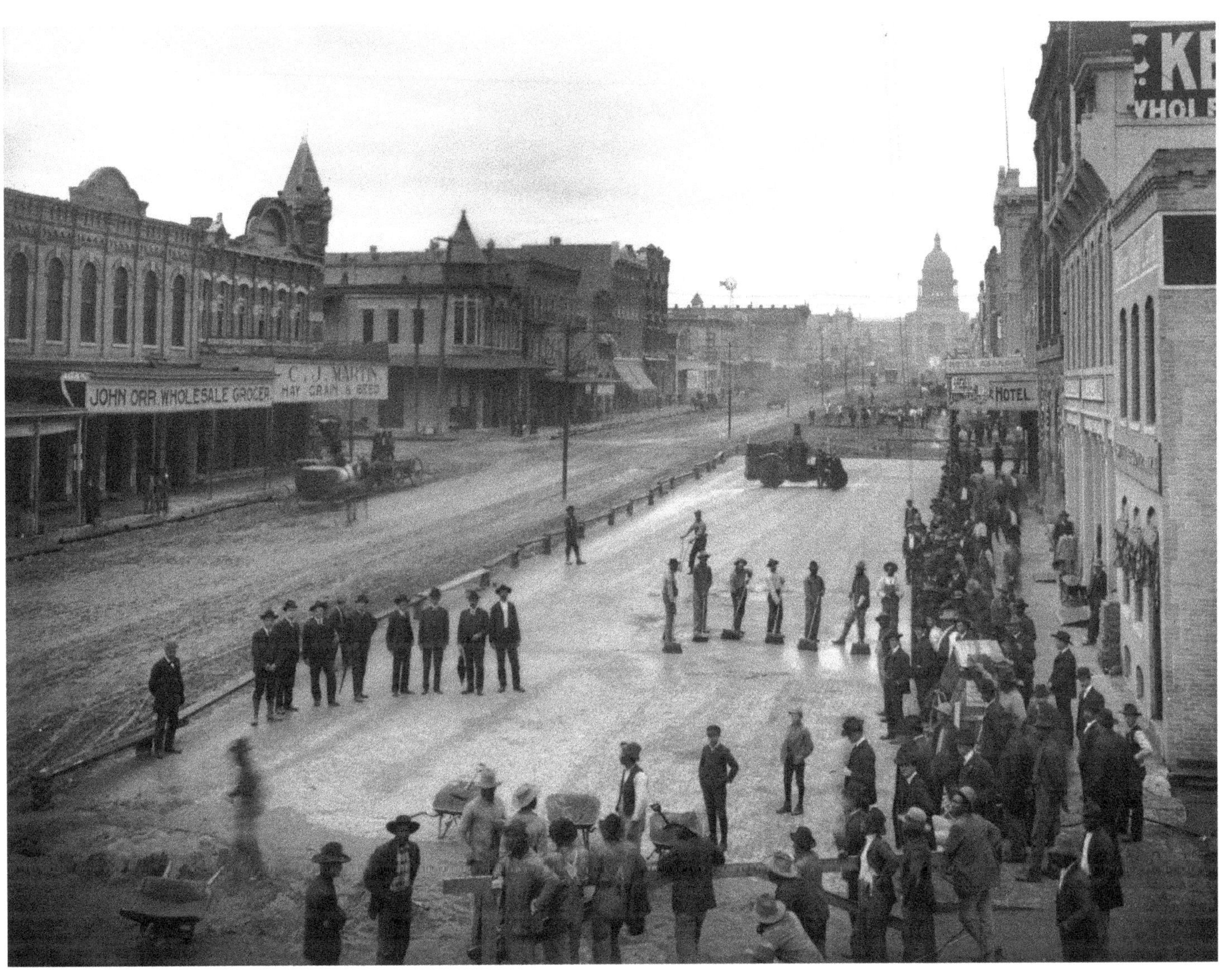

It was 1905 when Congress Avenue was paved for the first time—with brick. This event was viewed as Austin's debut as a bona fide city, rather than just a provincial town, and the bricking of Sixth Street quickly followed. Those who had automobiles, which began arriving in Austin around 1900, were thrilled, but buggy drivers and horse riders sometimes took spills when traveling too fast on the smooth new streets.

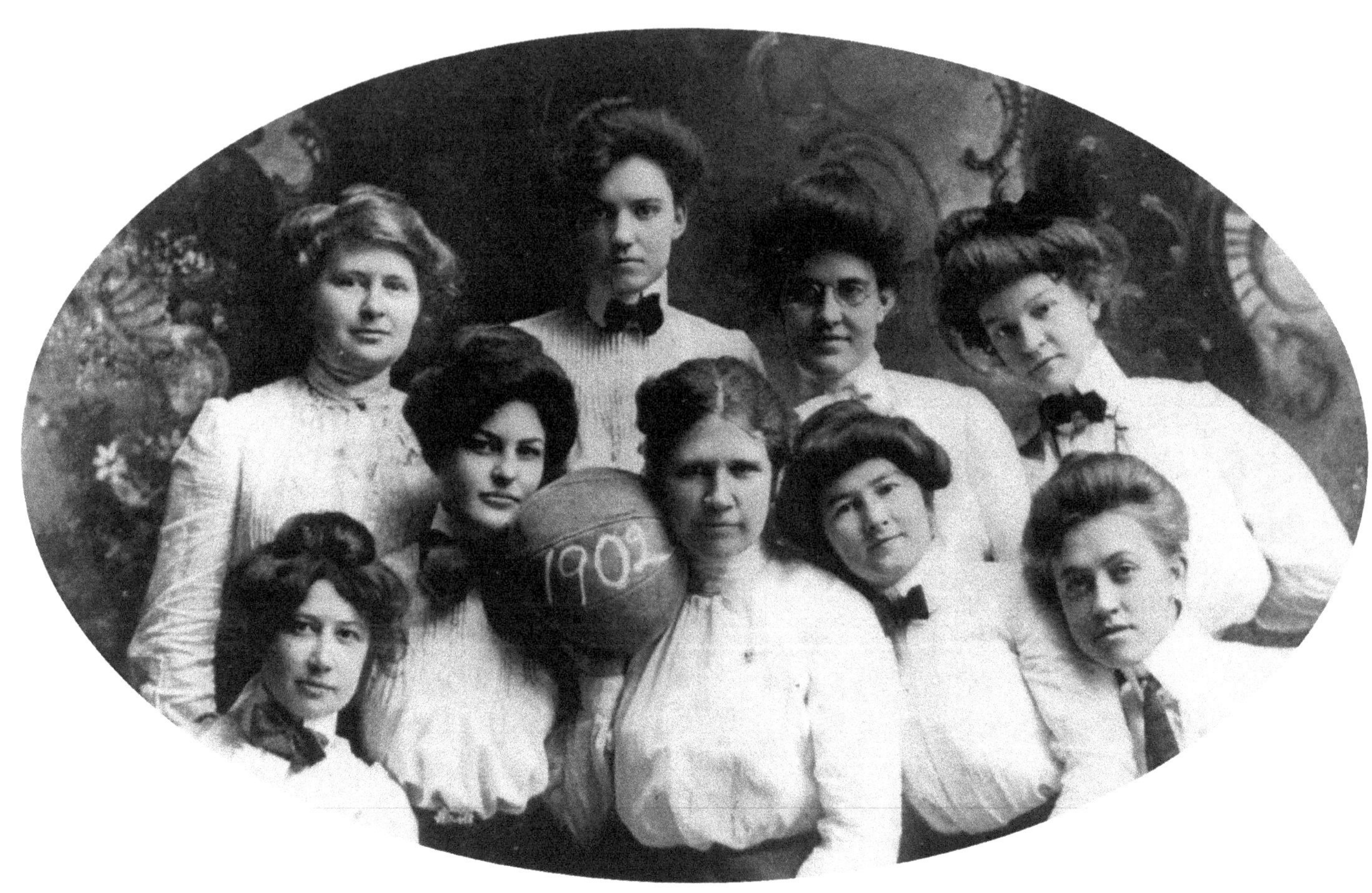

The current popularity of women's basketball at the University of Texas is not new. This photograph shows the women's basketball team in 1902, when they played their first game, but it took some time before the "Lady Longhorns" would receive the attention and support they enjoy today.

In May 1901, the twenty-fifth president of the United States, William McKinley, visited Austin, and thousands turned out to welcome him. A special arch was erected in his honor at the Capitol gate, and the president's carriage was accompanied by a military escort as he paraded up Congress Avenue. Four months later, Austin mourned when President McKinley was assassinated.

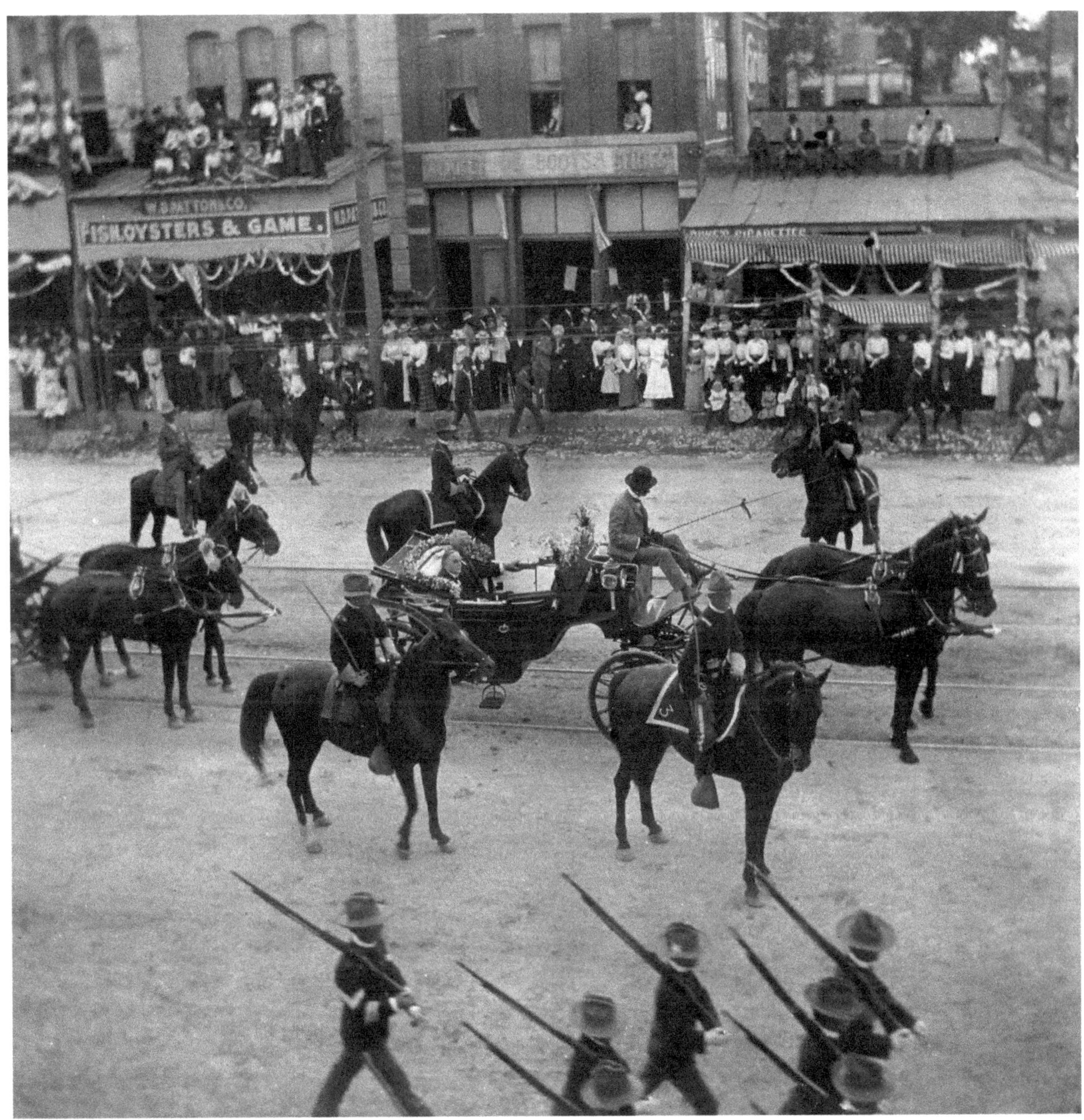

As the capital of Texas, Austin has often been honored by visits from nationally recognized politicians and dignitaries, including presidents. Always ready to make a speech, President Theodore "Teddy" Roosevelt is pictured speaking to Austinites from a specially decorated platform during his public appearance in 1905.

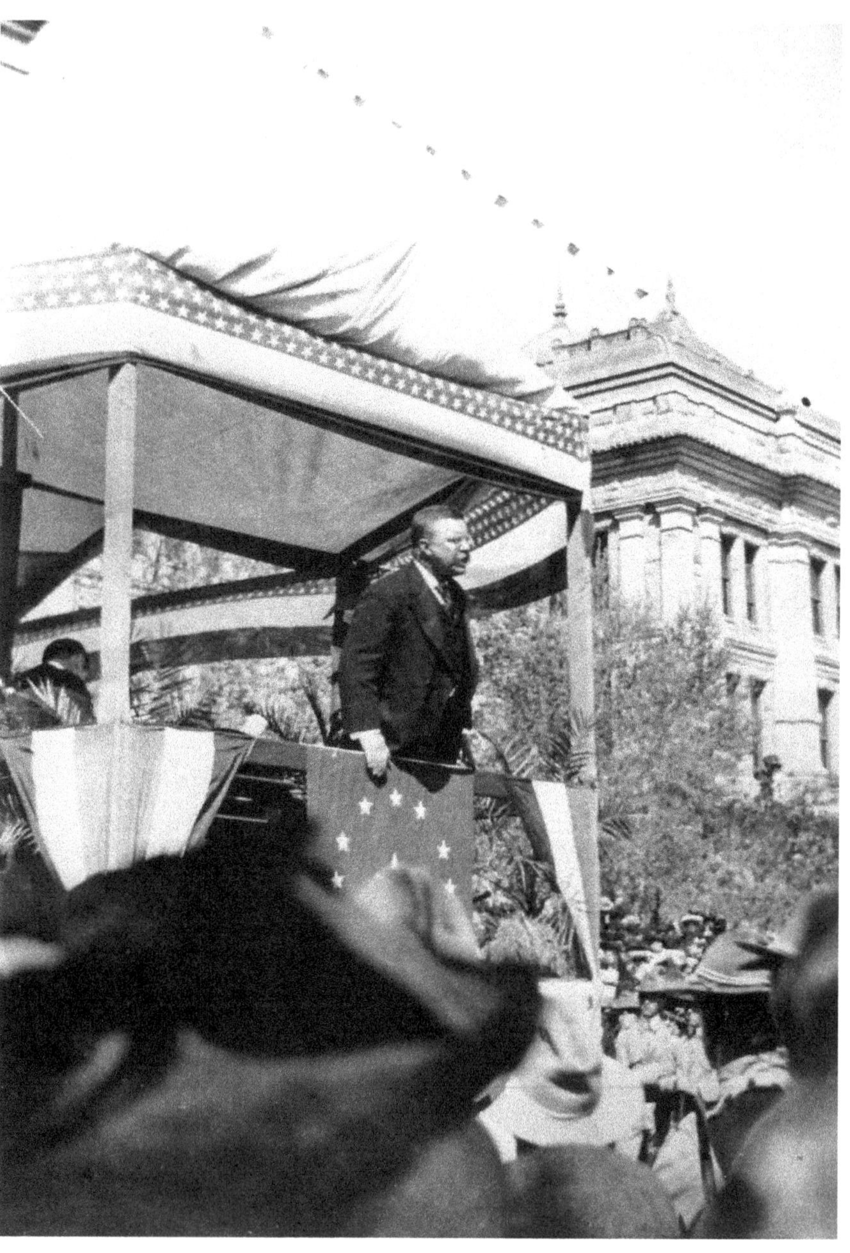

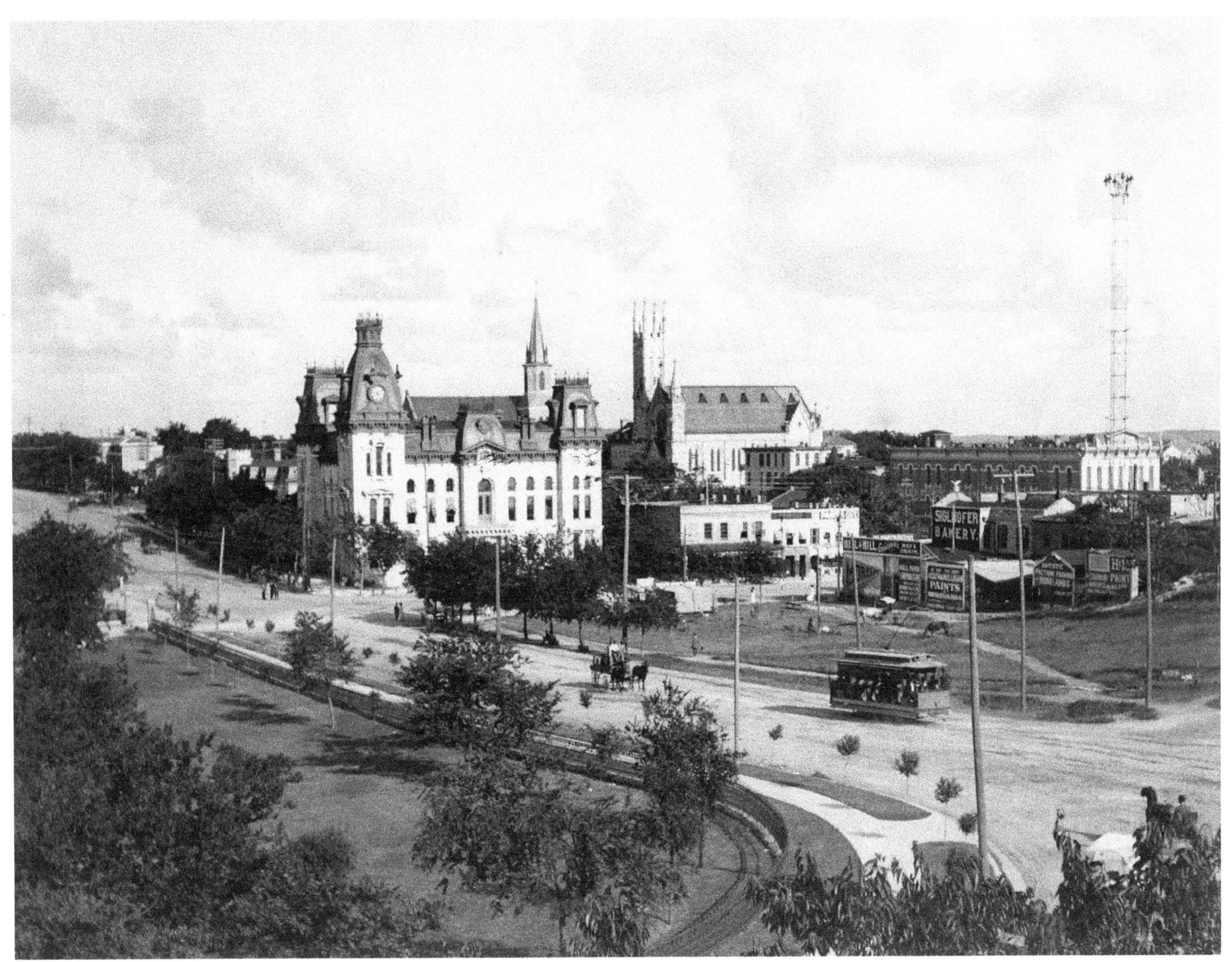

This view of Eleventh Street circa 1906 shows the Capitol grounds at left and the Travis County Courthouse, center, with the Methodist and Catholic church spires behind. To the right is a "moonlight tower" on Congress Avenue. By this time, the Lundberg Bakery had become Siglhofer's Bakery, as the sign on its side denotes, and its unique brass eagle is still visible.

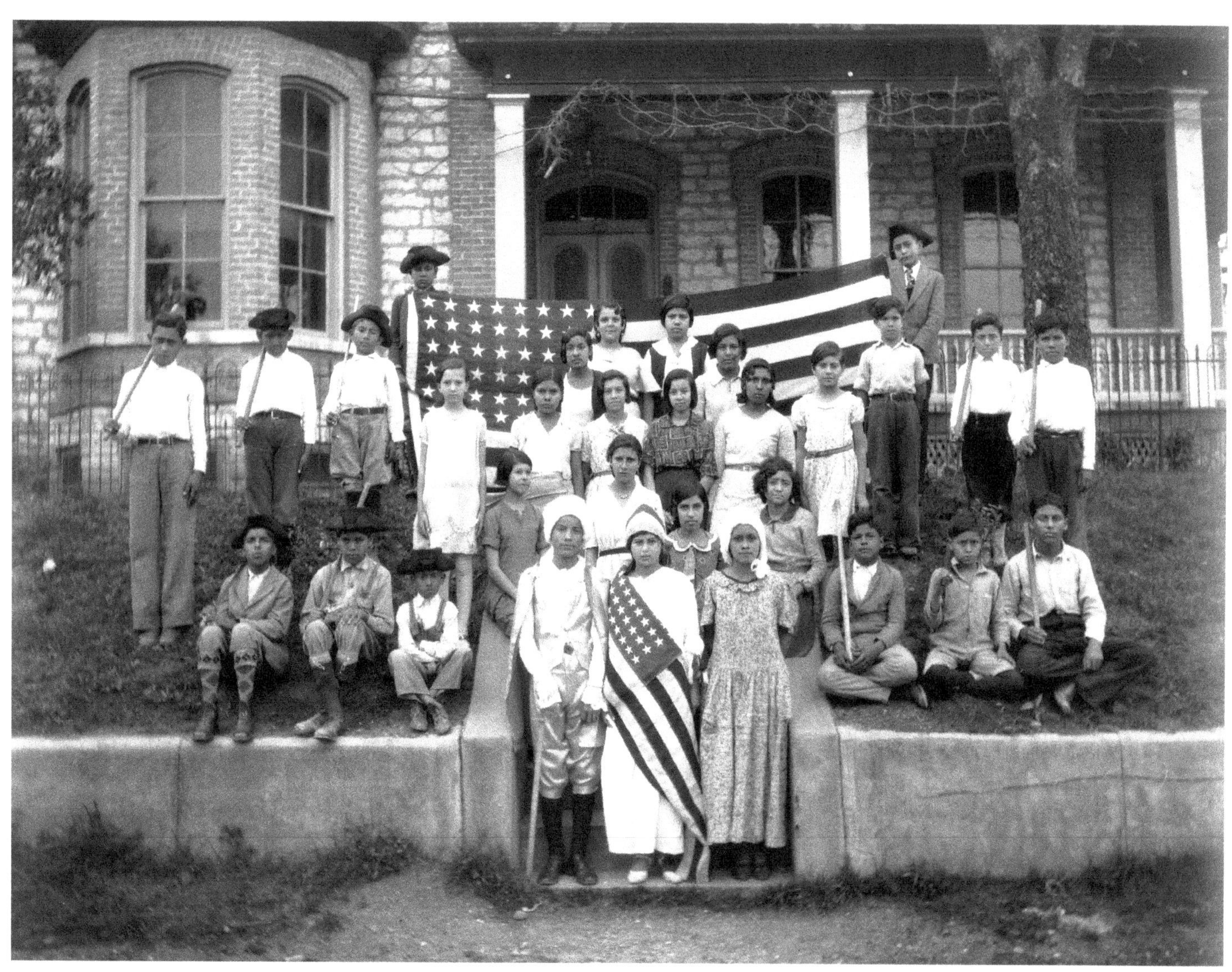

Students of Sisters of the Holy Cross Parochial School (also called Guadalupe School) pose in costume for a performance celebrating U.S. independence. This school was operated by Our Lady of Guadalupe (Catholic) Church, which was founded in 1907 on East Ninth Street in East Austin, to minister to the growing Mexican American community.

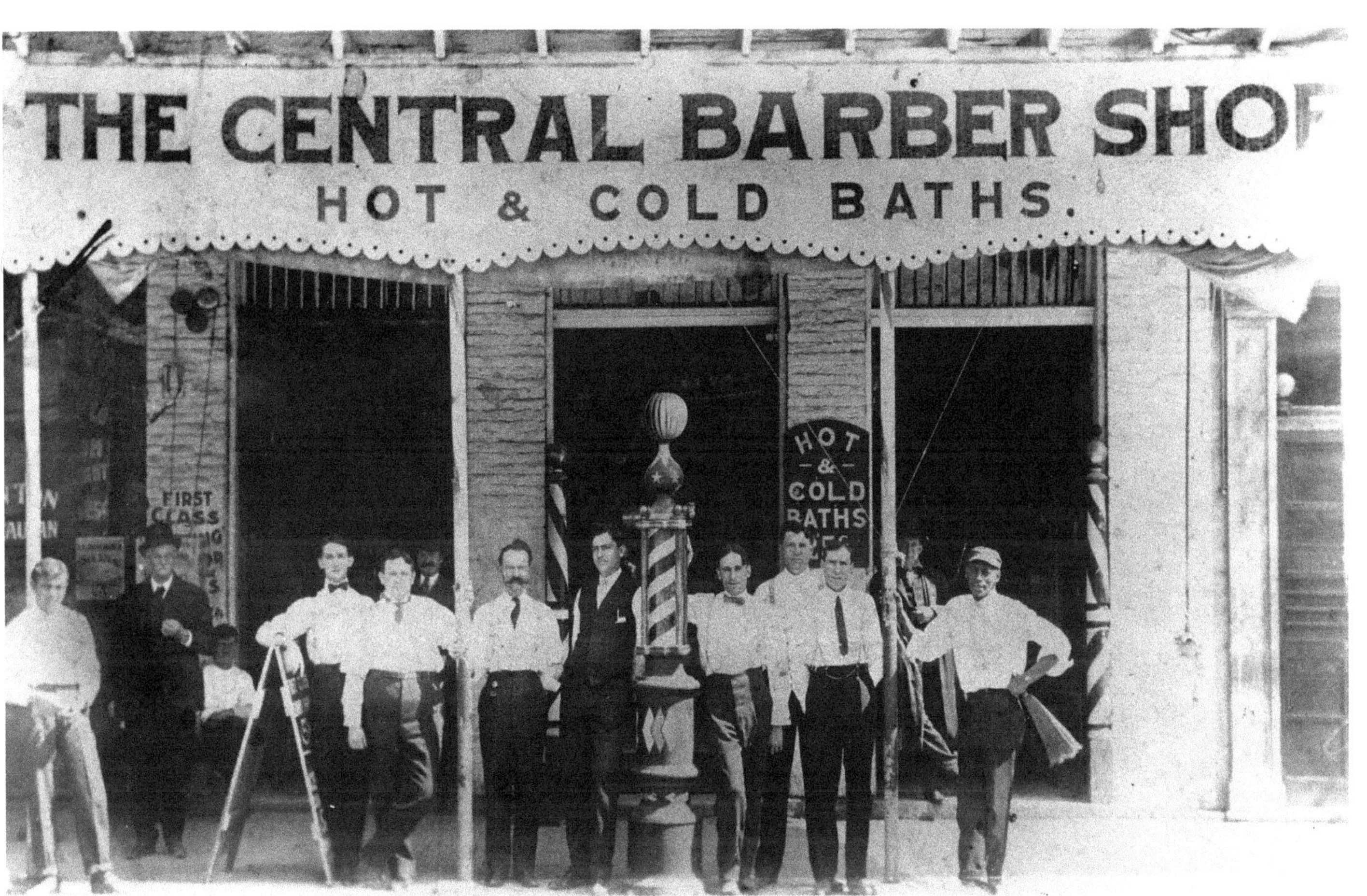

According to the signs, a fellow could get more than just a shave and a haircut at Reasonover's Central Barber Shop, pictured circa 1907.

The Austin depot for the International and Great Northern Railroad underwent reconstruction in the early 1900s. Originally built in 1888, Union Depot was located on Third Street at the corner of Congress Avenue and was distinguished by its rotunda.

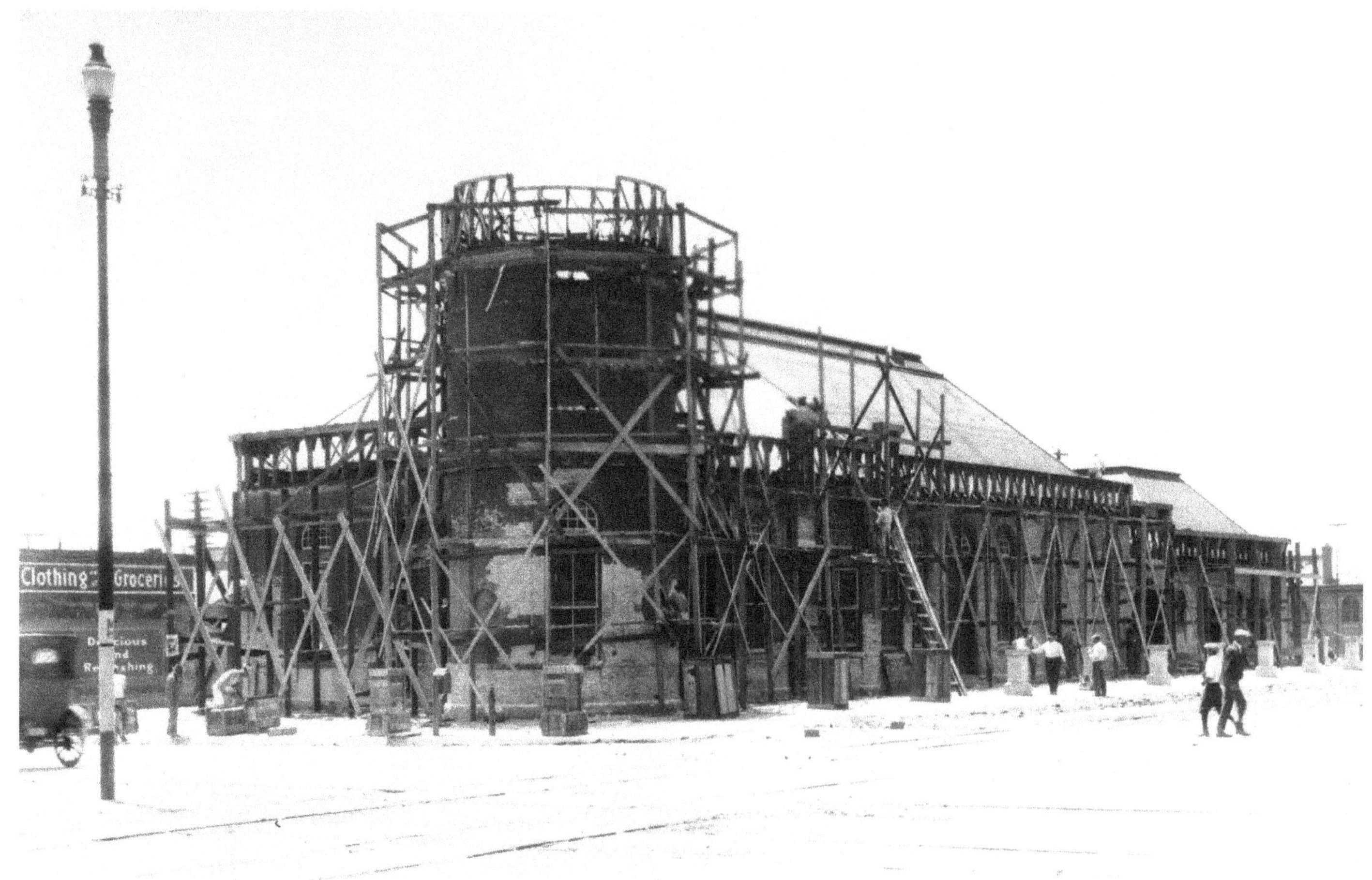

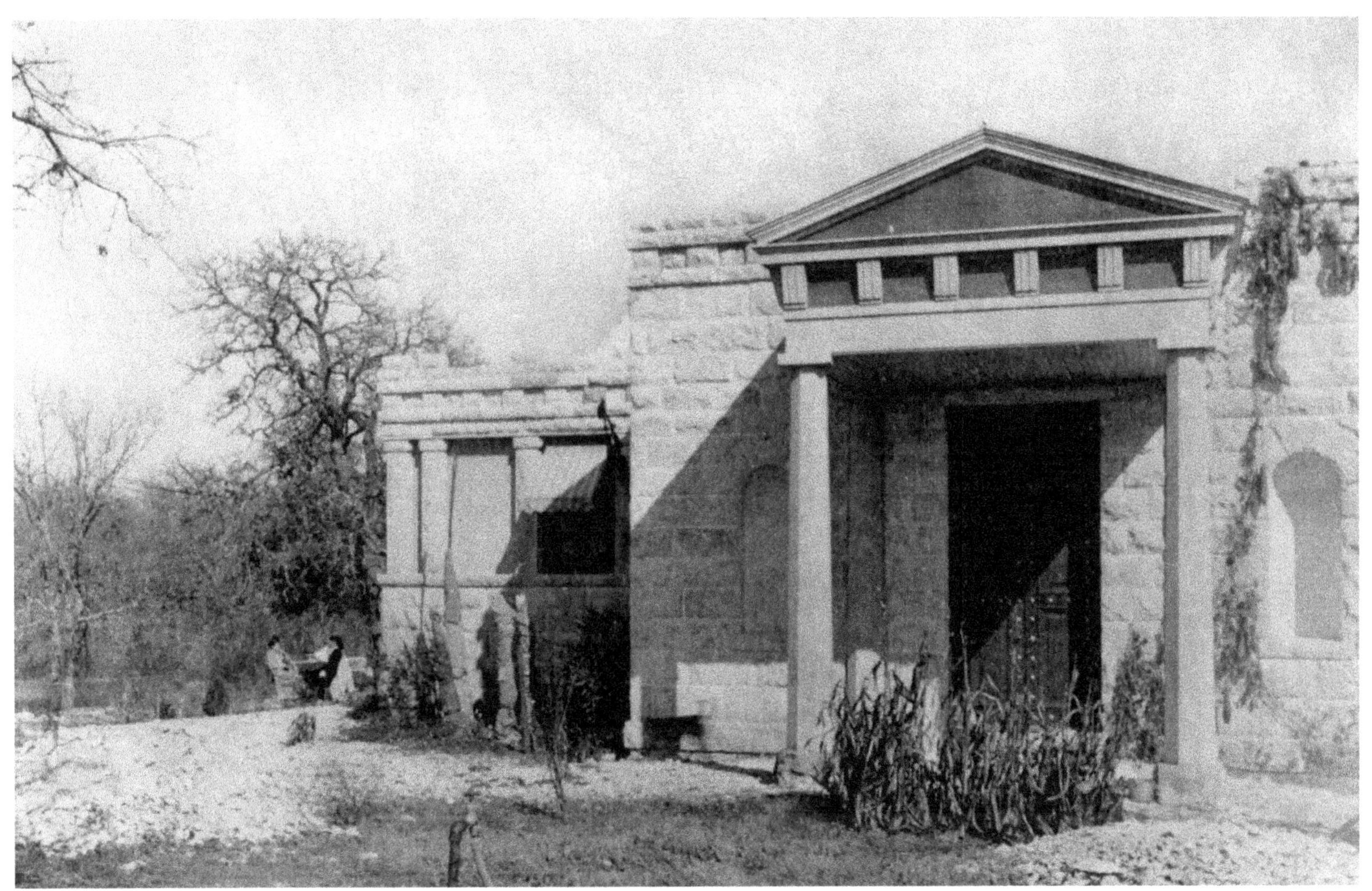

European sculptor Elisabet Ney built her studio-home, Formosa, in Hyde Park. She moved to Austin after receiving a commission for the 1893 world's fair to create statues of Sam Houston and Stephen F. Austin, which later were placed in the Capitol. Although Ney shocked neighbors when she slept on her flat roof, her reputation as an artist attracted many celebrities. After her death in 1907, Formosa became a museum.

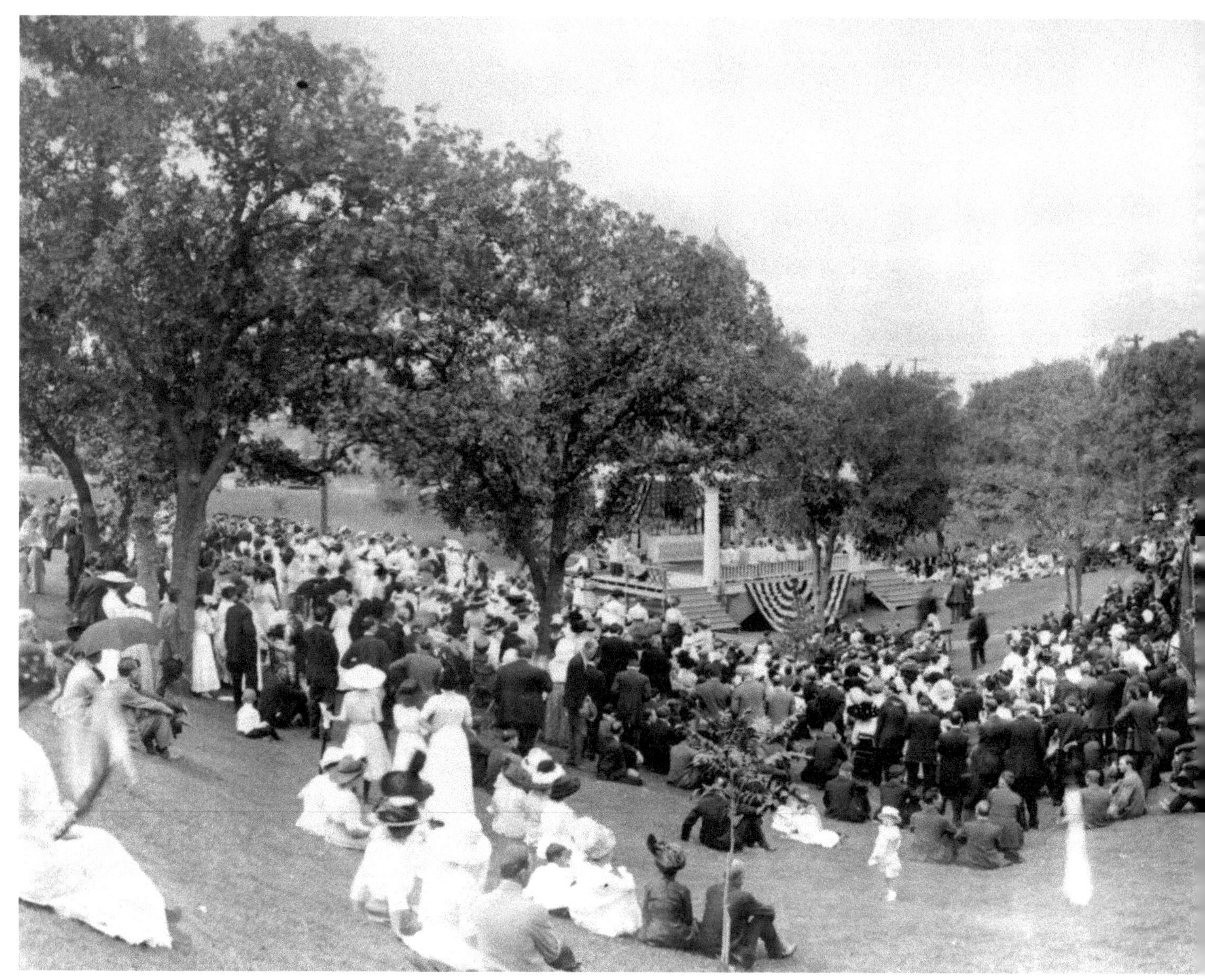

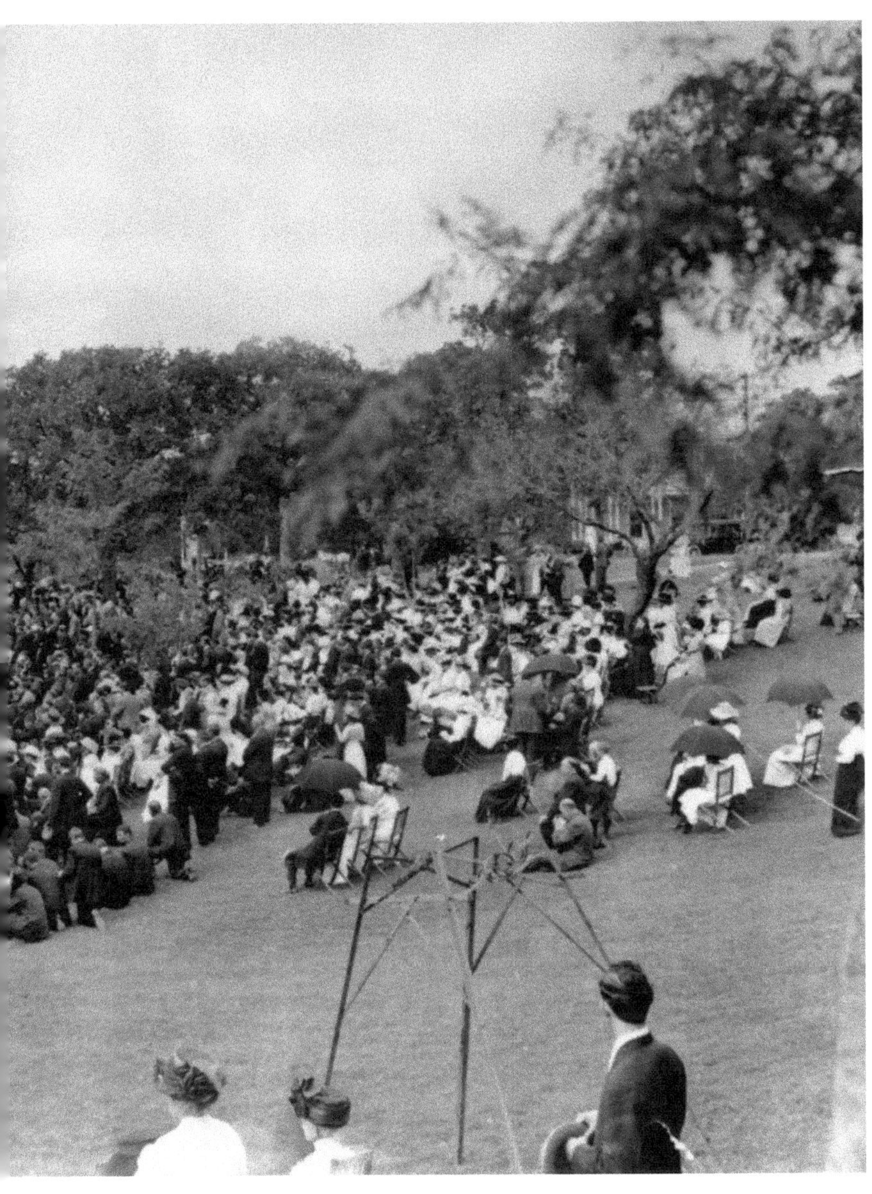

A public gathering takes place on the grassy slopes of Wooldridge Park, which in 1909 became Austin's first of many parks. It covers one of four city blocks designated as public squares in Edwin Waller's original city plan and was named for Alexander Penn Wooldridge, Austin's progressive mayor and civic leader. With its central bandstand, the park was often the site of political rallies and outdoor concerts.

A bird's-eye view from South Congress looking north circa 1908 shows construction of the concrete Congress Avenue bridge and the relatively sparse development south of the Colorado River. After this permanent bridge was completed in 1910, Austin began steadily to spread south.

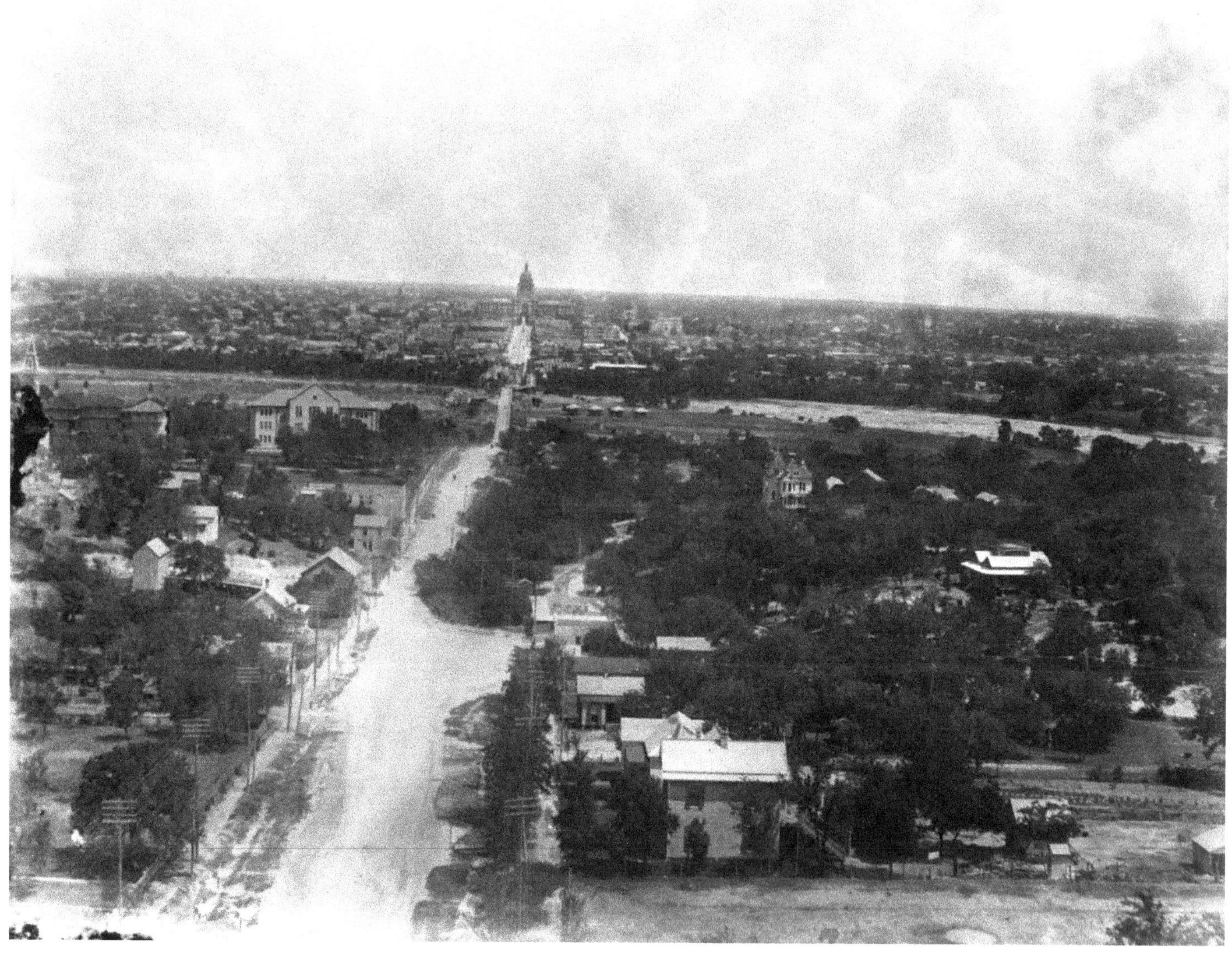

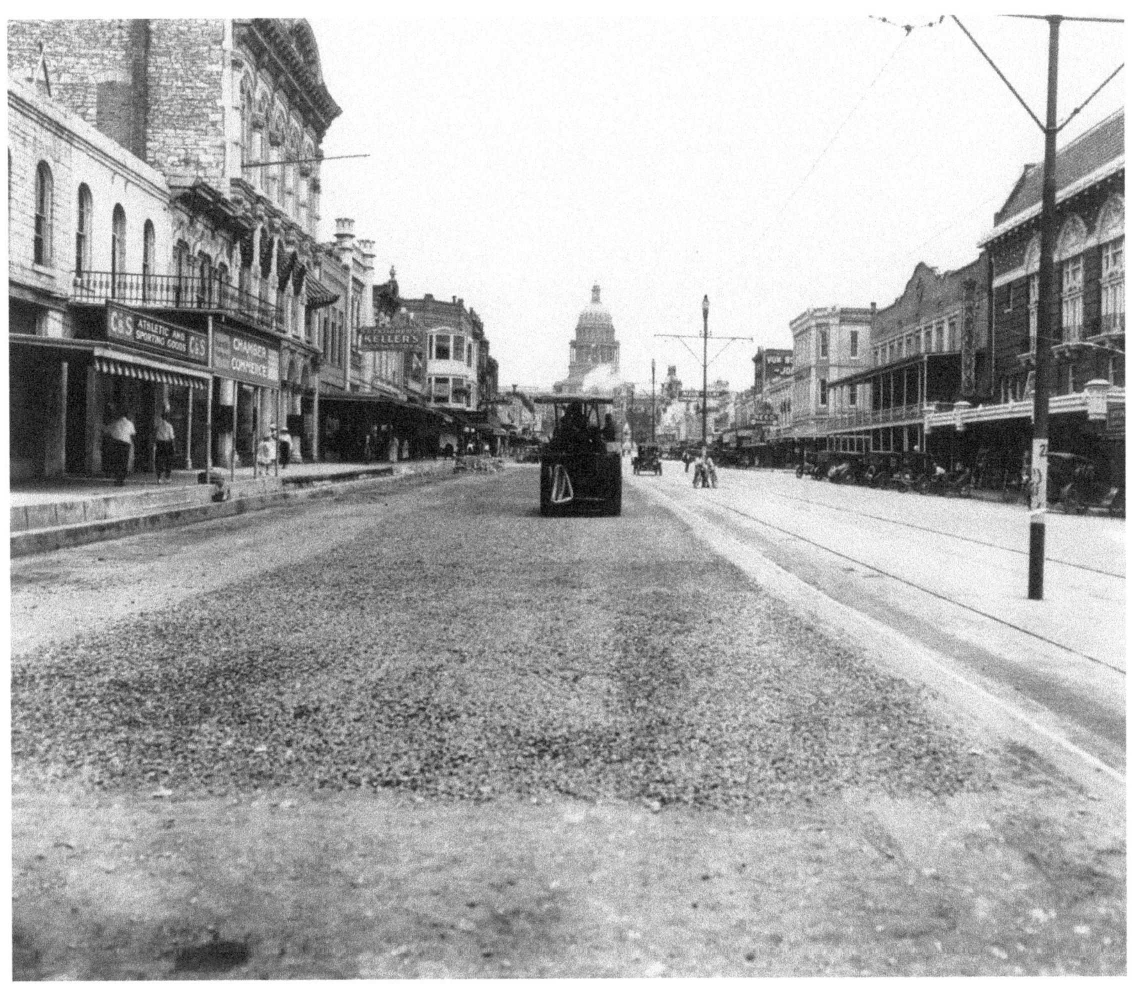

This is how Congress Avenue looked circa 1919. It appears that car parking was limited to the east side of the street at the time. The Majestic Theater (later renamed the Paramount) is on the right.

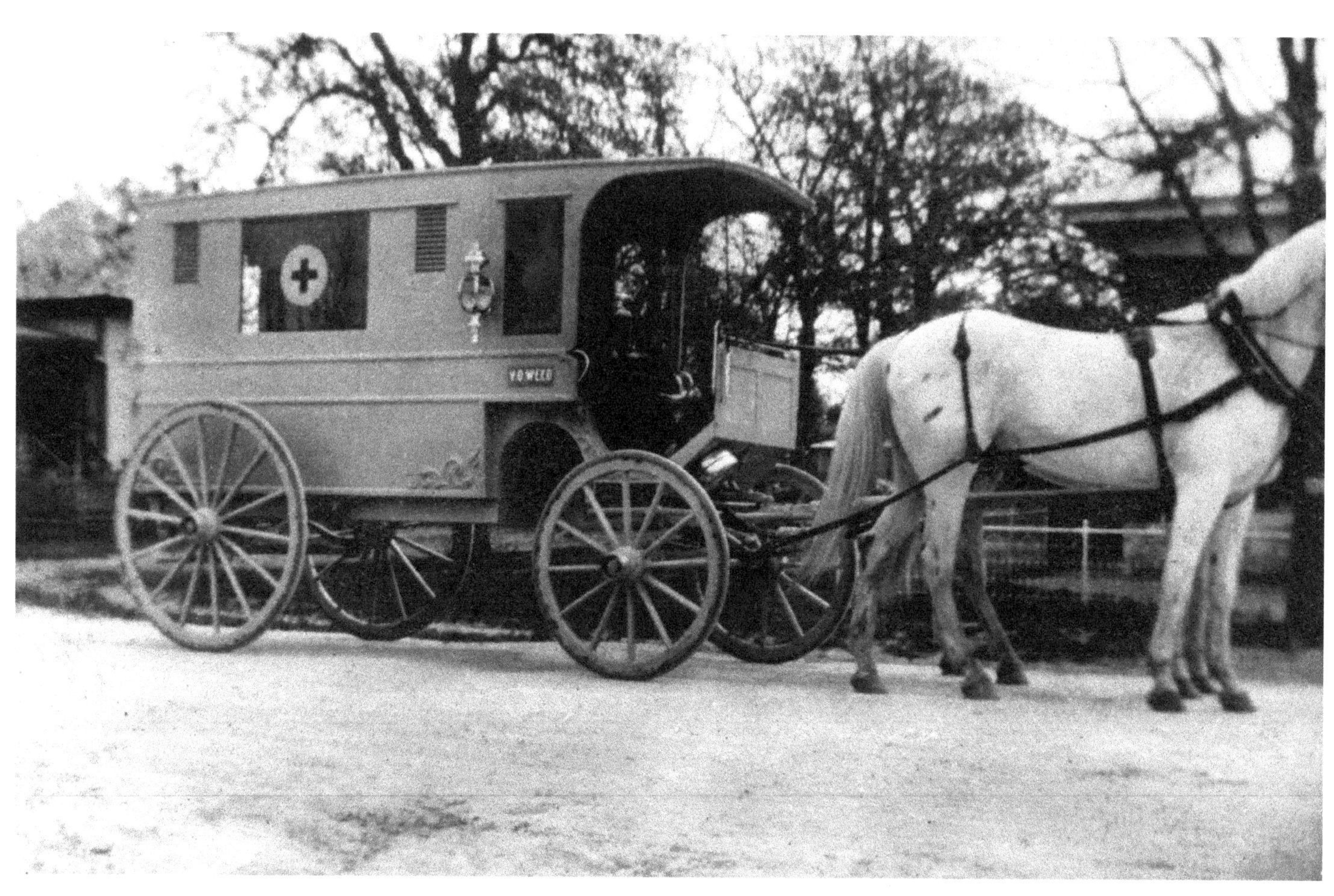

Owners of Austin funeral parlors provided horse-drawn hearses, which also were used as ambulances. This one, photographed in 1910, belonged to Mr. Turlow Weed's funeral home. It later became the city's first authentic ambulance when it was motorized.

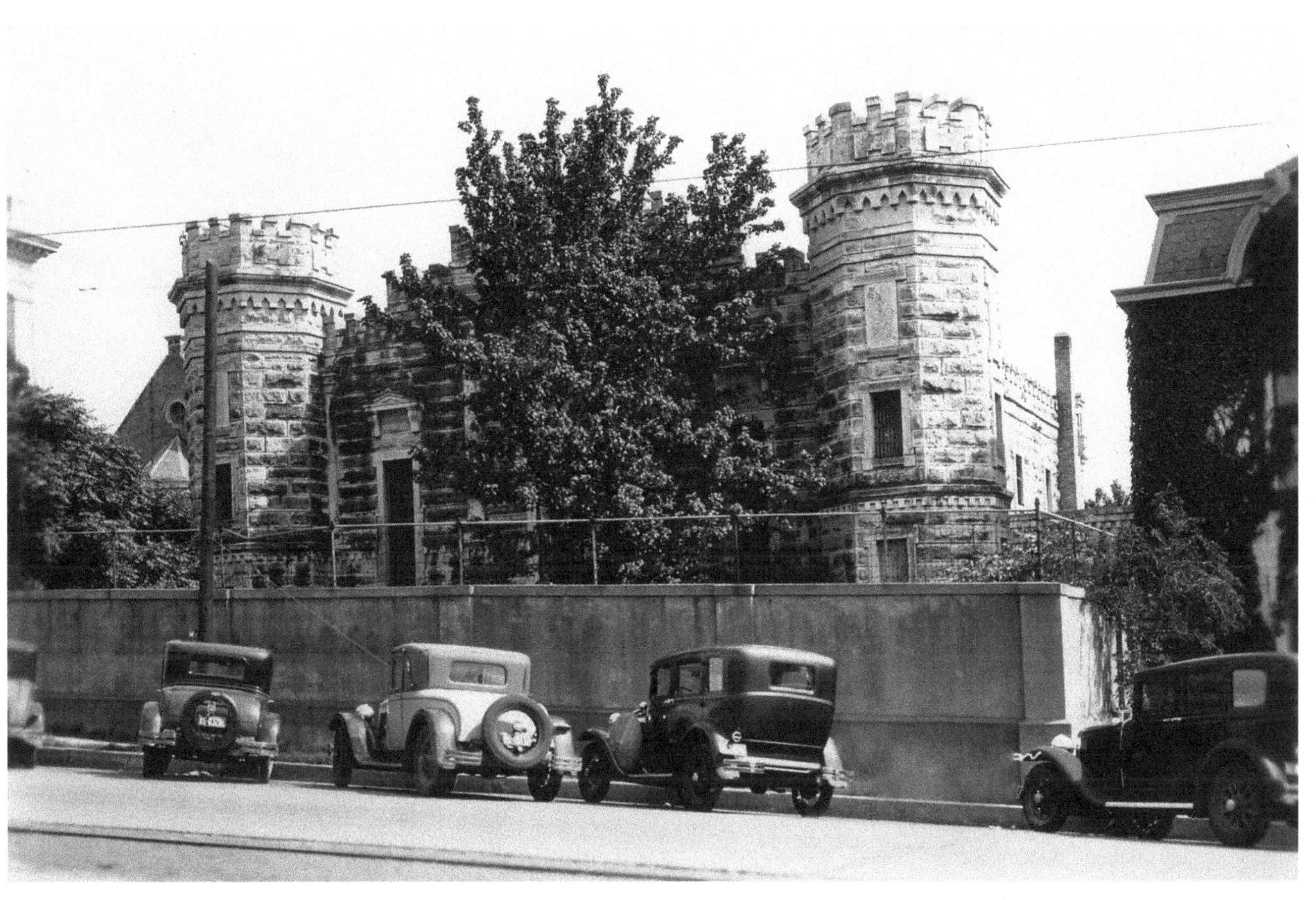

The fortresslike Travis County Jail stood in conveniently close proximity to the first Travis County Courthouse. Between the two was the jailer's house.

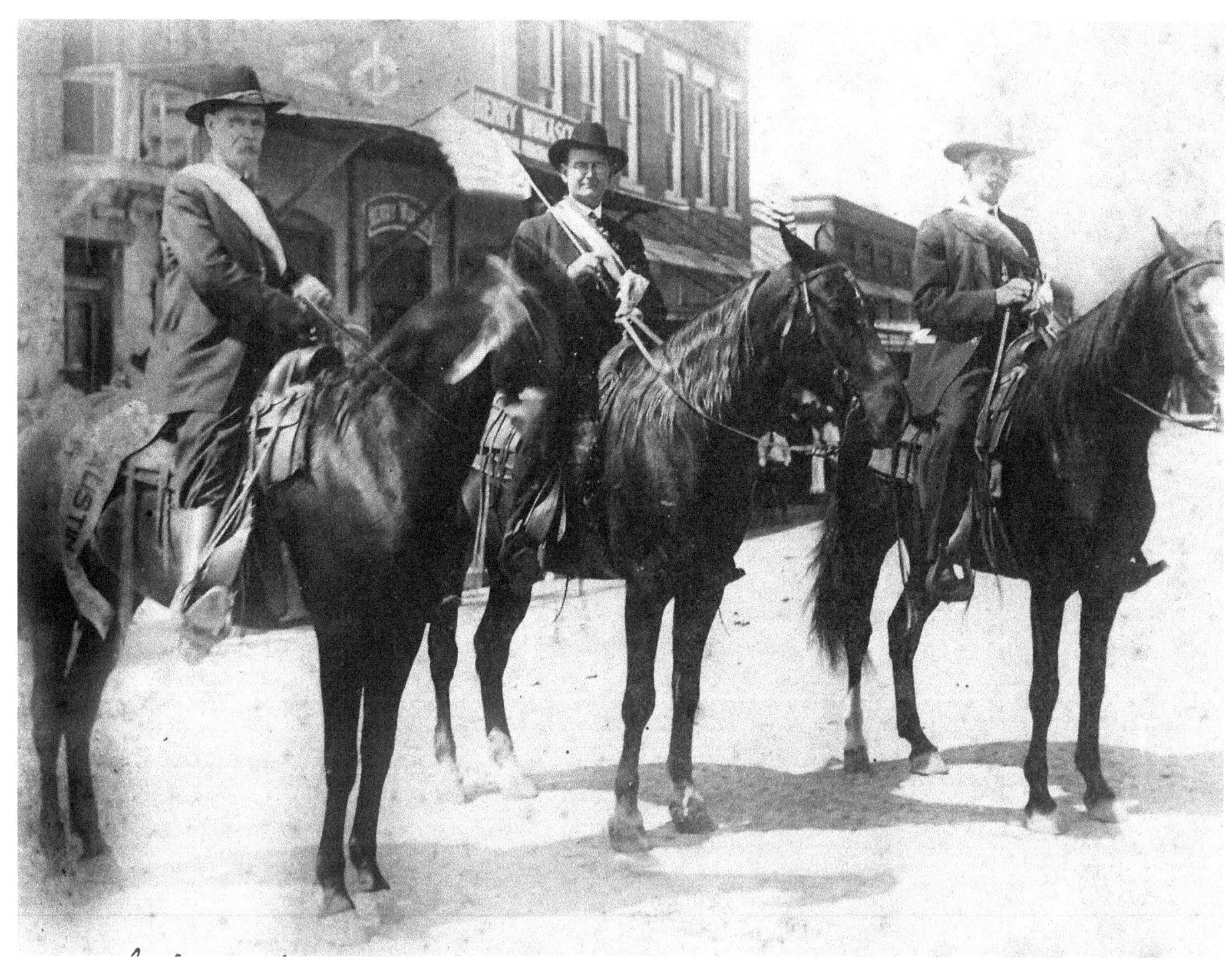

The chief of police, sheriff, and deputy sheriff pose on horseback, outfitted for a parade. By the beginning of the twentieth century, there were at least 20 members in the Austin police force. Under orders from Mayor Wooldridge, Chief of Police Will J. Morris (left) closed "Guy Town," the downtown red-light district, in 1913. It had flourished since the 1870s.

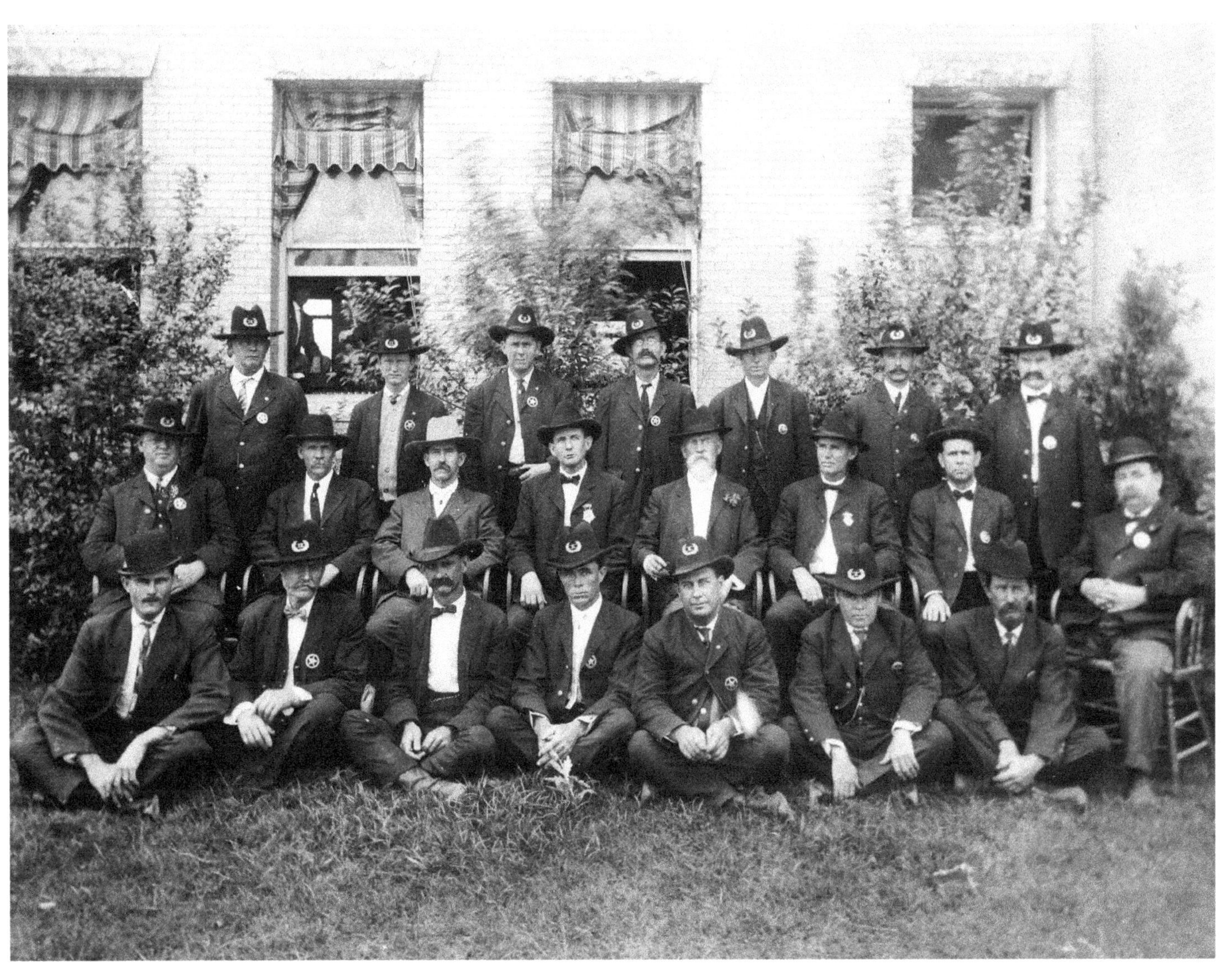

Austin law enforcement officers sit for a group photograph circa 1910, most of them dressed in distinctive uniforms. Fifth from left in the second row, with the white beard, is James P. Hart, commissioner of police.

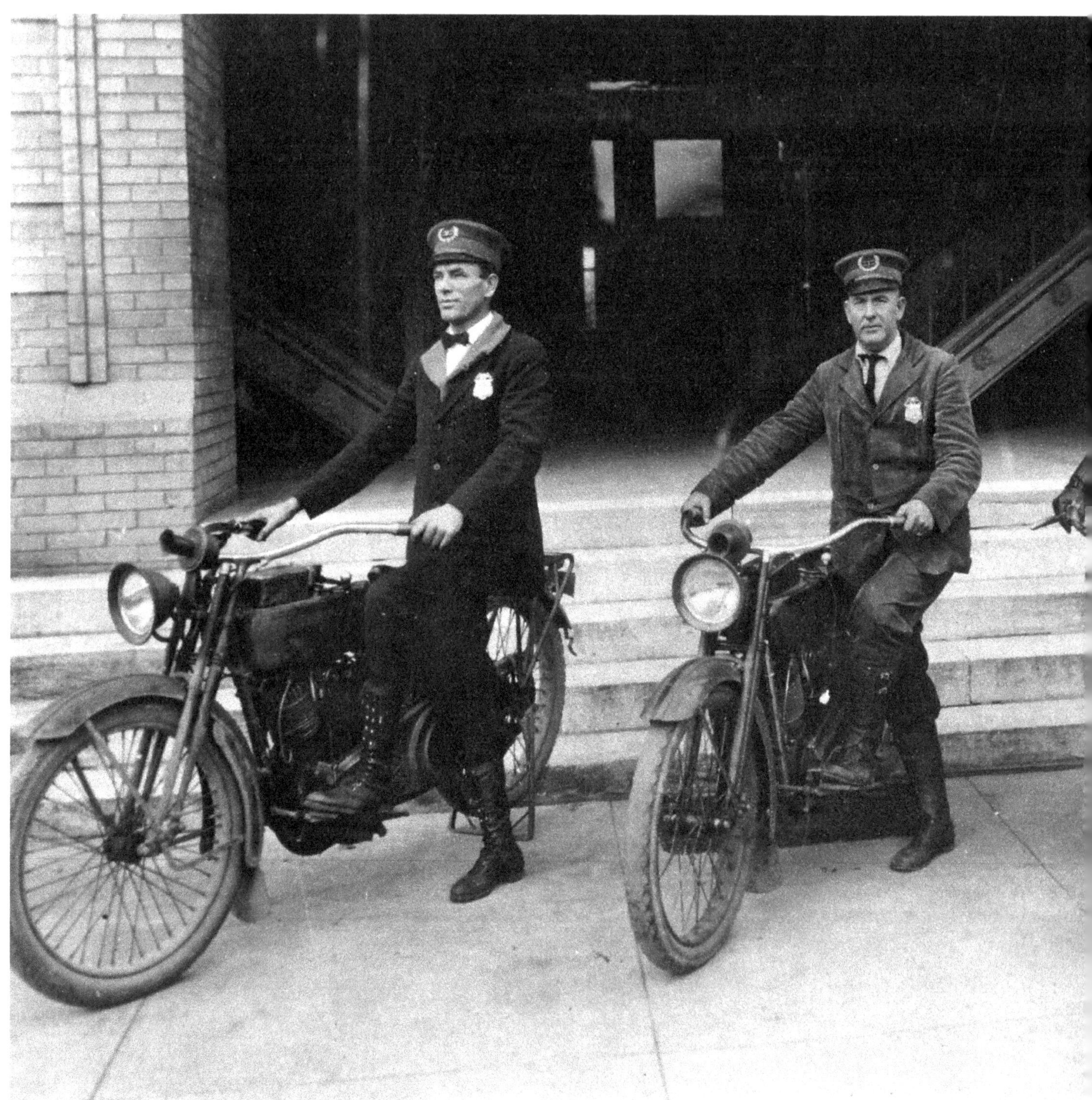

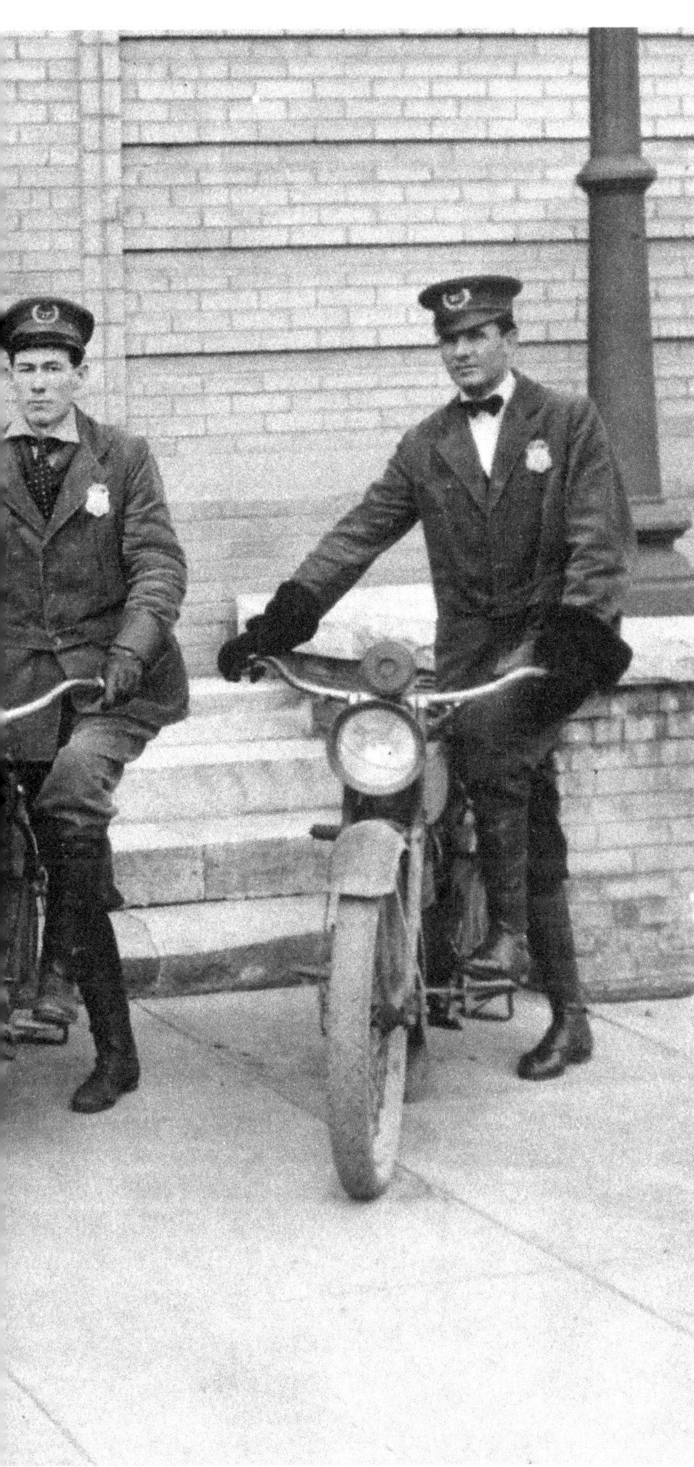

The growing number of automobiles on Austin streets in the early 1900s warranted at least four policemen on motorbikes.

This aerial view of the Capitol and surrounding area in the 1910s indicates how the Texas statehouse soared above the city's skyline. To the right are the steeple of the Tenth Street Methodist Church and spires of St. Mary's Cathedral.

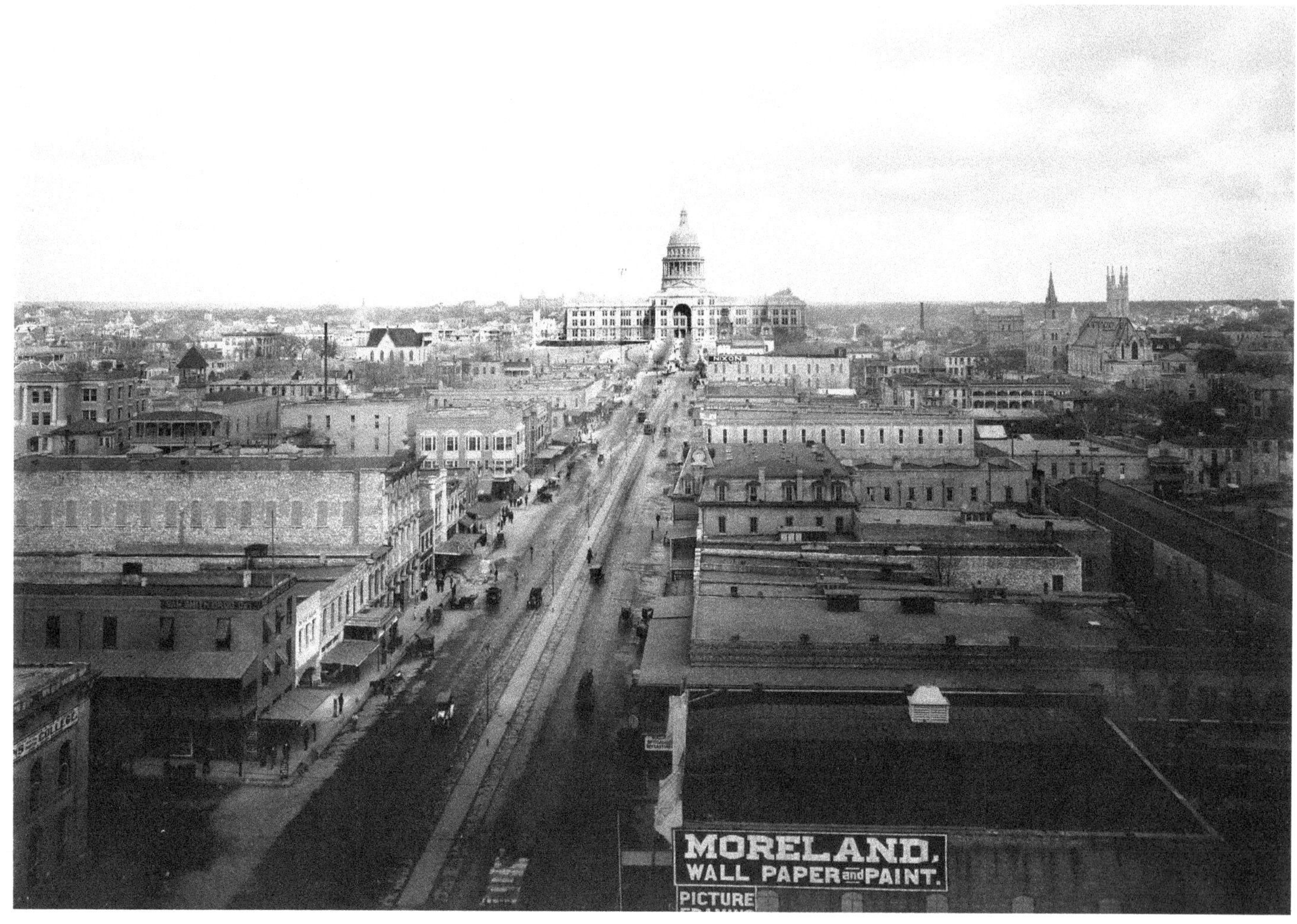

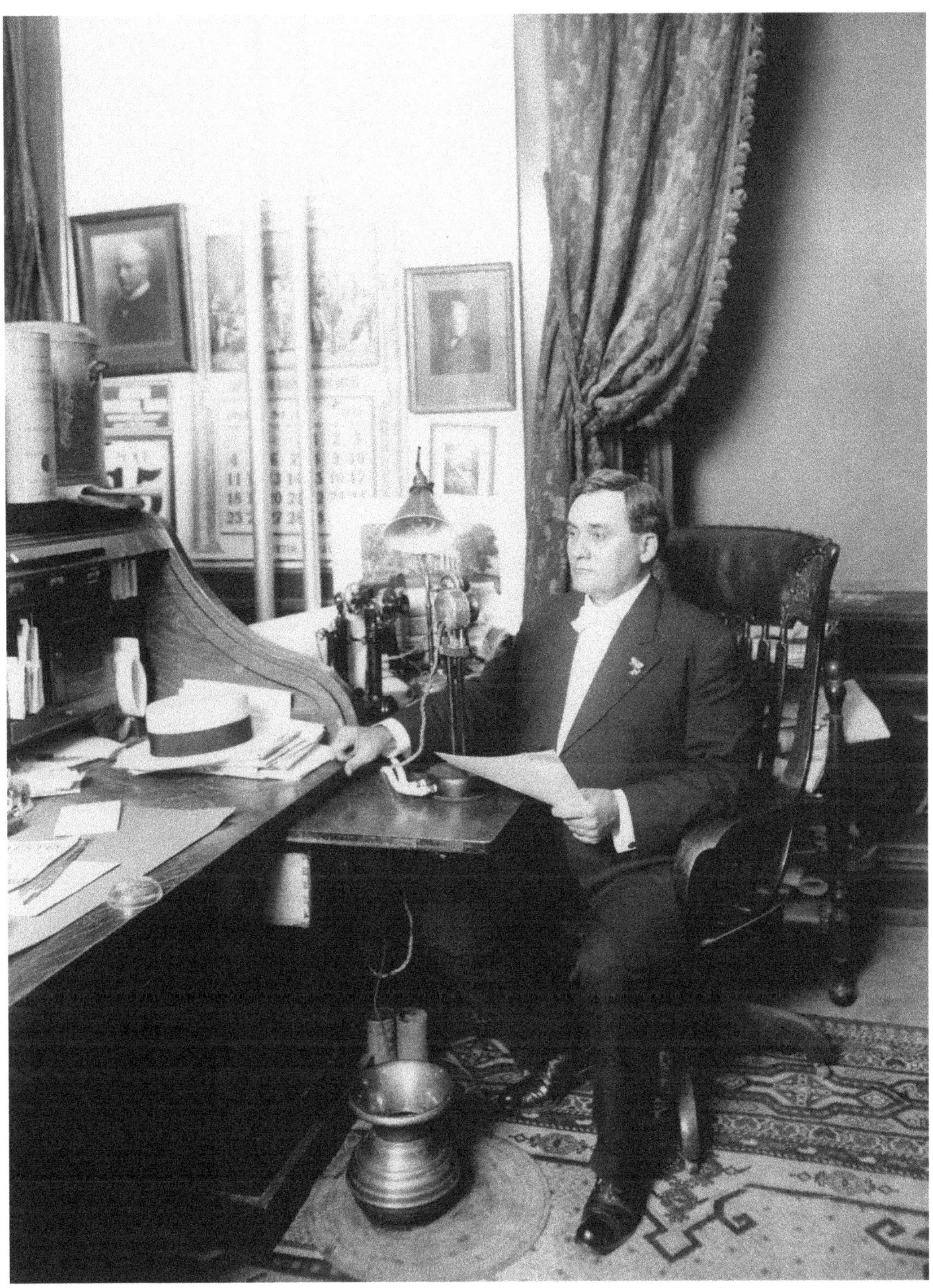

Posing in his richly appointed office in the Capitol, Governor Oscar Branch Colquitt displays all the trappings of a turn-of-the-century politician, including rolltop desk and spittoon. Colquitt was elected governor in 1910 as an anti-prohibitionist and reelected in 1912. His administration achieved advances in education, state institutions, and prison reform.

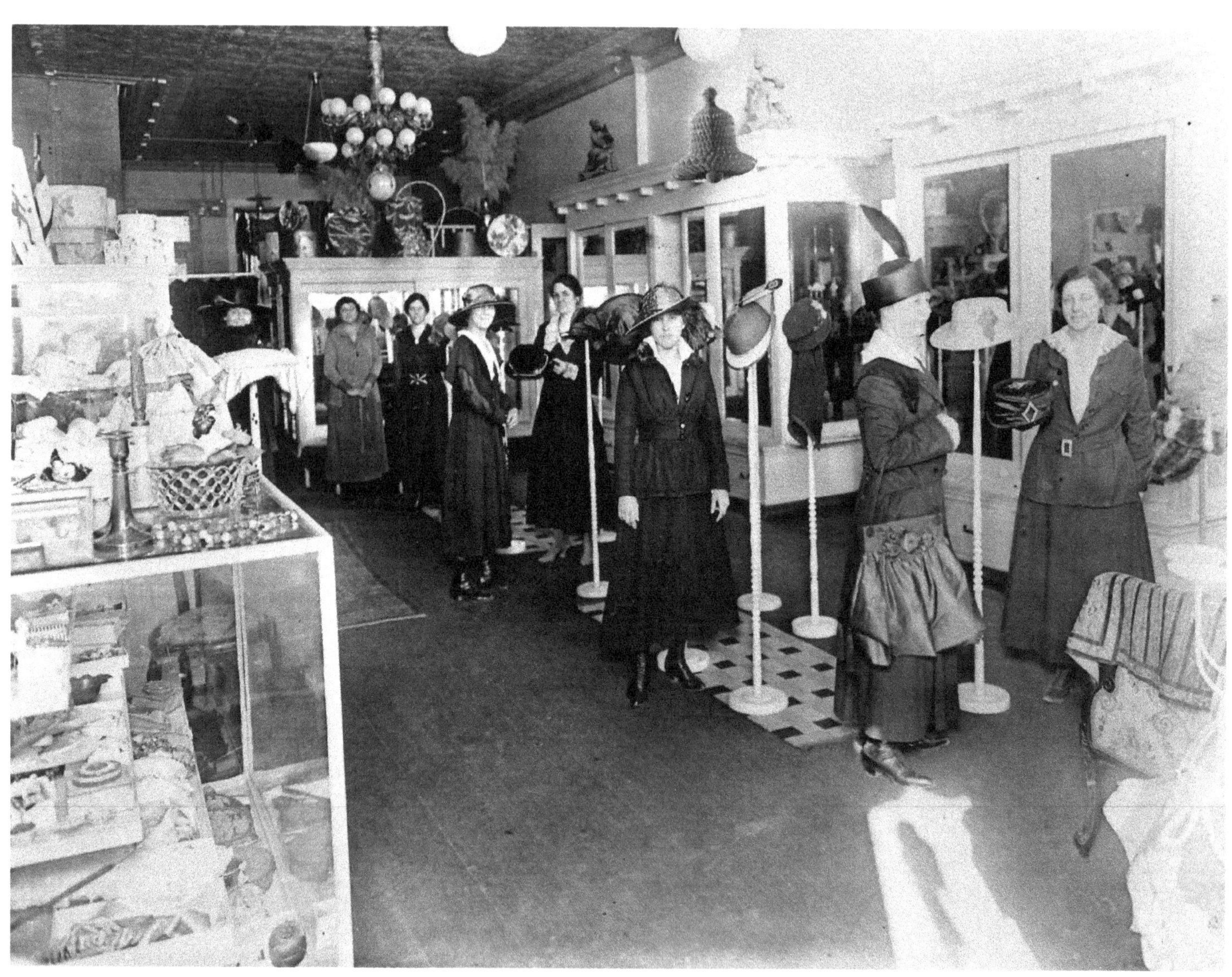

In the early 1900s, no self-respecting lady would allow herself to be seen in public without a "smart hat," and millinery shops such as this one did a thriving business in Austin.

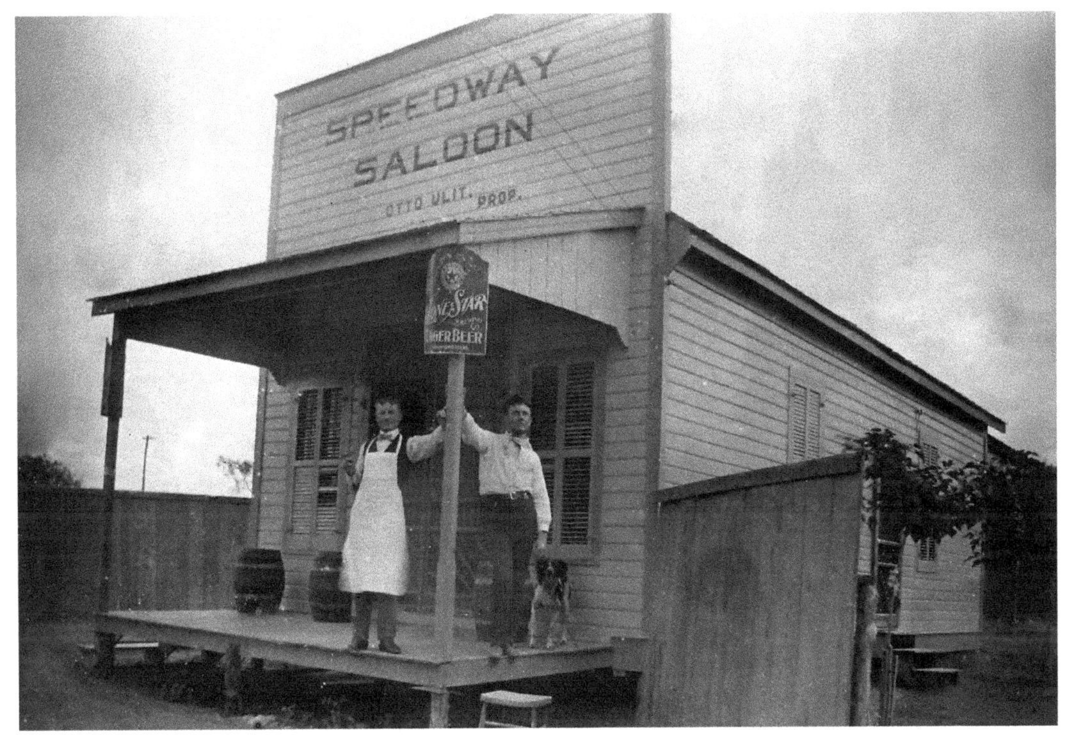

The modest Speedway Saloon, owned by Otto Ulit (at left in apron, with his brother William), was named for the street on which it was located. Speedway—a northward extension of Congress Avenue through Hyde Park, the city's first residential suburb—was paid for by its developer, Monroe M. Shipe, who named it "The Speedway" because it led to the Hyde Park racetrack. "The" has long been dropped from the street's name.

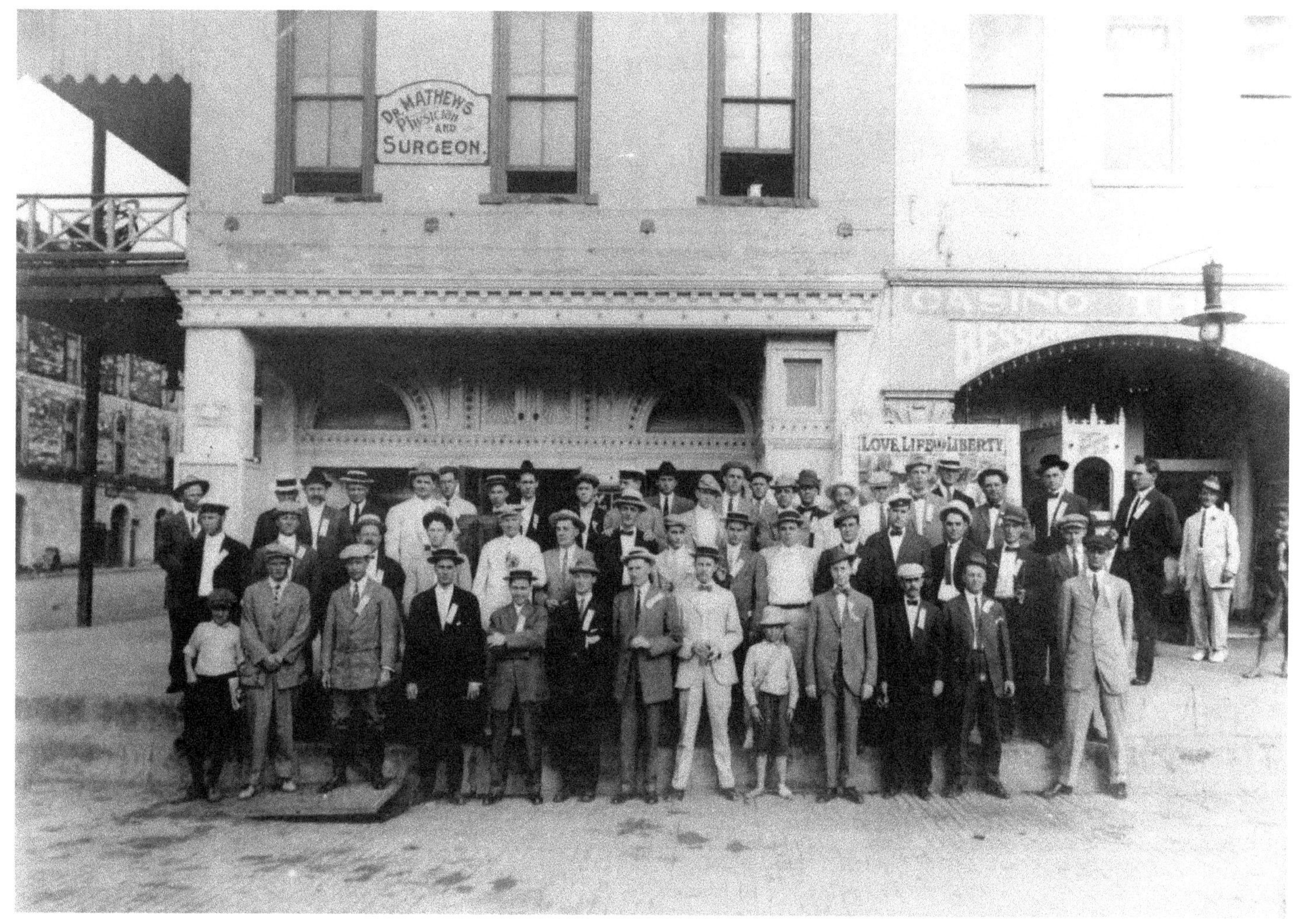

In 1913, the Young Men's Business League (later to merge with the Austin Chamber of Commerce) posed in front of the building in which Civil War veteran "Doc" Mathews had his office. Two newspaper boys seem to be junior members. Roy Bedichek was league secretary then, before going on to become a beloved folklorist and writer, as well as a major organizer and promoter of the University Interscholastic League.

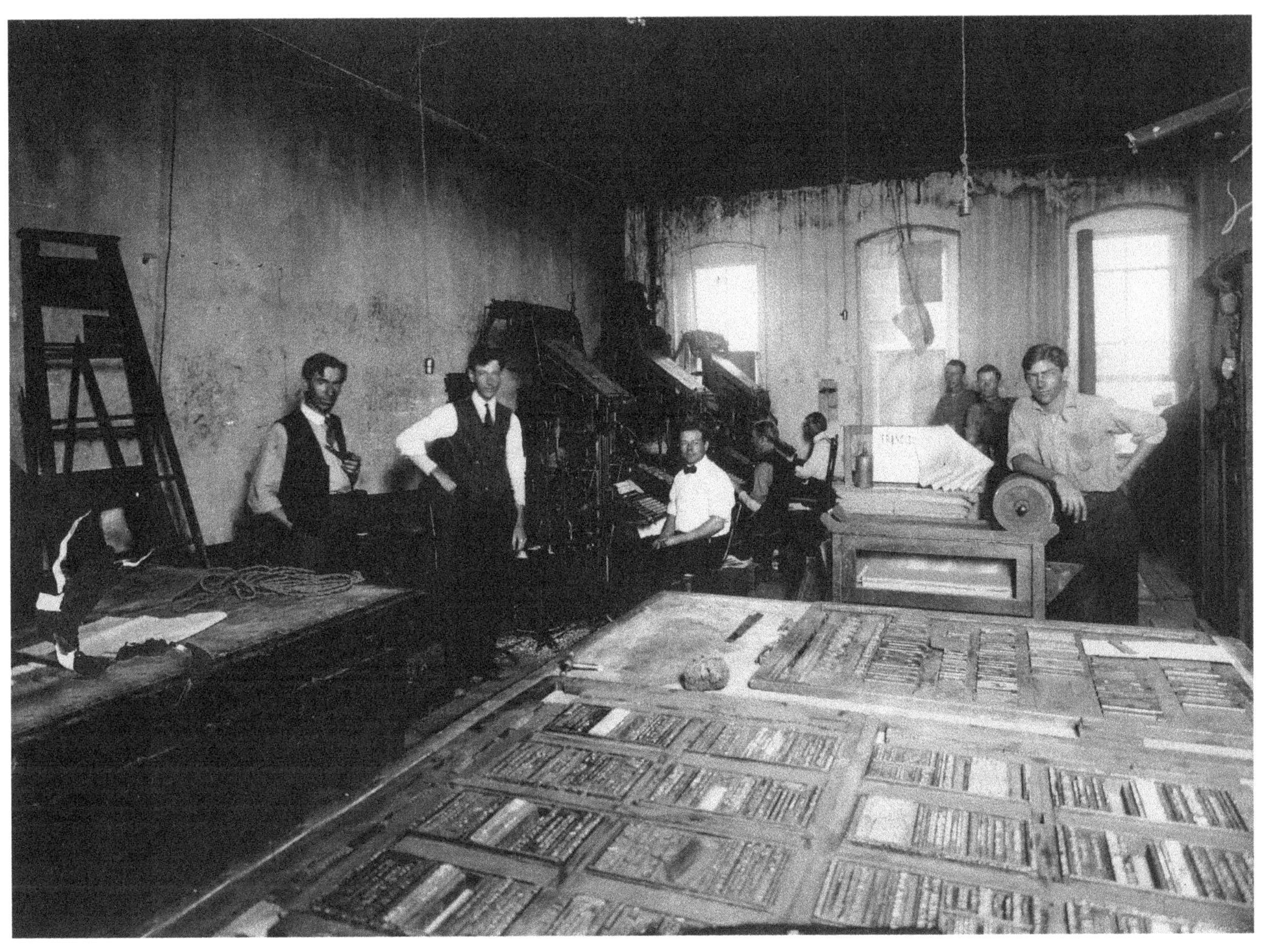

Newspapermen prepare to go to press in the *Statesman* office when it was on Congress Avenue between Seventh and Eighth streets. That space was replaced in 1915 by the Majestic Theater, later named the Paramount.

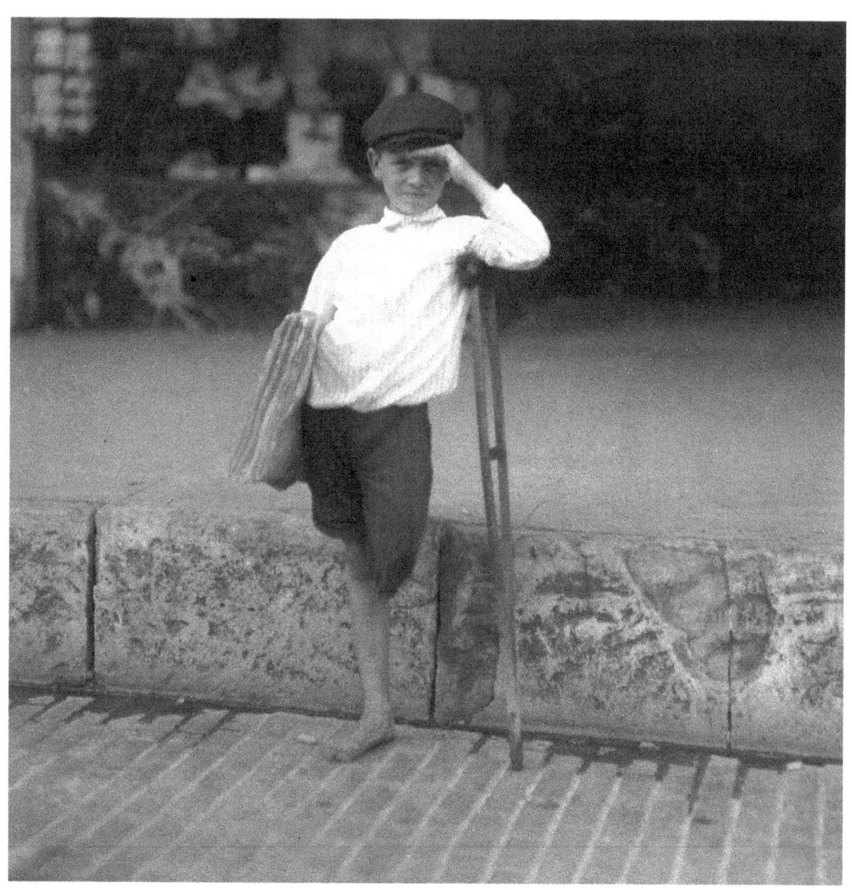

In October 1913, famed muckraker photographer Lewis Hine noted that this eight-year-old Austin newsboy, Alber Schafer, usually began selling Sunday papers at 8:00 A.M. Despite physical challenges, young Albert earned the grand sum of "one to two dollars a day." This photograph was part of Hine's documentation of working children undertaken for the National Child Labor Committee.

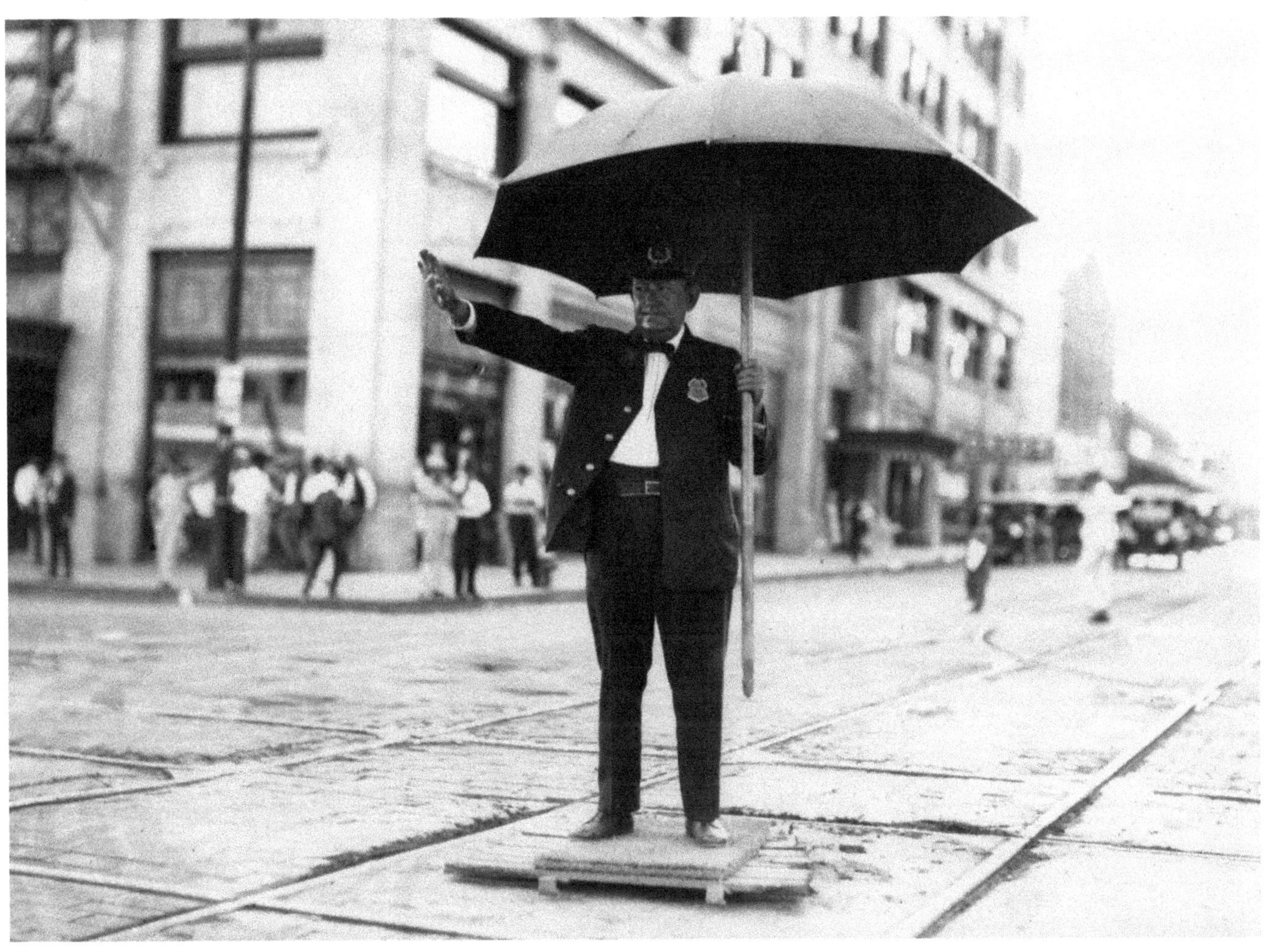

The city's first traffic cop, Officer Kelley, arrived from Atlanta in 1913 to direct Austin's increasing automobile traffic downtown. He stands at the intersection of Austin's two busiest paved thoroughfares, Sixth and Congress (note the trolley tracks). During rush hours, Kelley introduced Austin's first traffic light, which was battery powered and portable. Permanent electric traffic signals would not be installed until 1924.

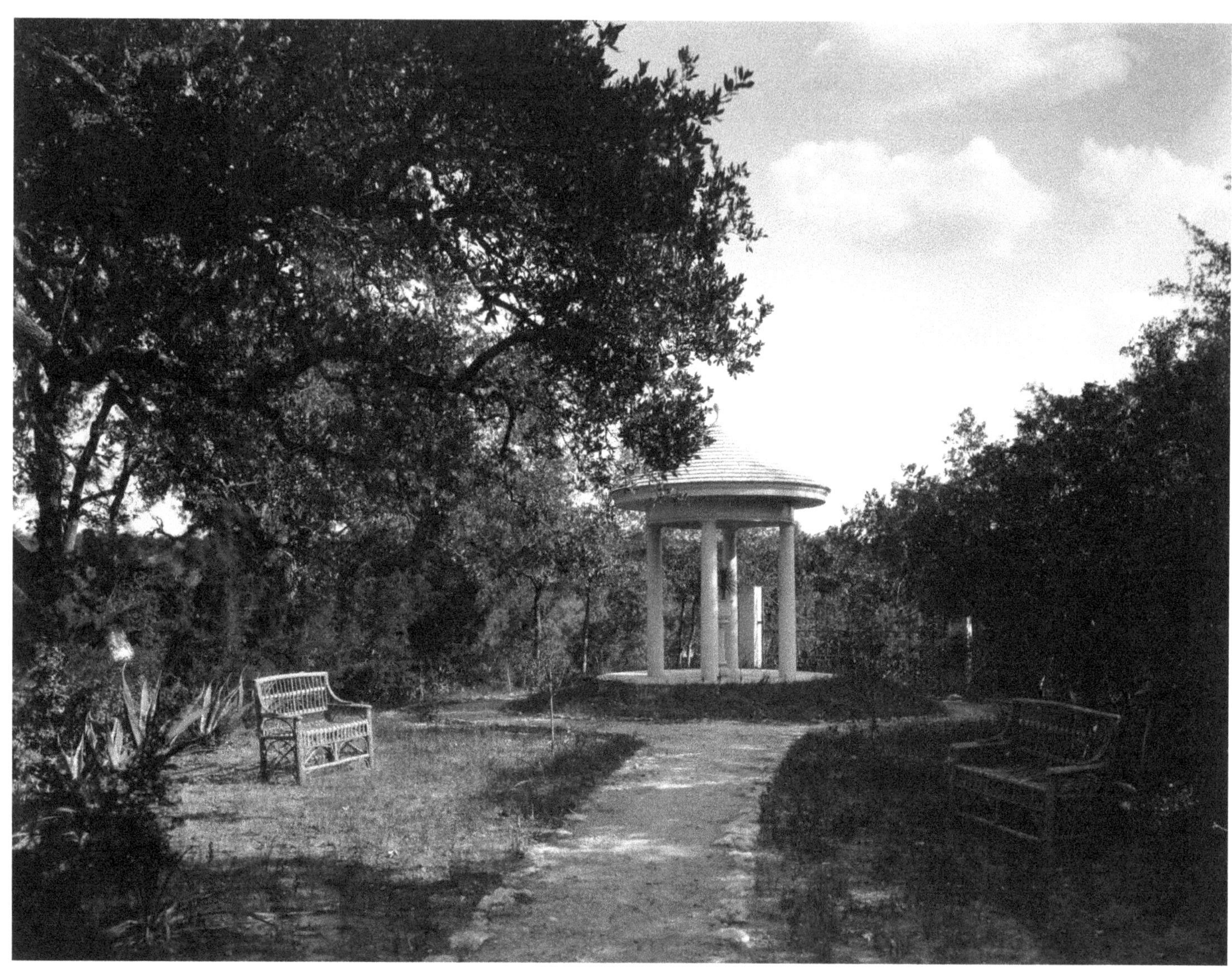

Laguna Gloria, a Mediterranean-style villa overlooking Lake Austin on West Thirty-fifth Street, was built in 1916 on land that Stephen F. Austin had once planned as his homesite. It was the home of Henry H. Sevier and Clara Driscoll Sevier. In 1943, Clara conveyed the property to the Texas Fine Arts Association, and by 1966 it was Laguna Gloria Art Museum, specializing in educating Austinites of all ages about contemporary art.

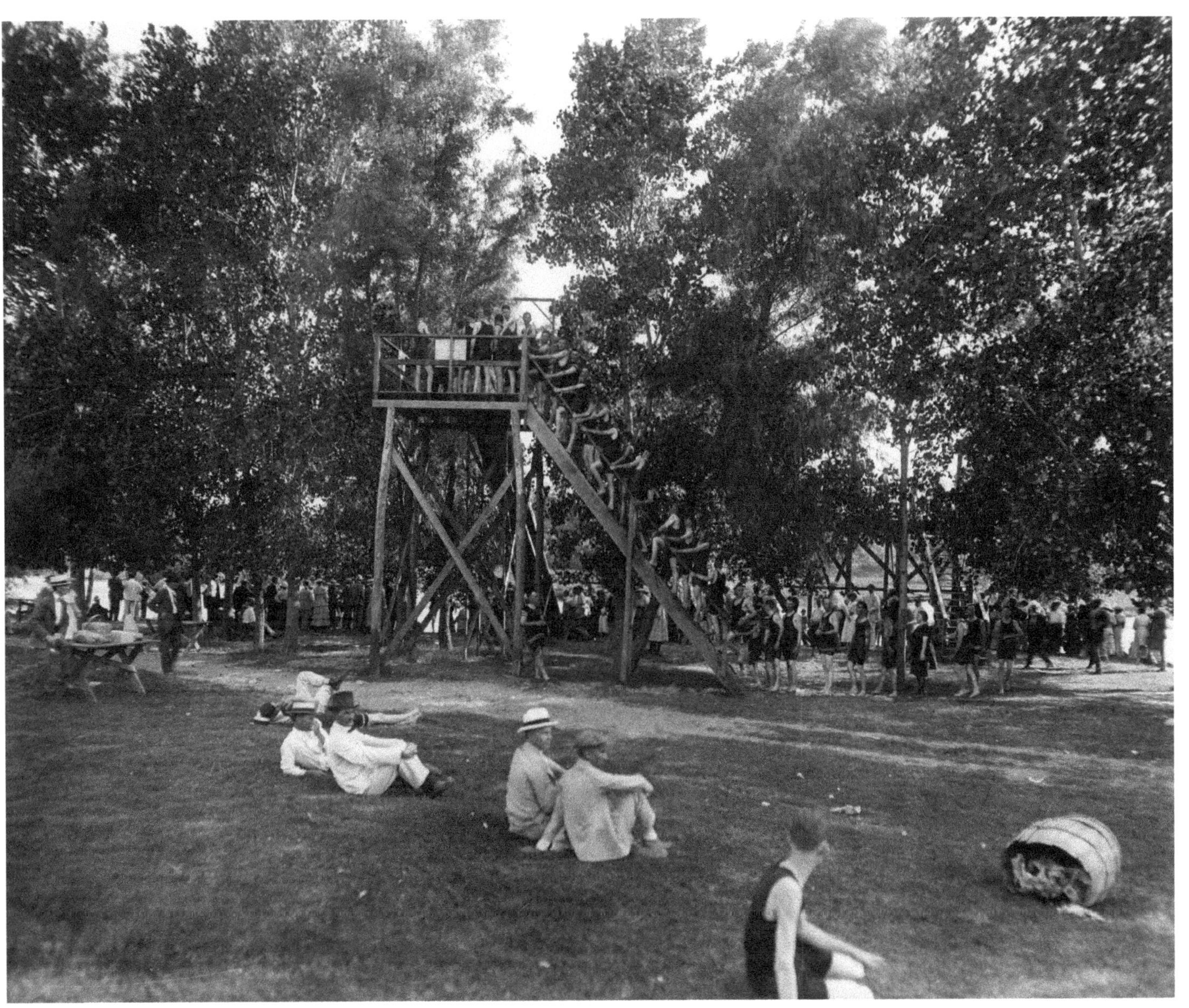

Deep Eddy could boast the first open-air concrete swimming pool in Texas in 1916, when owner A. J. Eilers developed the natural-spring area as a tourist resort. The City of Austin purchased Deep Eddy from Eilers in 1935, when Austin's first WPA project began: construction of a $25,000 bath house for swimmers. The pool's cold spring water and tall shade trees still make it a popular spot on hot summer days.

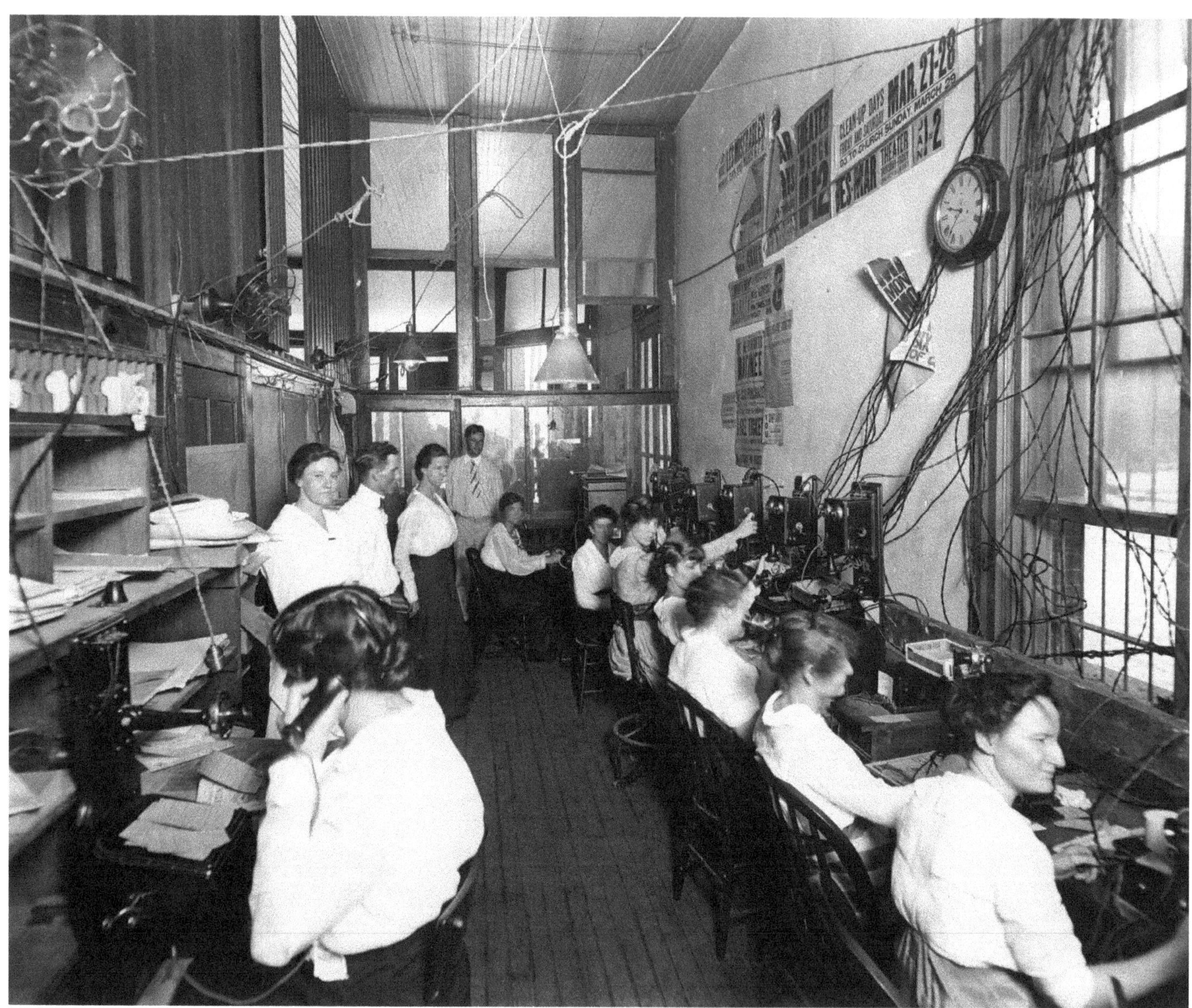

After a destructive fire at the telephone office, telephone operators worked in temporary quarters. Austin was the site of the Southwest's first experimental telephone communication in 1877, when a minister's daughter sang "Almost Persuaded" from Dr. Clark's store in South Austin to the telegraph office on Congress Avenue, about six miles away. Austin claimed almost 5,000 telephones by 1916.

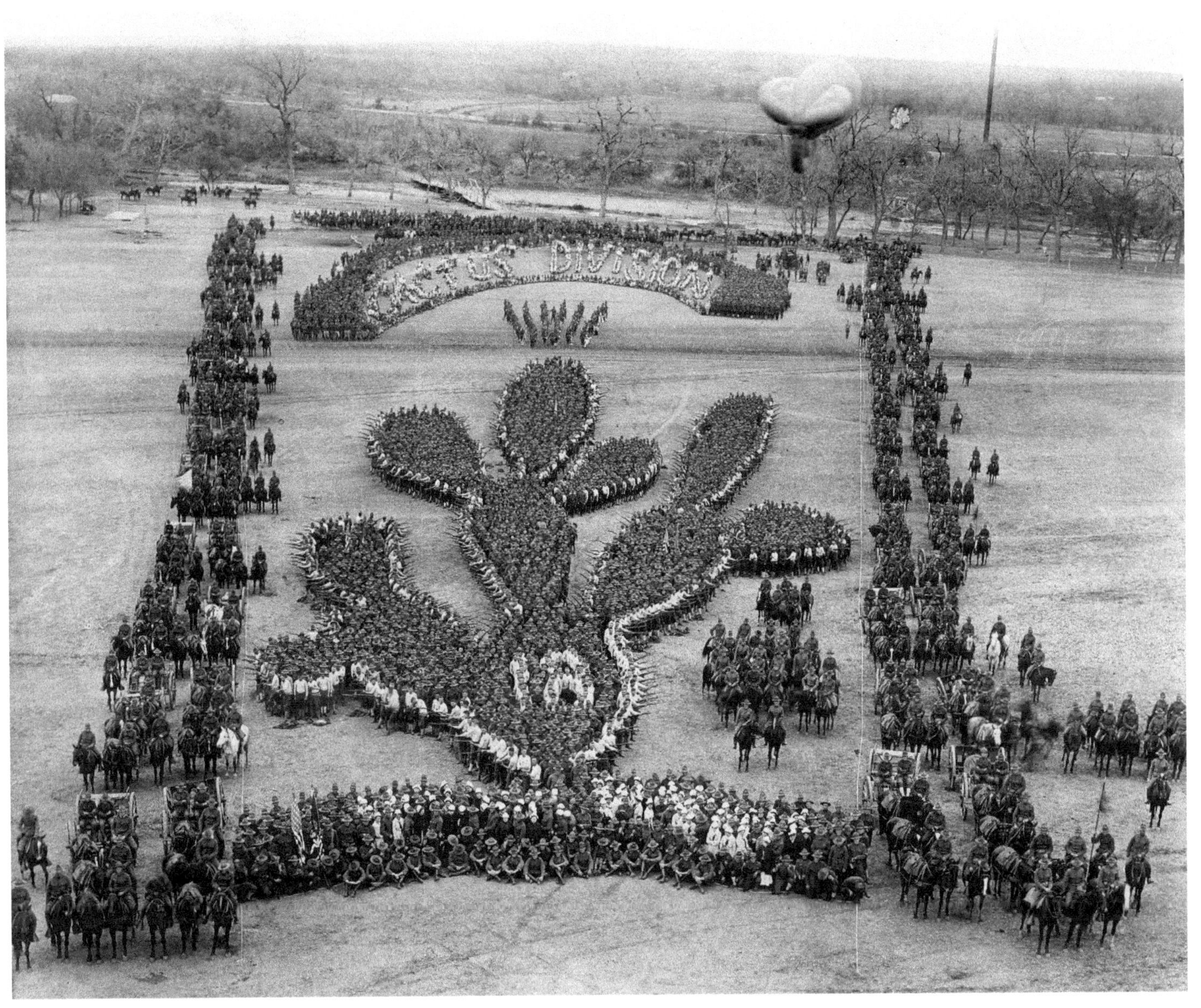

World War I doughboys pose circa 1916 in a graphic display of their nickname, the Cactus Division. General Woodford H. Mabry had introduced Austin spectators to military drills, dress parades, and battle enactments around 1891 at a military encampment near Hyde Park. The following year, Camp Mabry was founded as the Texas Volunteer Guard facility, often the site of displays for the public such as this.

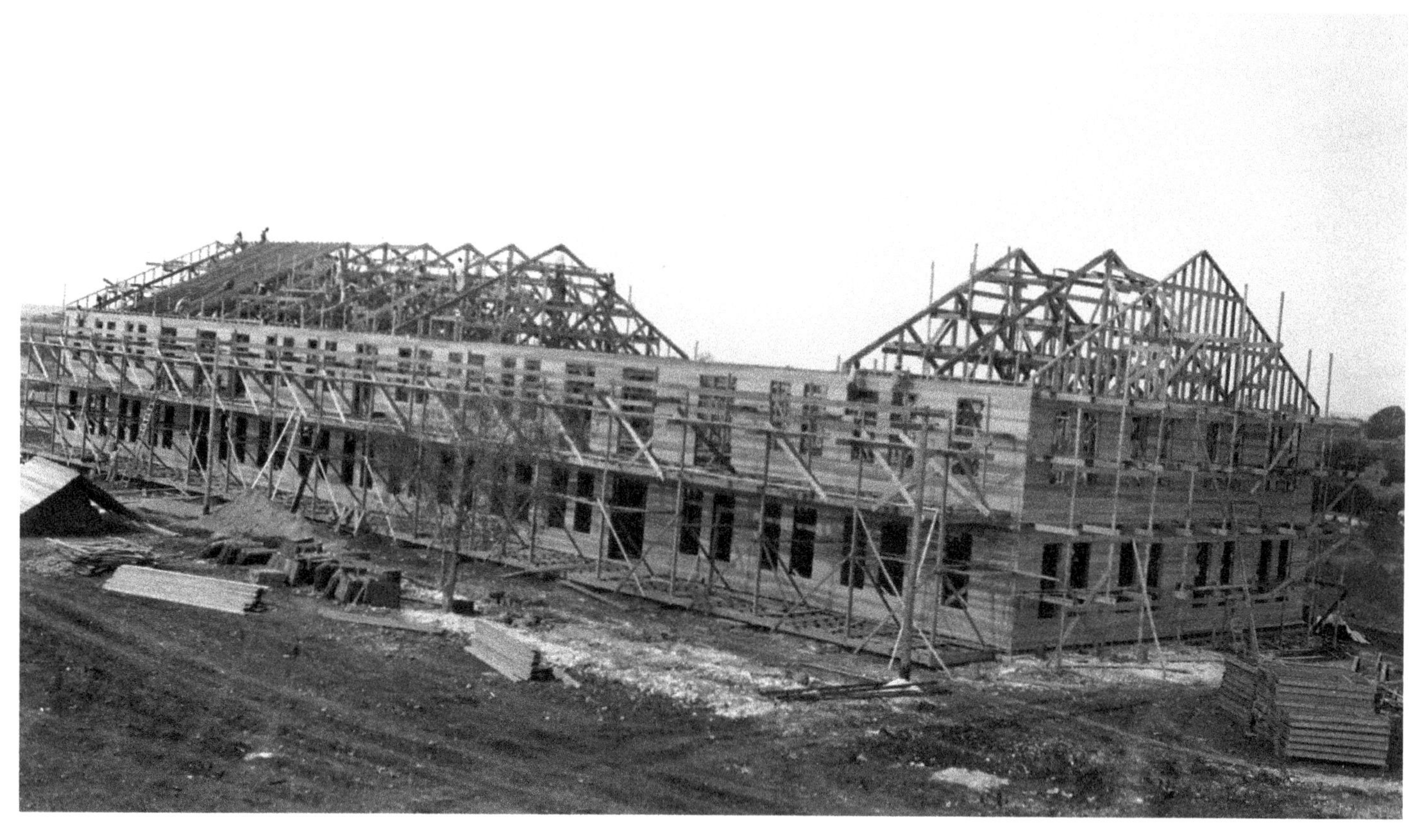

Penn Field, an aircraft-landing field south of Austin, was under construction circa 1917. Established for flight training by UT's School of Military Aeronautics, it was named for Austin cadet Eugene Doak Penn. Volunteers, including Boy Scouts and boys from the School for the Deaf, cleared the land of rocks and cornstalks. After World War I, the field was sold, and during the 1930s it housed the Woodward Furniture Factory.

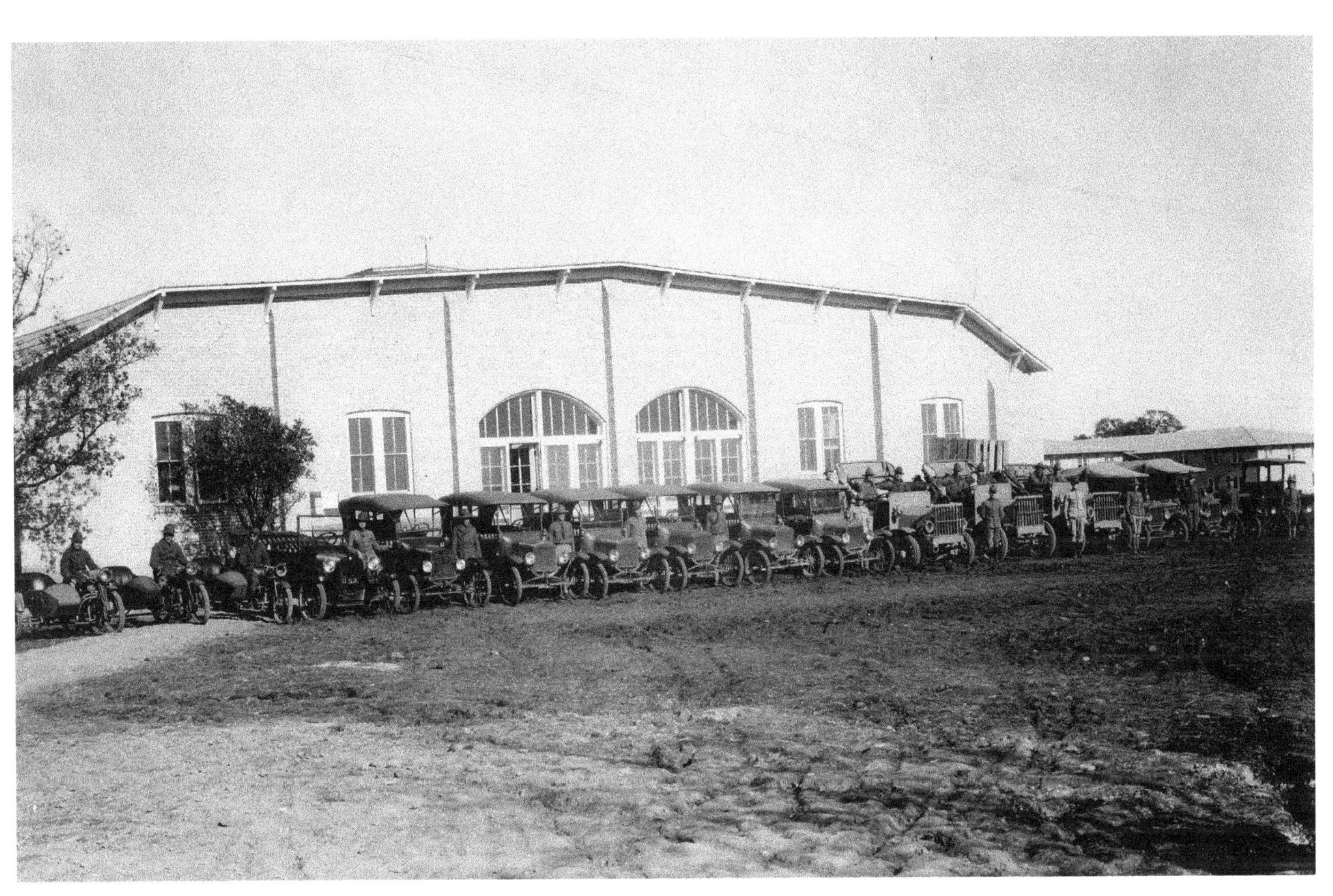

This photograph taken at Penn Field after construction was complete shows a lineup of well-cared-for automobiles and early motorcycles. The men are World War I students at the School of Automobile Mechanics, circa 1918.

Signs such as this one at the American National Bank building were prevalent among Austin businesses during World War I, reminding citizens to do their part to help the war effort.

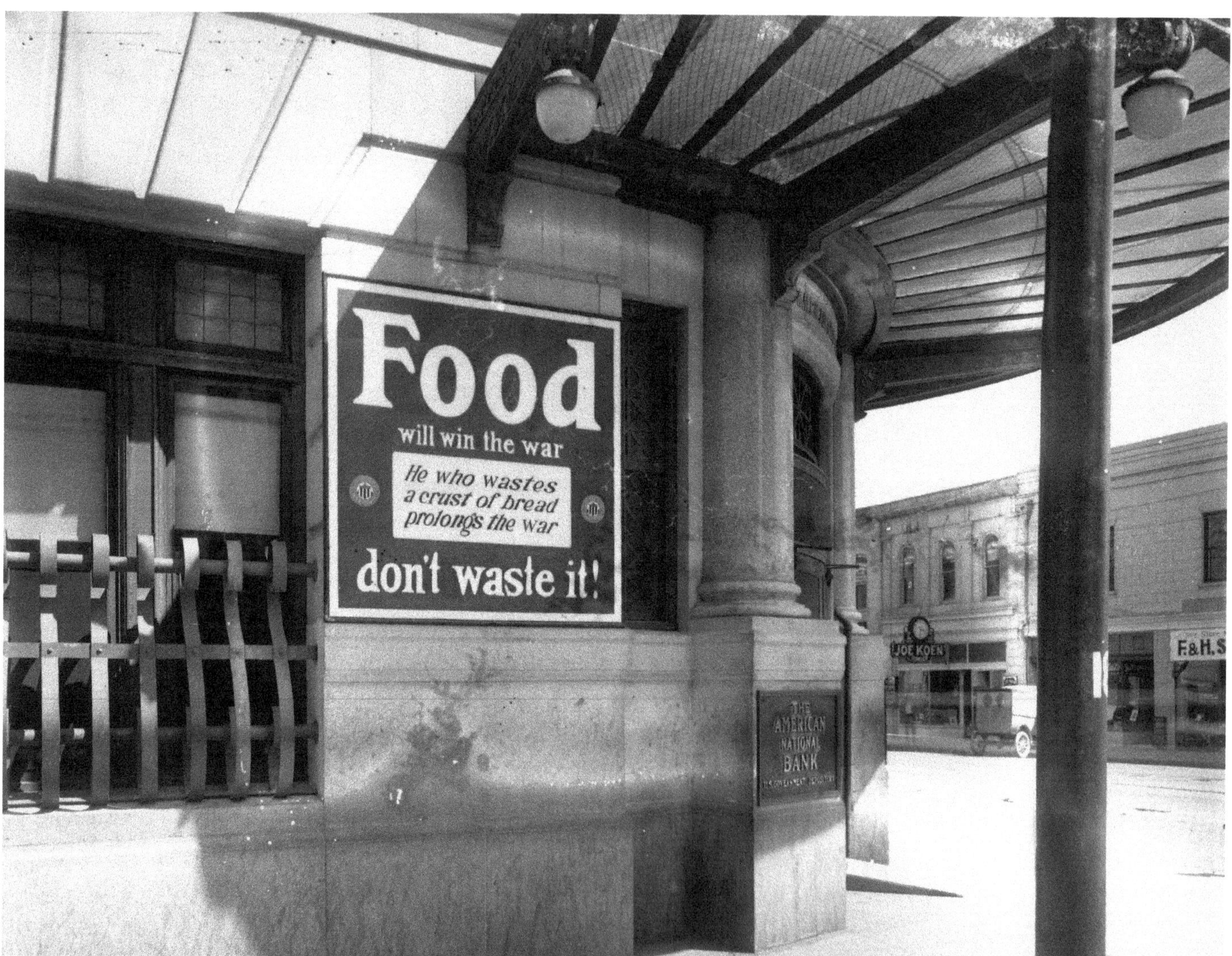

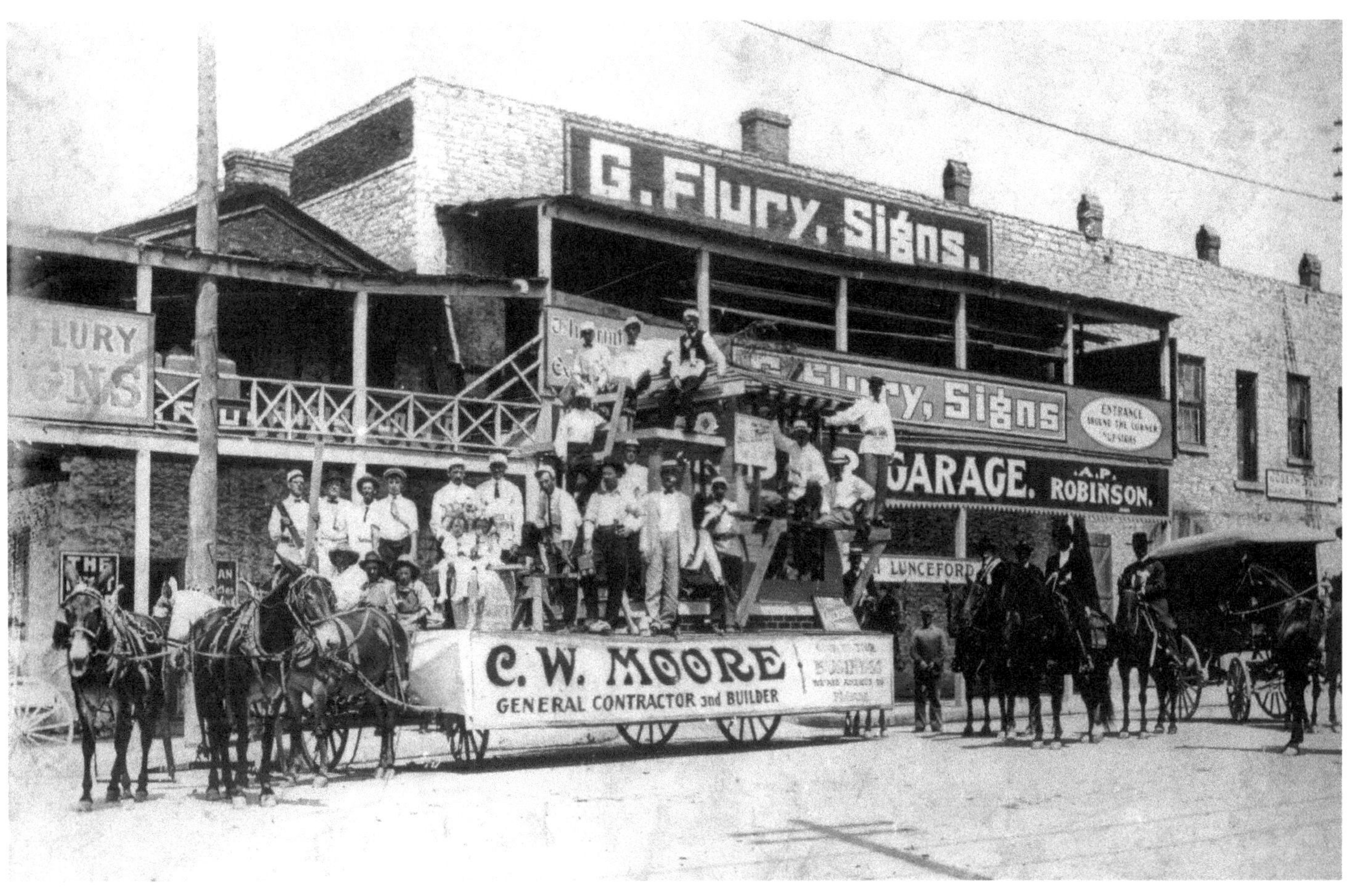

Even though automobiles were becoming more common, Austin's parades often featured teams of horses and mules. This parade float, sponsored by contractor and builder C. W. Moore circa 1918, featured carpenters on a miniature house they built expressly for the Labor Day parade.

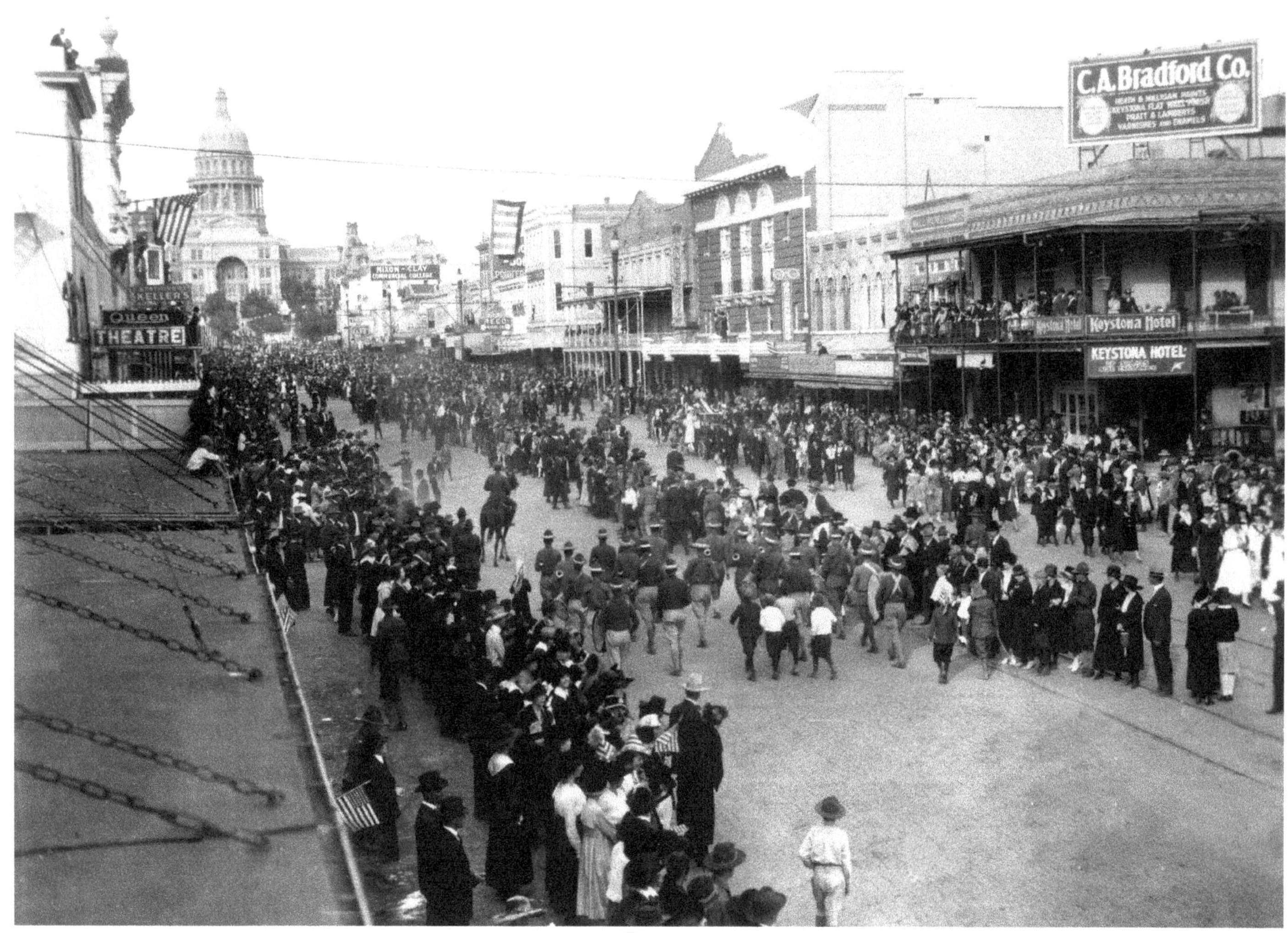

When World War I ended with the armistice on November 11, 1918, Austinites quickly organized a Victory parade on Congress Avenue. Spectators gathered not only on both sides of the street but also in the middle along the streetcar tracks, and the parade moved both north and south. A privileged few watched from the Keystona Hotel's second-floor balcony, and almost everyone dressed up for the joyous occasion.

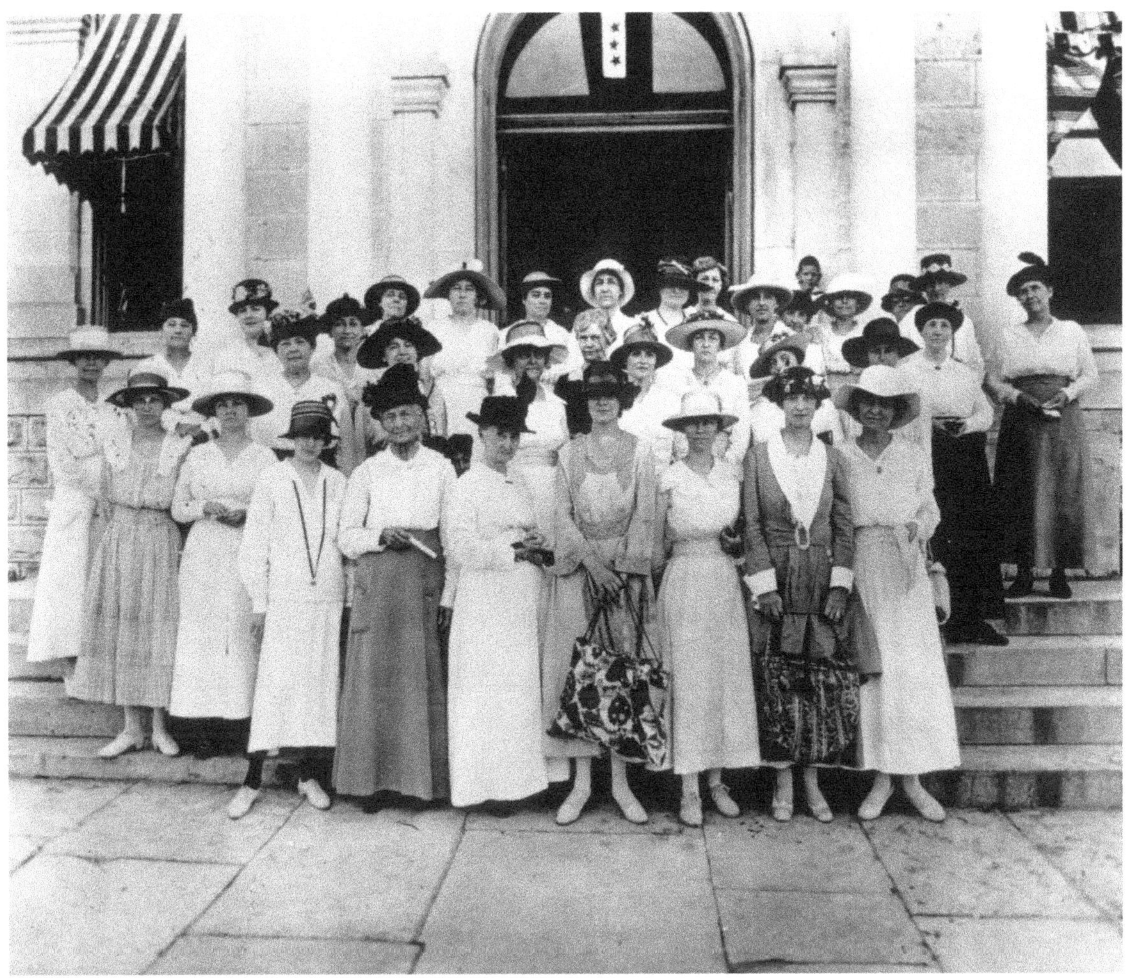

Standing on the steps of the first Travis County Courthouse, these well-dressed Austin women pose after registering to vote for the first time. The woman fourth from right, front row, is identified as Jane Y. McCallum, a president of the Austin Woman Suffrage Association who lobbied, spoke publicly, and wrote fervently to win full enfranchisement in 1919 for Texas women.

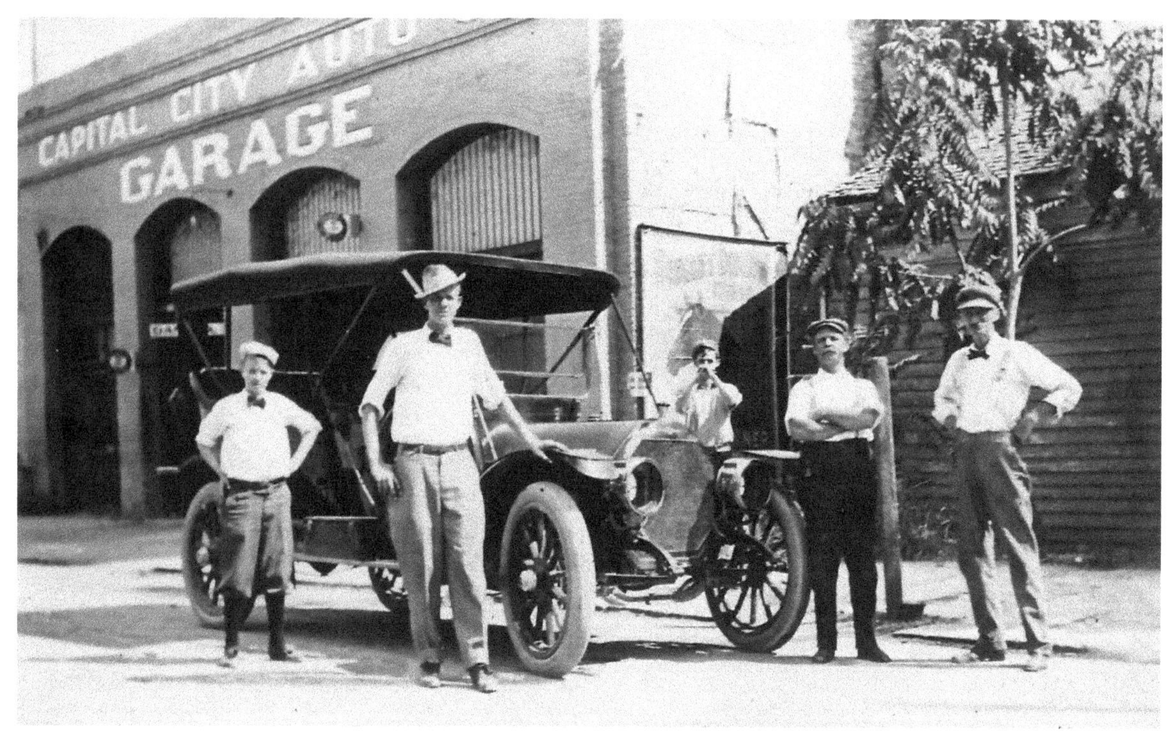

William Jennings Bryan—senator, three-time presidential candidate, and secretary of state—is believed to have lived in Austin between 1898 and 1899. This photograph shows his aides ("Senator Bryan's Boys") with local taxi drivers. Gifted at oratory, Bryan is best remembered in history for the 1925 Scopes "Monkey Trial" in Dayton, Tennessee, a staged contest between the ACLU and evolutionists against average, churchgoing Americans, represented by Bryan, waged to determine whether evolution or creation would be taught in public school classrooms.

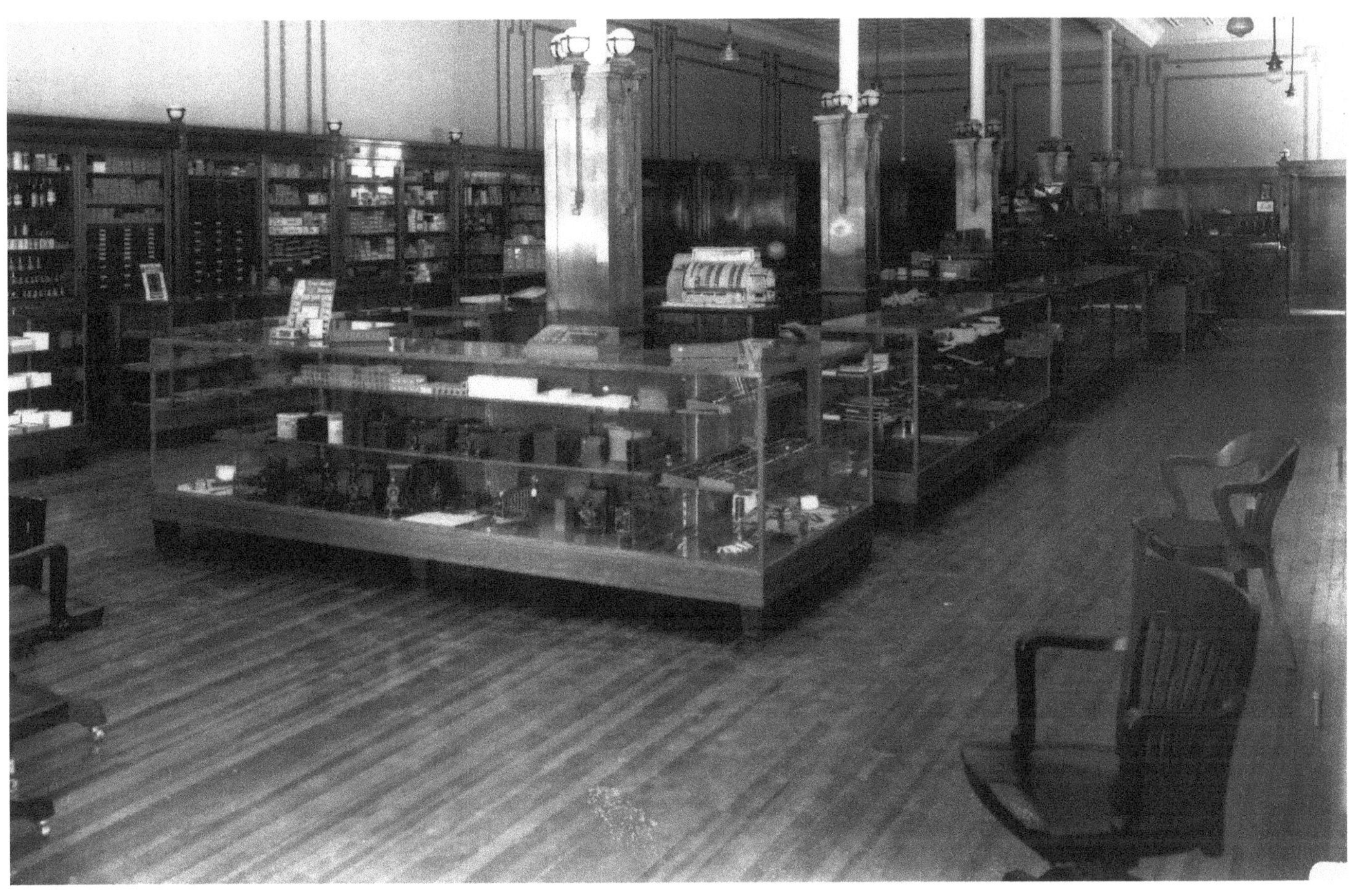

Many people who come to Austin to attend the University of Texas, Huston-Tillotson College, Concordia College, or St. Edward's University decide that they want to stay in the city permanently. Consequently, Austin can boast a relatively well-educated population, and bookstores are popular haunts. Some thrive, but others come and go. This is the interior of Tobin's Book Store, one that went.

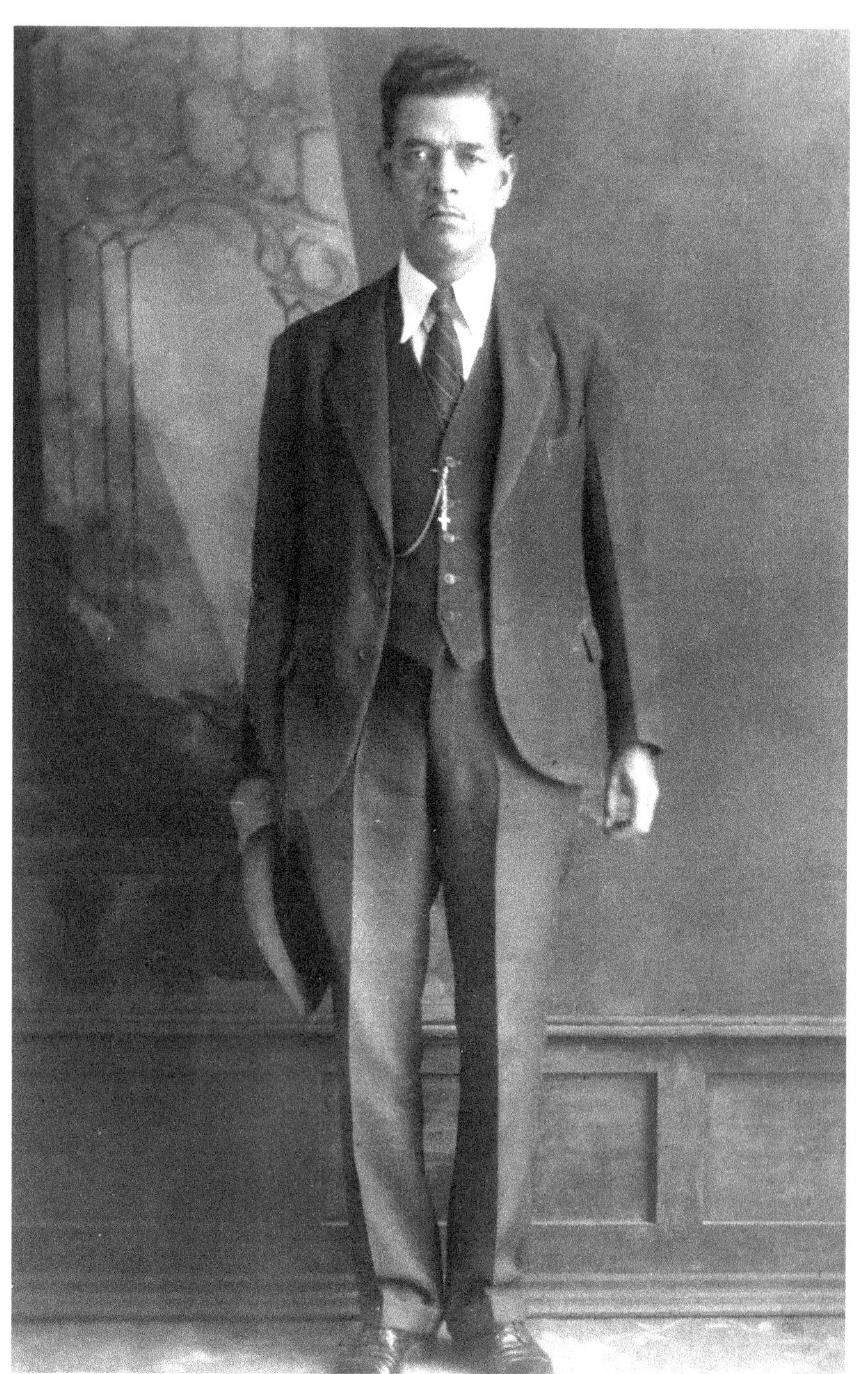

Pictured circa 1925, Eustacio Cepeda (1897–1972), was one of Austin's outstanding Mexican American citizens. In 1940, he established the Mexican consulate in Austin, after having spent years as unofficial consul to Mexicans immigrating to Central Texas. Fluent in English and skilled at diplomacy, he helped Latino families make the transition to their new life, despite language barriers and discrimination.

Elation and Depression

(1920–1940)

The Roaring Twenties were perhaps a little quieter in Austin than elsewhere, and the Depression years were less severe than in other Texas cities. Austin's government and education bases provided work through massive municipal construction projects and New Deal programs. The city's population actually grew during the 1930s, by 66 percent, and enrollment doubled at the University of Texas.

In 1920, however, Austin was ranked only tenth in population among Texas cities. Still, Austinites continued the tradition of holding a parade down Congress Avenue at every opportunity. The new dial telephones arrived in early 1922, giving Austinites plenty to talk about. That same year, a fierce tornado demolished buildings, killing 13 people and injuring 44. In 1923, Santa Rita Number One—an oil well on West Texas land owned by the University of Texas—came a gusher. The proceeds initiated a building boom that would dramatically expand the campus.

Austinites voted to change their city government again, this time to the city manager form. With an inventory of 1,700 books, the American Association of University Women started Austin's first library in 1926, the same year that Concordia Lutheran College was founded. The new Austin Municipal Airport, which had gravel runways, opened in 1930. The next year, Roy Velasquez started Roy's Taxi company with one cab, and by 1932 he had 35 vehicles transporting hundreds of Austinites daily. In 1933, Austin's first permanent public library building, Wooldridge Library, opened at Ninth and Guadalupe streets; the site's temporary structure was moved east to become the George Washington Carver branch library.

City council member Tom Miller was named mayor in 1933; he would serve in that office for 22 years. In 1936, President Franklin D. Roosevelt, making a brief whistle-stop late at night, was greeted by 30,000 residents. The following year, a young Lyndon Johnson won his first election to the U.S. House of Representatives from the Tenth Congressional District (which included Austin), and UT's imposing new tower, 307 feet tall, was completed and lit for the first time. In 1938, the new Austin Symphony Orchestra played its first concert to a packed auditorium. The reconstructed Austin dam was dedicated in 1940 and renamed Tom Miller Dam in honor of the mayor.

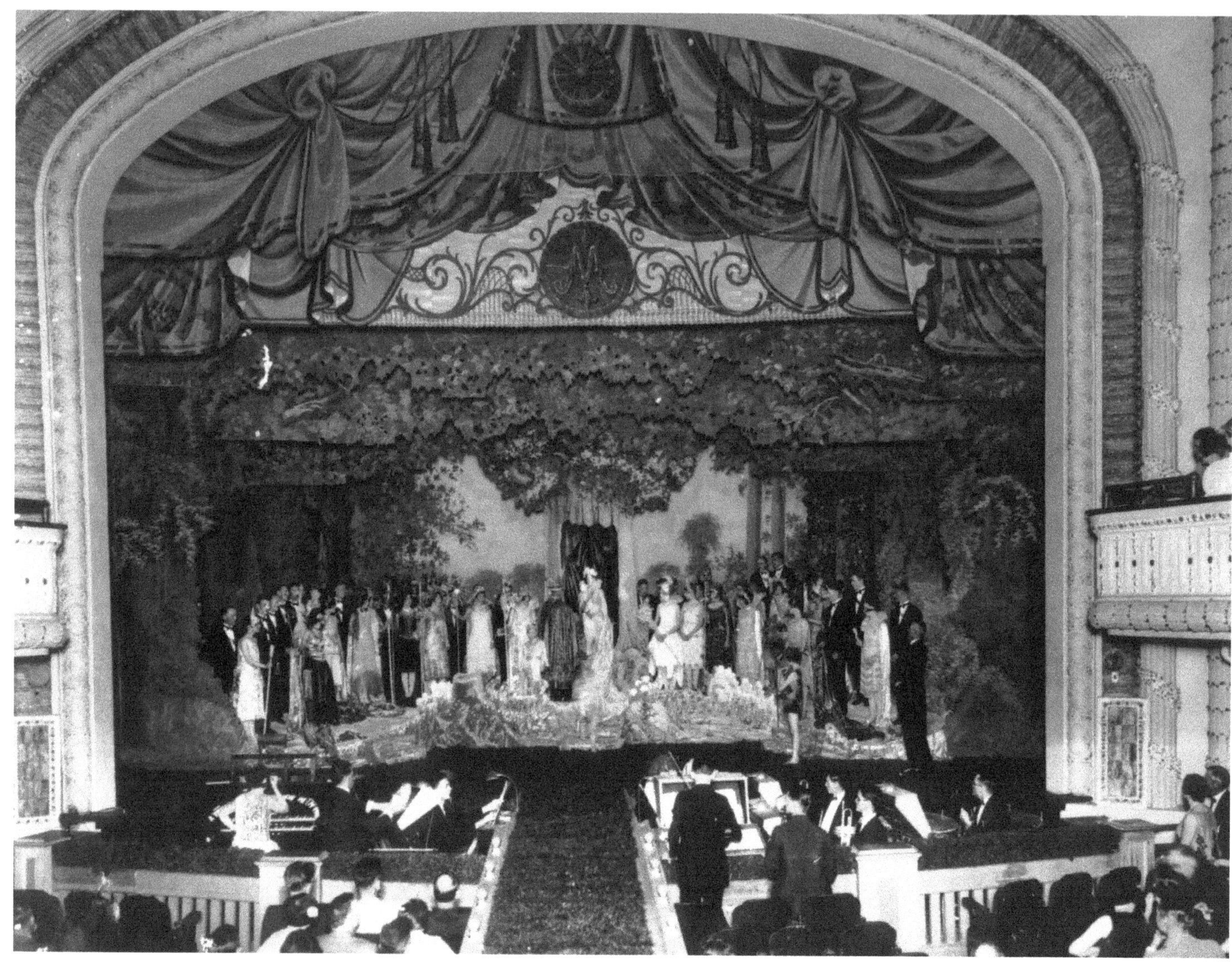

This 1920s performance at the Paramount Theater (originally called the Majestic), was just one of hundreds of stage productions seen there during its illustrious history. The theater hosted appearances by many famous performers, including opera singer Enrico Caruso, escape artist Harry Houdini, and those zany comics known as the Marx Brothers.

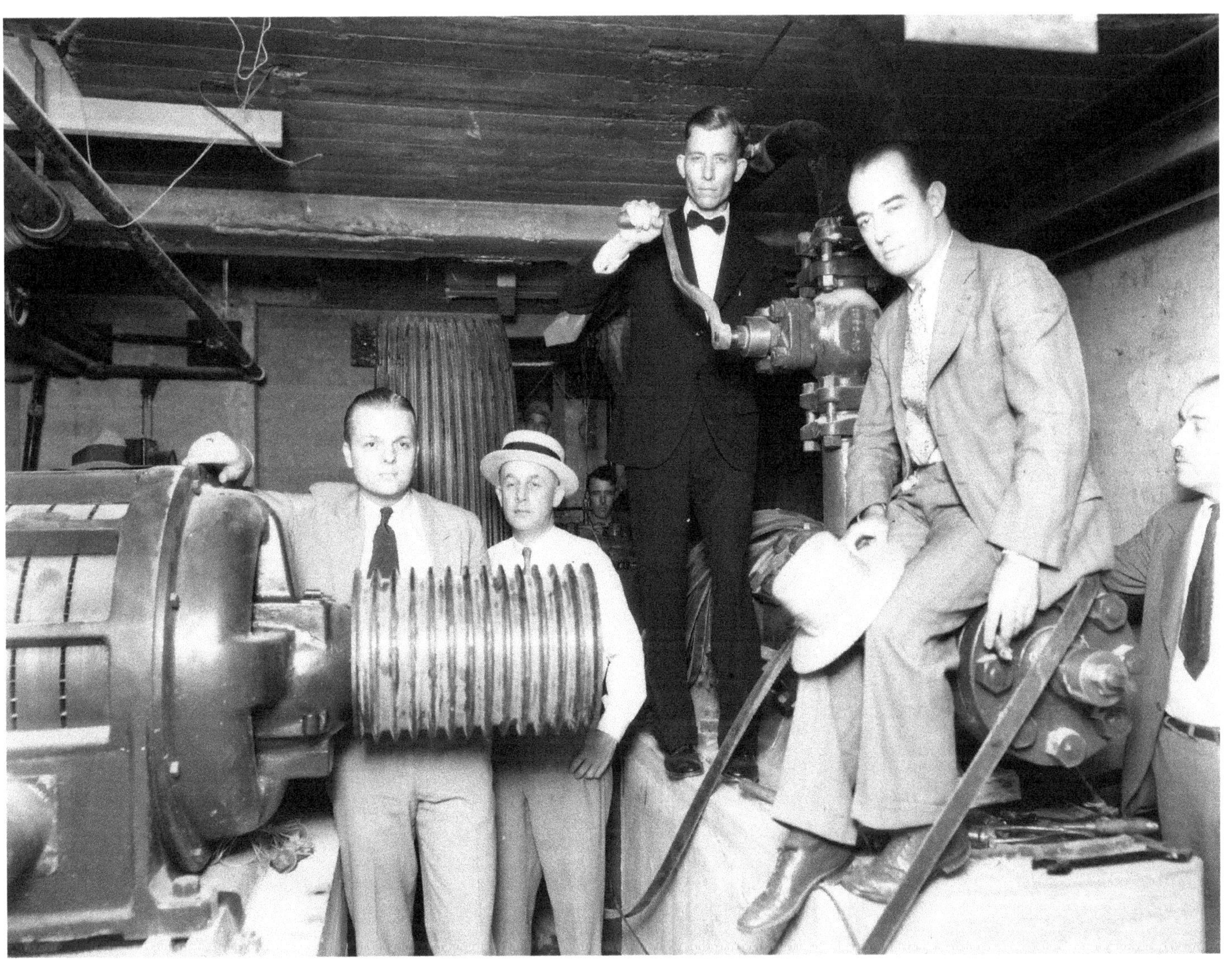

In the Paramount's heyday as a movie theater, it took several skilled hands to project the films without a hitch. Some of them are pictured here with their managers in what may be the basement of the theater.

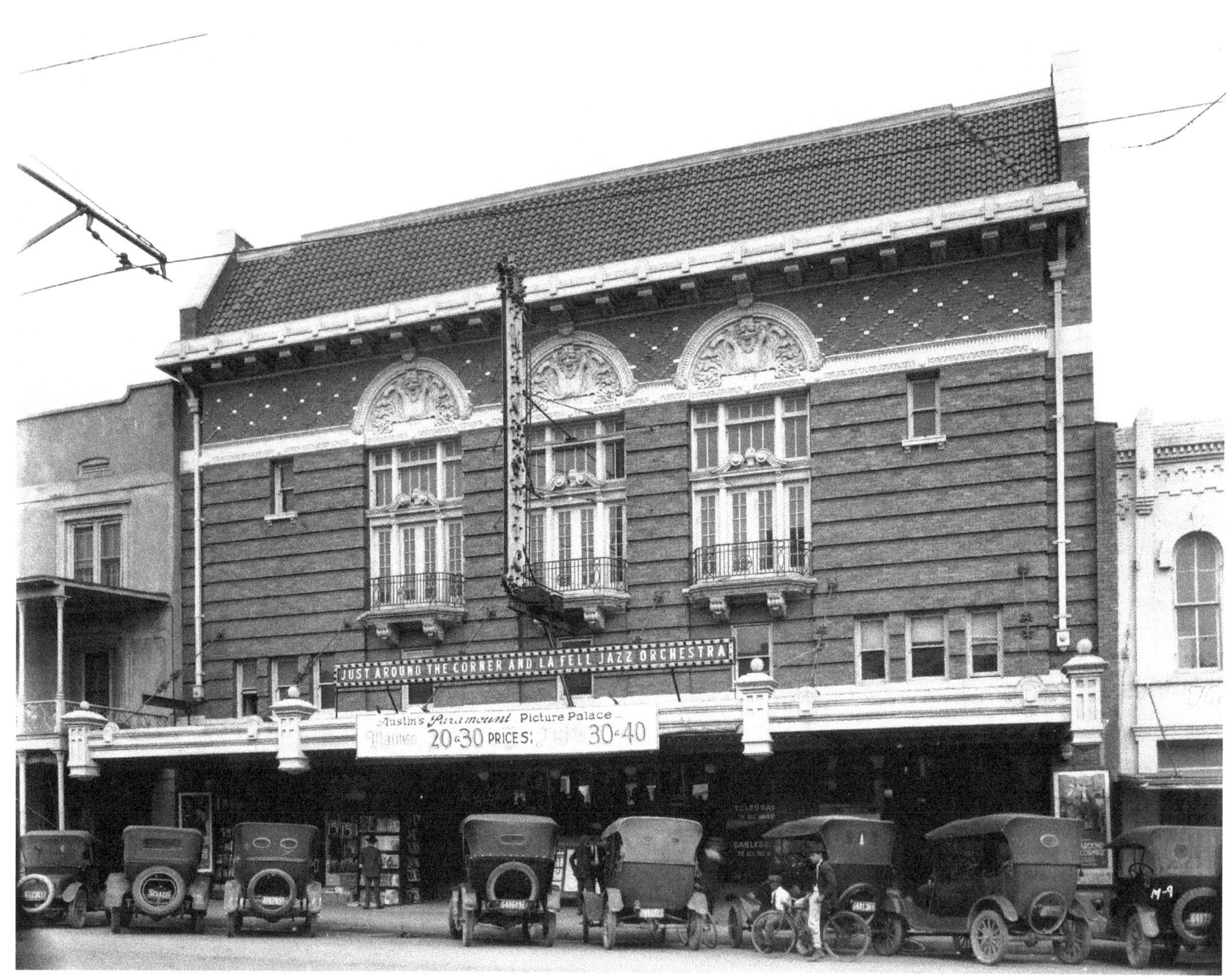

This exterior view of the Paramount Theater circa 1920 shows its handsome architectural detailing in days when automobiles were still relatively new to Austin. The marquee seems remarkably subtle by today's standards. Built in 1915 by local banker Ernest Nalle, this "Picture Palace" was restored to its original glory and reopened during the downtown renaissance of the 1980s.

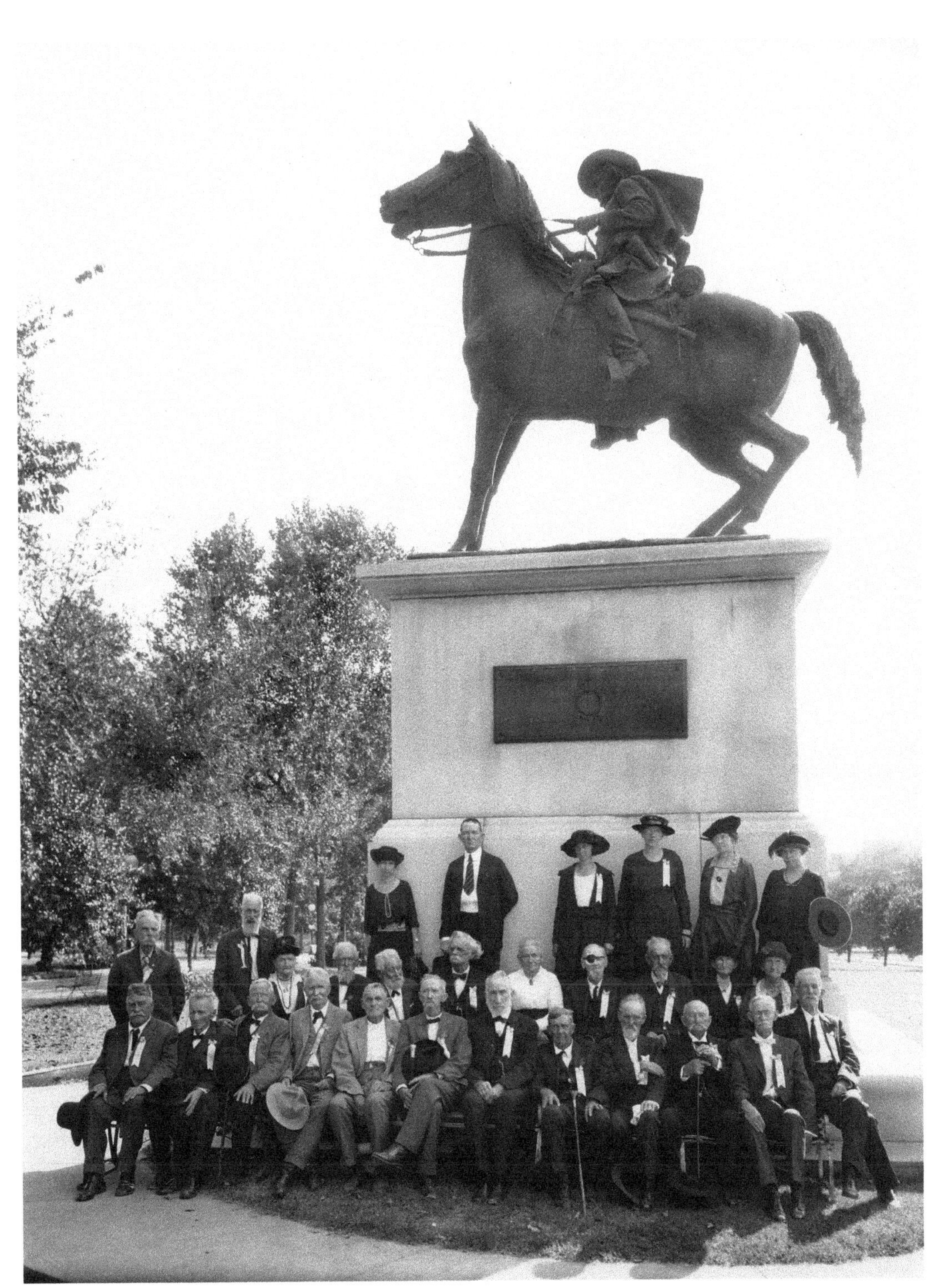

In 1921, surviving members of Terry's Texas Rangers, a company of Confederate cavalrymen during the Civil War, gathered at the foot of the statue erected in their honor on the Capitol grounds. Pictured in this reunion photograph are veterans from Austin and nearby towns, along with some of their female relatives.

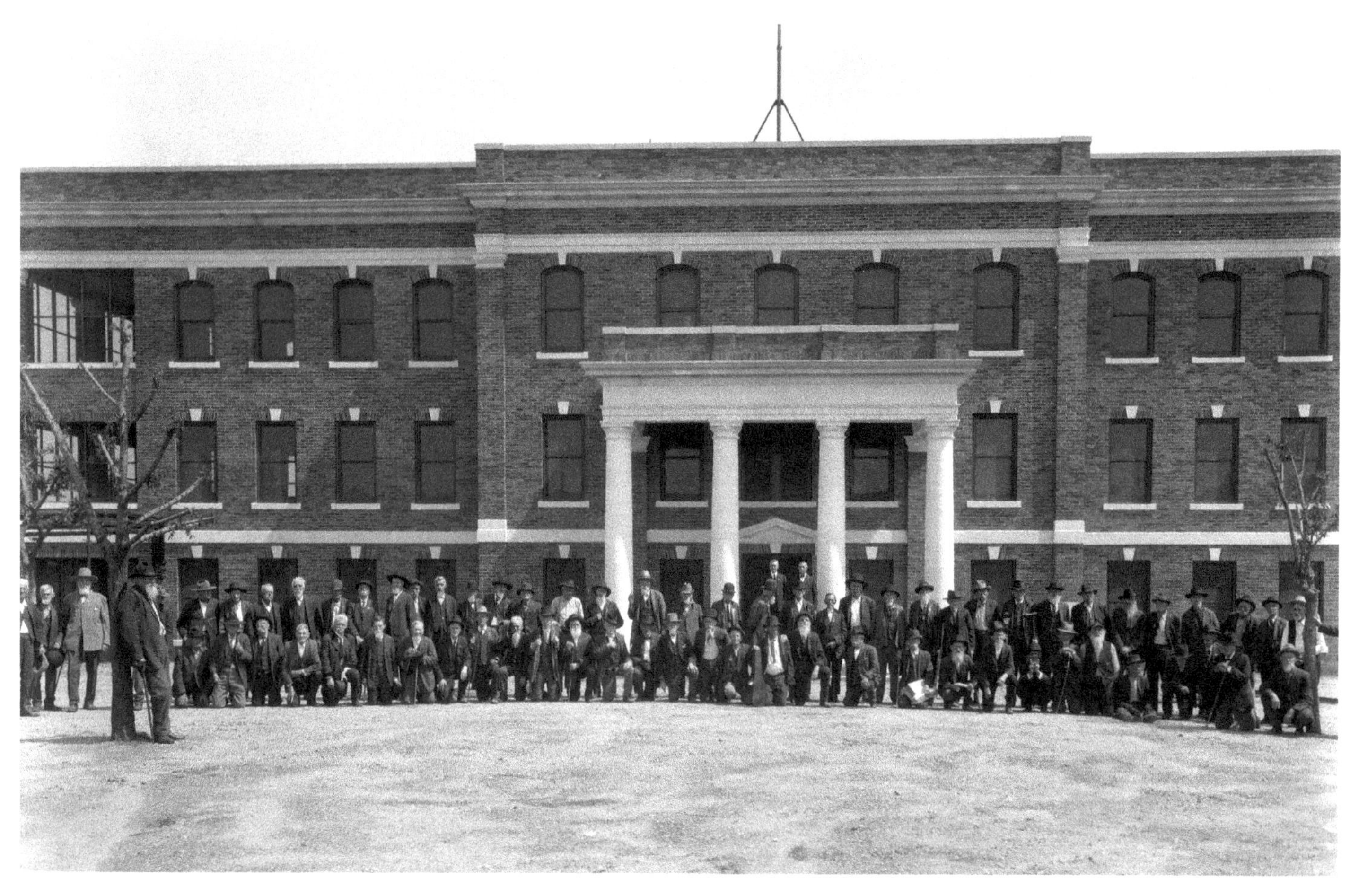

Residents pose in 1921 in front of the Texas Confederate Home, opened in 1886 on West Sixth Street. Funds to establish this home for disabled and indigent veterans were raised by the John B. Hood Camp of United Confederate Veterans and the United Daughters of the Confederacy. Between 1887 and 1953, more than 2,000 former Confederates lived at the facility. The last resident, Thomas Riddle, died at age 108.

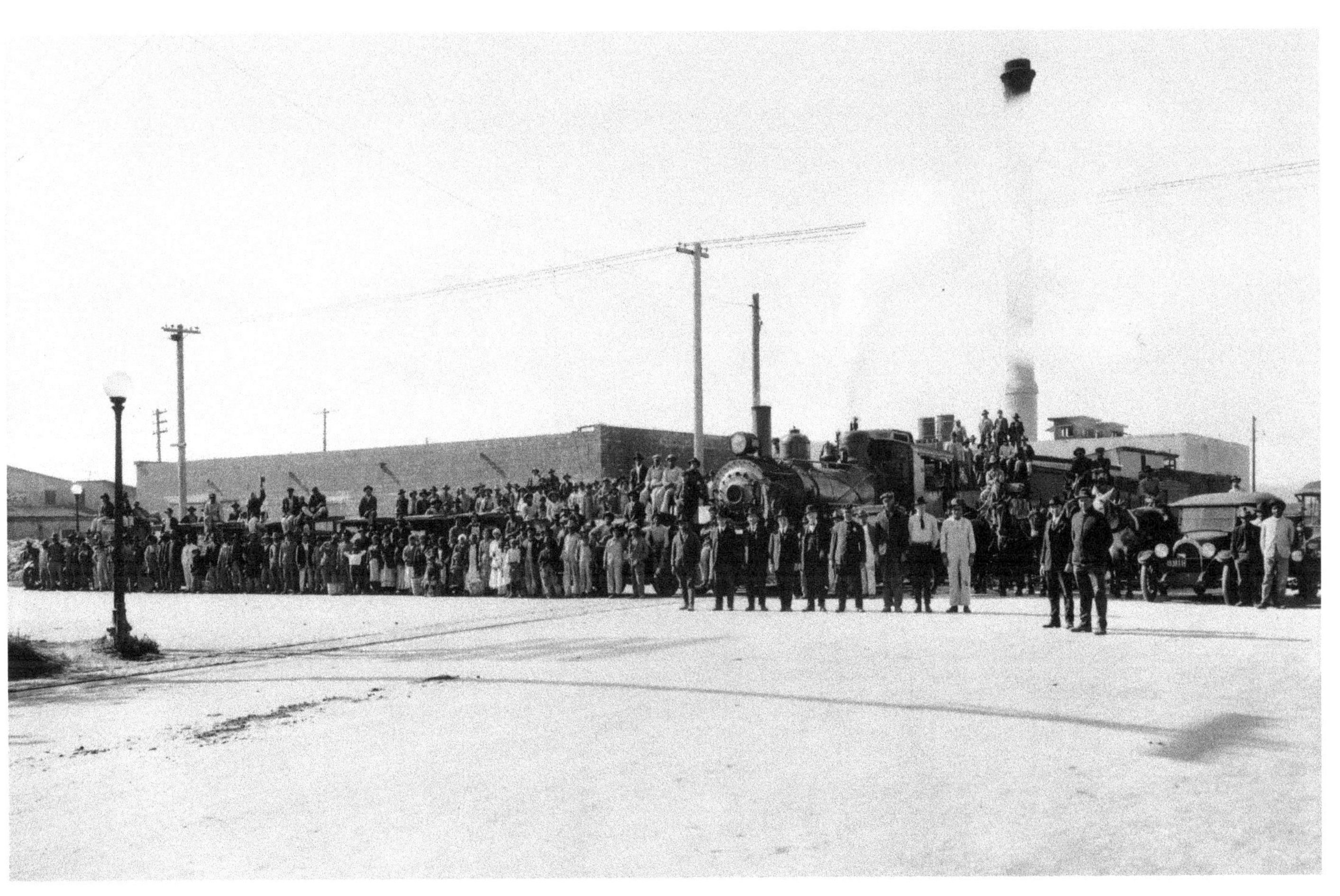

Photographed in the spring of 1921, field hands employed by the Crockett Produce Company's packing house prepare to board a train to the spinach field.

It looks as if these 1920s Austinites were so delighted by the visit of humorist Will Rogers that they couldn't drive straight! Rogers is wearing a hat and riding in the backseat of the convertible in the foreground, with his elbow on the ledge.

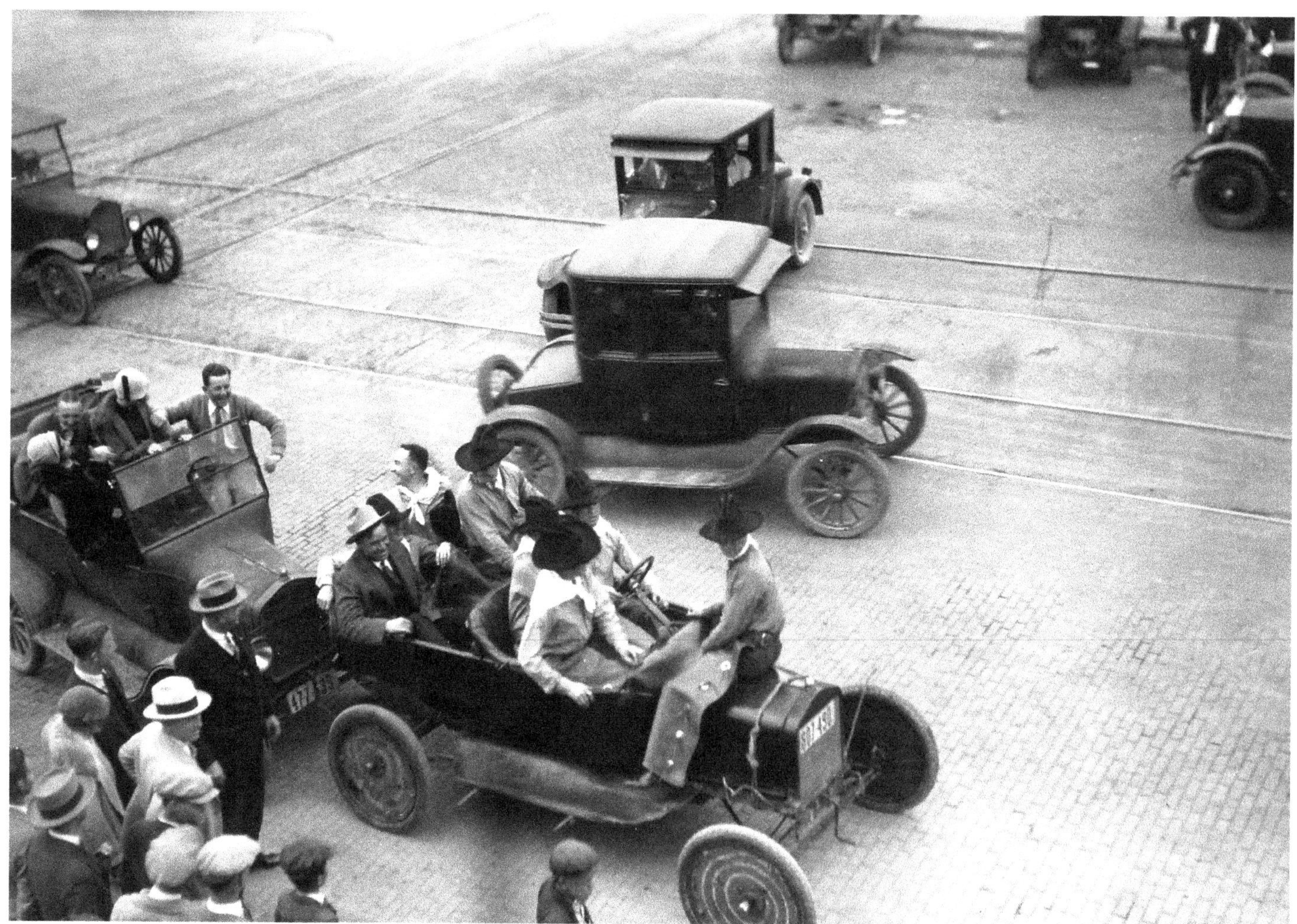

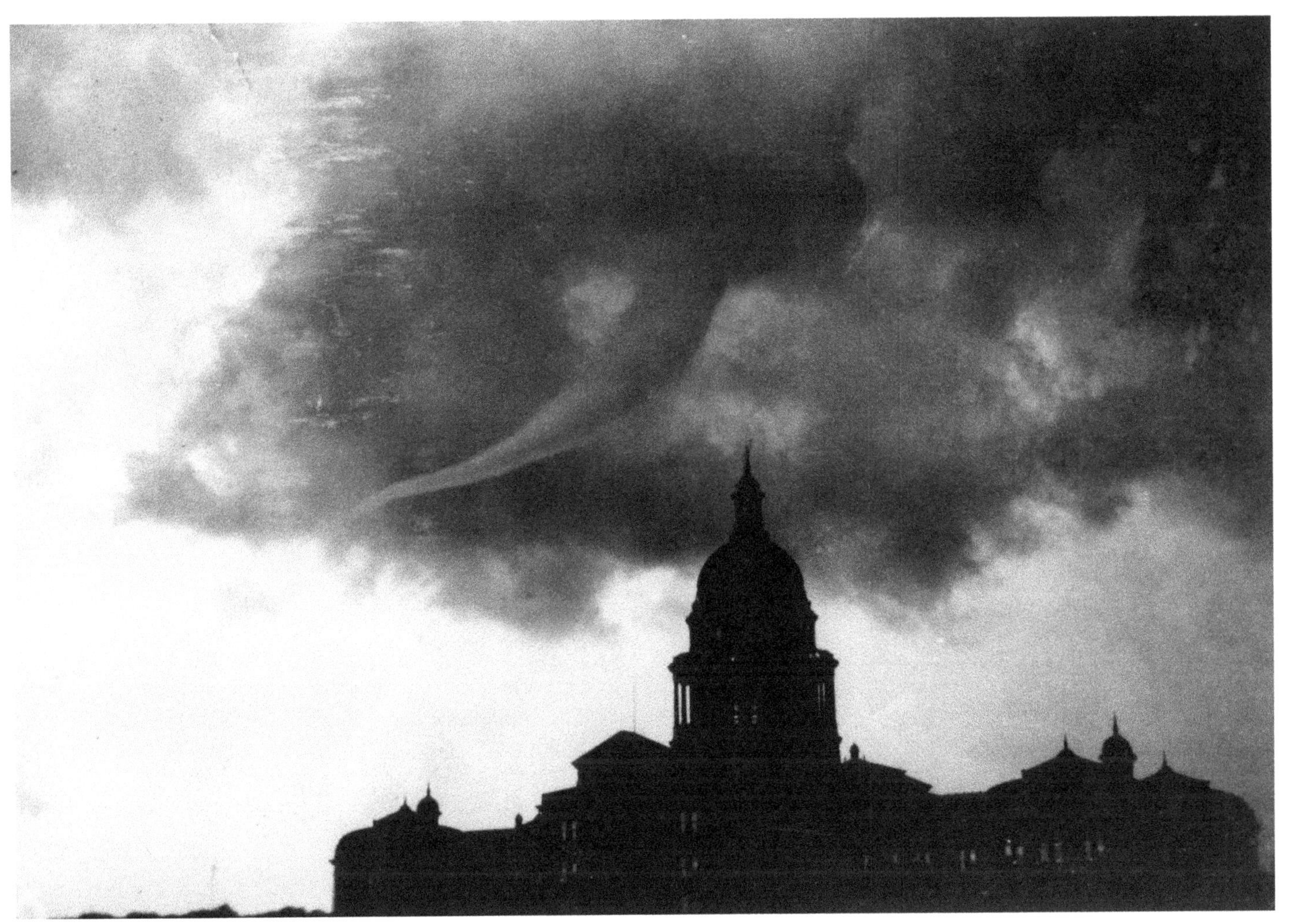

On May 4, 1922, a courageous photographer captured this dramatic shot of the tornado that threatened the Capitol, destroyed many other buildings, wounded 44 people, and killed 13.

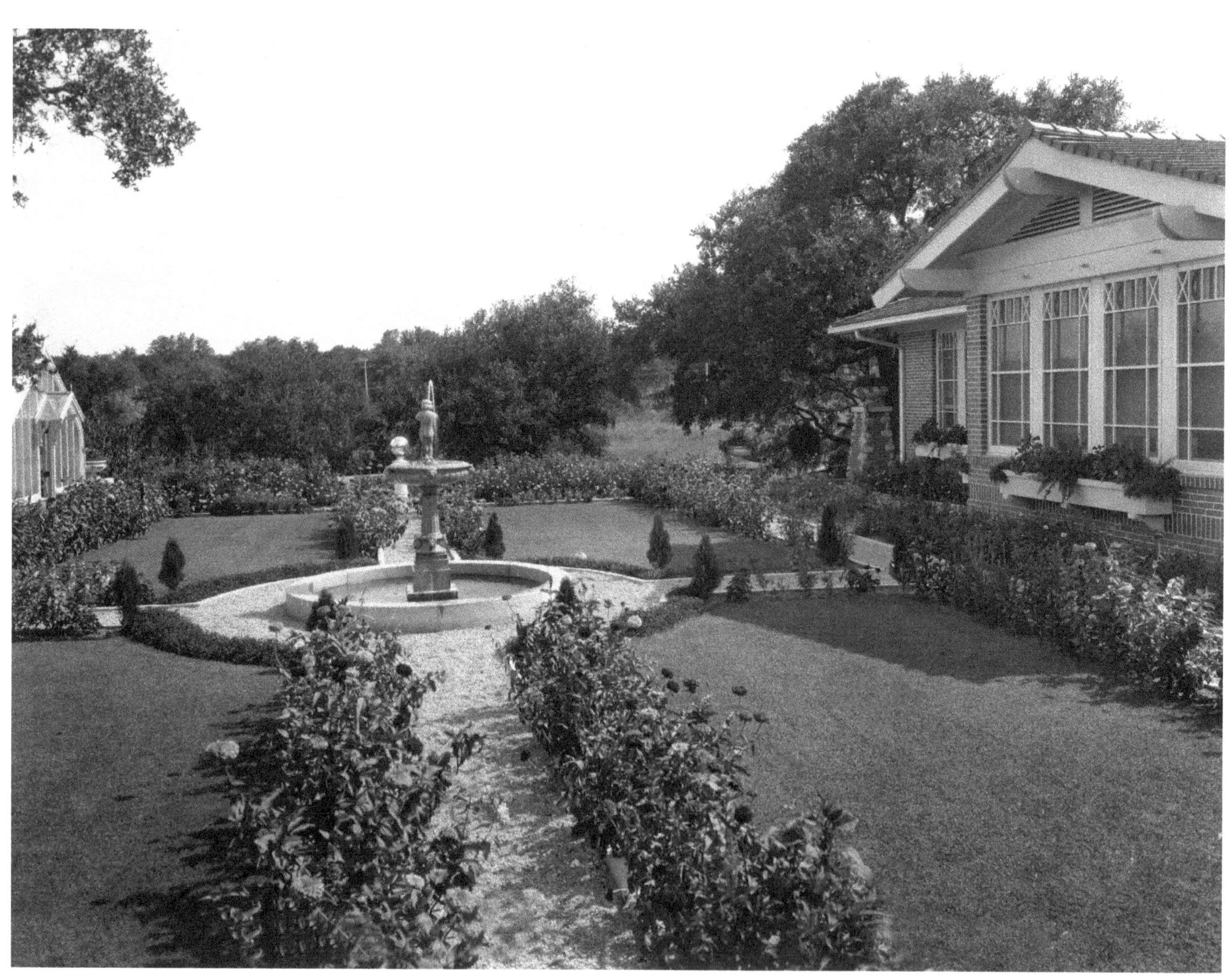

Travis Heights, in South Austin, was the setting of O. O. Norwood's estate, 1012 Edgecliff. Before constructing his "skyscraper" downtown, Norwood engaged architect Hugo Franz Kuehne to design his bungalow, completed in 1922. It was distinguished by gardens overlooking the river, with fountains, manicured lawns, and flower-lined paths. Kuehne was a founder of UT's School of Architecture.

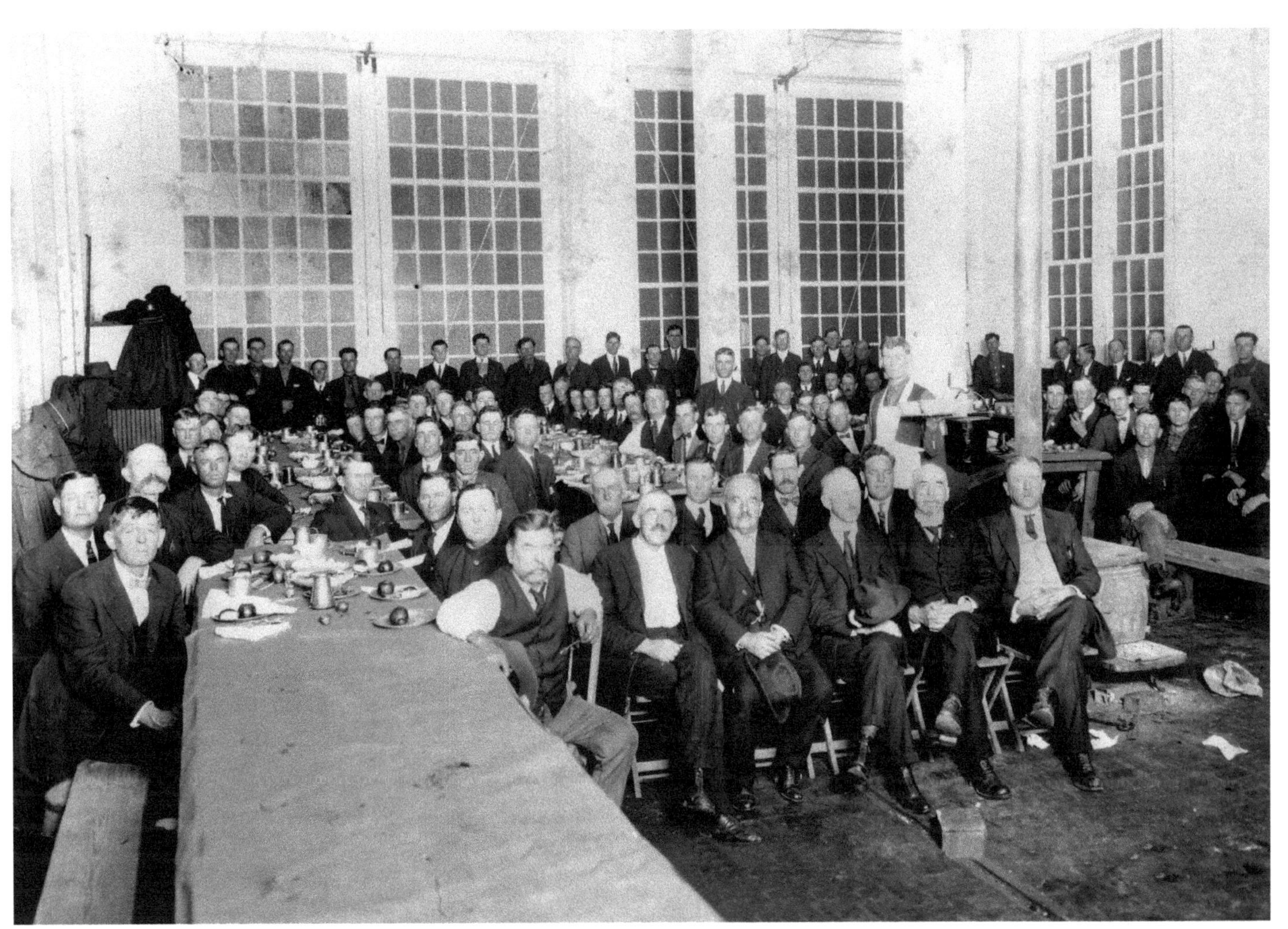

Employees of the Austin Street Railway Company gather in 1922 for a banquet at the elegant Driskill Hotel.

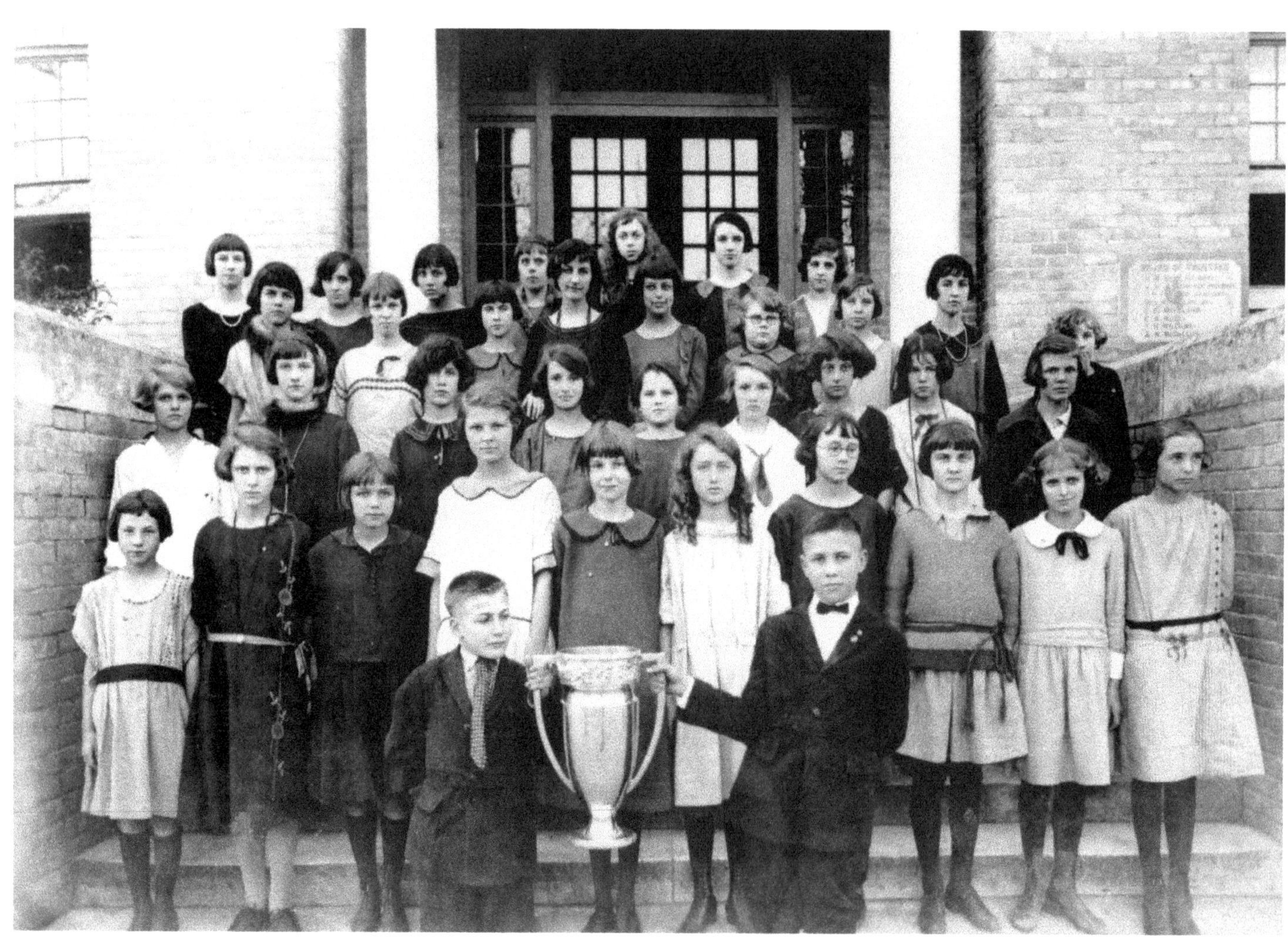

In 1923, students at Baker School won the Music Memory Contest (still being held annually) for three years in a row, which entitled them to keep the trophy. Baker School was built in Hyde Park in 1911.

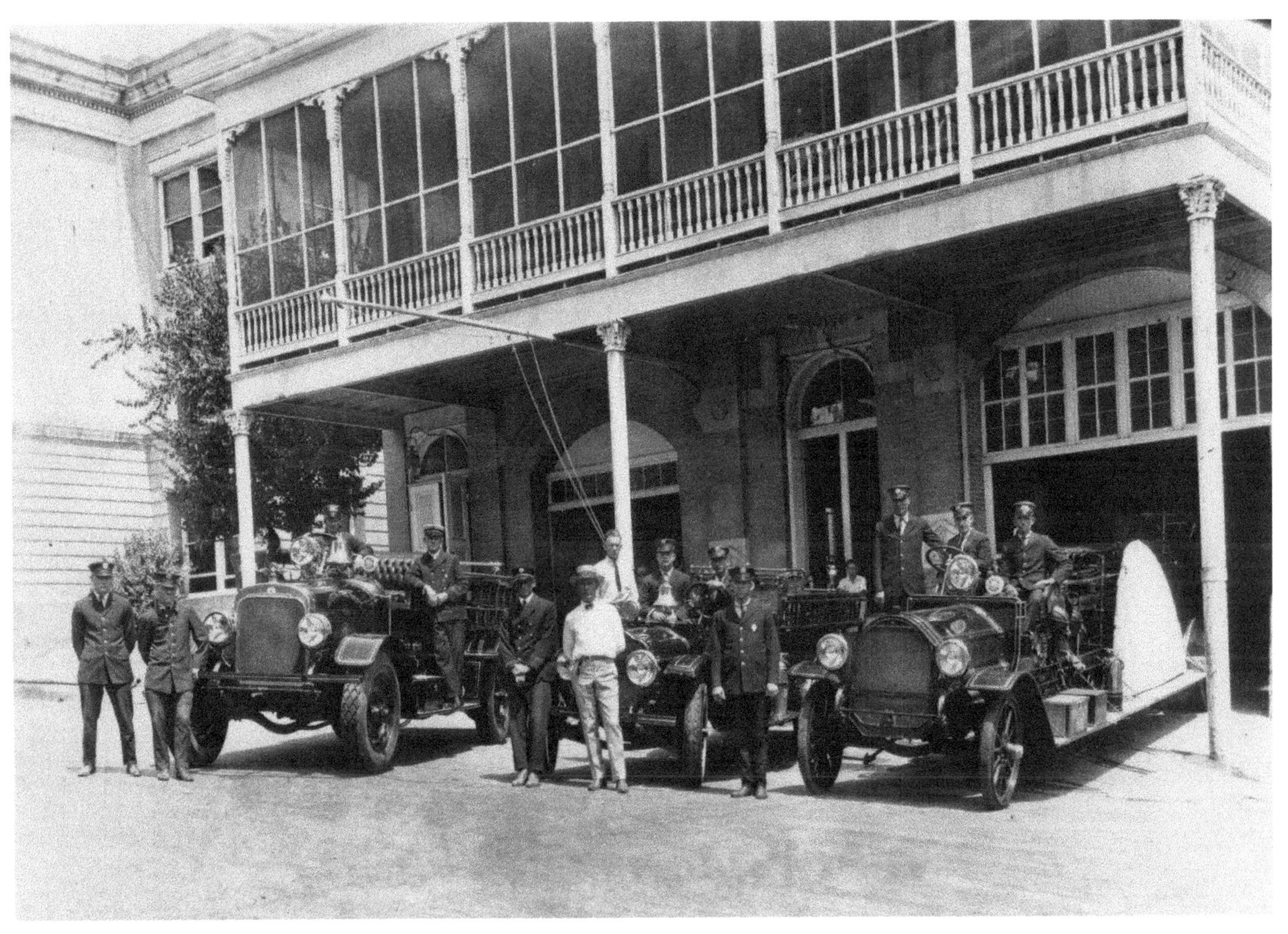

Members of the Austin Fire Department pose with their vehicles in 1923. The hatted man not wearing a uniform, center, is Fire Commissioner H. W. Nolan. In 1916, Austin voters had approved the change from a volunteer force to a paid force. The new fire department began with 27 firefighters, 5 motorized vehicles, and 3 pieces of horse-drawn fire equipment left over from volunteer days.

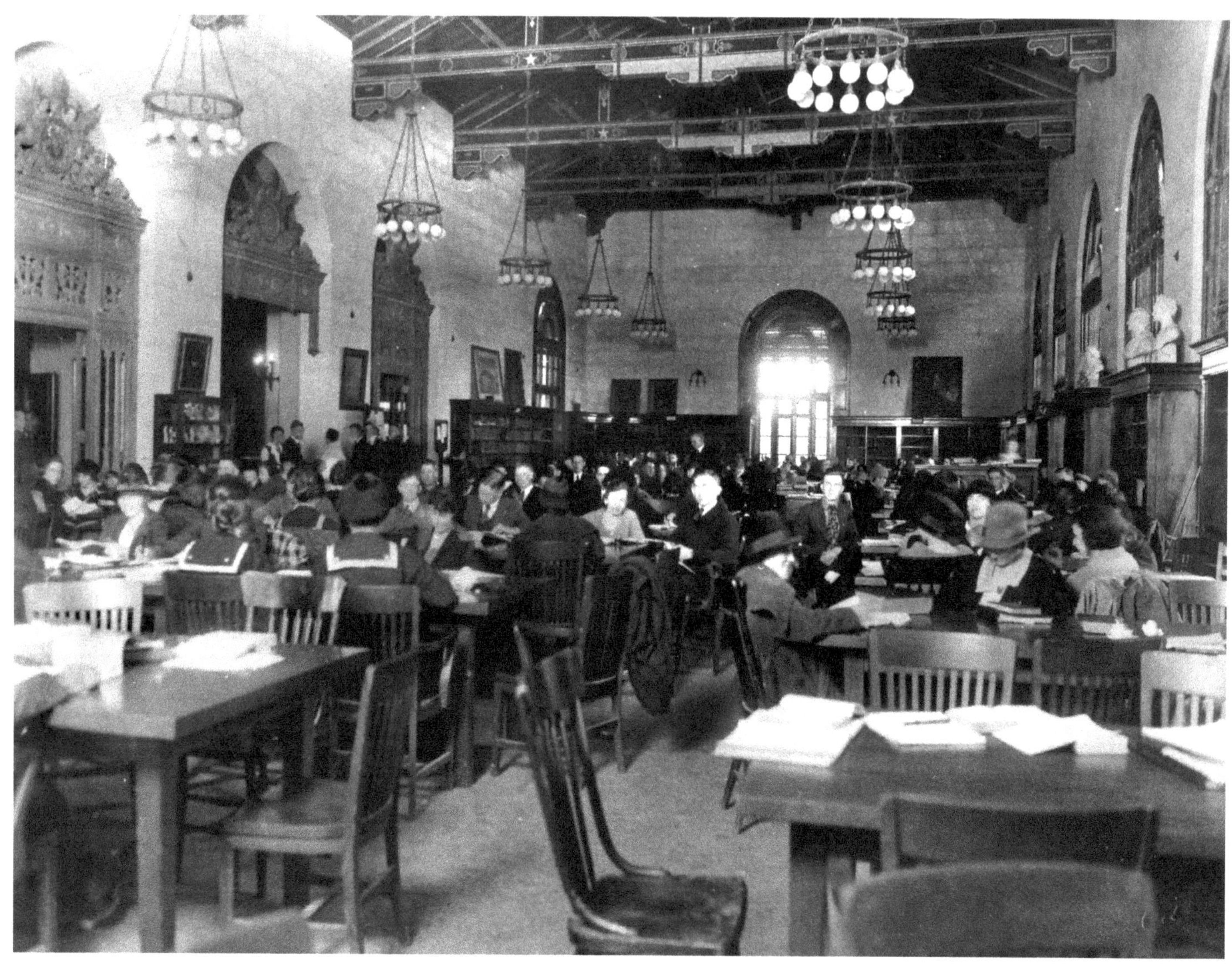

University of Texas students circa the early 1920s study at Battle Hall, the university's original library. Designed in 1910 in the Spanish Renaissance style by architect Cass Gilbert, it was lauded as one of the finest buildings in the state. Battle Hall influenced the campus building style well into the 1930s. It was named for William James Battle, professor of Greek and acting president of UT from 1914 to 1916.

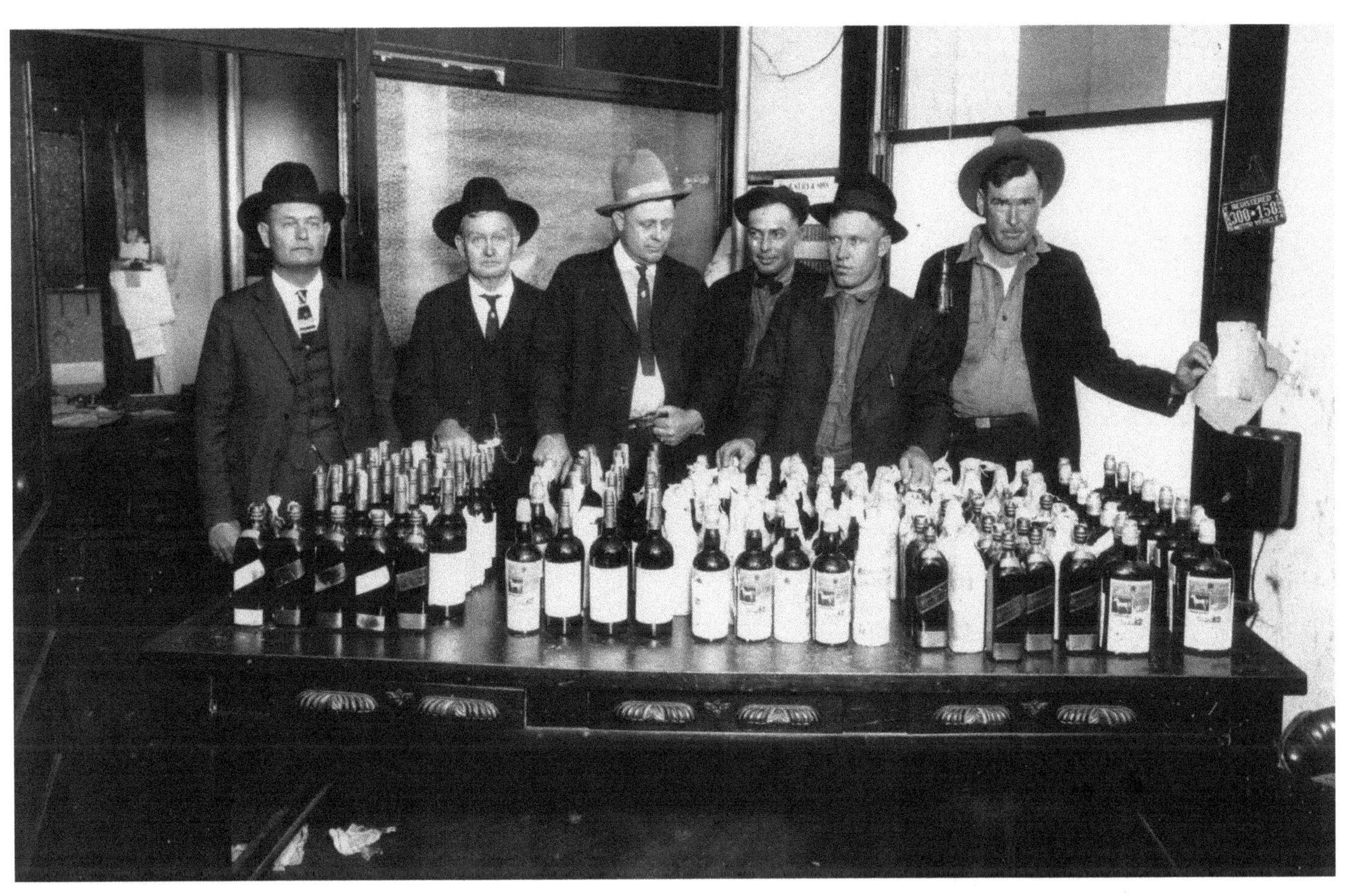

In April 1924, Prohibition in Austin was in full swing. This photograph shows Austin policemen and Texas Rangers after they seized 157 quarts of whiskey and other liquor. Pictured (from left) are officers R. R. Fowler, W. M. Bowden, O. B. Chesshir, L. D. McClain, A. H. Von Rosenberg, and W. E. Mayberry.

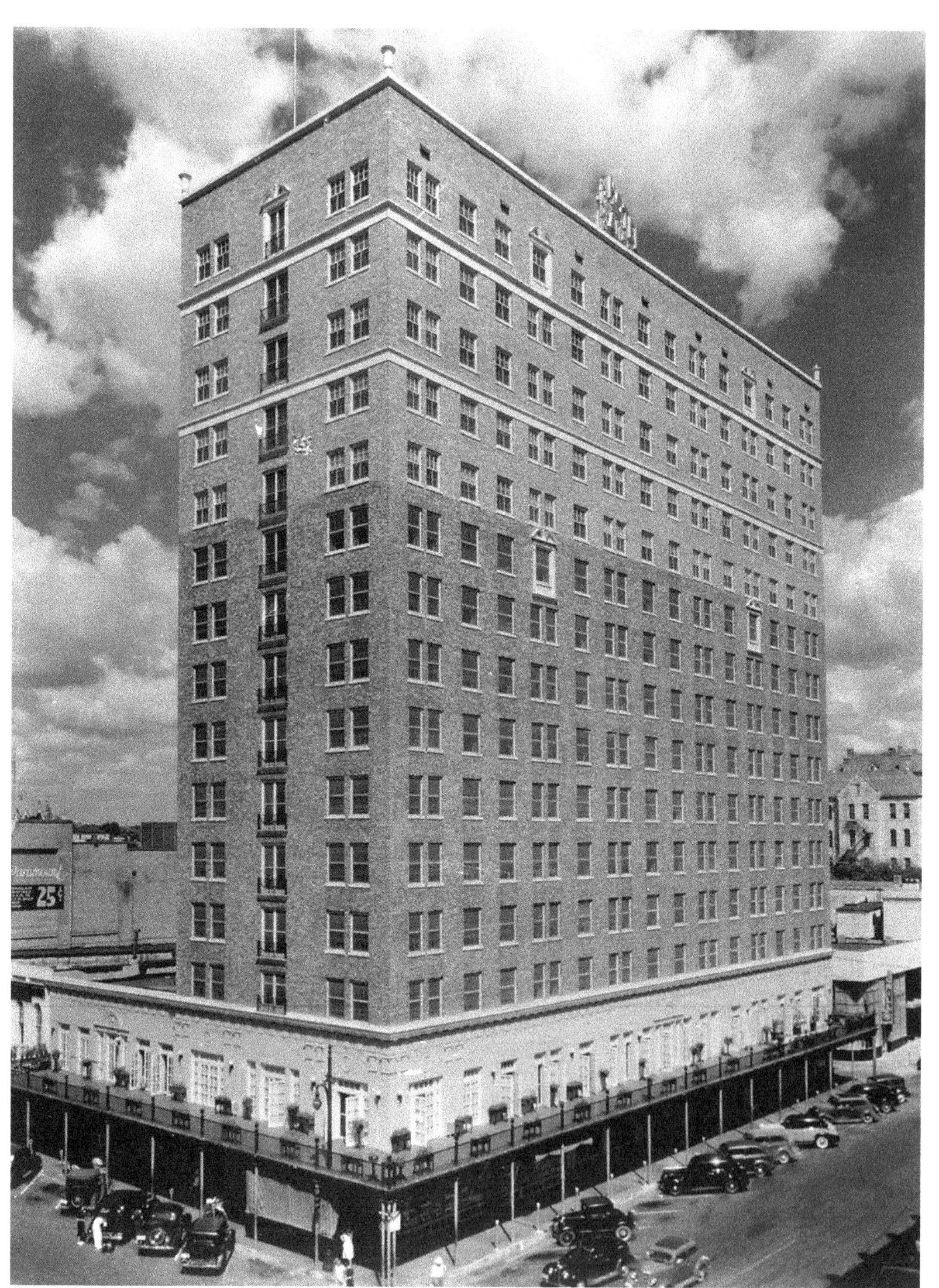

The Stephen F. Austin Hotel, distinguished by a balcony wrapping around two sides of the second-floor ballroom, opened in 1924 on Congress Avenue's east side. It later became the Bradford Hotel.

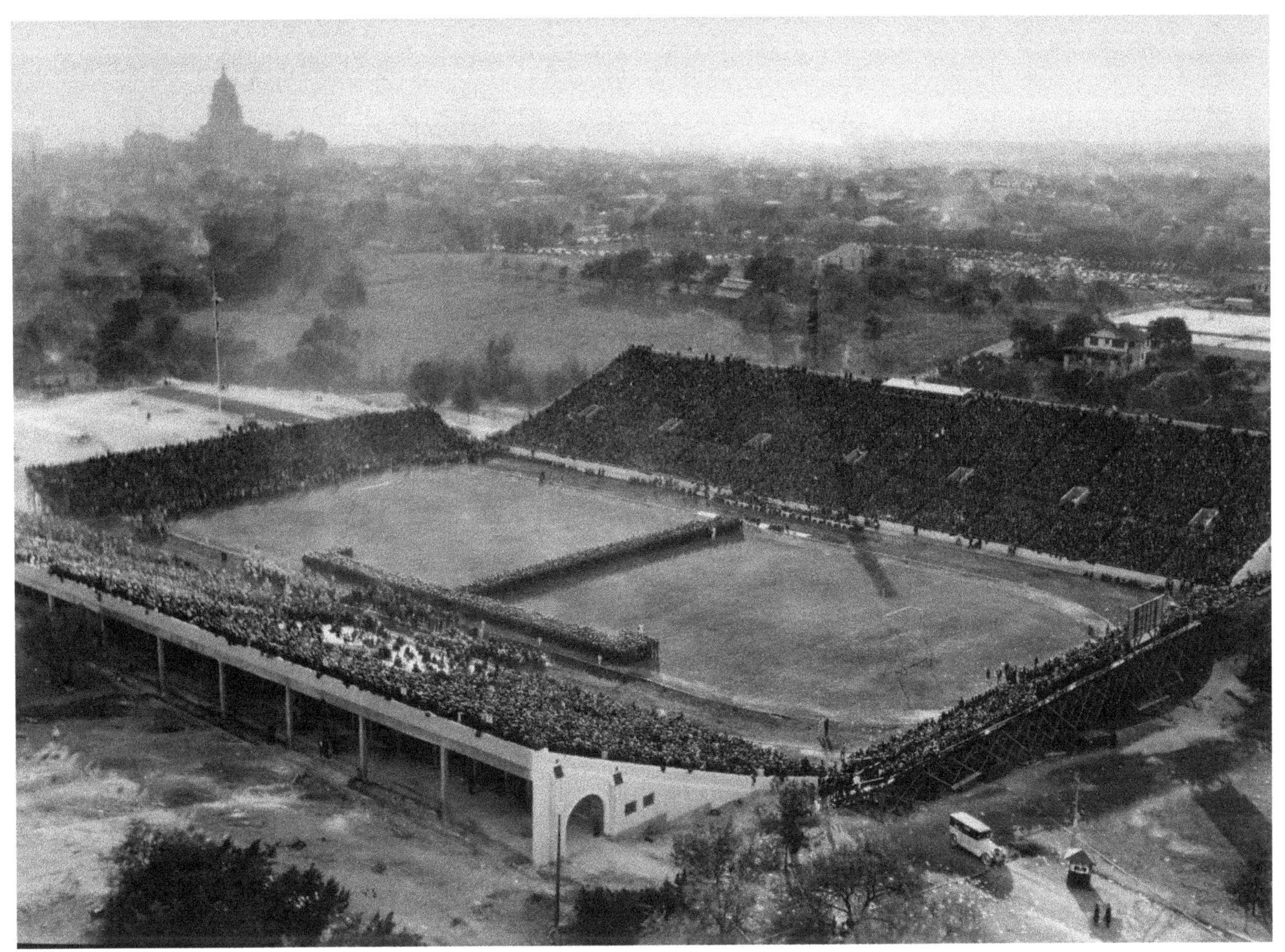

The proceeds from a productive oil well on West Texas land owned by the University of Texas initiated a building boom that dramatically expanded the Austin campus. On November 27, 1924, UT dedicated its Memorial Stadium during the annual Thanksgiving Day football game against Texas A&M University. The Texas A&M Aggies have traditionally been the major rivals of the University of Texas Longhorns.

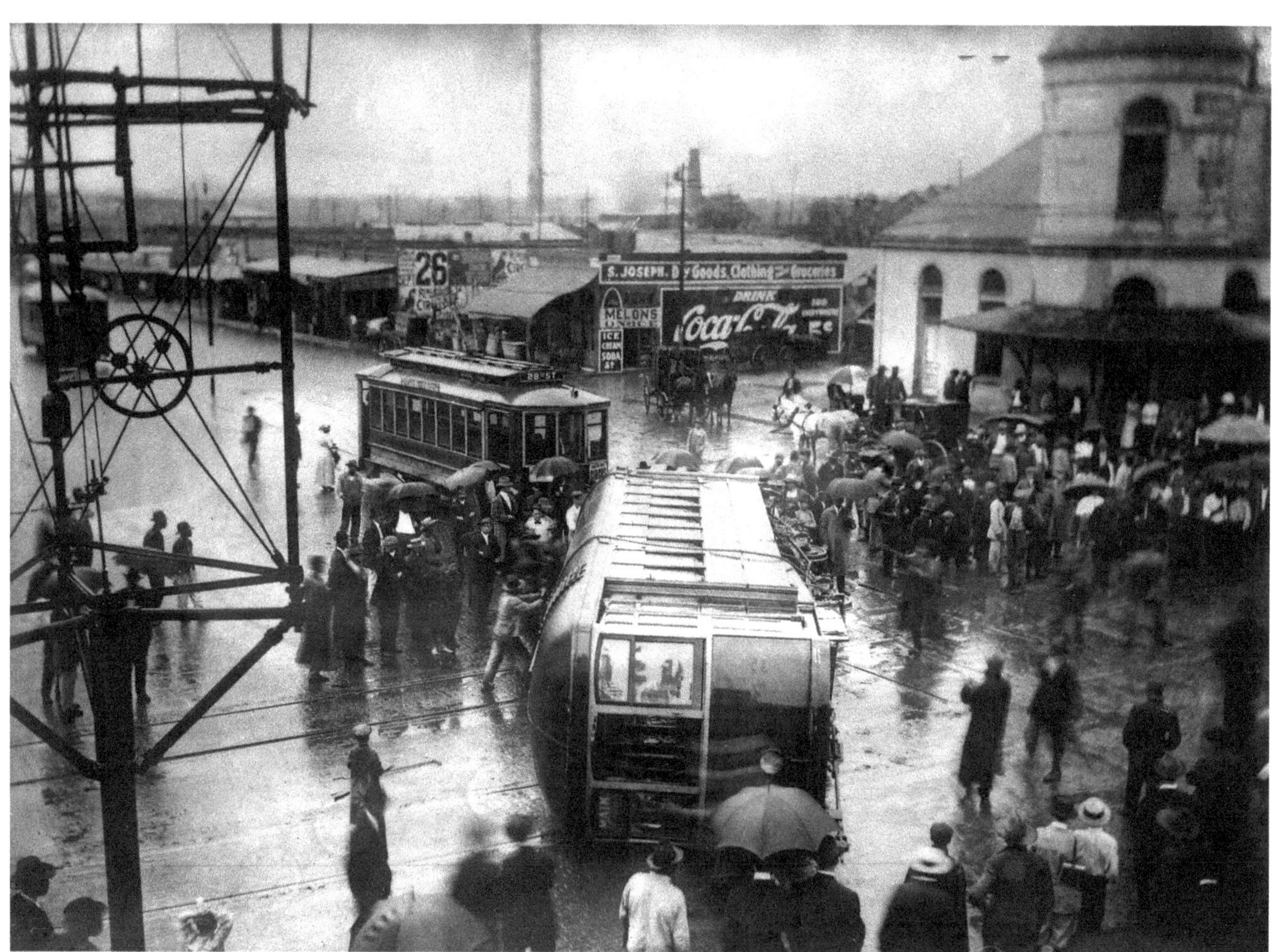

Crowds gathered at Congress and Eleventh Street circa 1925 after a new streetcar derailed and overturned during its inaugural inspection tour by company directors. It was a rainy day. Note that the older streetcar, behind the new streamlined model, is still upright. The Austin Street Railway Company, which introduced the city to mass transit with mule-drawn streetcars, served Austin for 50 years with its electric streetcars.

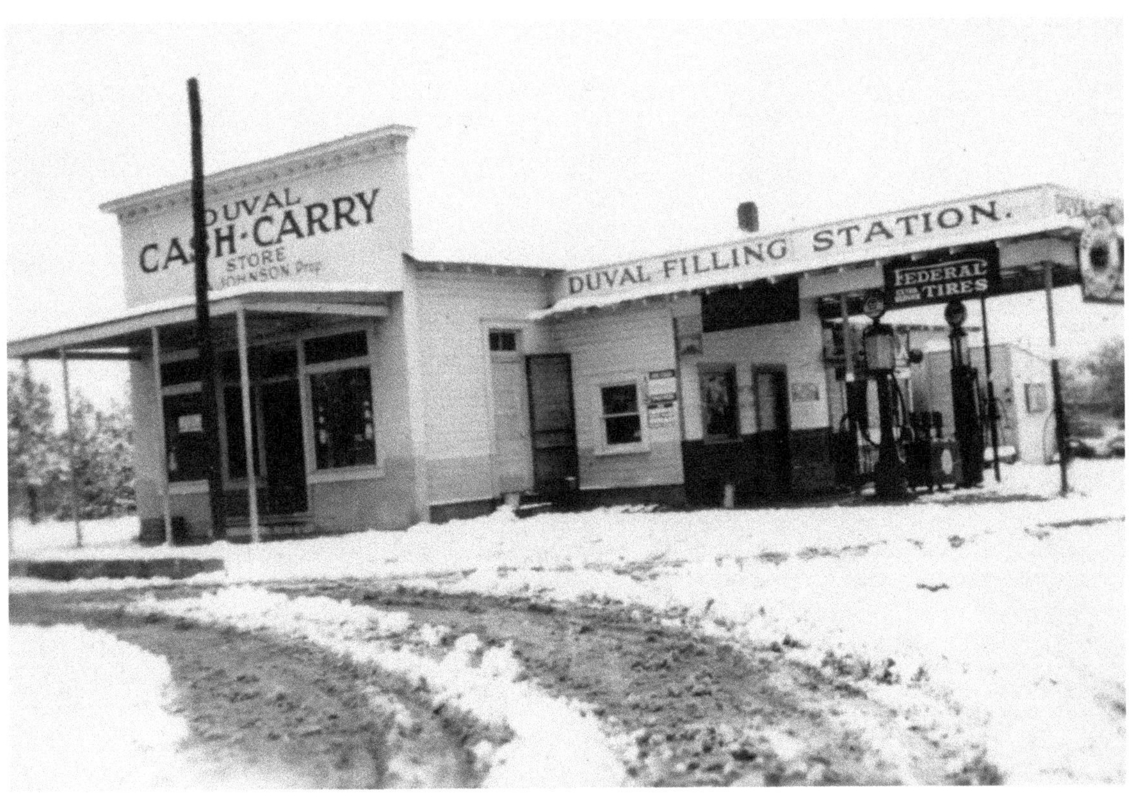

This grocery store with its added-on filling station was on East Forty-third Street but probably was named for its proximity to Duval Street, one of the boundaries of the Hyde Park residential suburb. The photograph was taken in the 1920s on one of Austin's rare snow days.

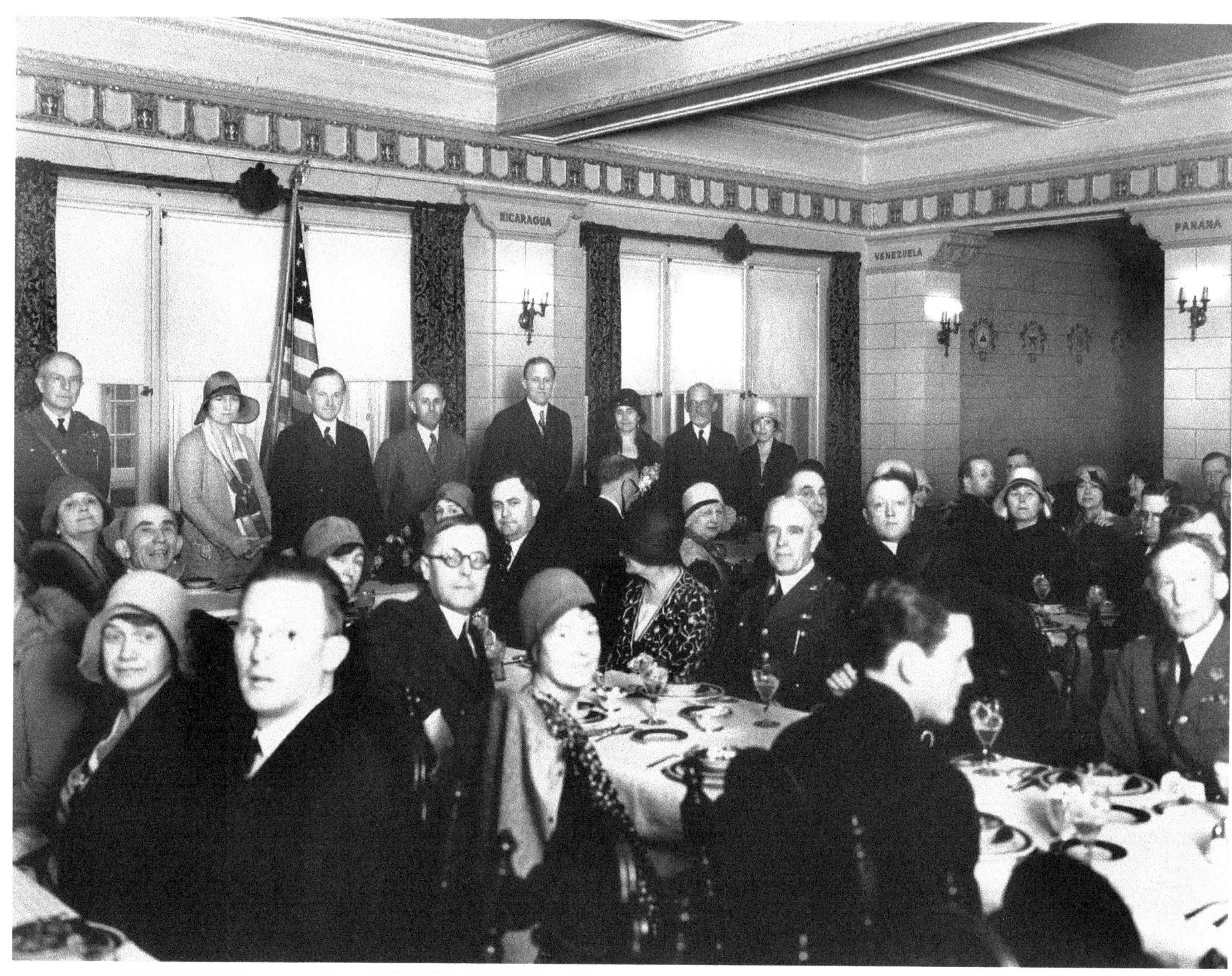

Among the nation's presidents who graced Austin with their presence was Calvin Coolidge ("Silent Cal"), pictured during his term of office (1923–1929) at a banquet in his honor. The president stands in front of the flag beside Mrs. Coolidge, who wears a chic hat.

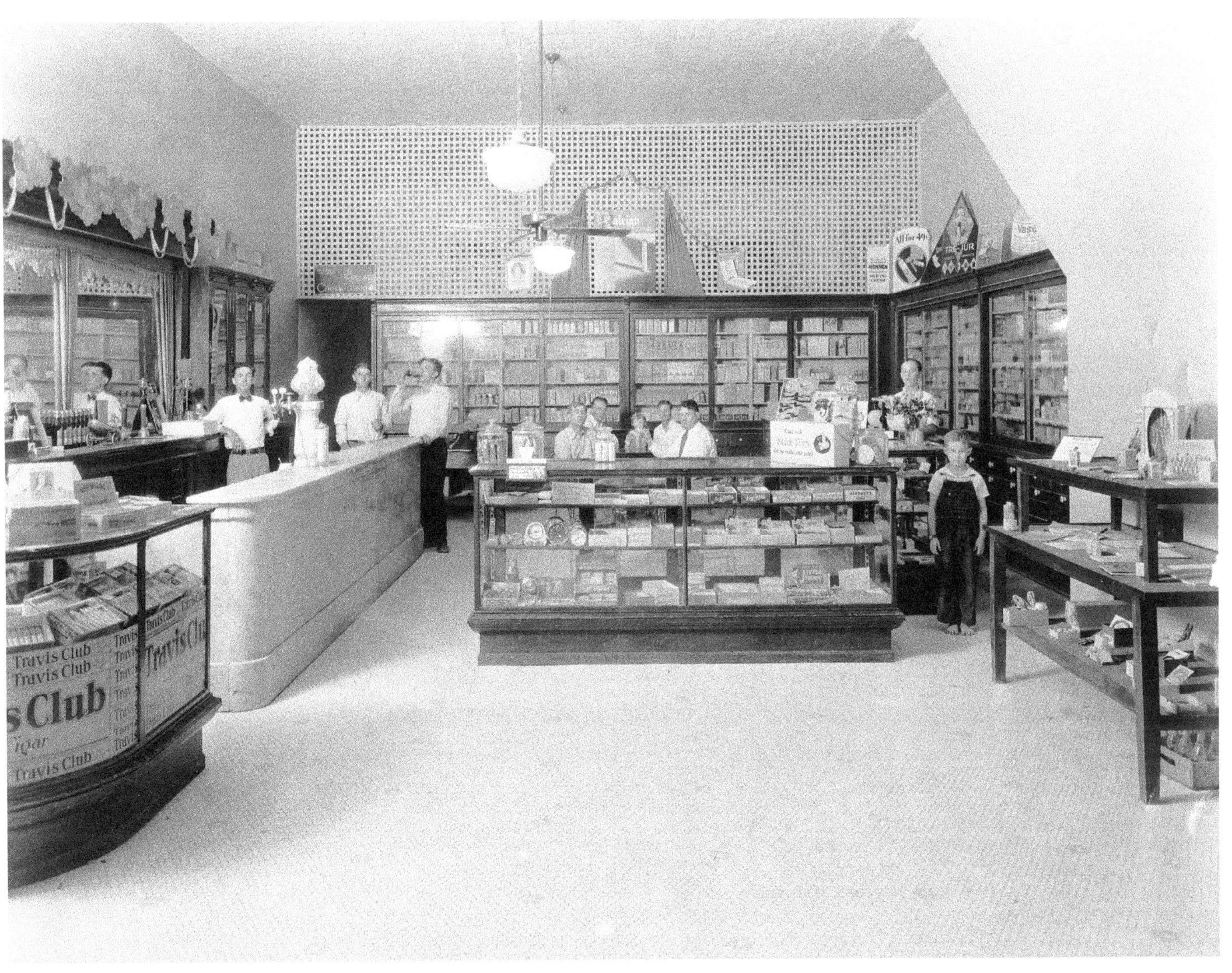

It would appear that this South Austin drugstore circa 1925 offered almost everything a customer could possibly want—except, perhaps, a friendly smile.

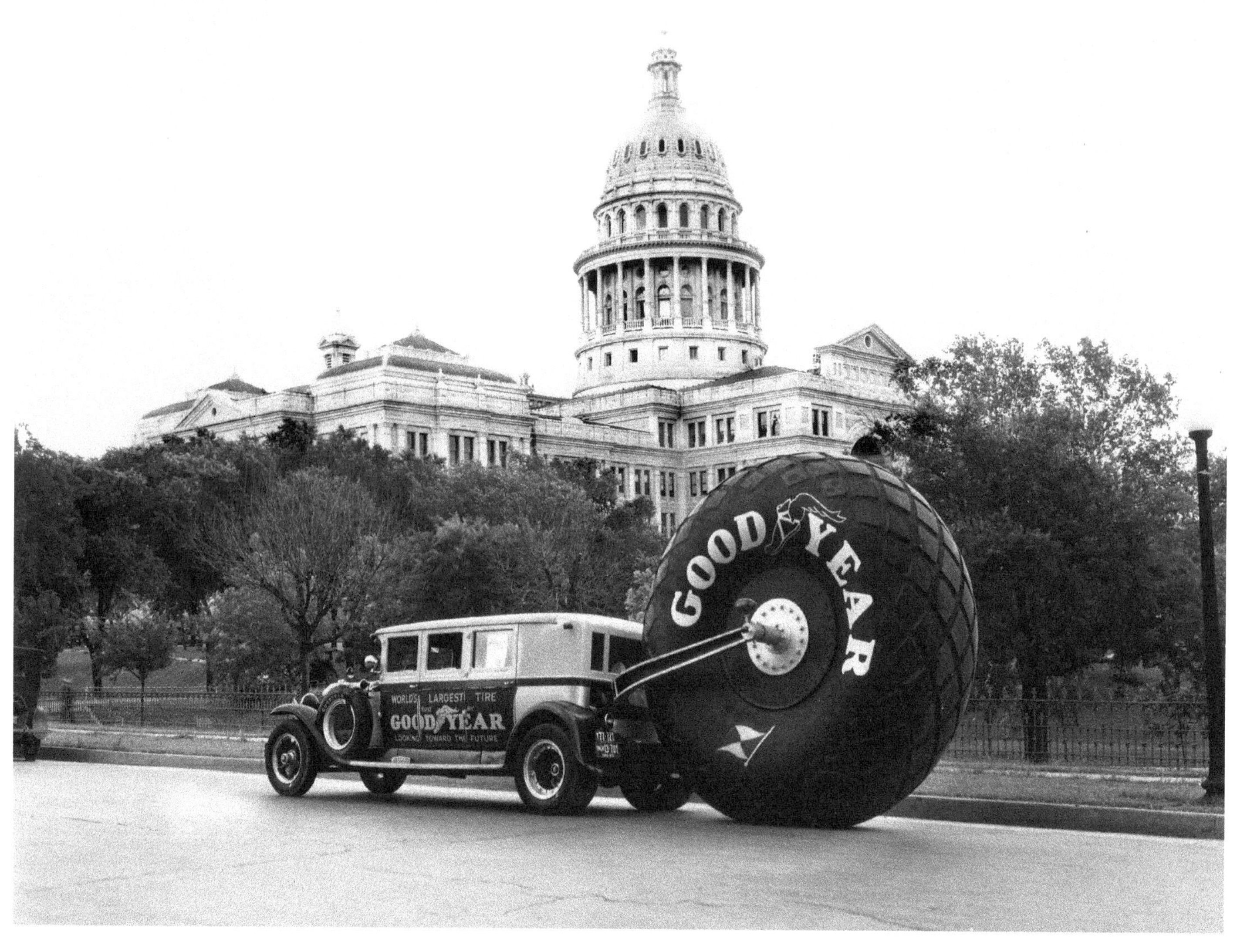

Before there was a Goodyear blimp, there was the oversized Goodyear tire, purportedly "The World's Largest Tire," attached to the back of an early truck. This photograph shows the eye-catching advertising gimmick on a street in front of the Capitol.

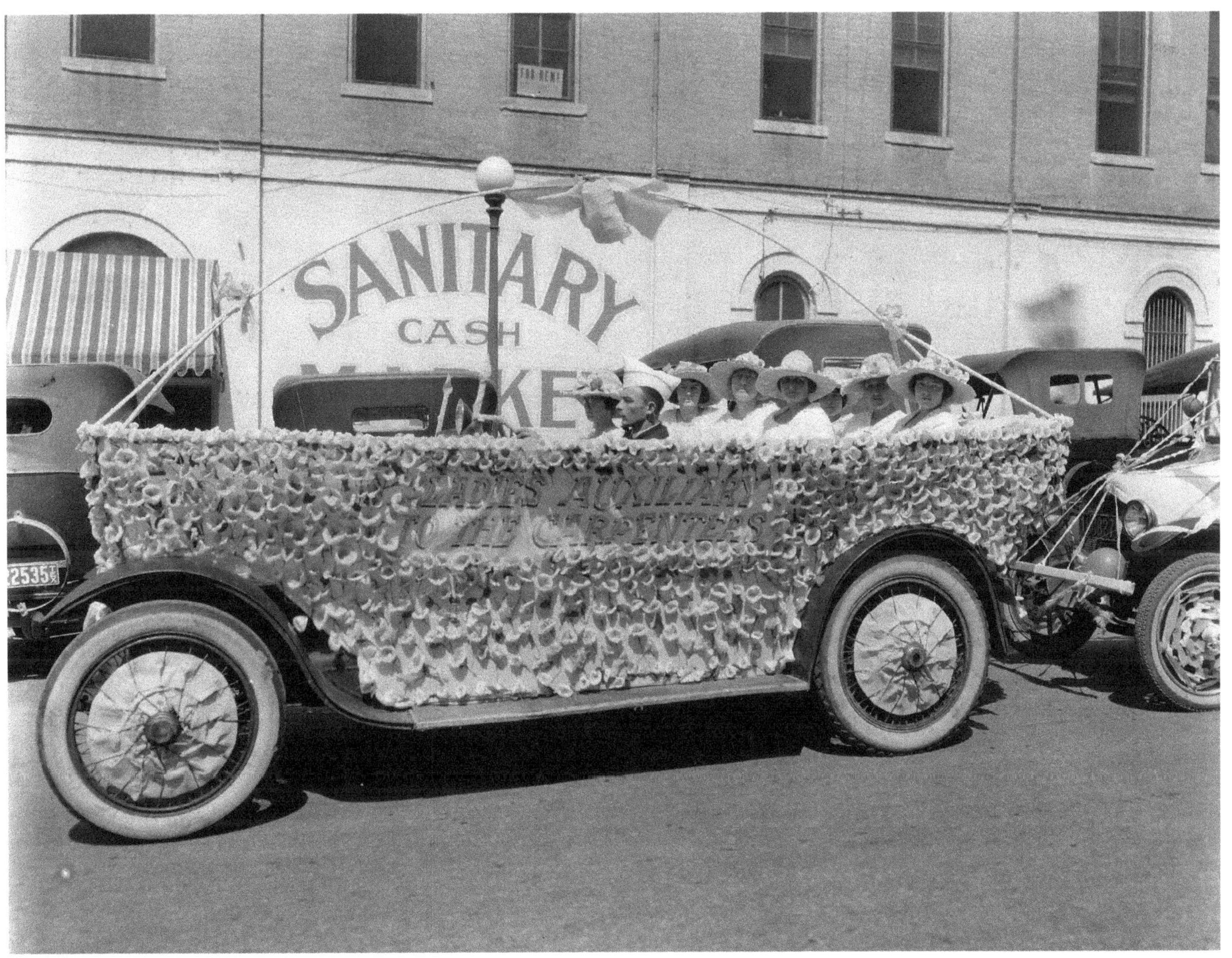

Wearing their decorated picture hats, these members of the Ladies' Auxiliary to the Carpenters face the camera as their chauffeured car, covered with crepe-paper calla lilies, makes its way in a 1920s spring parade. Austin's penchant for parades, begun in the nineteenth century, has continued into the twenty-first.

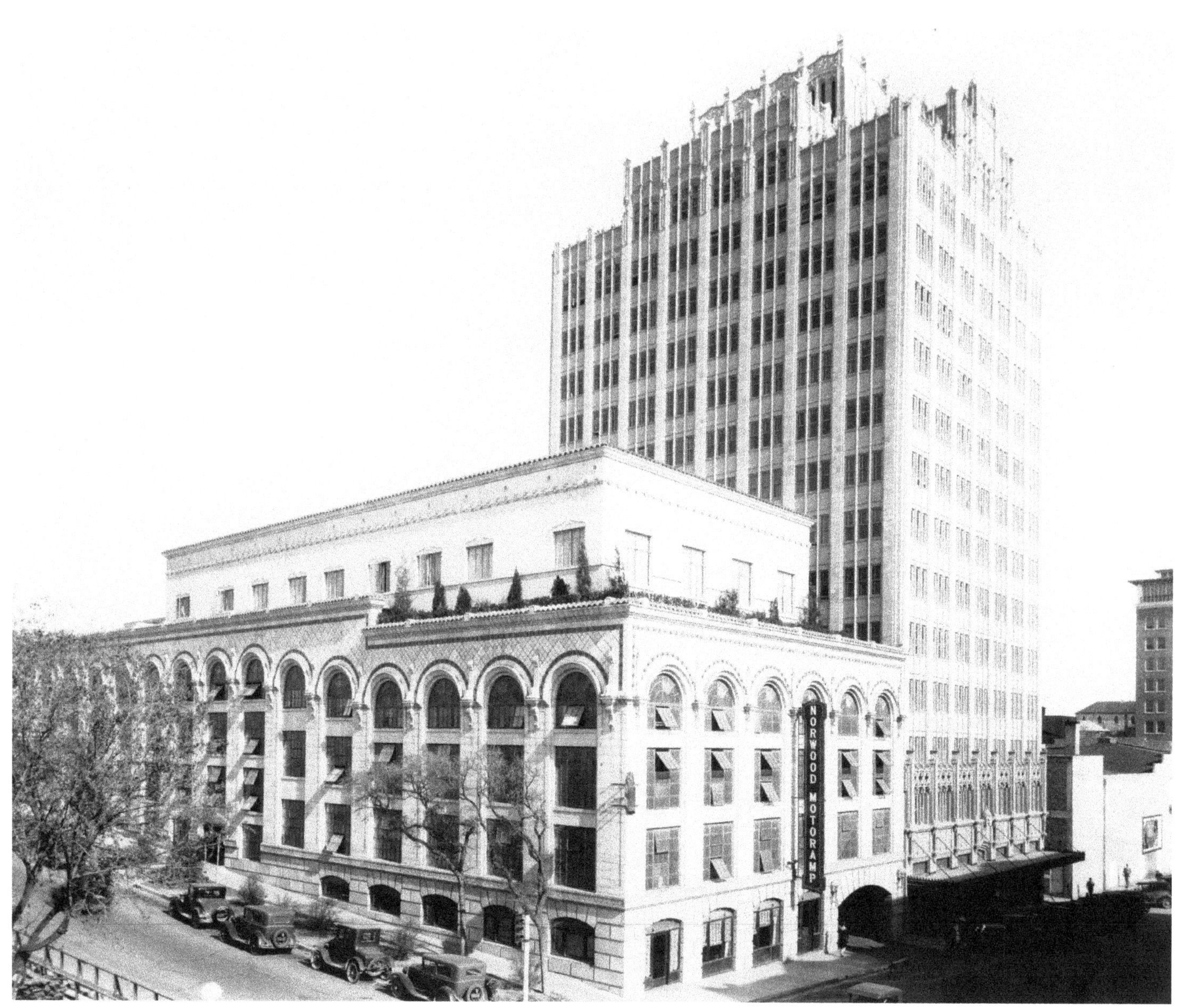

The splendid 14-story Norwood Building, 808 West Tenth Street, with its early art-deco influence, was completed in 1929. It was Austin's first air-conditioned office building and boasted the city's first self-parking ramped automobile garage (called the Motoramp). Earlier parking garages had used large elevators to move cars up and down.

This view shows Congress Avenue, looking south from the corner of Seventh Street, probably in the late 1920s.

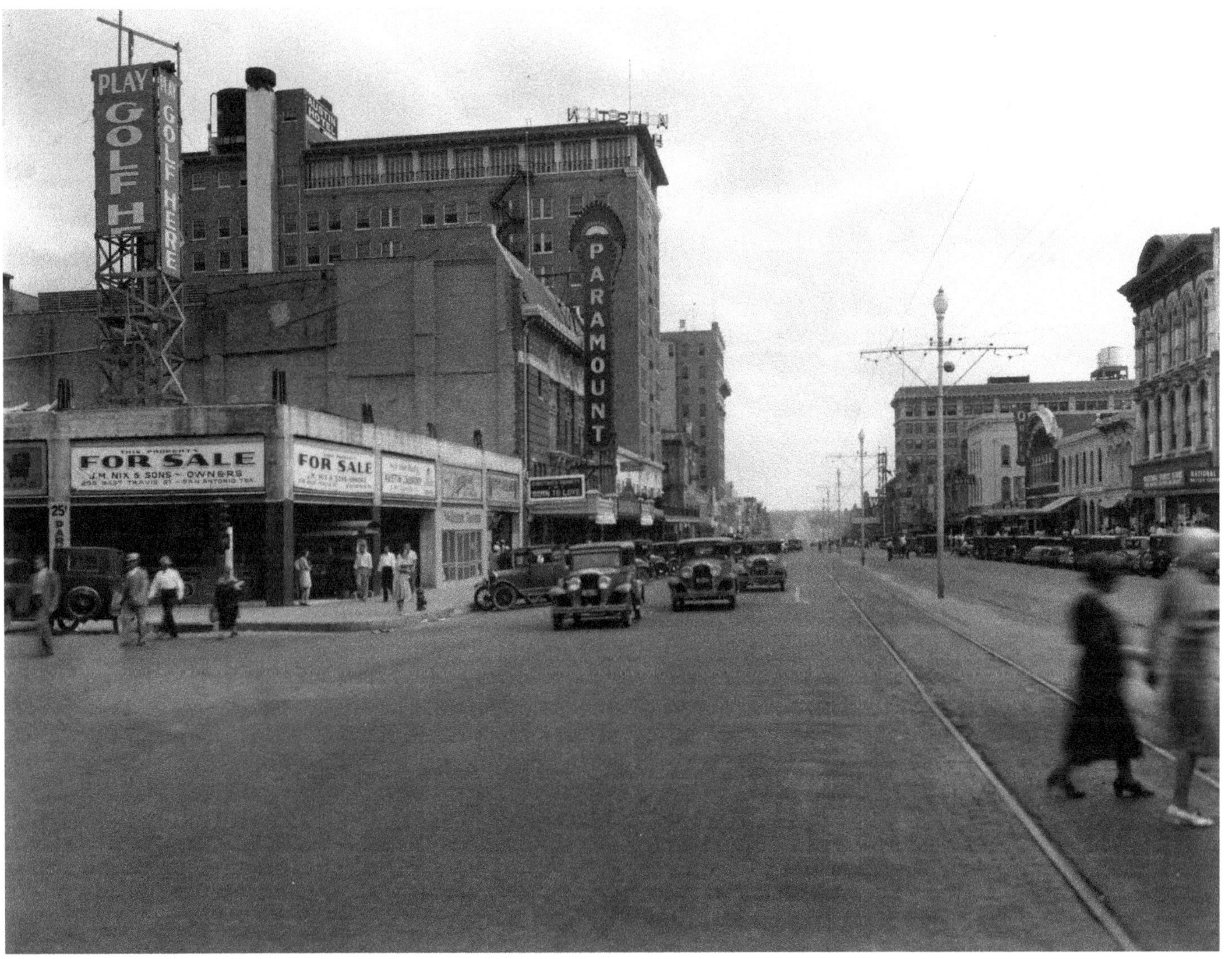

Members of the Travis County 4H Club and their sponsors parade on Congress Avenue in support of farms. Notice that many members on the right carry sapling trees for planting.

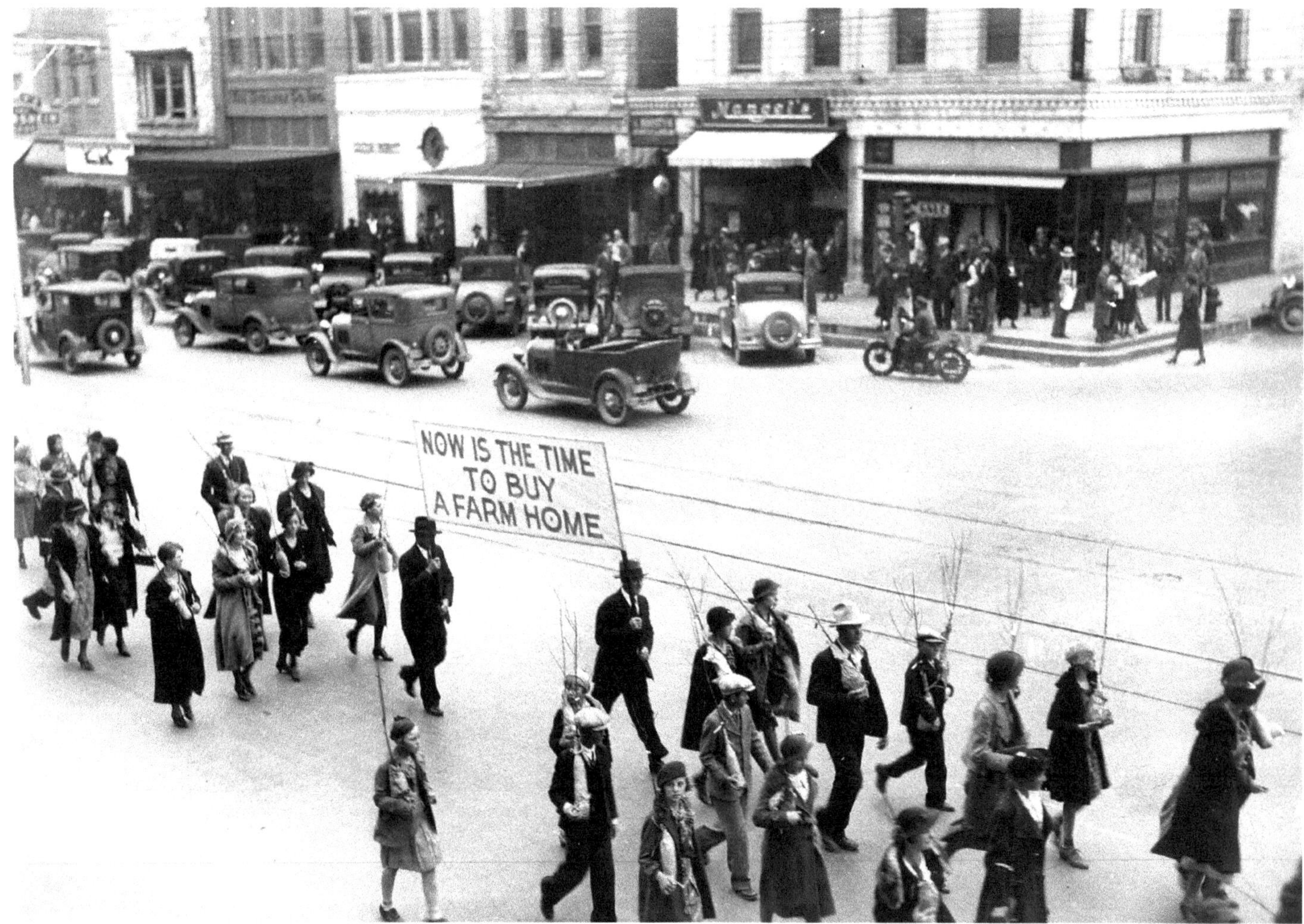

In October 1930, Austin's new Municipal Airport opened near the northeast section of town. It was dedicated in honor of former city councilman Robert Mueller and marked the beginning of airmail service for the city. This photograph shows the decidedly homey Braniff Airways terminal in 1938.

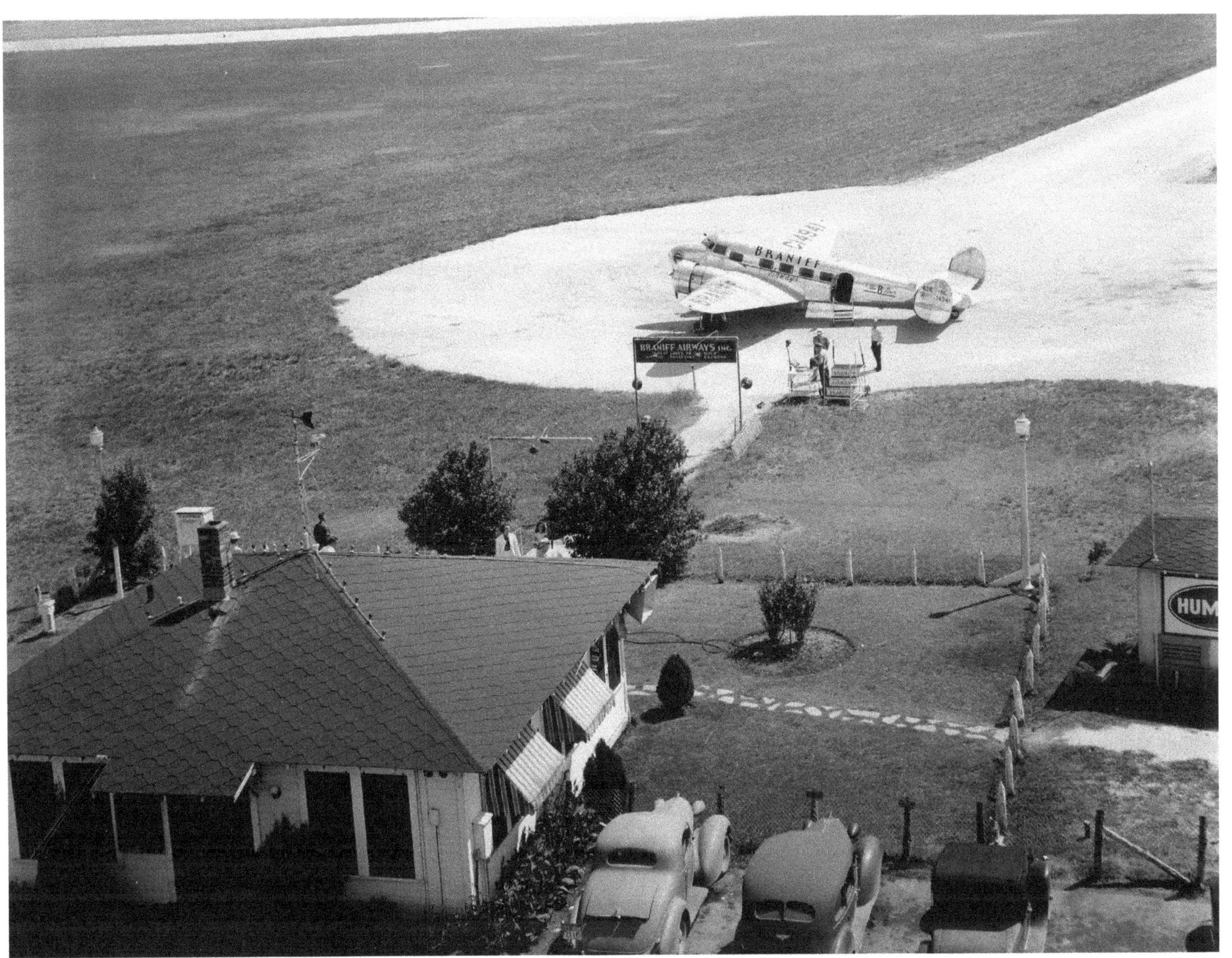

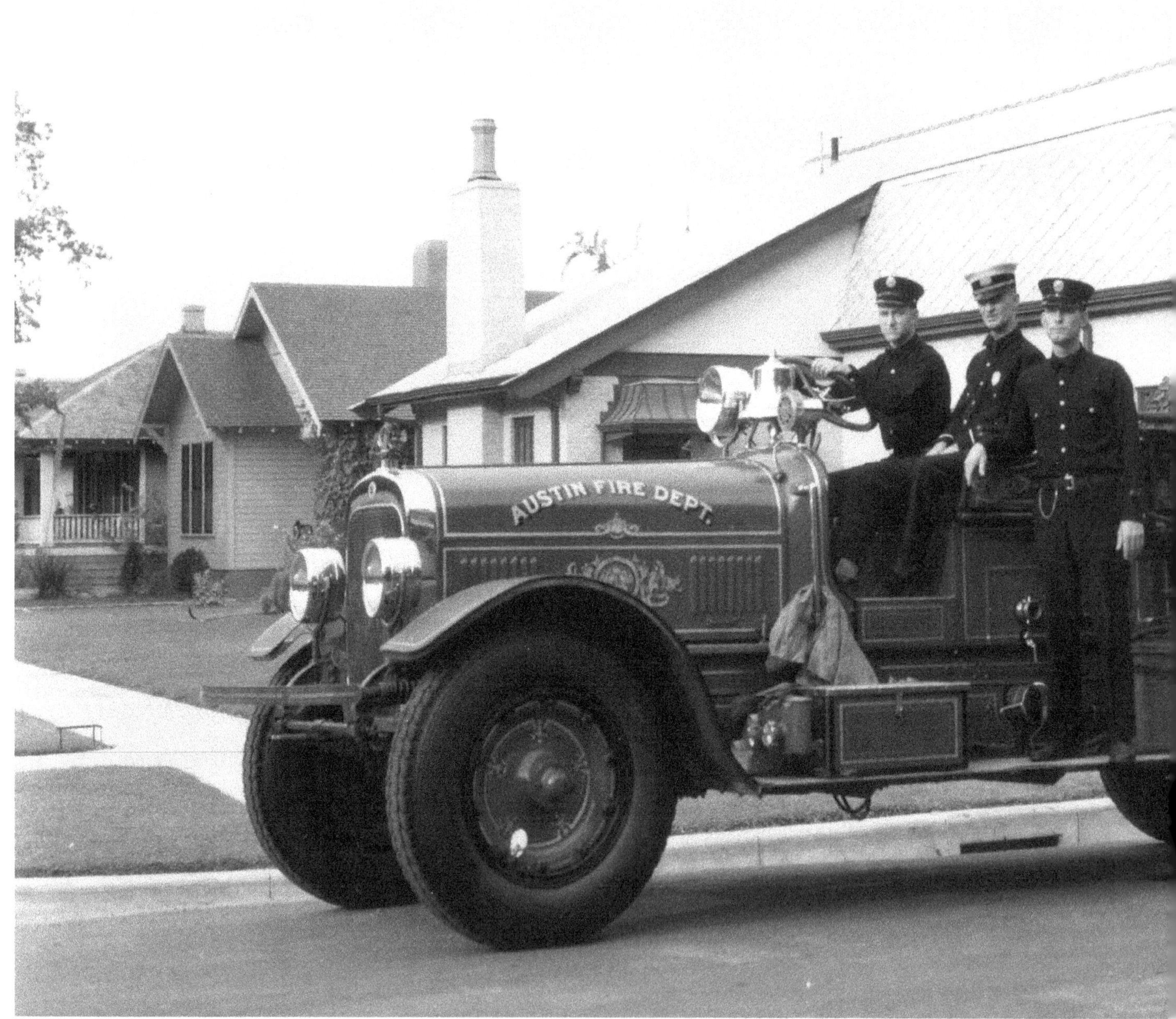
AUSTIN FIRE DEPT.

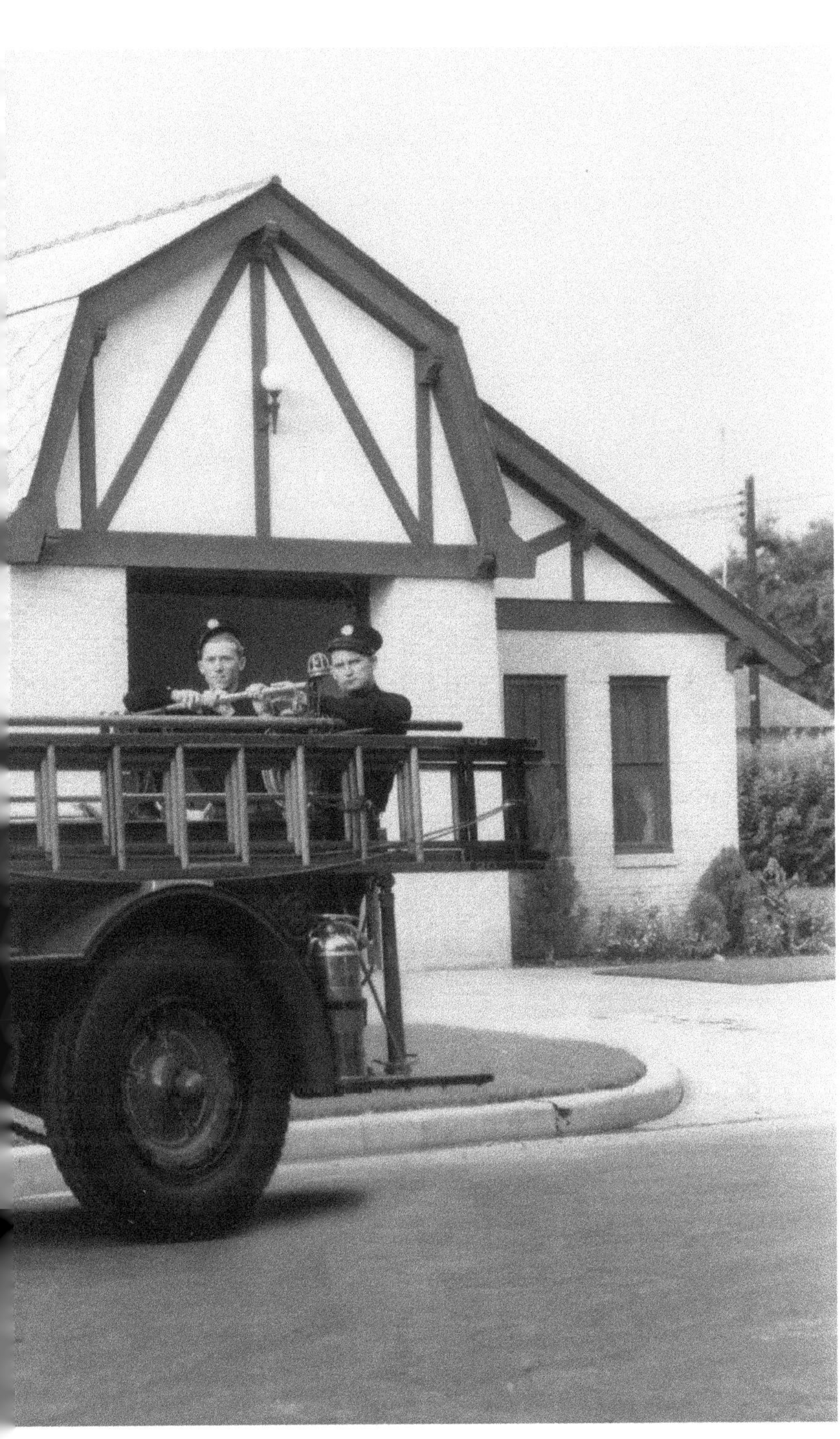

Members of the Austin Fire Department in 1930 display their shiny new firetruck at Fire Station Number Nine, located in Hyde Park.

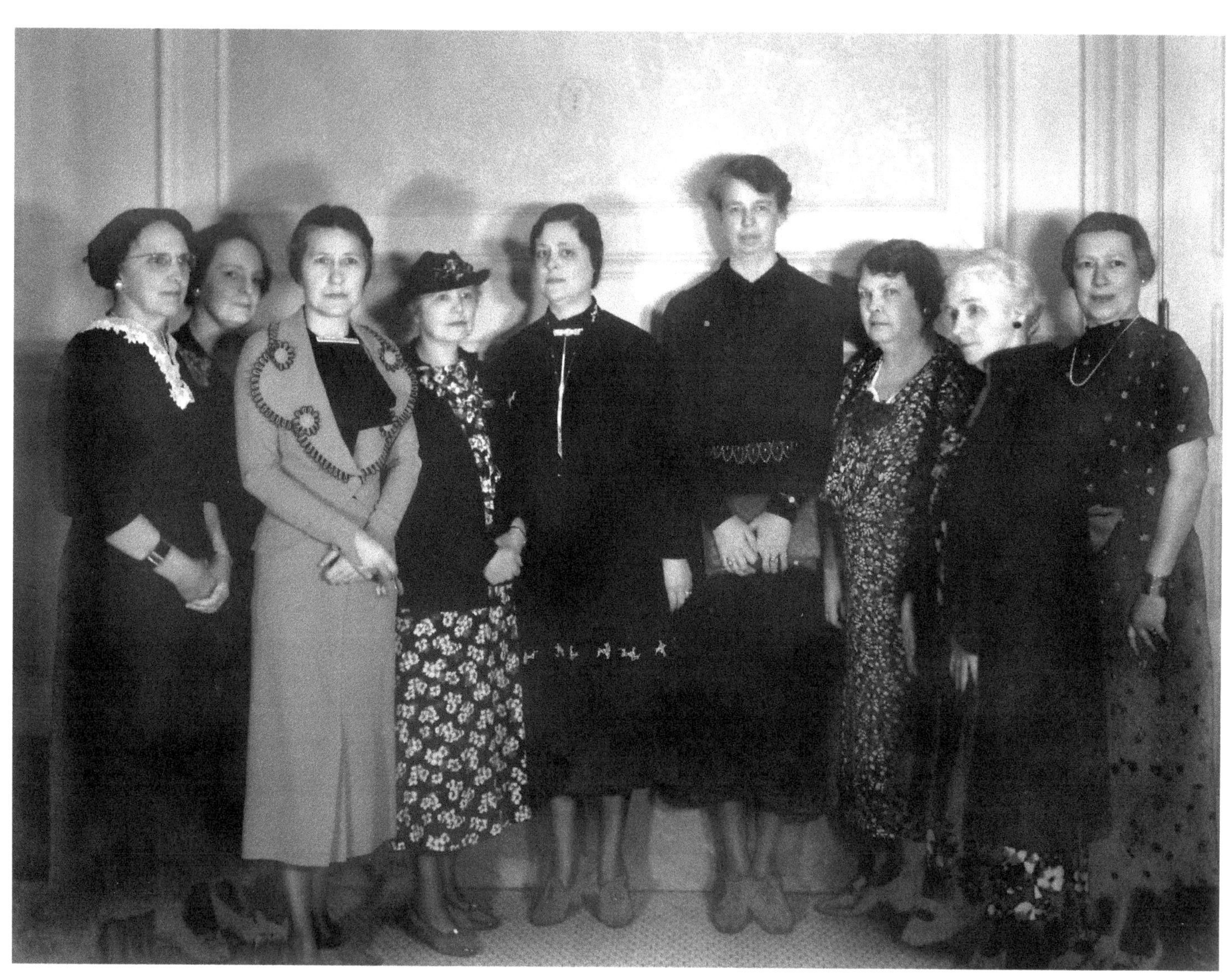

During the Depression years, first lady Eleanor Roosevelt served as goodwill ambassador for the administration of her husband, Franklin D. Roosevelt. She (the tallest) was photographed while meeting with some of Austin's leading women (from left): Mrs. W. R. Long, Velma Hunter, Mint Reed, Nina Bremond, Camille Butler, Dot Wilcox, Lutie Perry, and Mrs. Bickler.

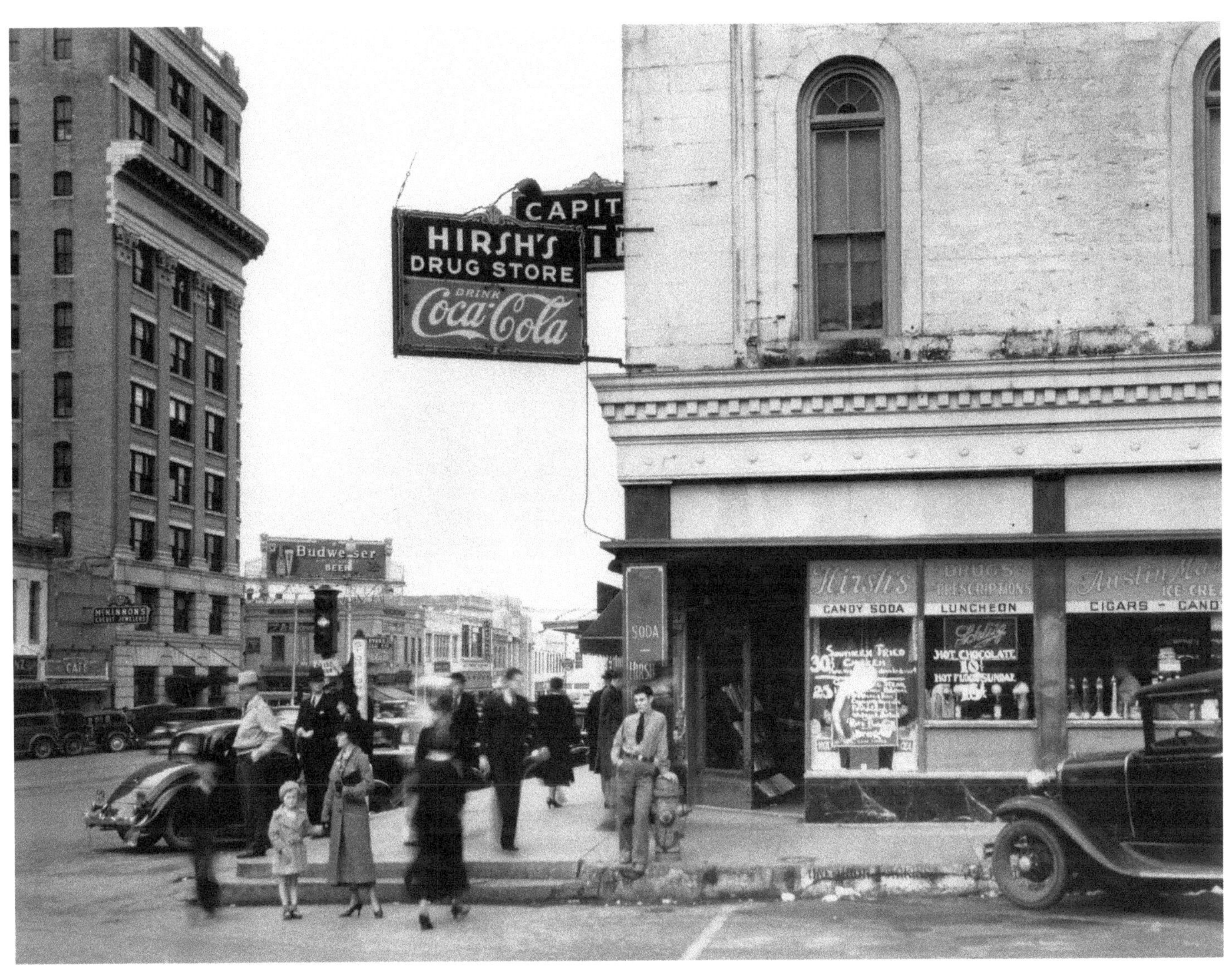

Hirsh's Drug Store, pictured here in the Depression days, was on a busy corner of Congress Avenue.

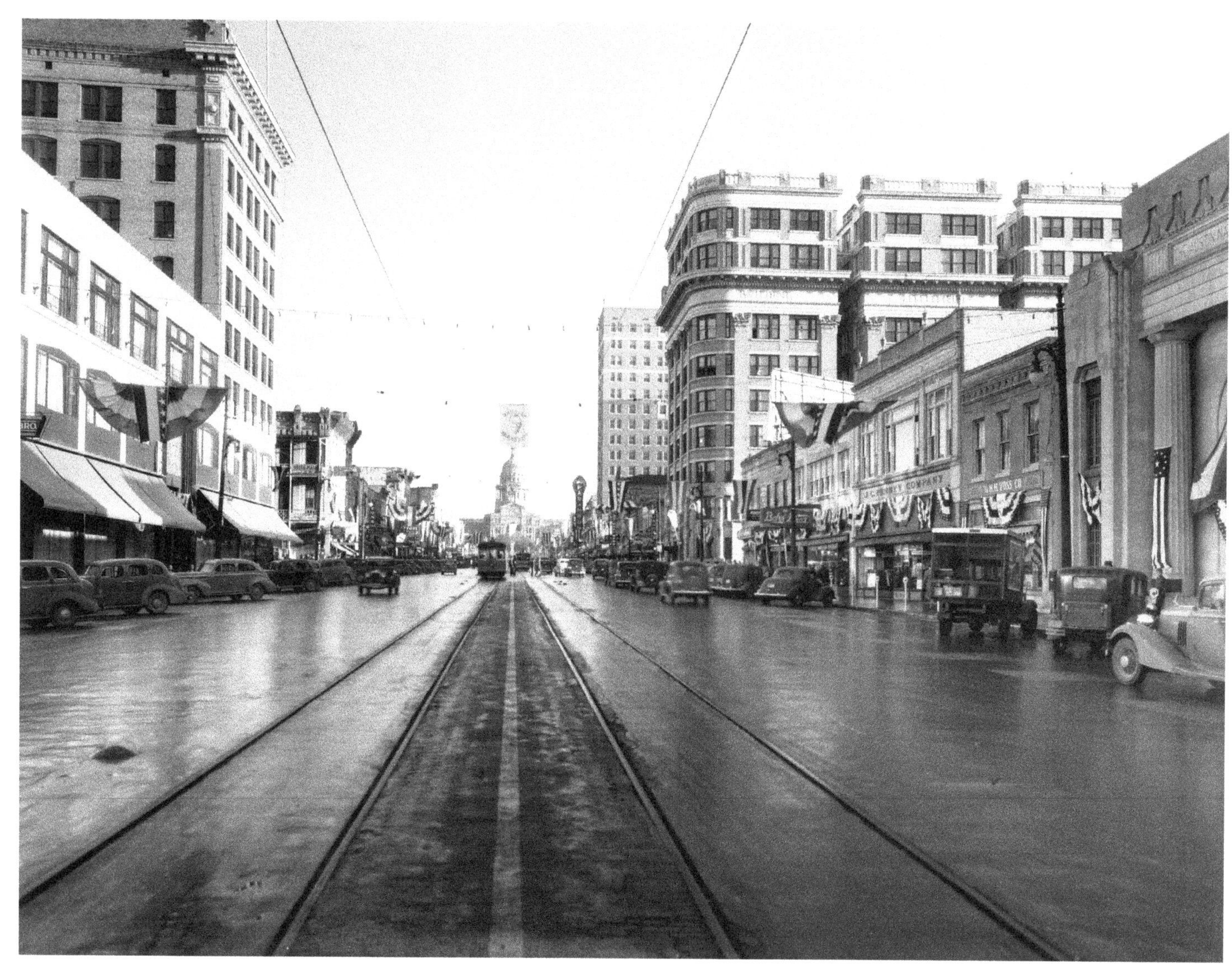

This view shows how Congress Avenue appeared looking north on a rainy day in 1939, decorated for the inauguration of Governor W. Lee "Pappy" O'Daniel, self-proclaimed "hillbilly" singer and radio personality.

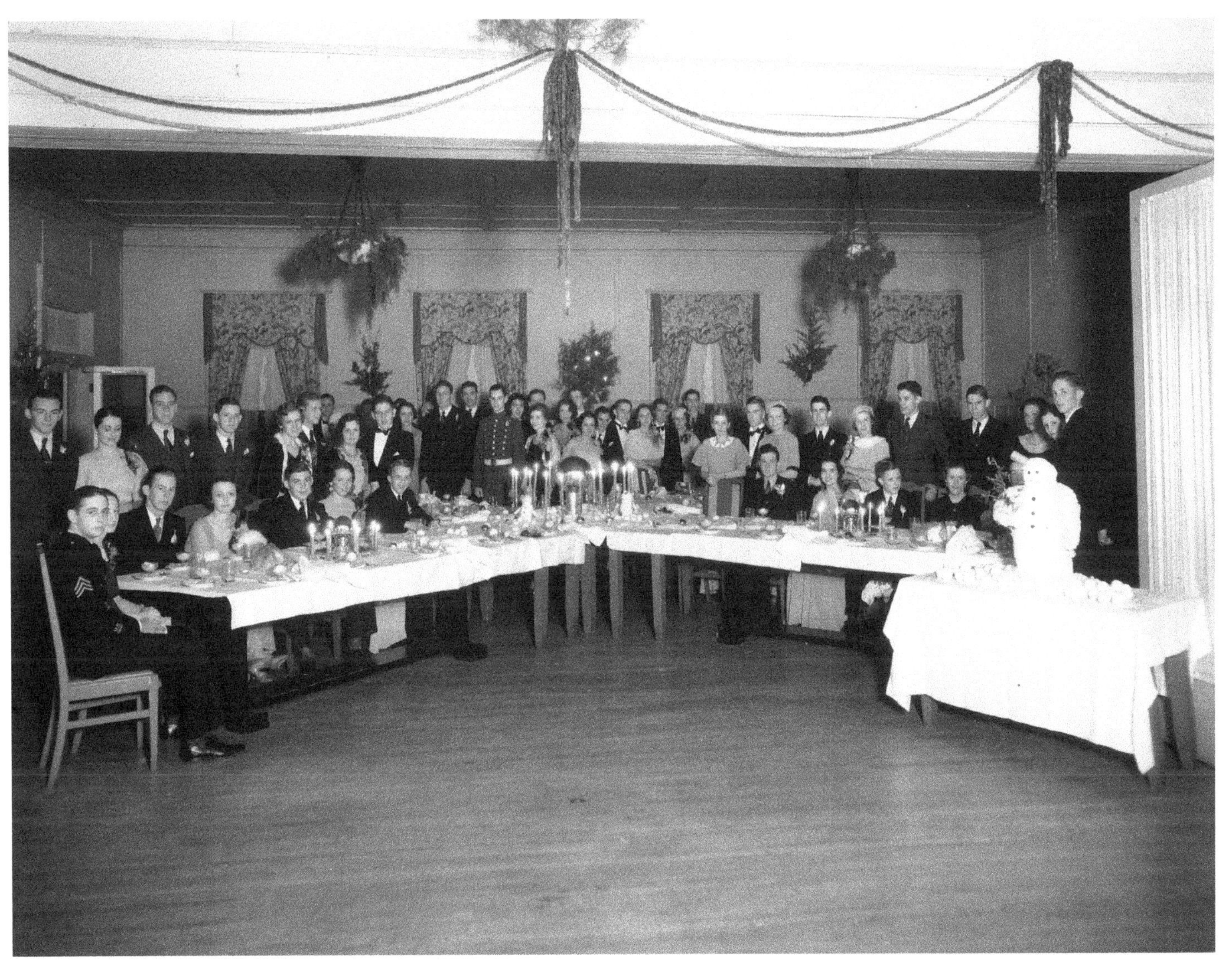

In December 1932, well-dressed young men and women pose near the dance floor during a holiday party at the Austin Country Club, located in the Tarrytown neighborhood west of downtown.

The appearance of Congress Avenue and other Austin commercial streets changed noticeably in the 1930s, when architecture began reflecting art-moderne and art-deco designs. Some structures, such as the new Austin National Bank, were built in the contemporary style, while others simply added modernized facades to existing nineteenth-century storefronts.

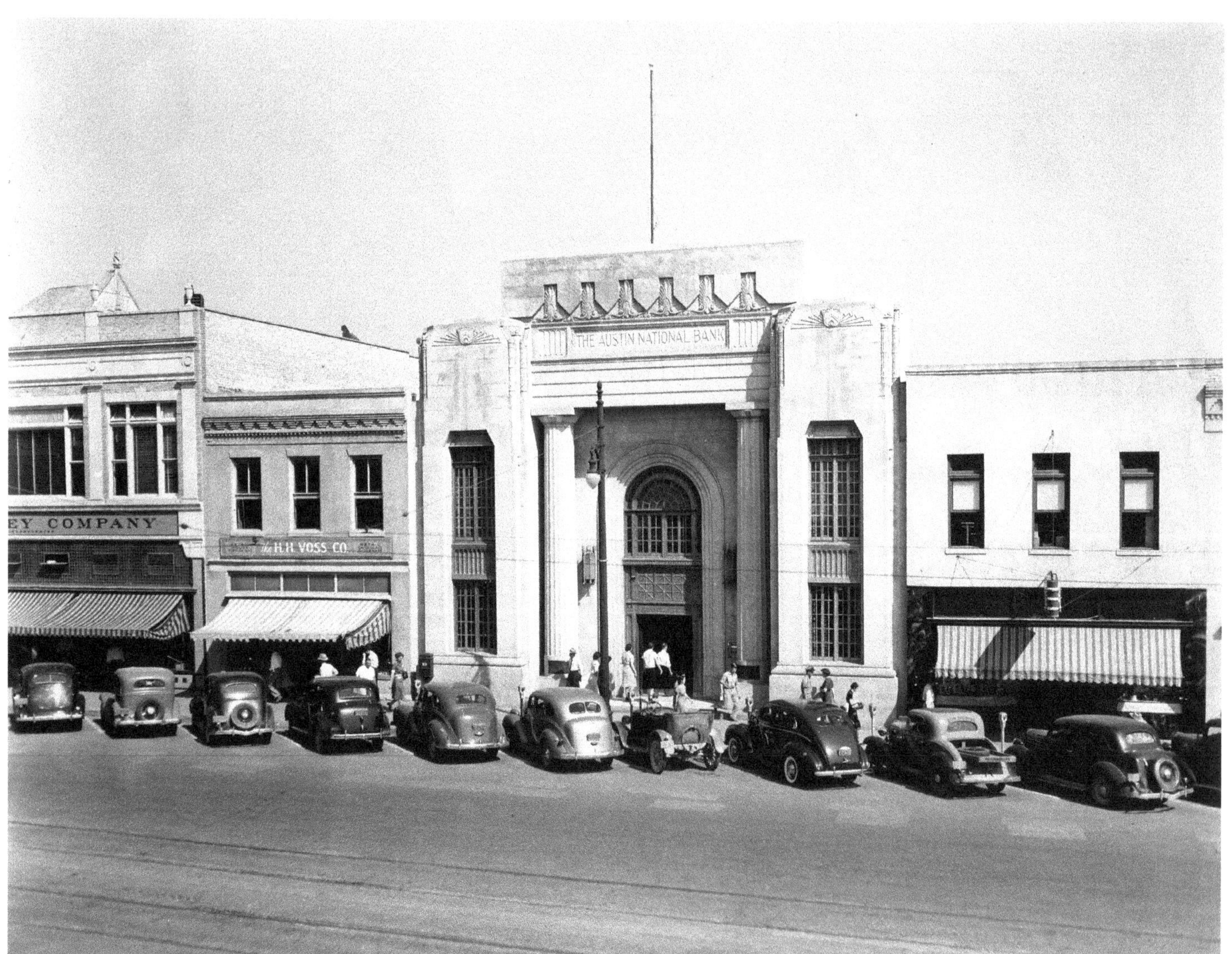

Harry Aiken, a former Hollywood actor, opened his first Night Hawk restaurant in 1933, emulating late-night cafés in California. He soon had several of them around town. This photograph shows employees at the second Night Hawk, on Guadalupe, popular with university students. In 1958 Aiken was the first Austin restaurateur to integrate, serving African Americans years before any other local restaurant followed suit.

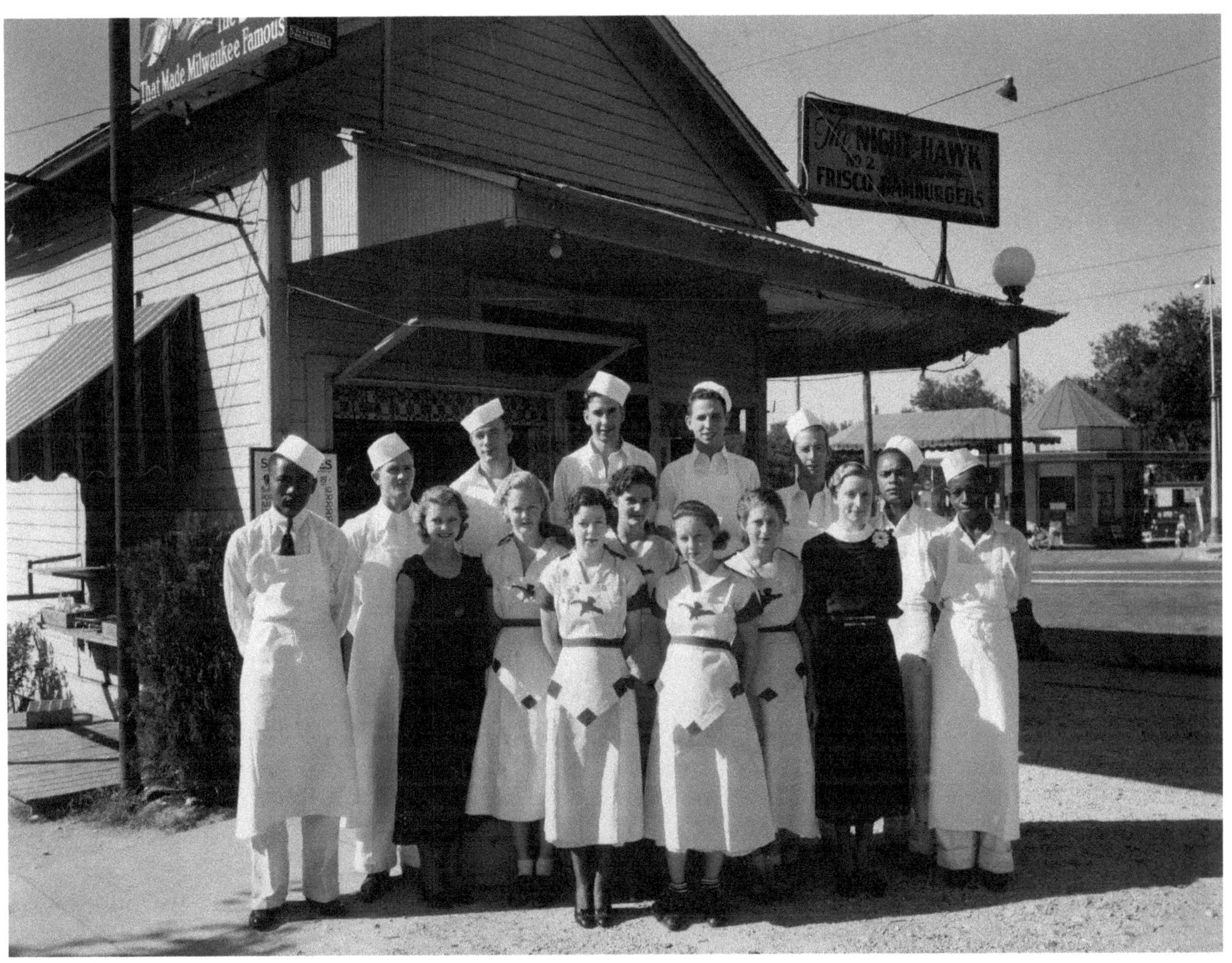

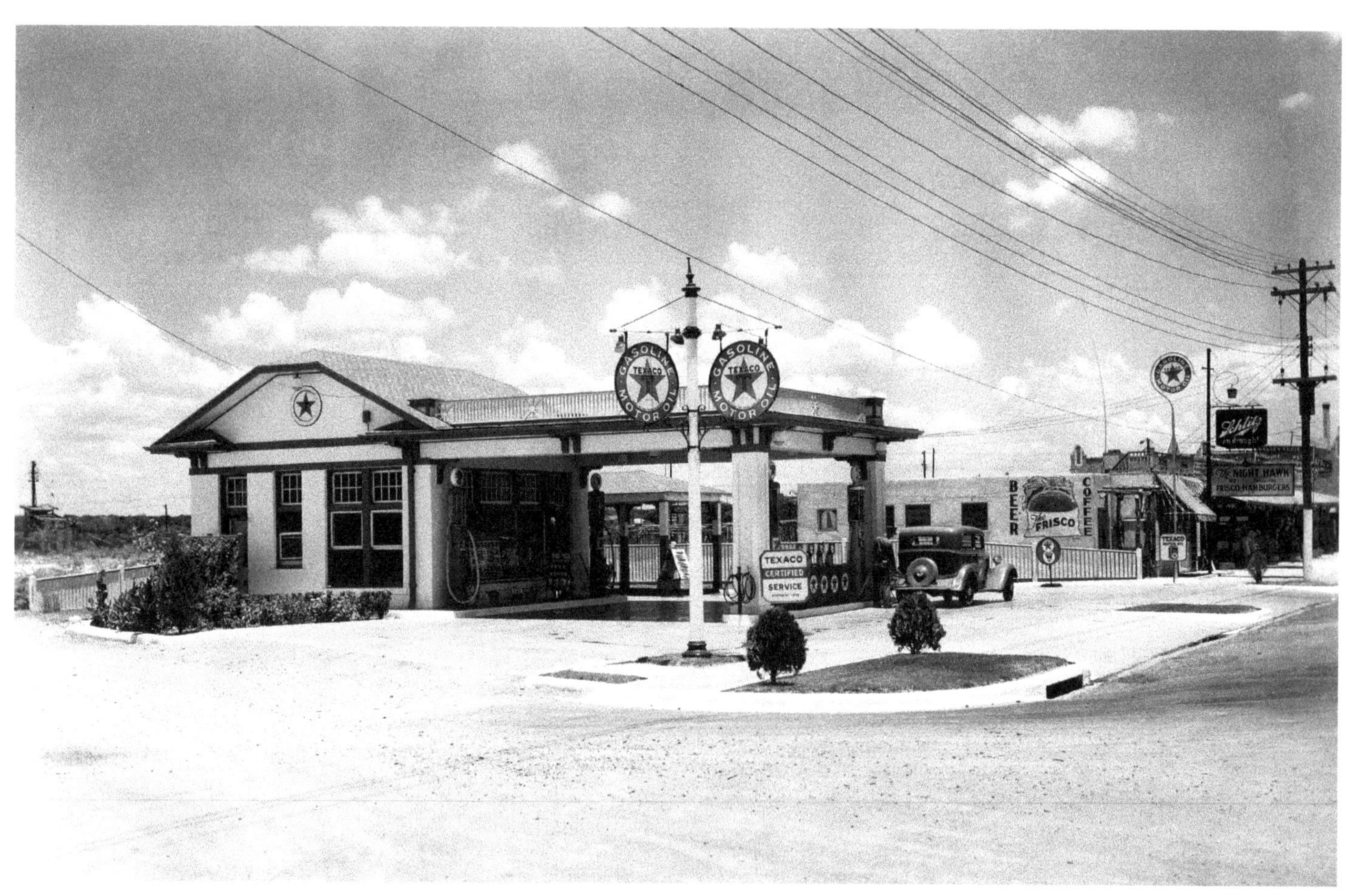

By 1934, when this photograph was taken, gasoline stations such as this Texaco in South Austin were common sights. Note its next-door neighbor, the Frisco, possibly the first of several such popular and locally owned hamburger cafés around town.

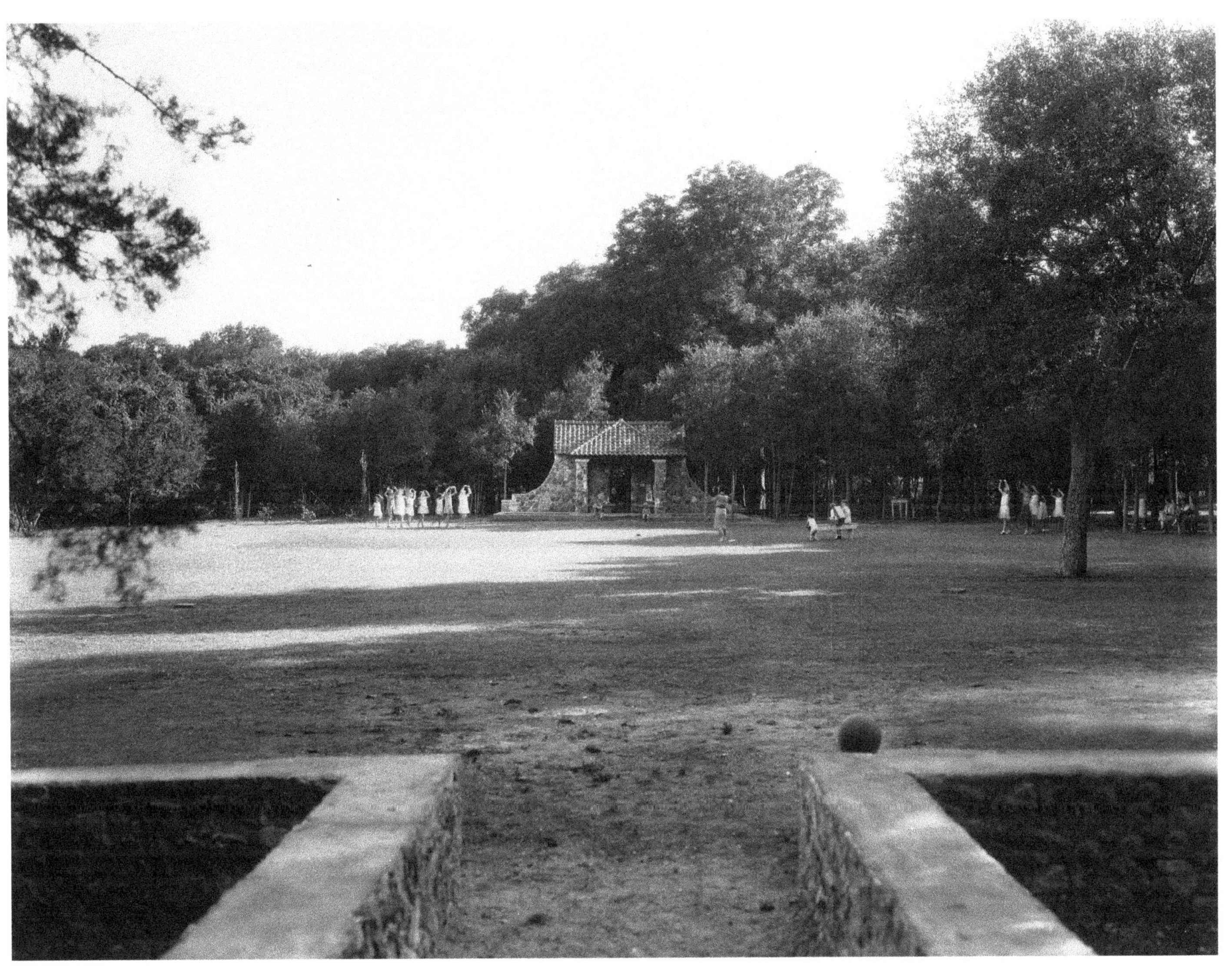

Dance students dressed as sylphs rehearse for a recital on the lawn at Eastwoods Park circa 1935. Many of the city's parks were enhanced by stonework structures and walls, created by government-employed stonemasons during the Depression years. This park is located just north of the University of Texas campus.

Pictured circa 1934 is petite performer Sally Rand, posing on the Capitol steps in Hollywood's idea of a cowgirl outfit and surrounded by her welcoming committee. Miss Rand was a silent-screen actress in the 1920s, but she was best known for creating a sensation at the 1933 world's fair in Chicago by dancing with two large ostrich-plume fans—and what appeared to be nothing else. The man at far left is identified as Wiley Post, famous aviator from Texas.

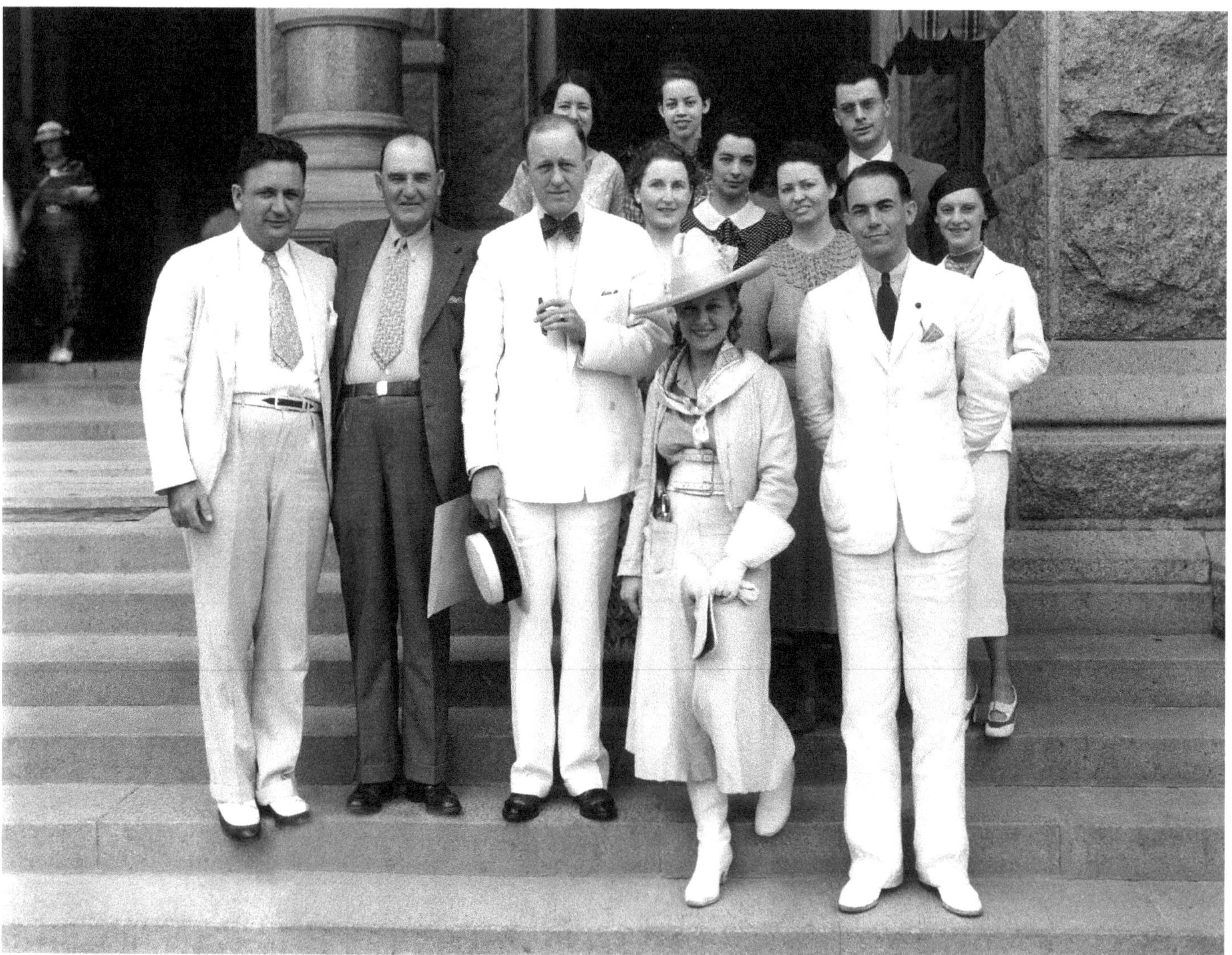

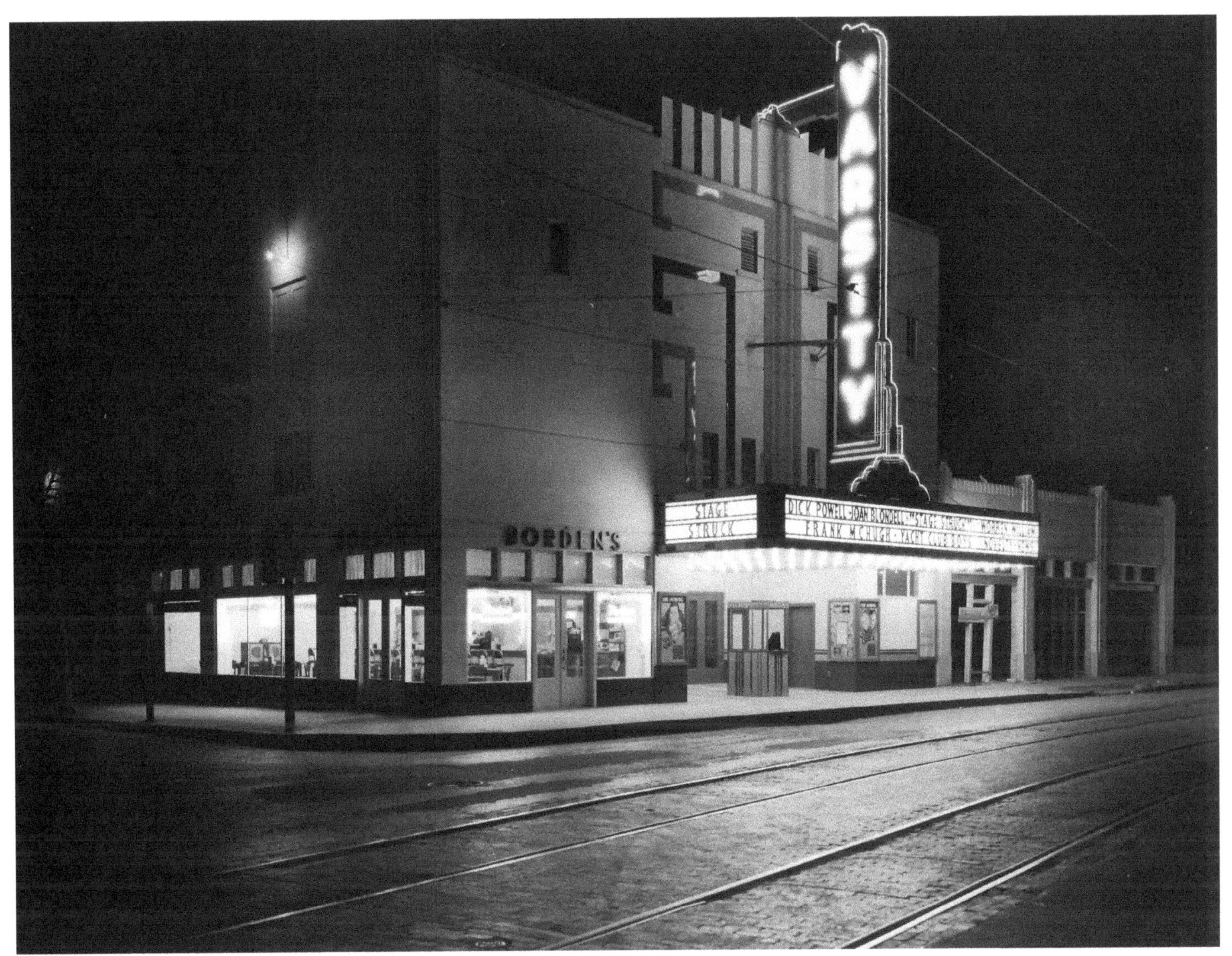

The Varsity Theater was across from the University of Texas campus, on the section of Guadalupe Street that has long been called "The Drag." This photo shows how the Varsity looked in 1936, when Dick Powell and Joan Blondell were Hollywood stars and Borden's ice cream and soda-fountain shop was next door.

This City of Austin parade truck in the 1930s featured a sign reminding citizens just how fortunate they were to have an efficient system of water, electricity, and sewage disposal—even when days of the Great Depression were tough.

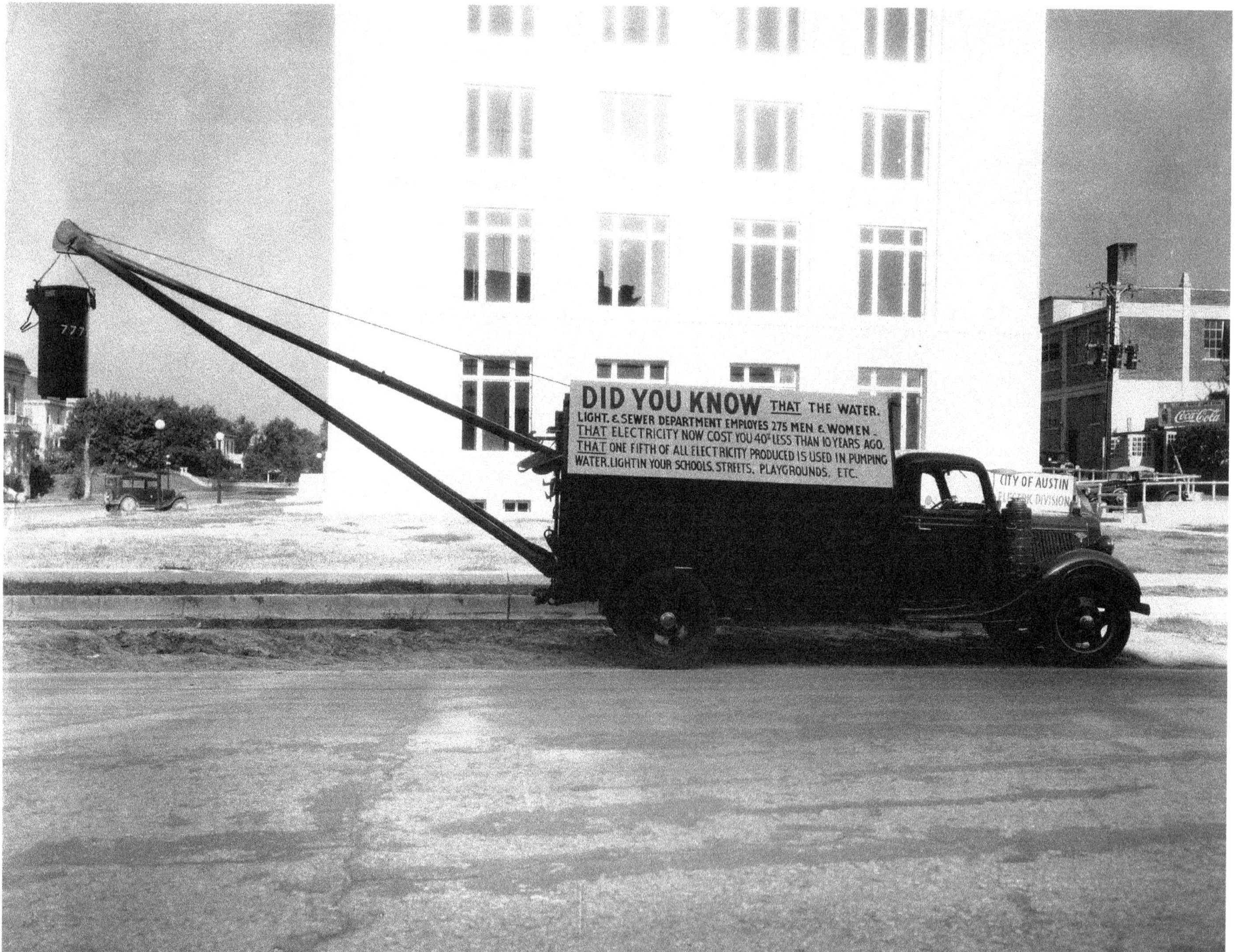

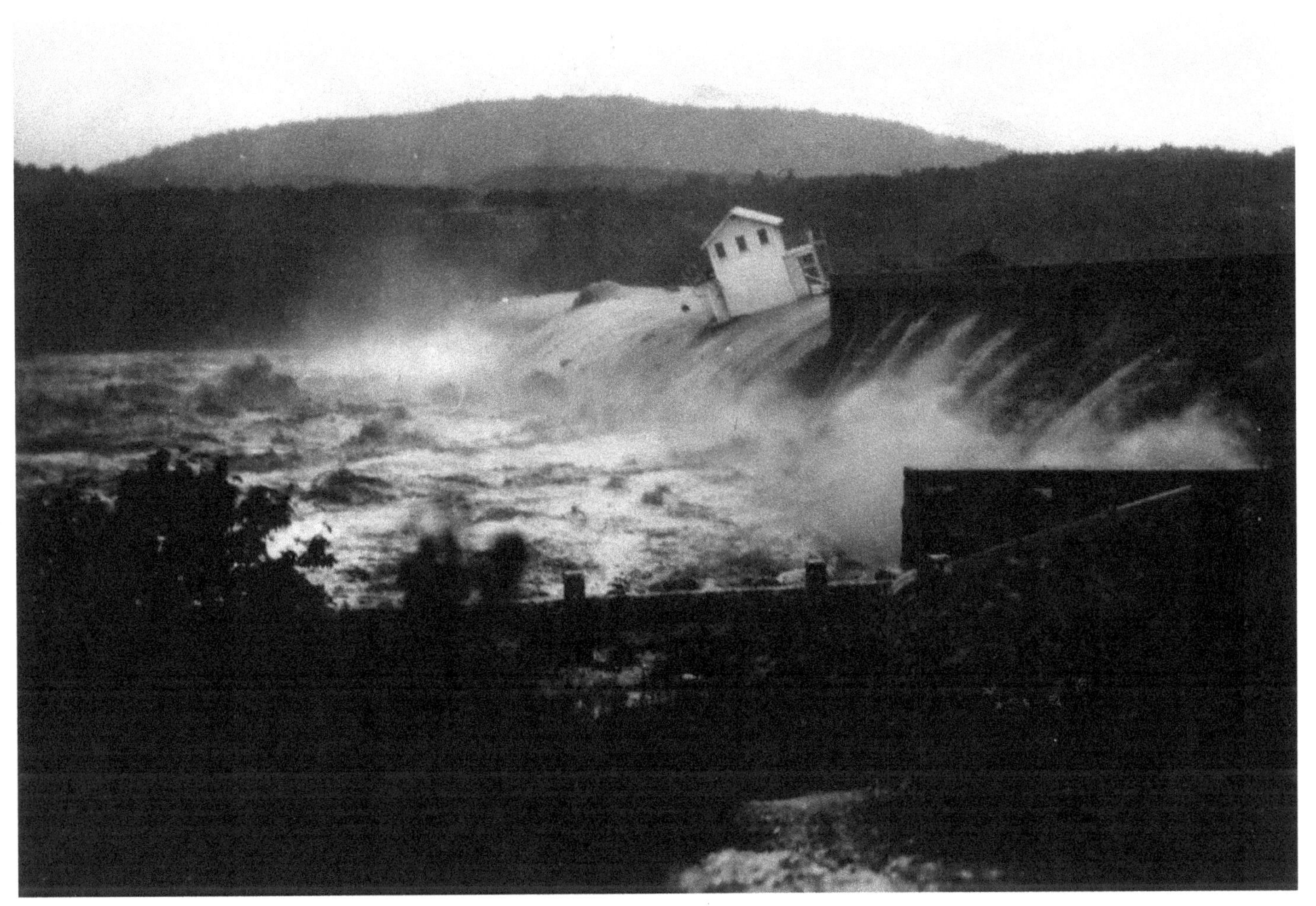

As if the Great Depression were not stressful enough, the Colorado River flooded in 1935.

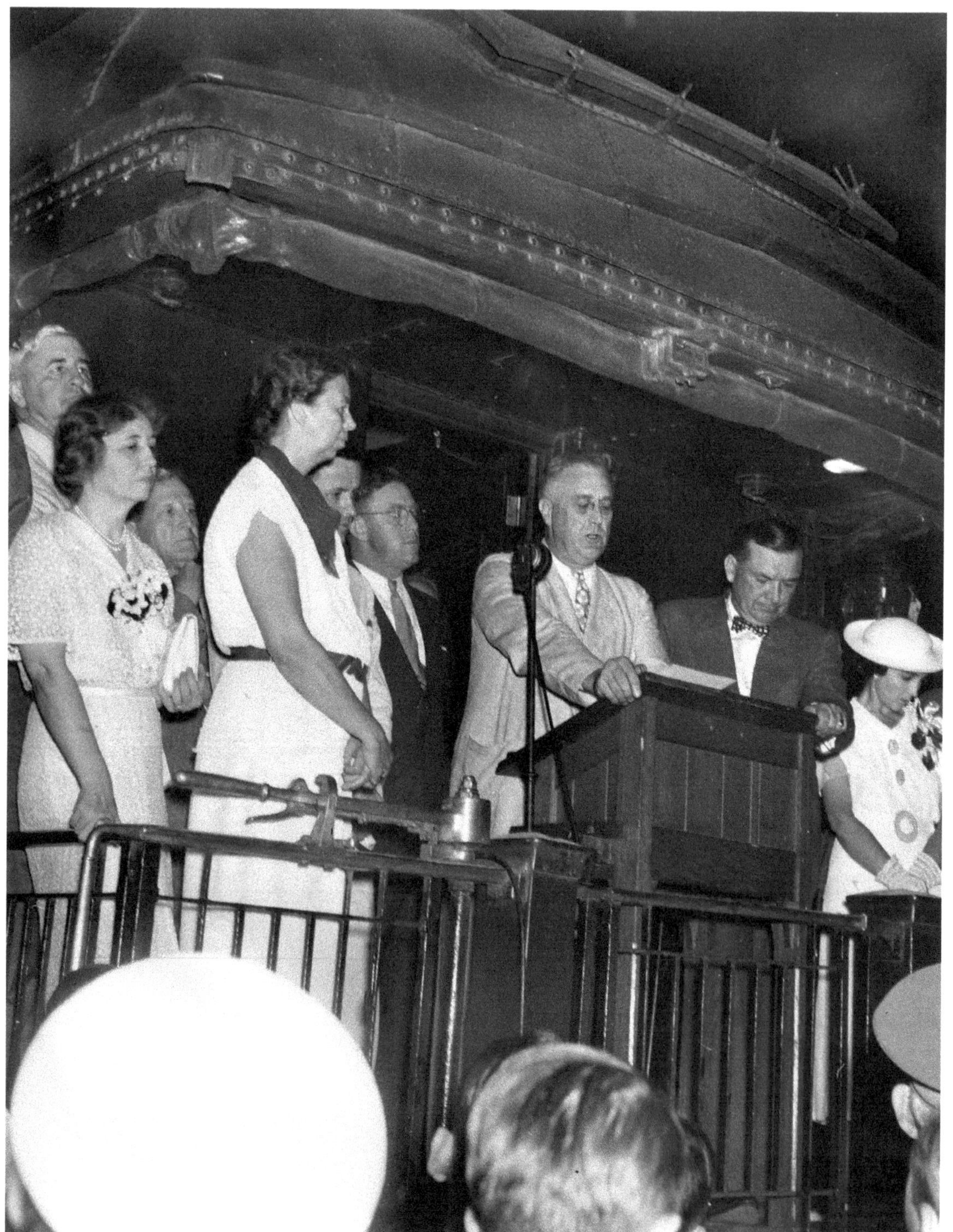

In 1936, President Franklin D. Roosevelt made a brief whistle-stop in Austin while on a railway tour. Despite the late hour of the train's arrival, thousands of Austinites turned out to greet the president and first lady, Eleanor. Before leaving, FDR touched off a ceremonial dynamite explosion to break ground for the Texas Memorial Museum.

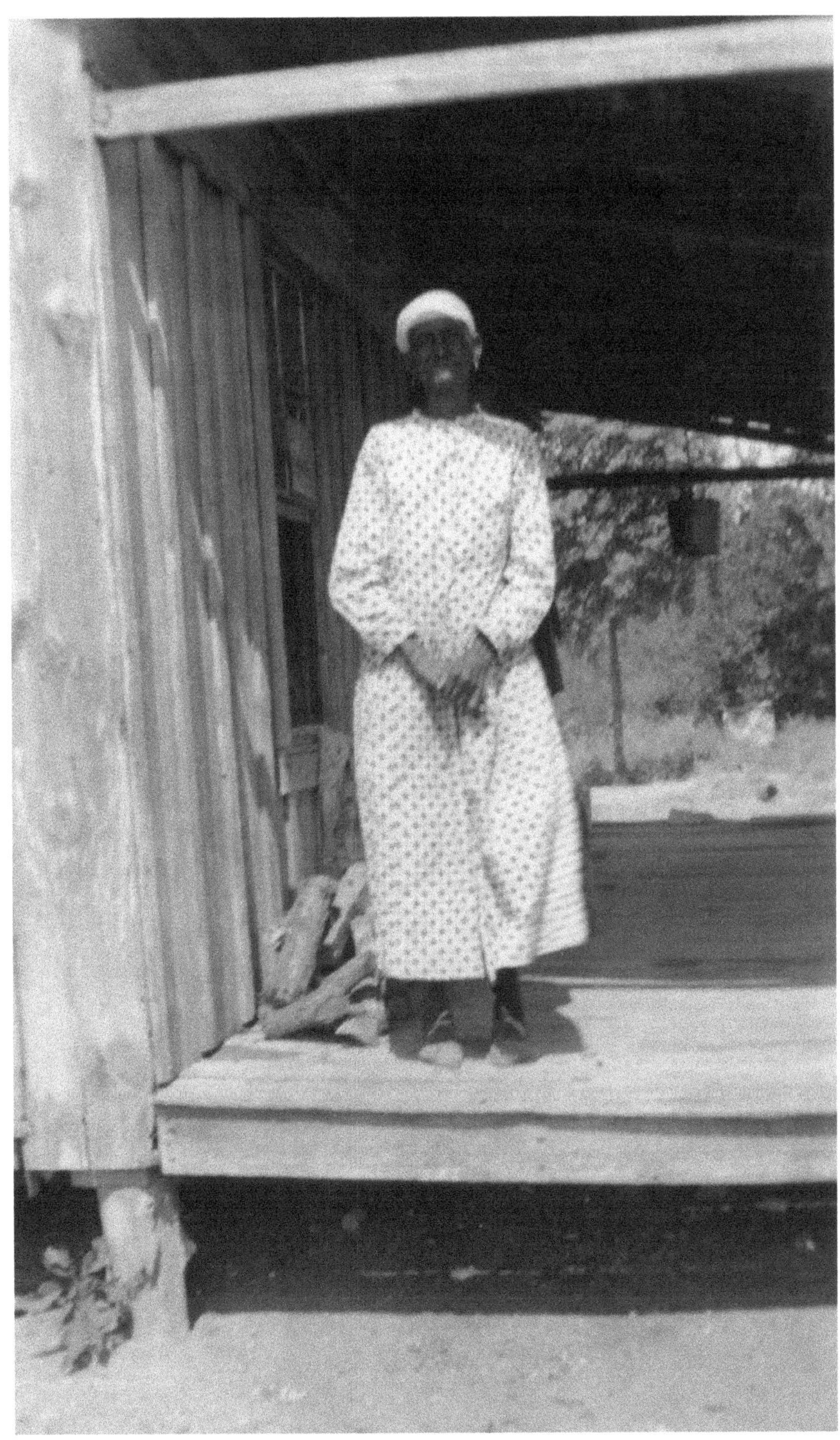

Austinite Sallie Wroe was photographed in 1937 or 1938 by a member of the Federal Writers' Project of the Works Progress Administration (WPA) to document African Americans who had been enslaved. The WPA was instituted by President Franklin D. Roosevelt to create jobs for the unemployed during the Depression.

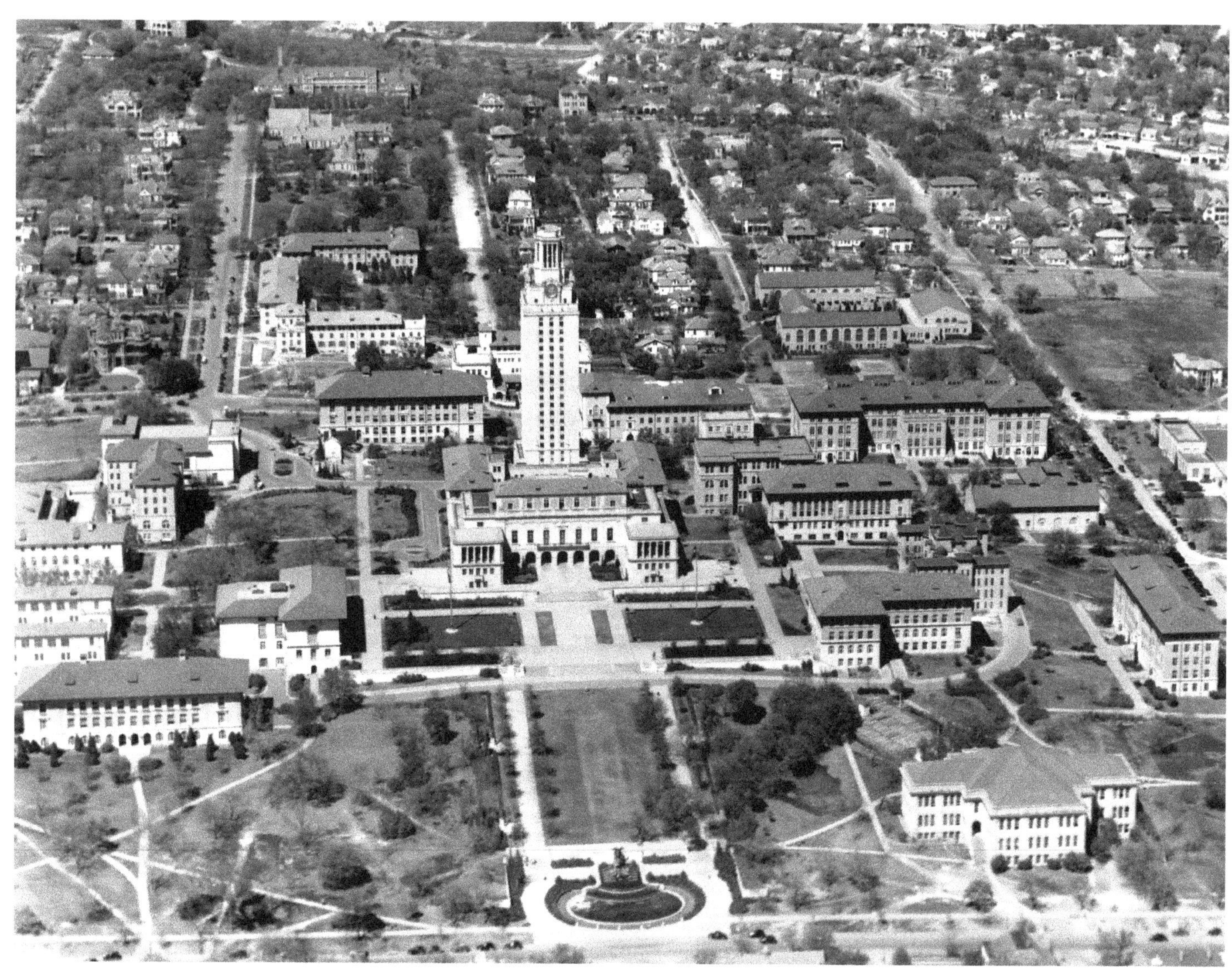

This bird's-eye view of the University of Texas campus shows the 307-foot tower of the Administration building, completed in 1937. Note the homogeneous architectural style of the campus buildings constructed in the 1930s, inspired by Cass Gilbert's Spanish Renaissance design of Battle Hall. The university's building boom and other construction projects helped keep many Austinites employed during the Depression years.

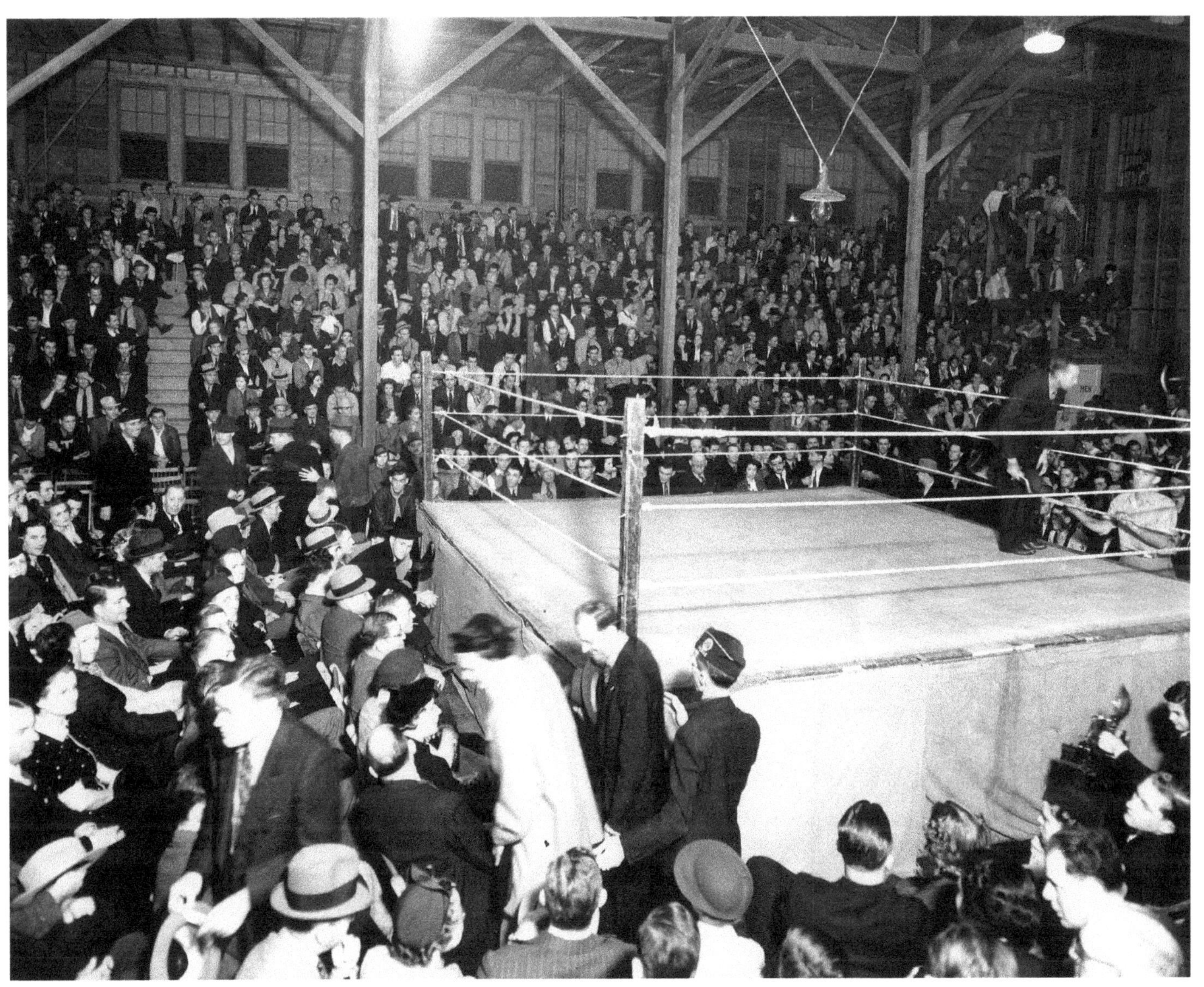

A crowd gathers for a Golden Gloves amateur boxing tournament in a local gymnasium circa 1938.

The first housing projects in the nation were built in Austin. Among them were the Santa Rita apartments for Mexican Americans (pictured) and the Rosewood project for African Americans. In 1939, 186 families moved into three projects, paying approximately $12 per month for rent and utilities. Congressman Lyndon Johnson had been instrumental in getting approval for the projects from the Federal Housing Authority.

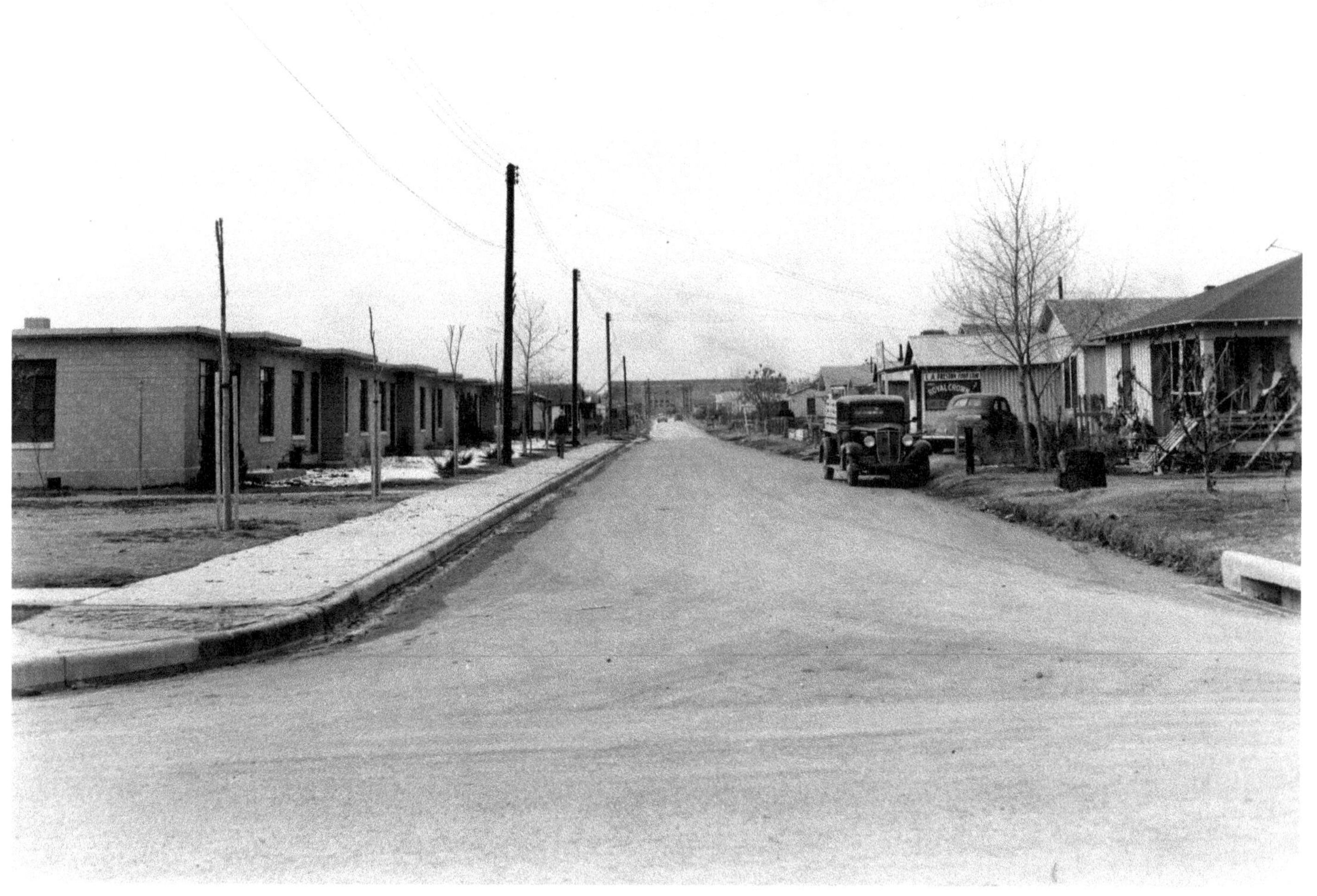

At 1:40 in the afternoon of February 7, 1940, Austinites gathered at Congress Avenue and Sixth Street for a last ride on the city's electric streetcars. This day meant a significant change in the lives of Austin commuters, who from then on would be riding the Austin Transit Company's new buses, rather than the streetcars that had served the city in one form or another since 1875.

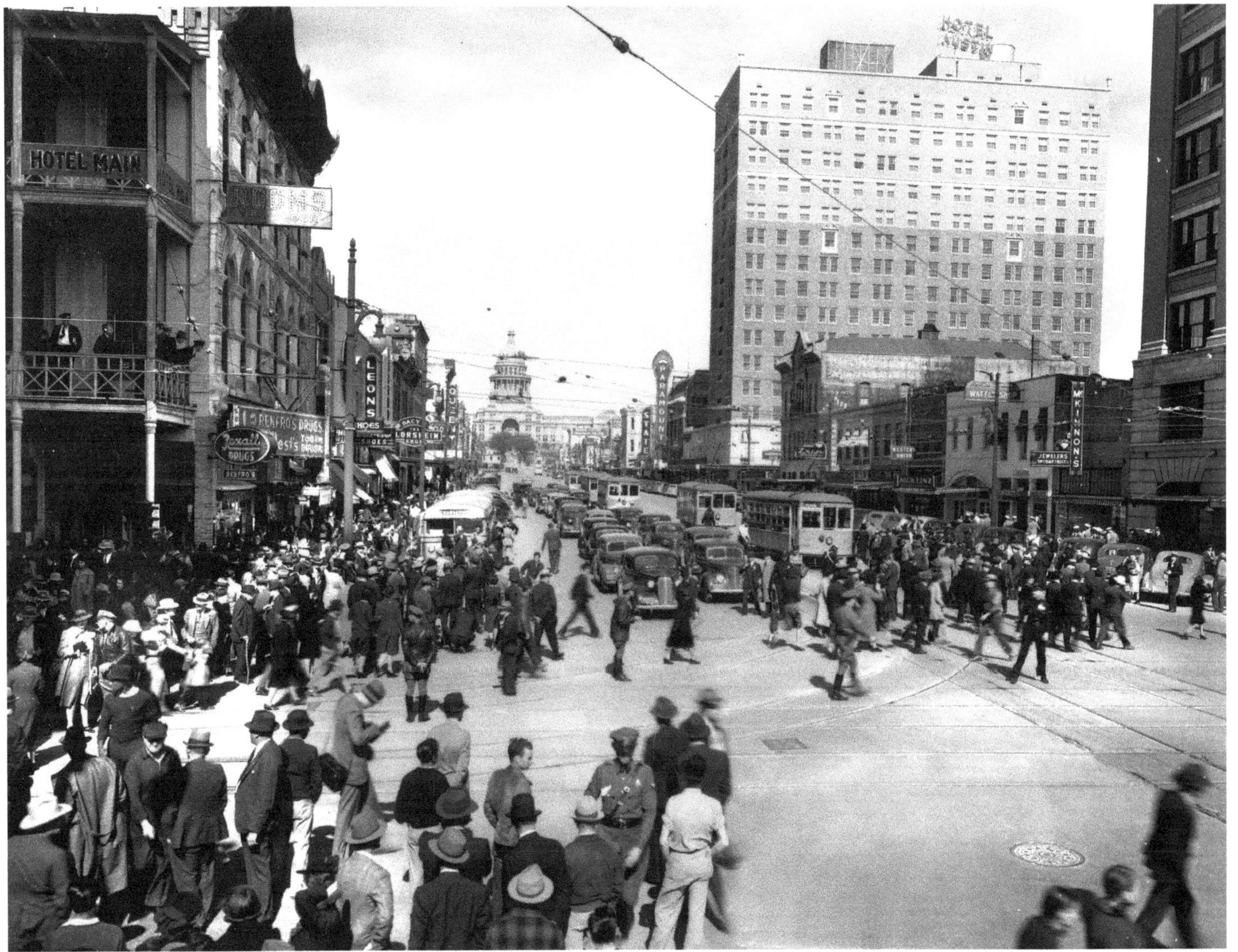

Looking down Sixth Street from the center of Congress circa 1940, you couldn't miss the Littlefield Building's curved facade (left) and the Driskill Hotel right behind it. Note that the trolley tracks have been removed and paved over.

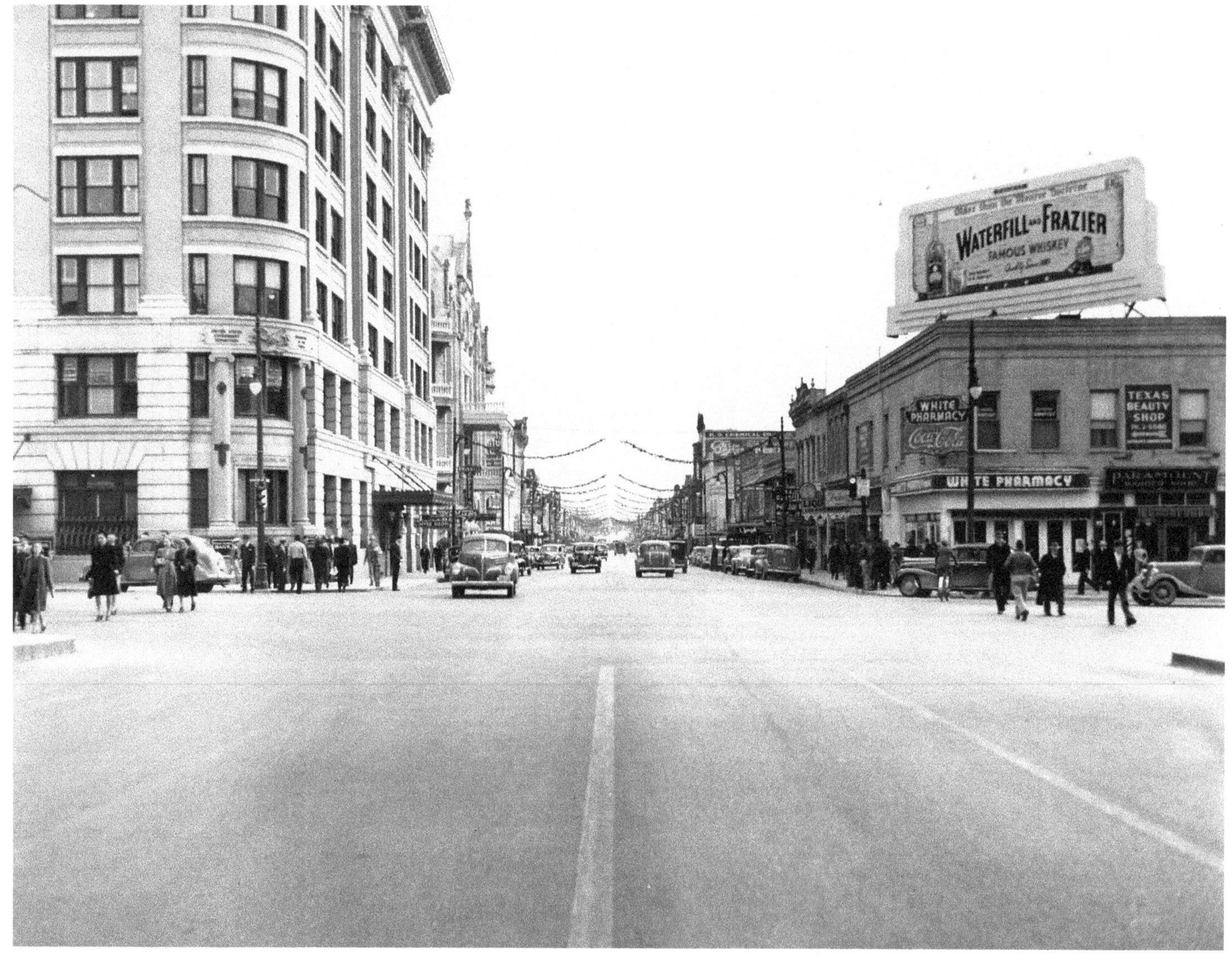

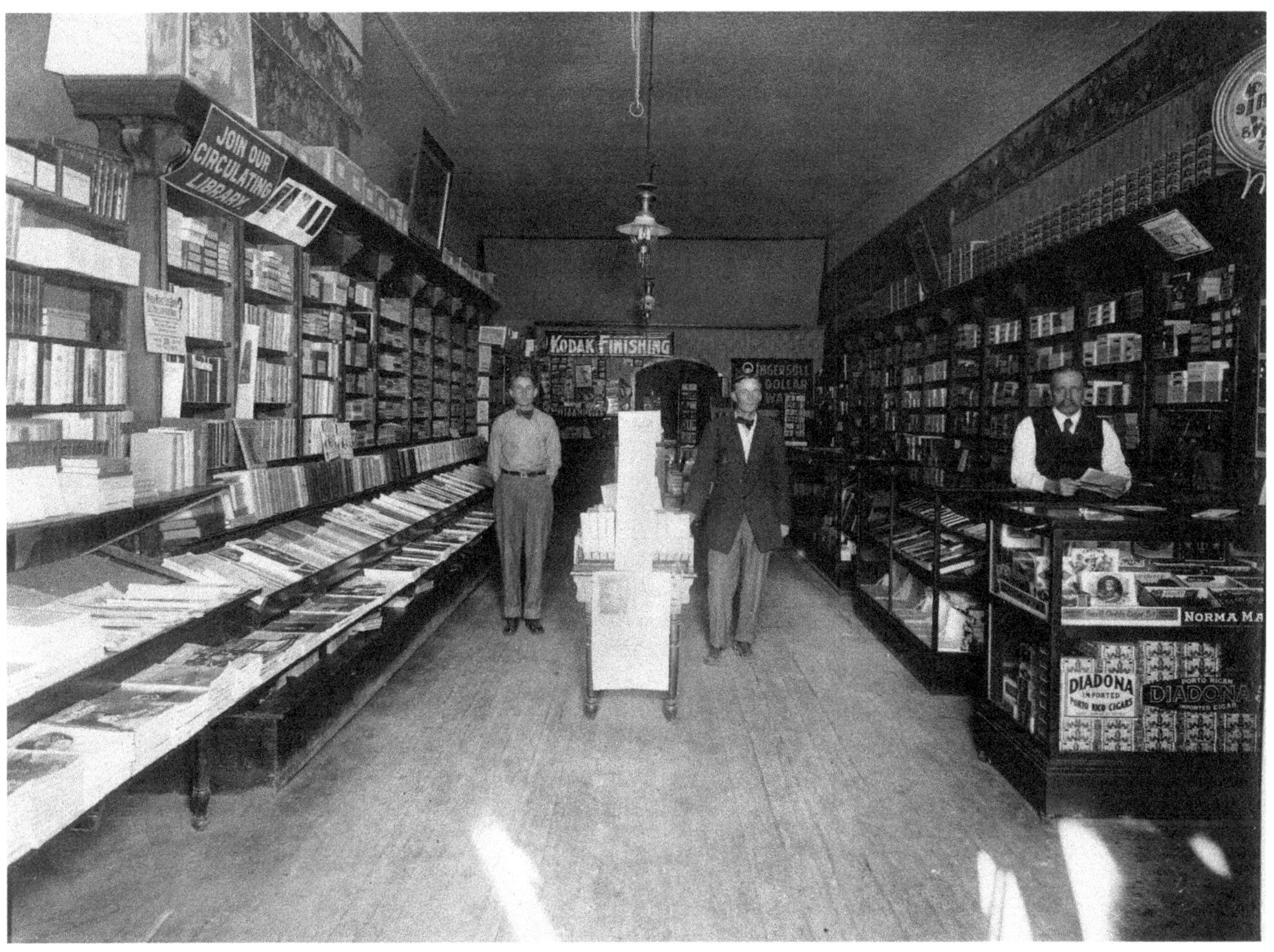

This photograph shows the interior of the City Book Store, where apparently cigars as well as books were sold and film developing was another sideline. The sign at left, "Join Our Circulating Library," indicates that the picture may have been taken before 1926, when the American Association of University Women started Austin's first library.

The Governor's Mansion, 1010 Colorado Street, is conveniently located within a block of the Capitol. Designed by local renowned architect Abner Cook in the Greek Revival style, it was completed in 1856. Its first resident was Governor Elisha Marshall Pease, and it has been the official home of the governors of Texas ever since. A rear addition was completed in 1914 during Governor Colquitt's term.

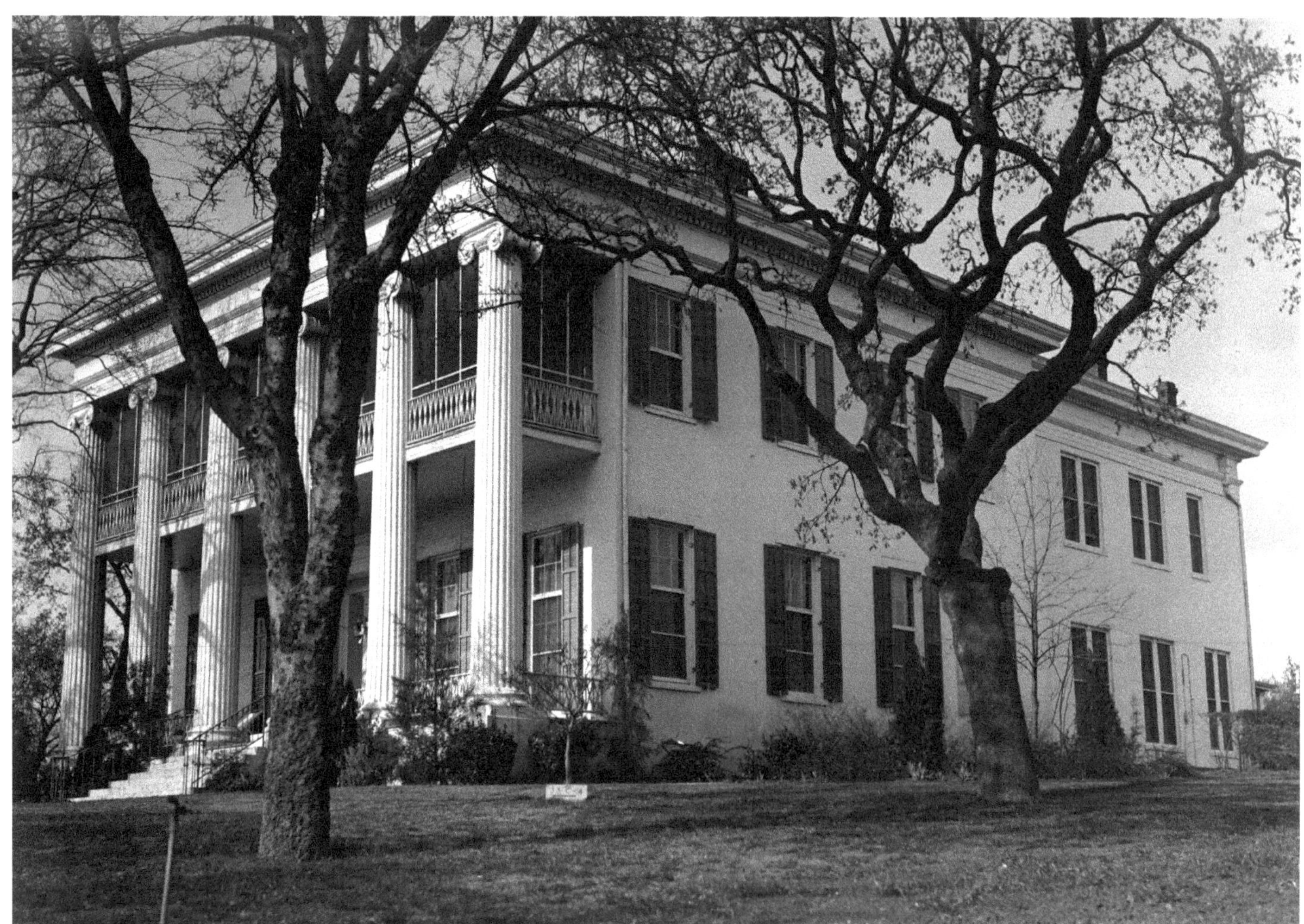

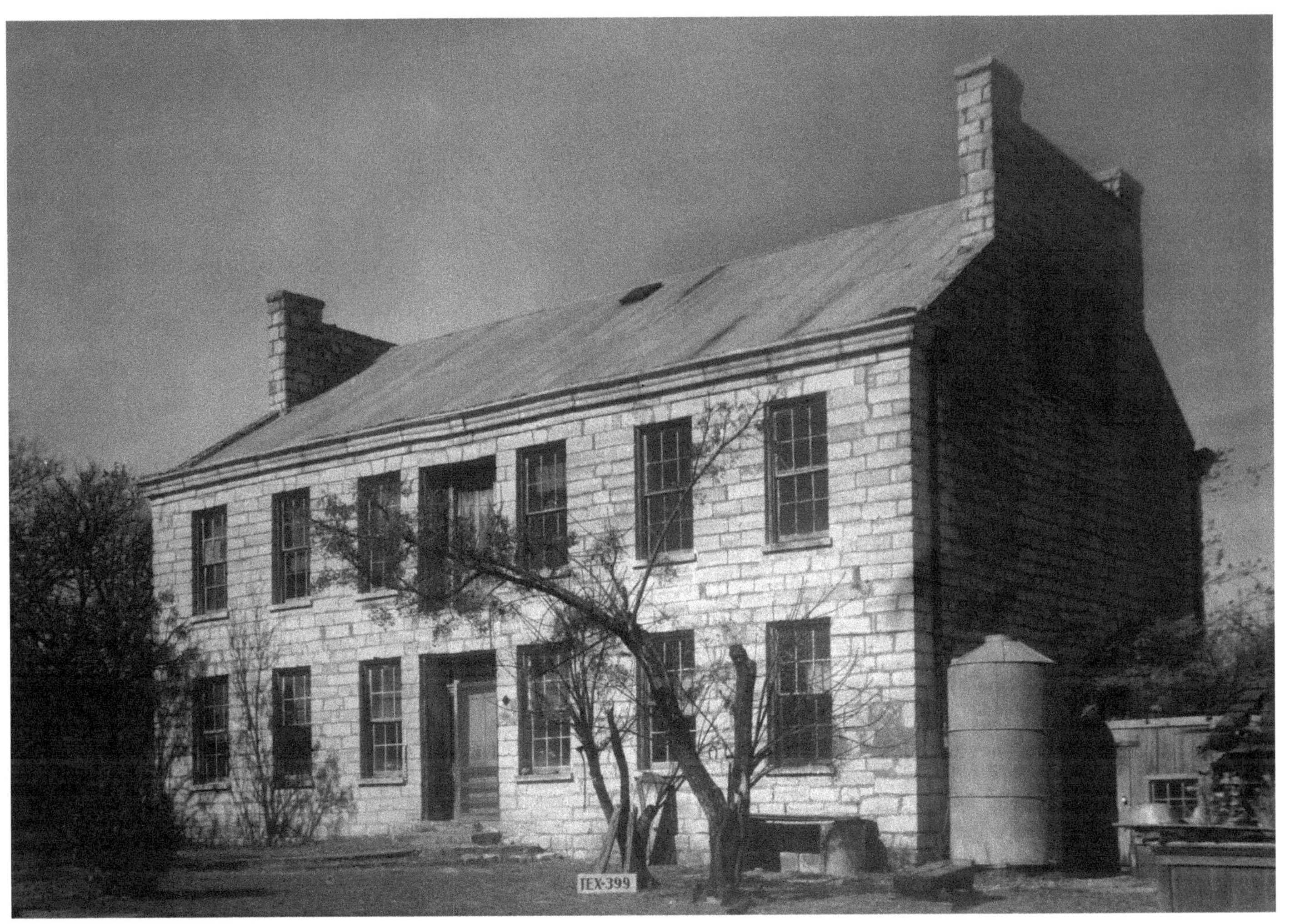

Judge Sebron G. Sneed acquired 470 acres south of Austin in 1854 and built this imposing 12-room house in 1857 with the aid of a mason and a carpenter. The limestone was quarried on the property by slaves, and the house featured eight fireplaces. Sneed brought his family and possessions from Arkansas to Austin by oxcart, and he was one of Austin's most respected criminal lawyers before becoming a judge.

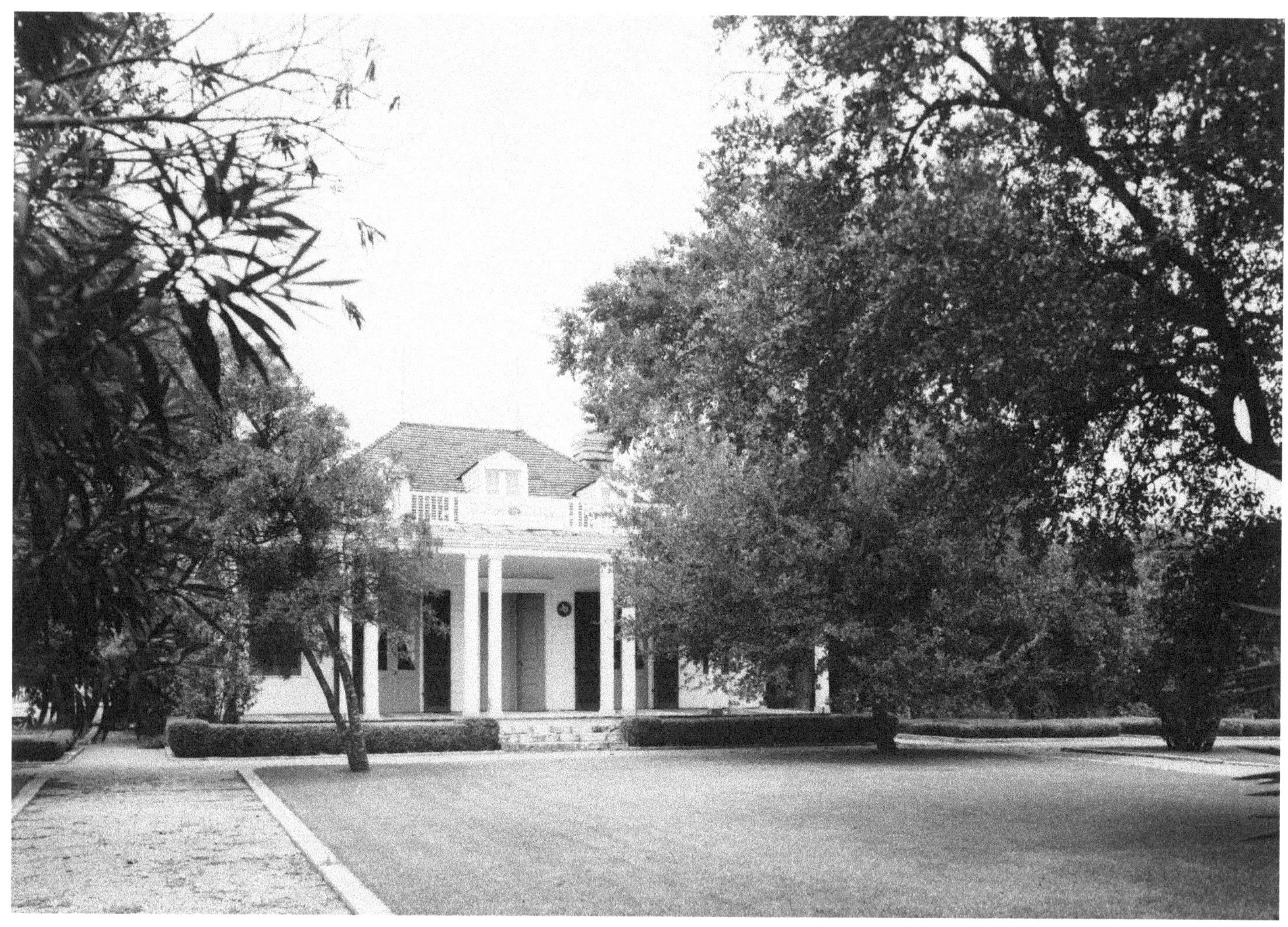

The French Legation, 802 San Marcos Street, is Austin's oldest documented structure still on its original site. Construction began in December 1840. It was the embassy and residence of Pierre Alphonse Dubois de Saligny, Chargé d'Affaires from France to the Republic of Texas. Staying only 15 months, the dapper Frenchman made the Legation a social center, lavishly entertaining the new city's most prominent residents.

West Avenue was the westernmost street in Judge Edwin Waller's original plan for Austin, and by the late 1800s many fine homes graced the street. Several were demolished in the mid twentieth century, however, including (pictured) the Angeline Townsend House at 1802 West Avenue, razed in 1962. Built circa 1869, the residence was representative of the post–Civil War Greek Revival style with Victorian influences.

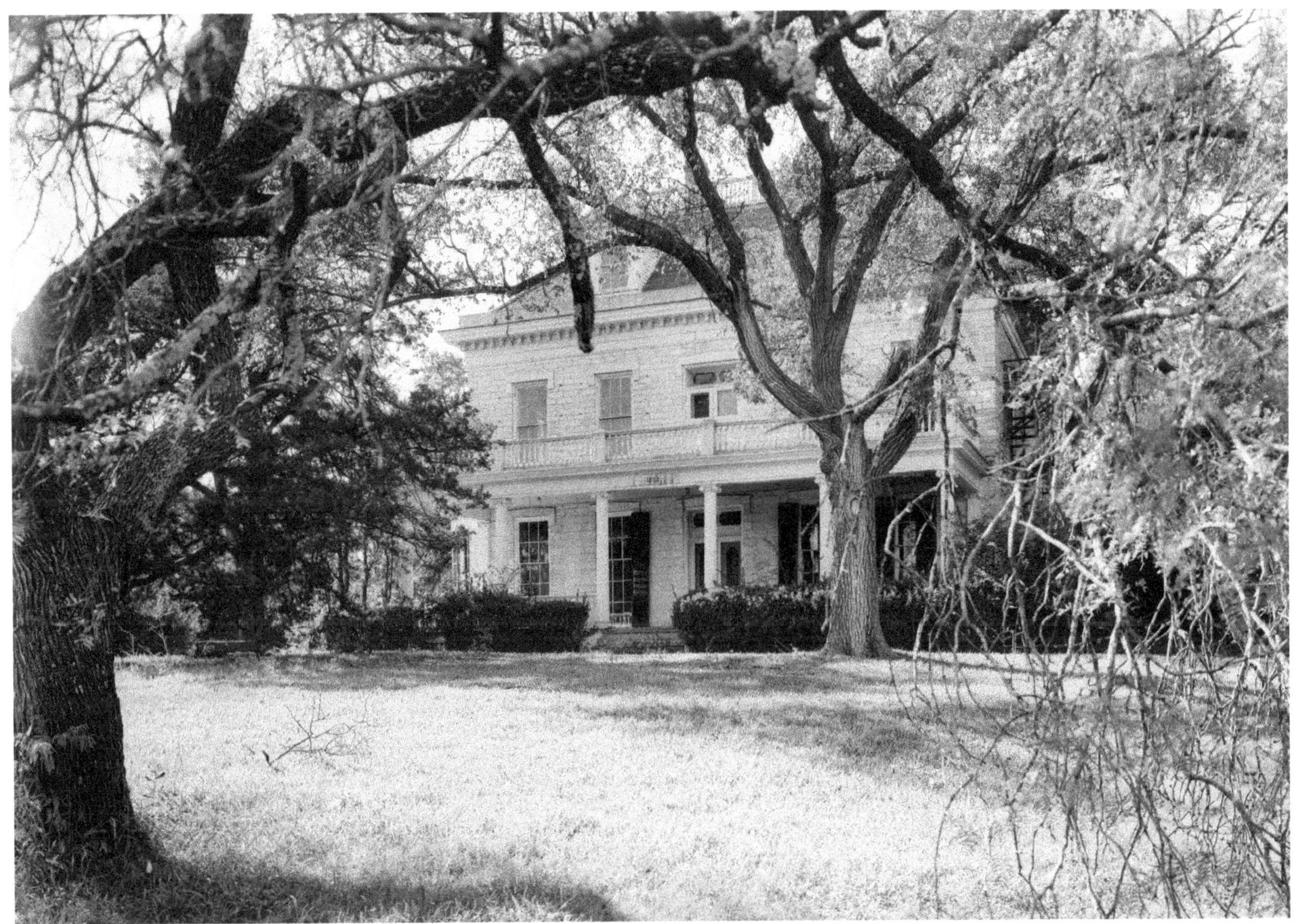

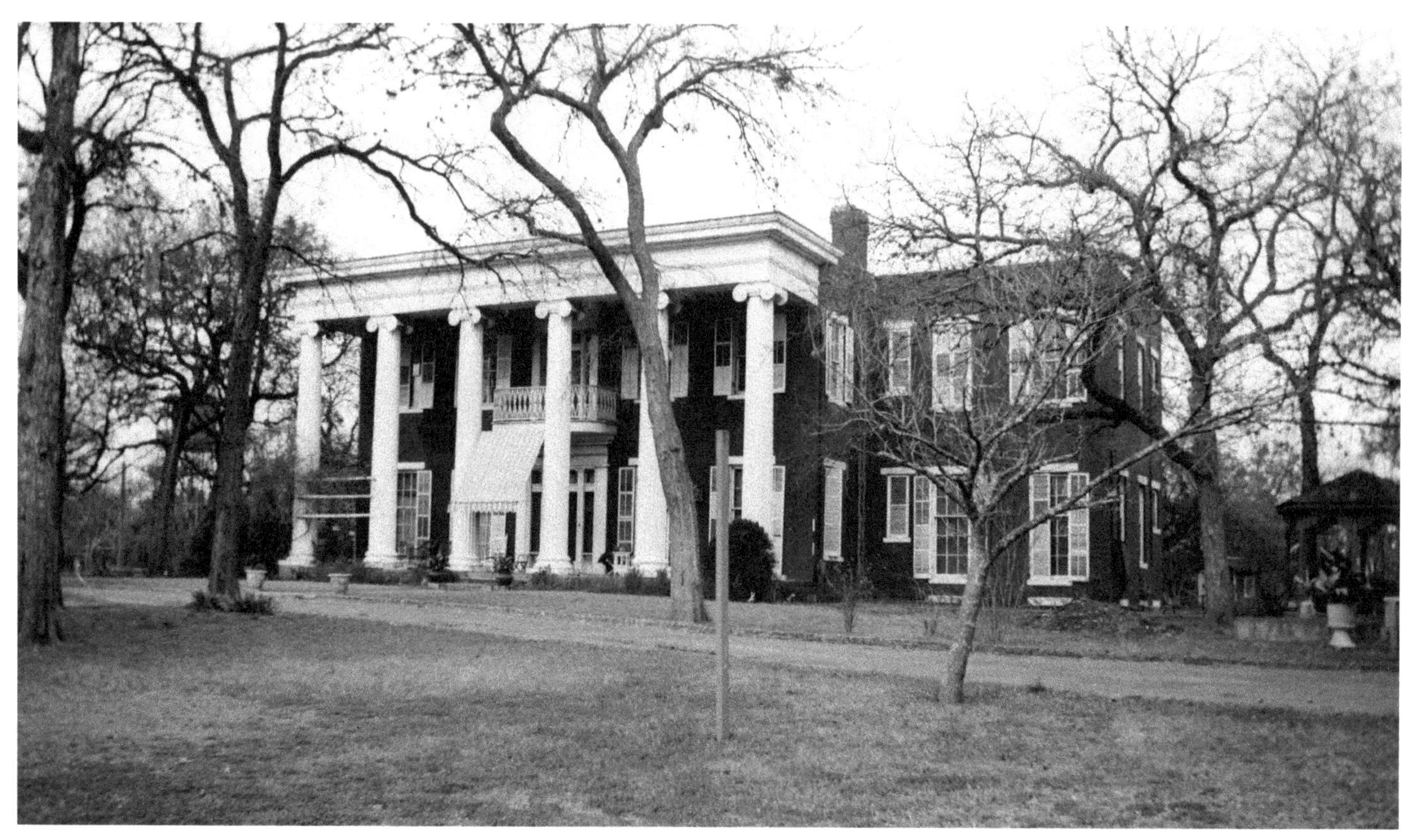

Woodlawn, the Pease Mansion, was built before 1853 by Abner Cook for James C. Shaw, who owned it briefly before selling it to Governor Elisha M. Pease. The Pease family and descendants lived there until 1956, when it was sold to Governor Allan Shivers. Today its brick is painted cream and its Doric columns remain white. The carriage path is now a driveway, and elegant landscaping includes graceful live-oak trees.

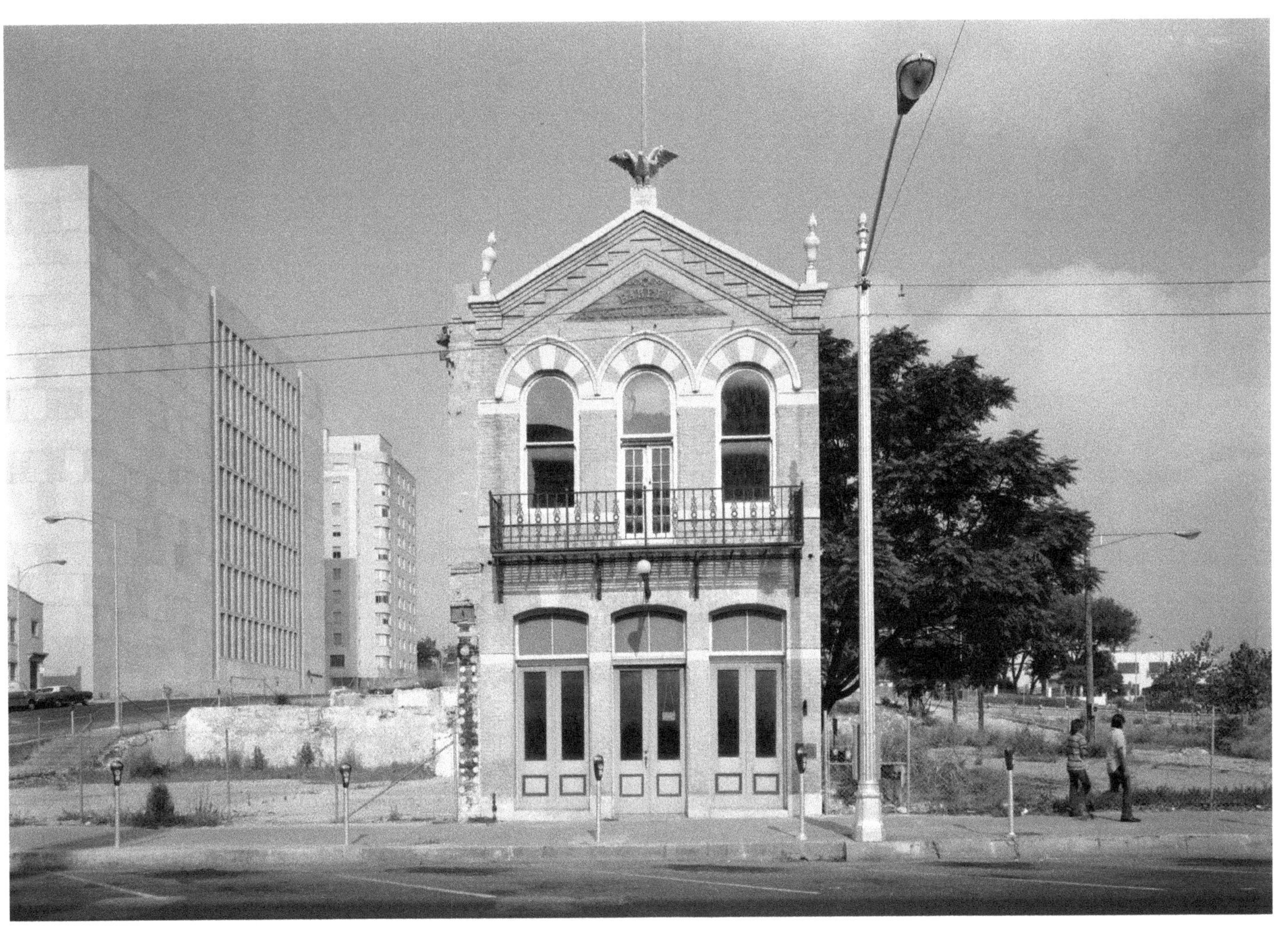

Swedish immigrant Charles Lundberg completed his New Orleans Bakery in 1876, soon adding an ice cream parlor and a huge bread oven. His chosen location on Congress Avenue was ideal, a mere stone's throw from the Capitol. Although the building changed hands several times after Lundberg's death, it remained a bakery until 1937. It is still known locally as the Lundberg Bakery building.

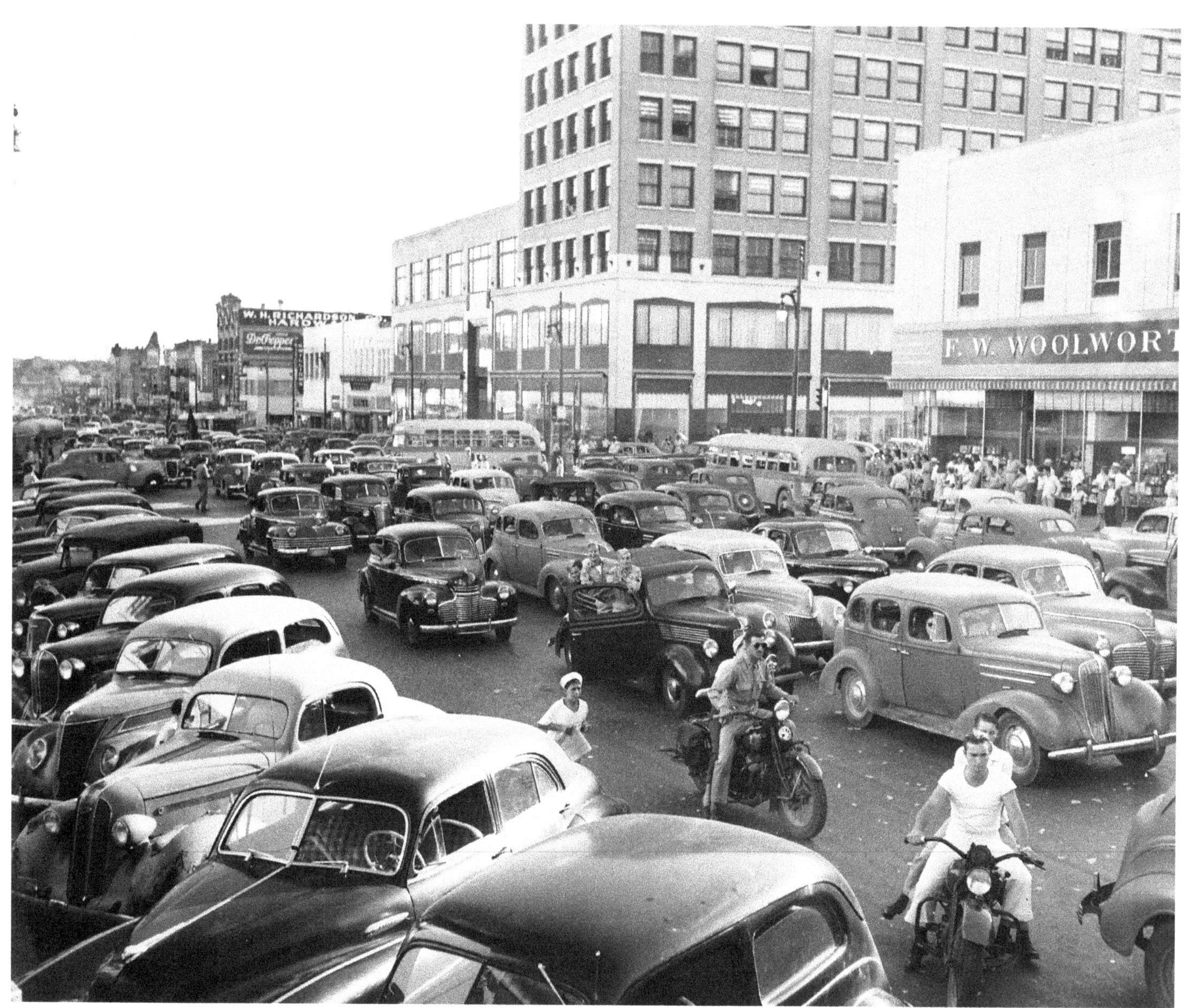

By 1945, Congress Avenue's old brick paving had long since been covered over with modern paving to withstand the traffic of automobiles, buses, and motorcycles. The corner in front of Woolworth's was a popular bus stop for downtown workers. The locally owned Scarbrough's Department Store was in the tall building at center, the city's first "skyscraper" of eight stories.

War, Peace, and Activism

(1941–1979)

During World War II, the University of Texas adopted a year-round curriculum and included war-related courses. Responding to the attack on Pearl Harbor, Austin held its first voluntary blackout in January 1942. The new Del Valle Army Base was completed in the fall, later renamed Bergstrom Army Air Field to honor the first Austinite killed in battle.

In 1946, Austin voters approved $940,000 in bonds to purchase the right-of-way through town for Interstate Highway 35, and the Balcones Research Center for scientific research opened in an abandoned wartime magnesium plant. In 1950, the U.S. Supreme Court found in favor of African American Herman M. Sweatt against the UT Law School for denying him admission. Consequently, UT admitted black people for the first time, but only to some programs. The television era began in Austin on Thanksgiving Day 1952, when KTBC aired the UT-A&M football game. In September 1956 the school board took initial steps to integrate Austin public schools, and in 1958, locally owned Night Hawk restaurants began serving blacks, becoming the first integrated restaurants in town.

The era of protest began in the spring of 1960, when UT students picketed segregated restaurants near campus and joined sit-ins at segregated lunch counters downtown. Austinites heatedly debated commercial development around newly formed Town Lake, and the city council banned gasoline-powered boats. In 1970, Austin's largest antiwar demonstration of the Vietnam era took place after four students were killed at Kent State University. In August, the Armadillo World Headquarters opened and quickly became Austin's best-known live-music venue, and in November, 2,000 demonstrators marched down Congress Avenue, supporting a labor strike by employees of the Economy Furniture Company, most of whom were Mexican Americans.

In 1971, Lady Bird Johnson began the Town Lake Beautification Program, which added a hike-and-bike trail, rest areas, and thousands of trees. More than 40,000 people attended Willie Nelson's first annual Fourth of July Picnic in 1973 near Dripping Springs. In 1974, the city council passed the Historic Zoning Ordinance and Creeks Ordinance to protect Austin's historic buildings and natural environment from escalating development, partly a response to destruction of some of its finest Victorian homes.

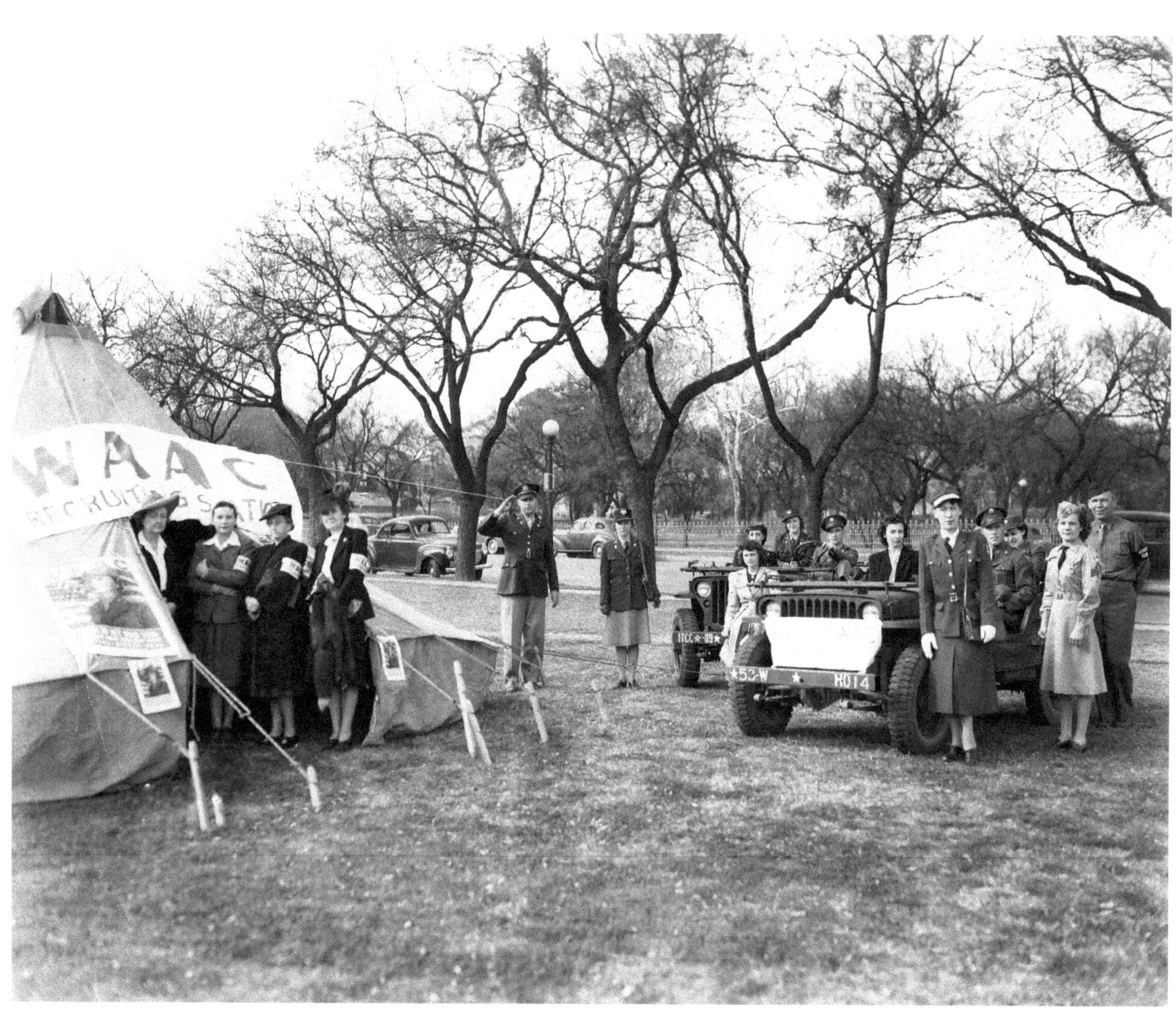

Members of the Women's Army Corps (and others) pose for a photographer at Camp Mabry during World War II. Military personnel also were stationed at Bergstrom Air Force Base, formerly Del Valle Army Air Field, and at Camp Swift, outside Bastrop, Texas, a nearby town east of Austin.

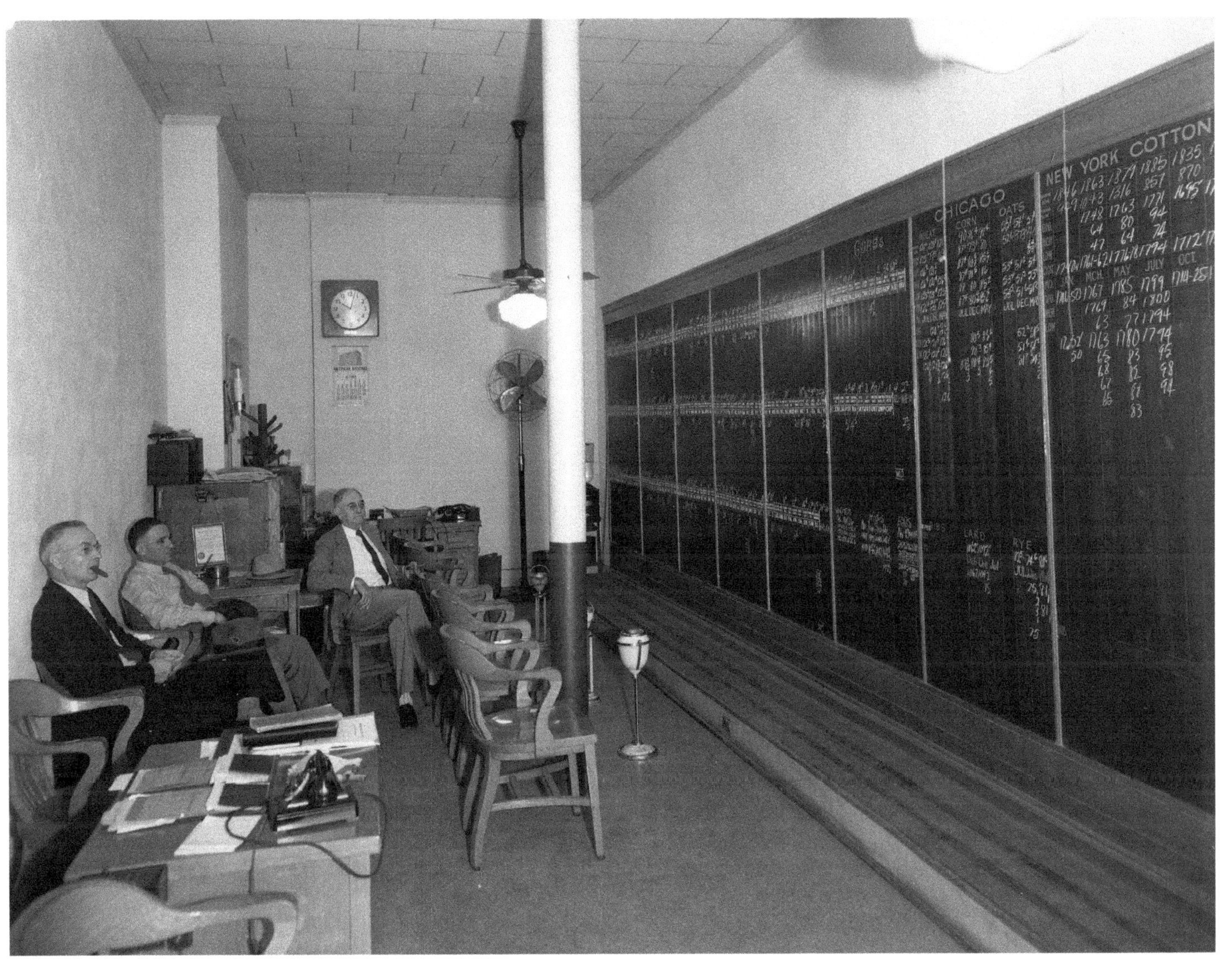

Cotton was the major cash crop in Central Texas, not only in the nineteenth century but well into the twentieth. These gentlemen are keeping track of the market in the Austin office of Merrill Lynch, Pierce, Fenner & Smith in 1941.

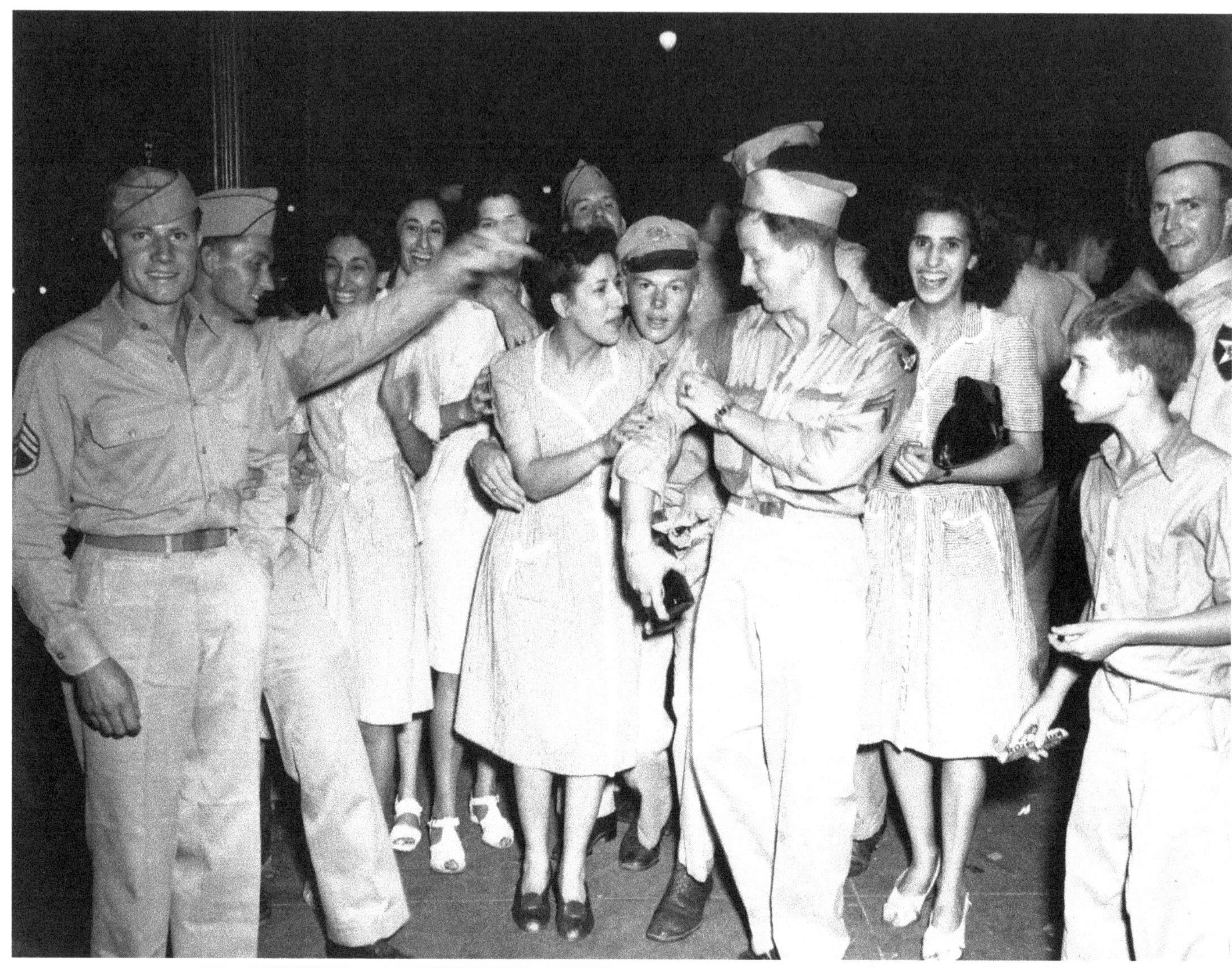

On August 14, 1945, President Truman announced that Japan had surrendered, thus ending World War II. Soldiers from local and nearby military bases joined Austinites in victory celebrations throughout the city. On downtown streets, the dancing, singing, and general merrymaking continued past "the wee small hours of the morning" of the following day.

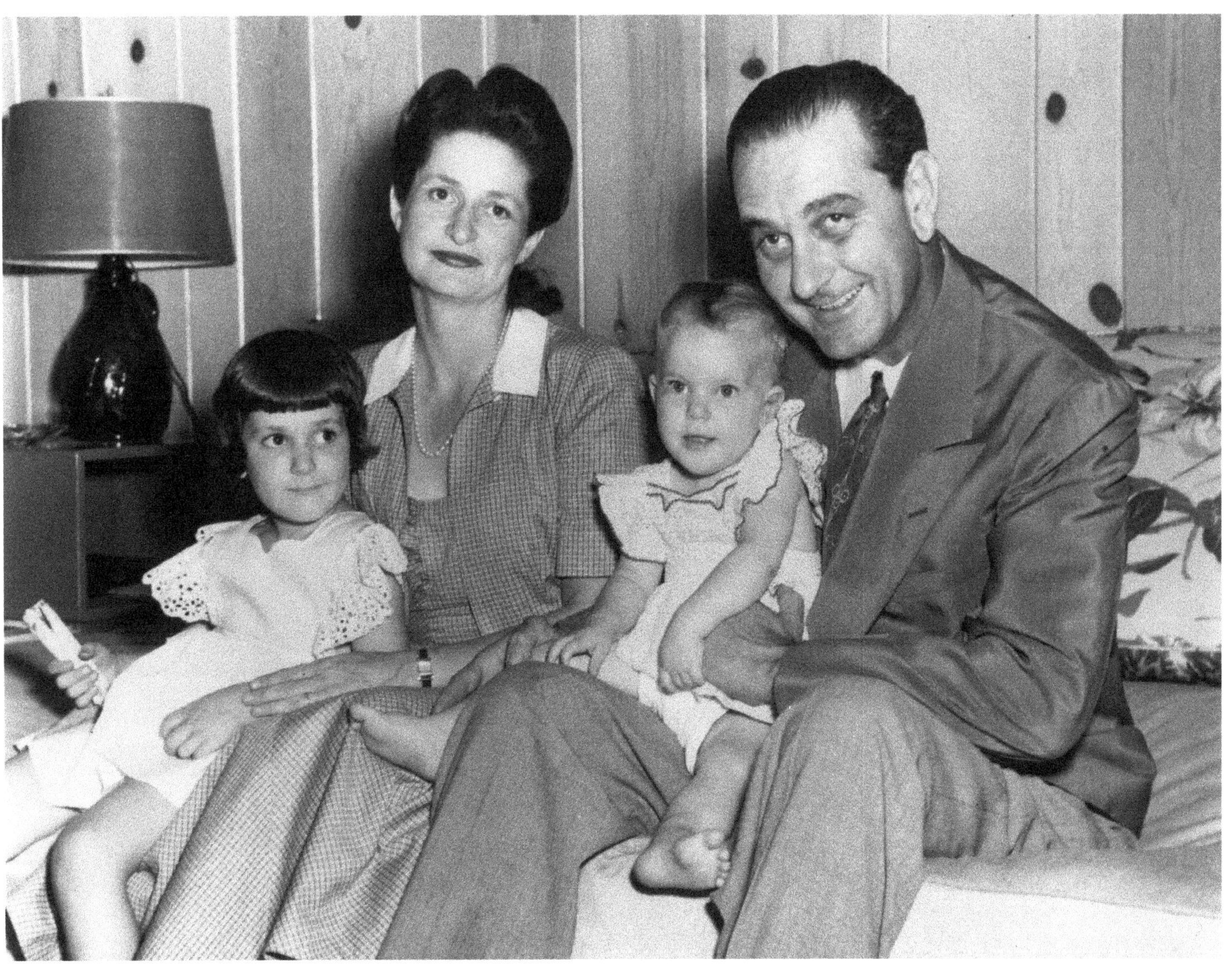

On election day in 1948, U.S. Senate candidate Lyndon B. Johnson awaits election returns with his wife, Lady Bird, and his two young daughters, Lynda (left) and Luci in their Austin home on Dillman Street. Johnson won and went on to be an effective senator, mastering the organization and rules of the Senate. He was elected majority whip in 1951 and became the youngest Senate minority leader in 1953.

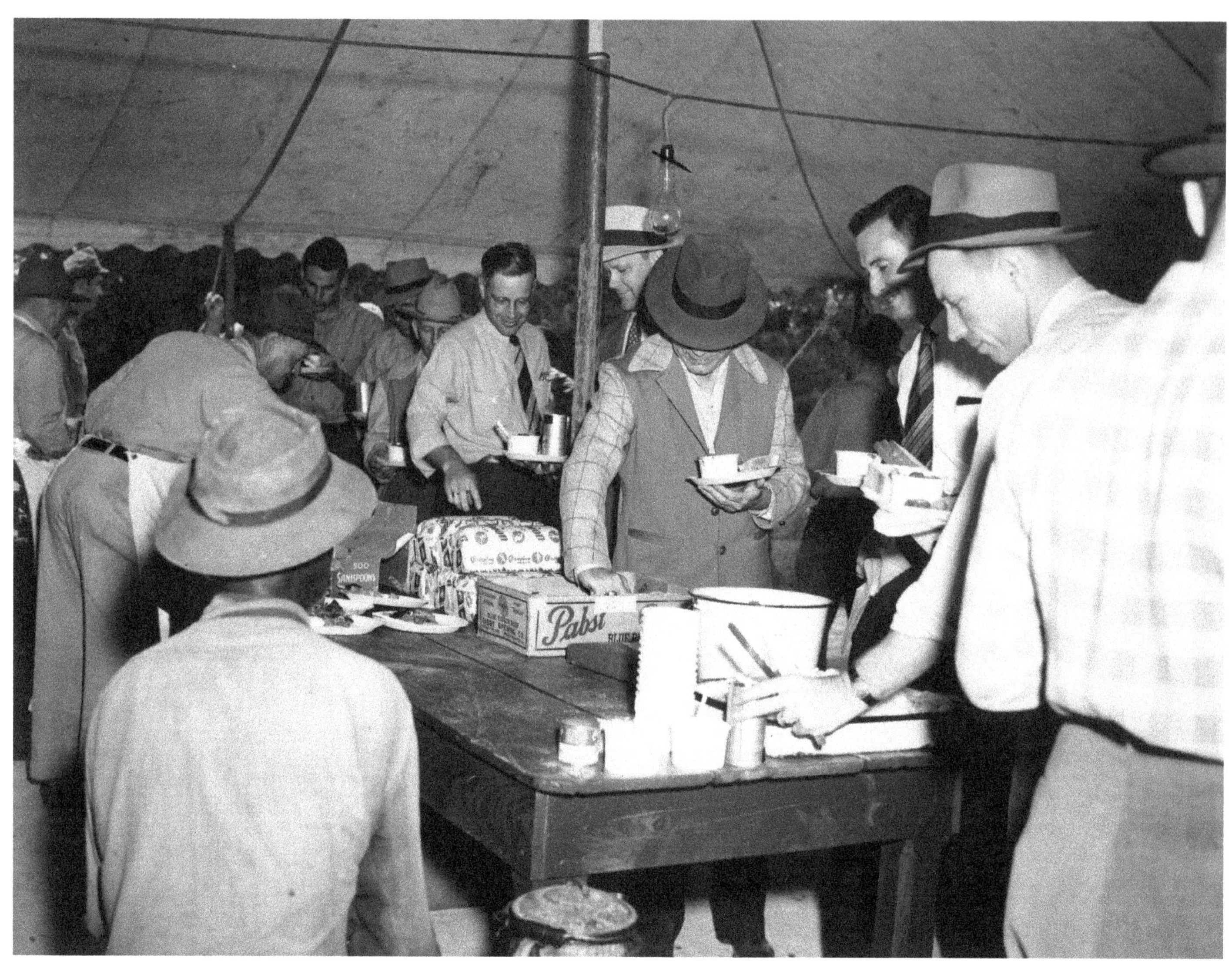

Judging from the fashionable two-patterned jacket worn by the man at center (face obscured by his hat), this Austin Police Department picnic, with food served inside a tent, was held in the late 1940s or early 1950s, probably at Zilker Park.

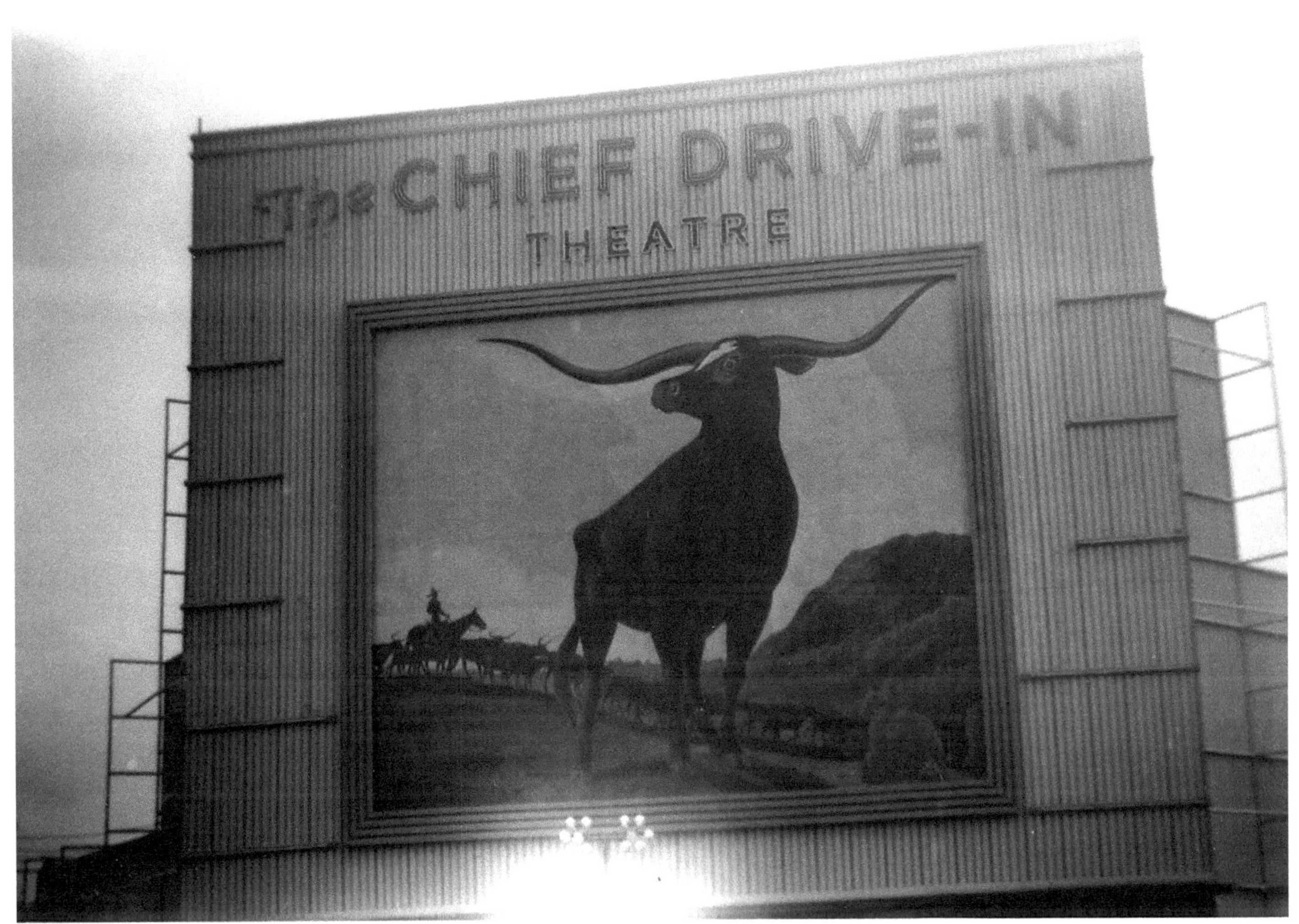

In the postwar years through the 1960s, drive-in movie theaters, located on spacious lots away from the center of town, were the precursors of watching movies at home on television and almost as comfortable. Austin's Chief Drive-In Theater featured, appropriately, a Texas longhorn steer as its design motif on the back of its mammoth screen in 1952.

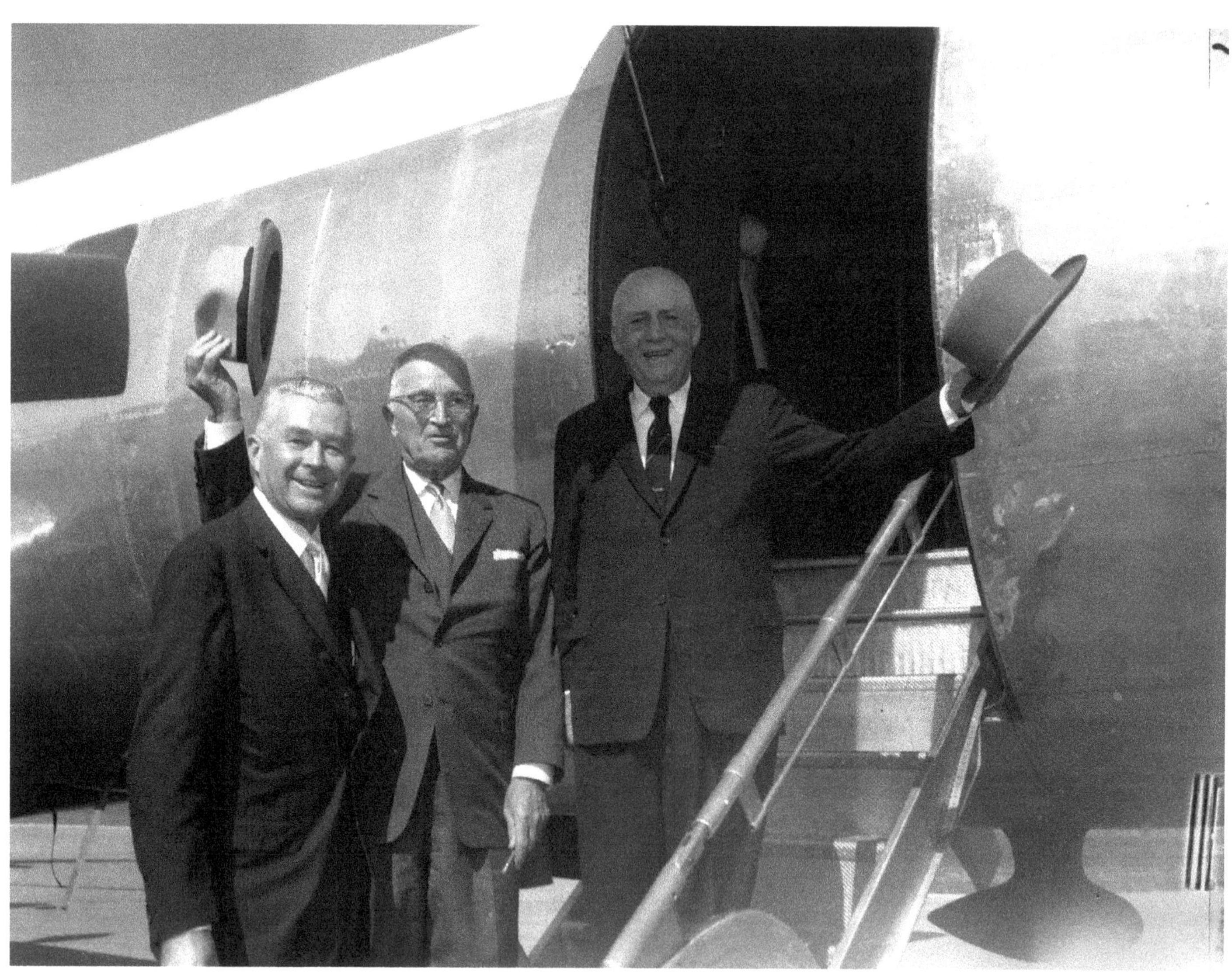

One of several U.S. presidents who visited Austin over the years was Harry Truman, photographed disembarking from his airplane. As vice-president, Truman became president when Franklin D. Roosevelt died in 1945 before World War II ended. Truman was reelected and served until 1953, when General Dwight D. Eisenhower succeeded him in holding the nation's highest office.

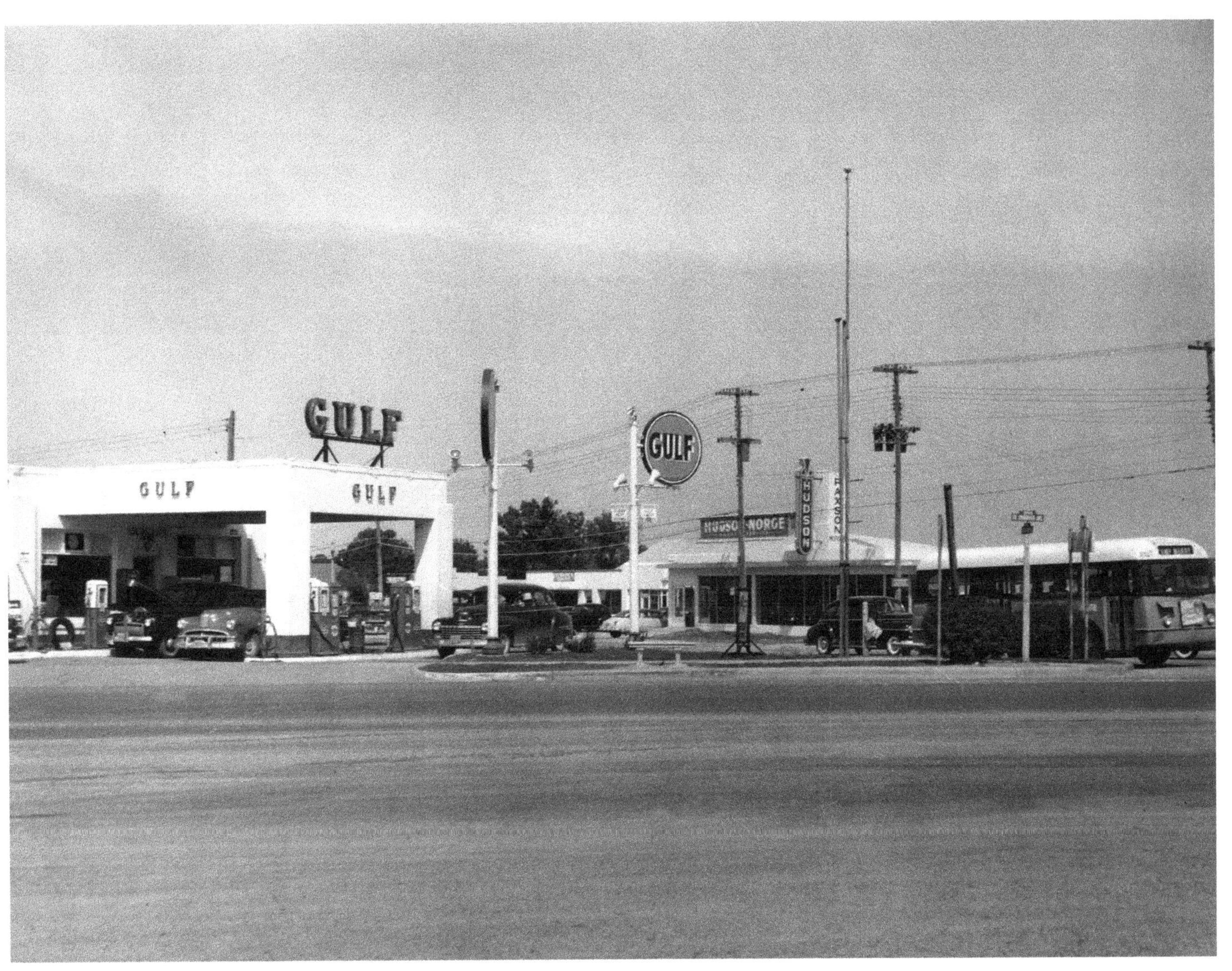

It's difficult to find a gasoline station in the central business district of Austin these days, but in 1951, motorists could have their tanks filled for them by uniformed attendants at this Gulf station at the corner of Riverside Drive and South Congress Avenue. Note the streamlined city bus at right. Buses had replaced electric streetcars in 1940.

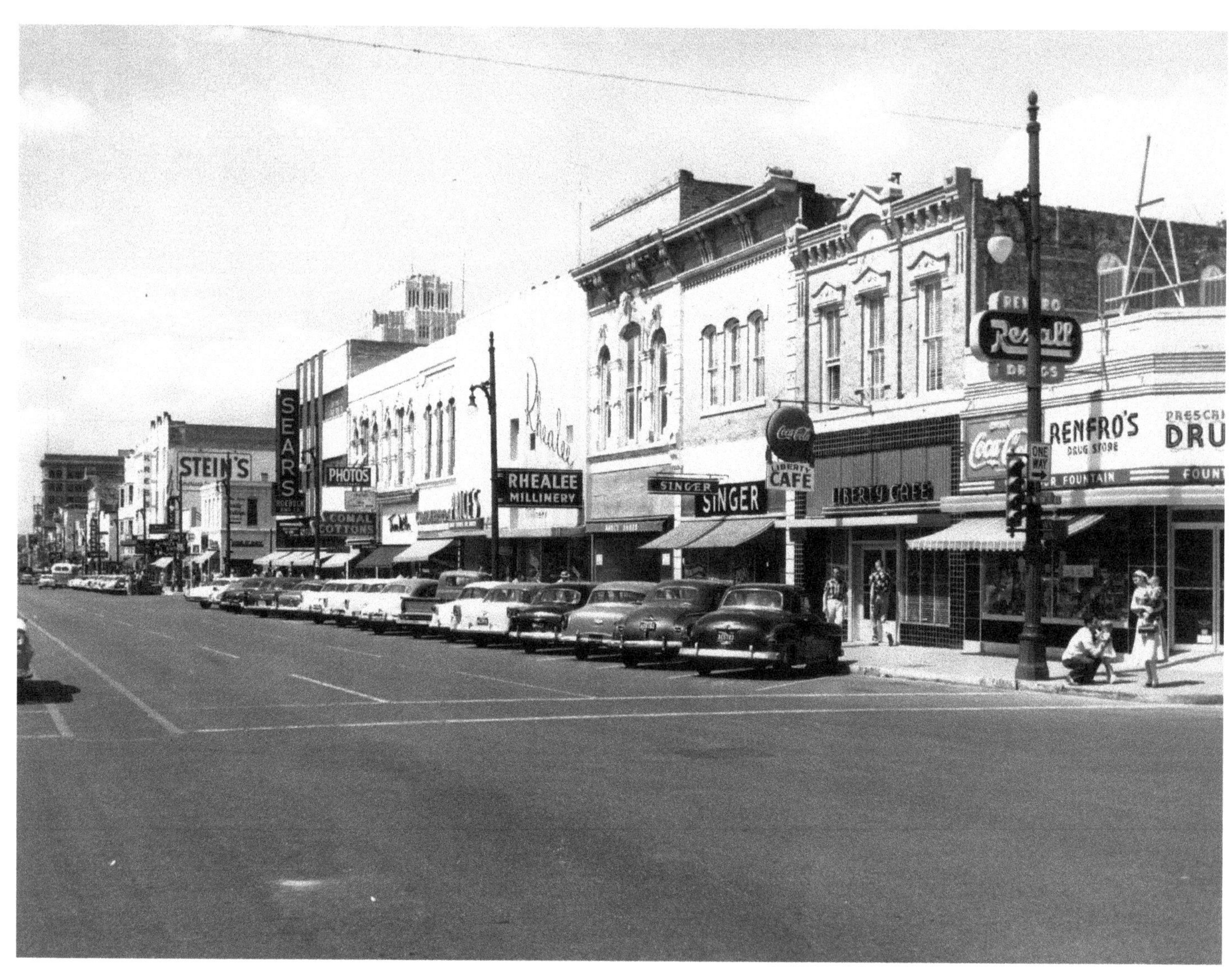

In the postwar years of the late 1940's and early 1950's, retail businesses on Congress Avenue—including clothing stores, Sears, and Renfro's Rexall Drug Store—were prospering. But suburbs were proliferating as well, and soon they would draw business away from the original downtown area.

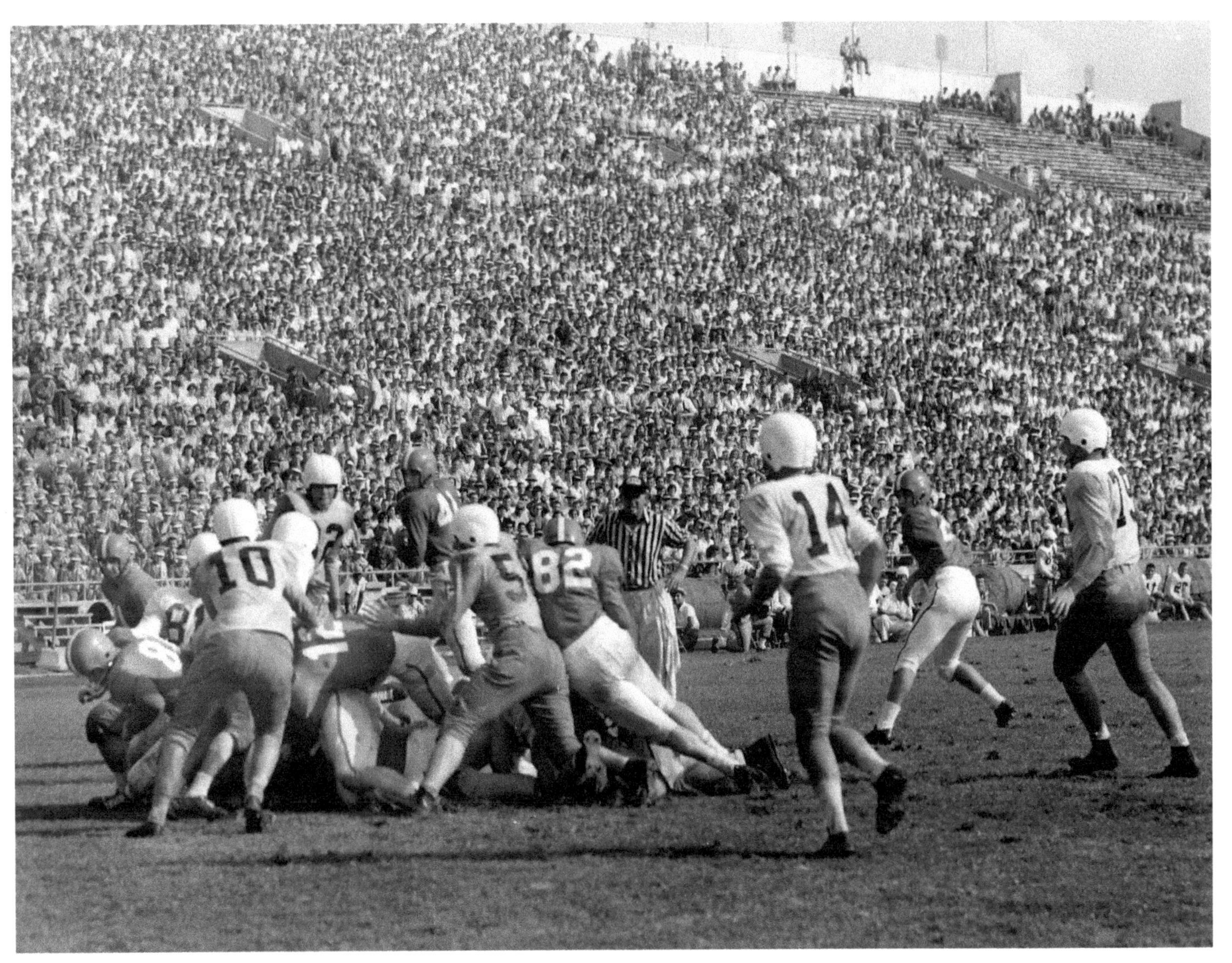

As the crowded stands clearly indicate, football was a favorite spectator sport at the University of Texas in the 1950s and 1960s. In December 1969, President Richard M. Nixon proclaimed the undefeated UT Longhorns the Number One college football team in the country.

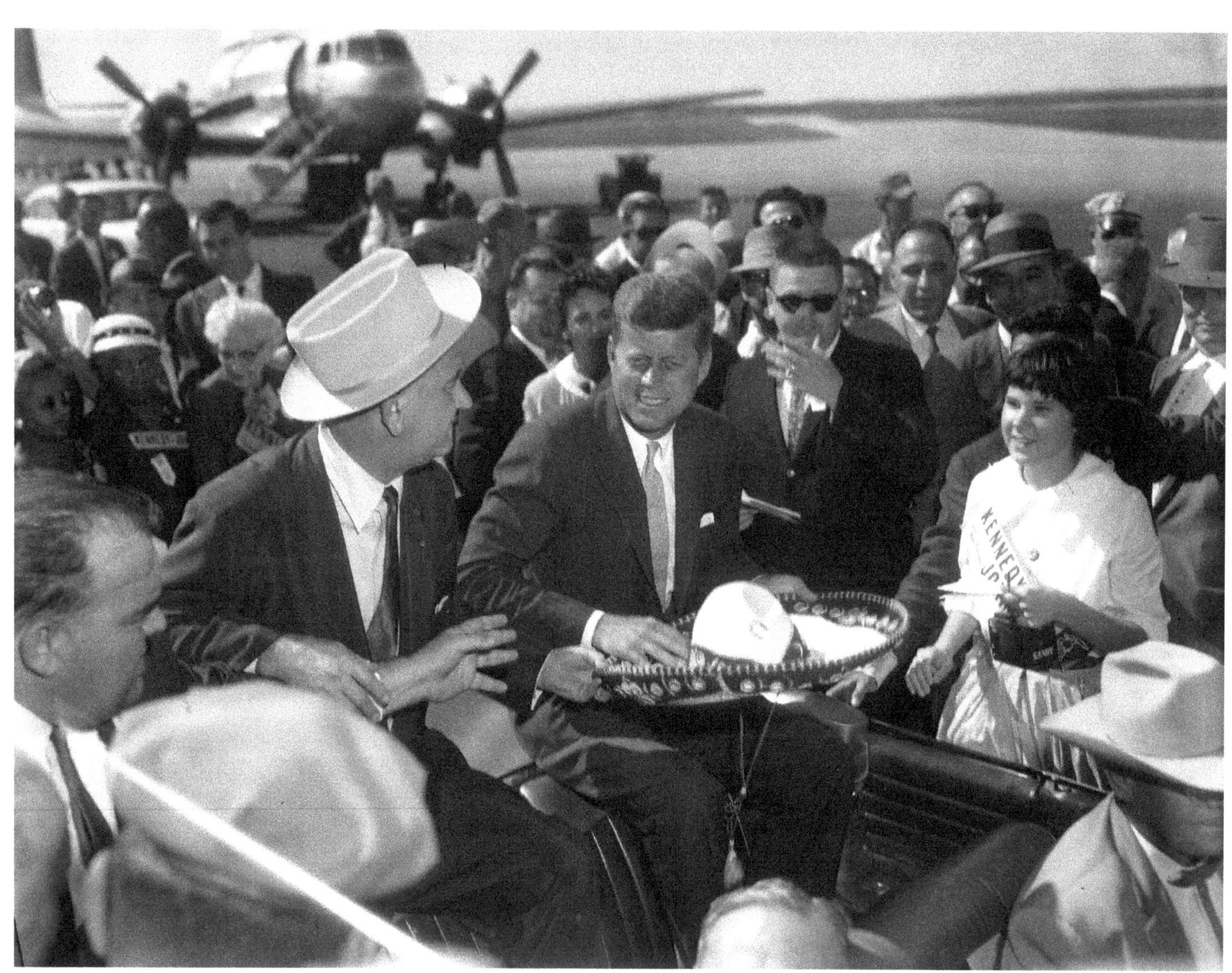

Presidential candidate John F. Kennedy receives a sombrero during a 1960 campaign stop in Austin with running mate Lyndon B. Johnson.

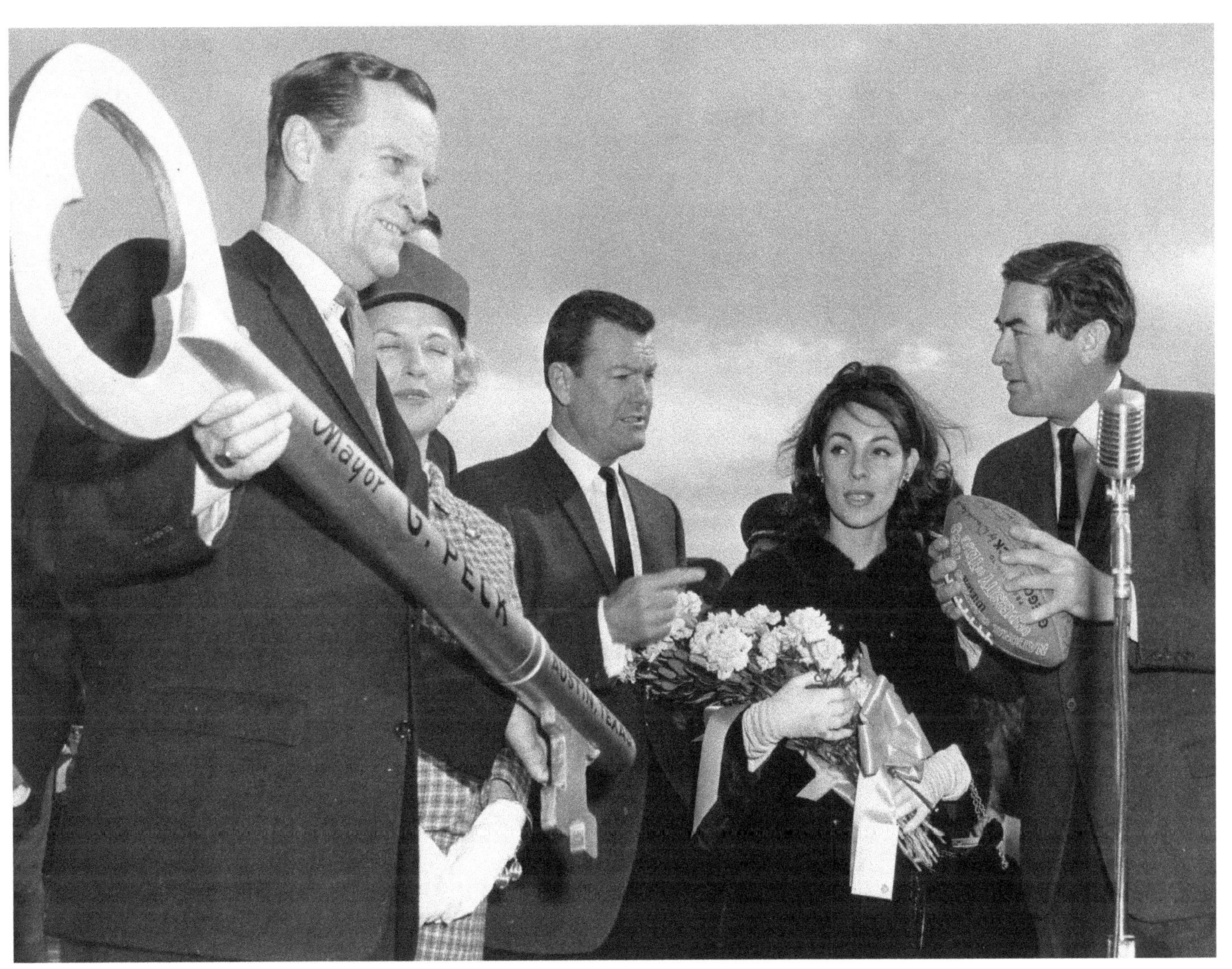

Visiting Austin in 1964, Hollywood leading man Gregory Peck (right), winner of the Academy Award for his performance in 1962's *To Kill a Mockingbird,* receives a signed Longhorn football from famed University of Texas coach Darrell K. Royal (center). Peck was presented with the key to the city as well. The university's Memorial Stadium would later be renamed in honor of Coach Royal.

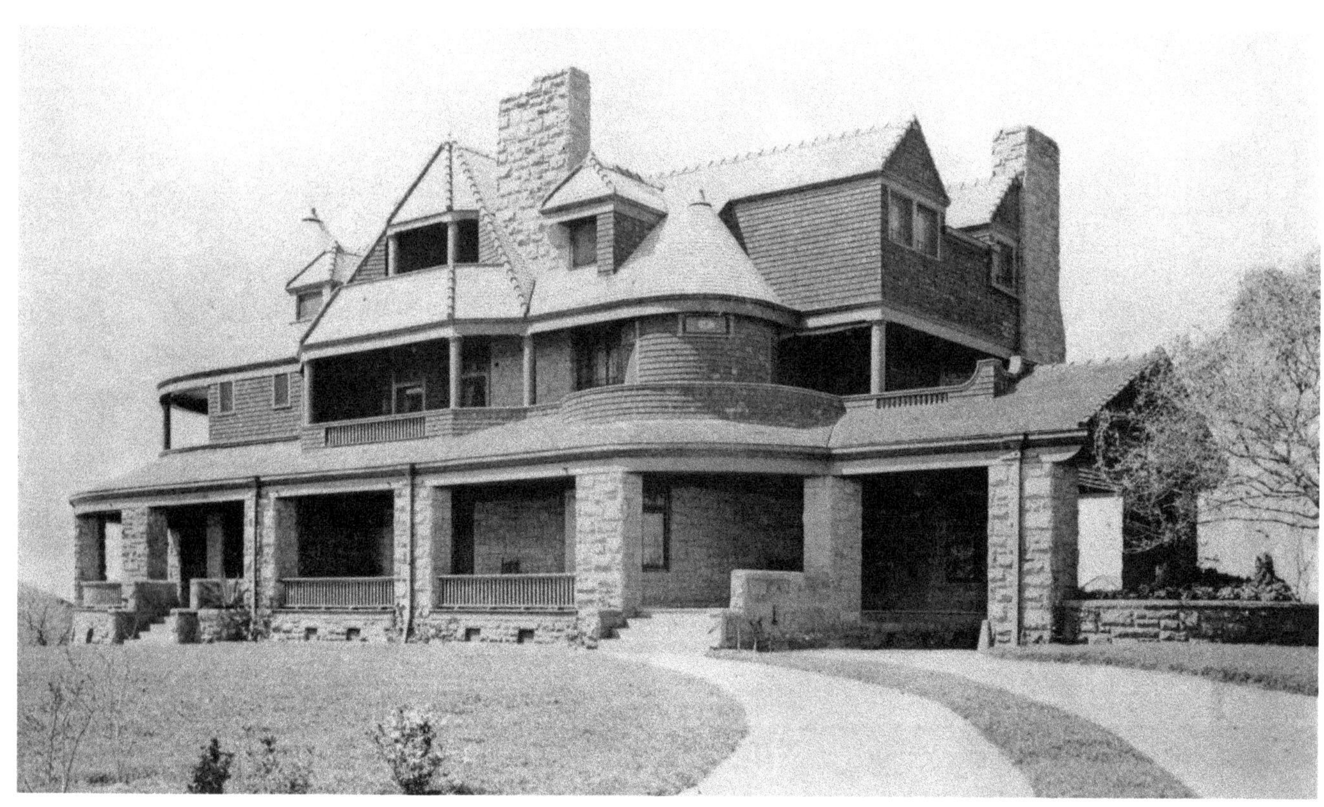

Built in 1891, the residence of Colonel Edward M. House, 1704 West Avenue, was designed by New York architect Frank Freeman in the Richardsonian shingle style with red sandstone masonry. An influential figure in the administration of President Woodrow Wilson, Colonel House had admired Freeman's work and apparently wanted a modern-style home. Unfortunately, the house was destroyed by fire in 1968.

With his own hands, no blueprints, and minimal assistance, Austinite Isamu Taniguchi created the peaceful Oriental Gardens and Teahouse at Zilker Park as his gift to the city. He completed the three-acre project in 1969. Taniguchi persuaded local businesses to donate everything needed for the site. It features waterfalls, paths, handhewn bridges, and six ponds subtly shaped to spell AUSTIN when viewed from above.

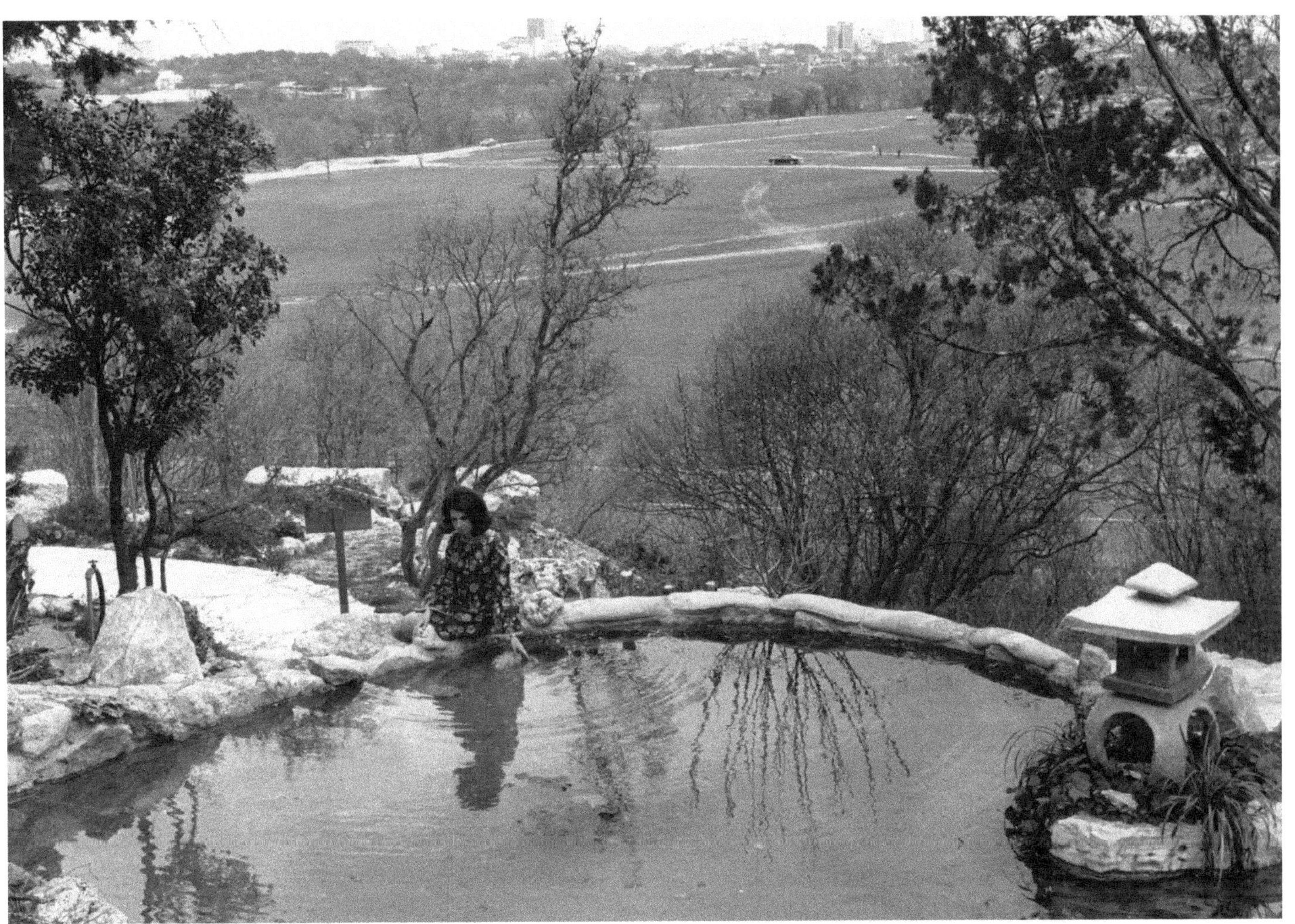

Isamu Taniguchi, creator of the Oriental Gardens in Zilker Gardens at Zilker Park, sits on his handmade Half-Moon bridge. Taniguchi arrived in Texas from California during World War II as a detainee at a Japanese-internment camp in South Texas. After the war, he settled and farmed near Harlingen before sending both his sons to the University of Texas. He later retired to Austin at their suggestion.

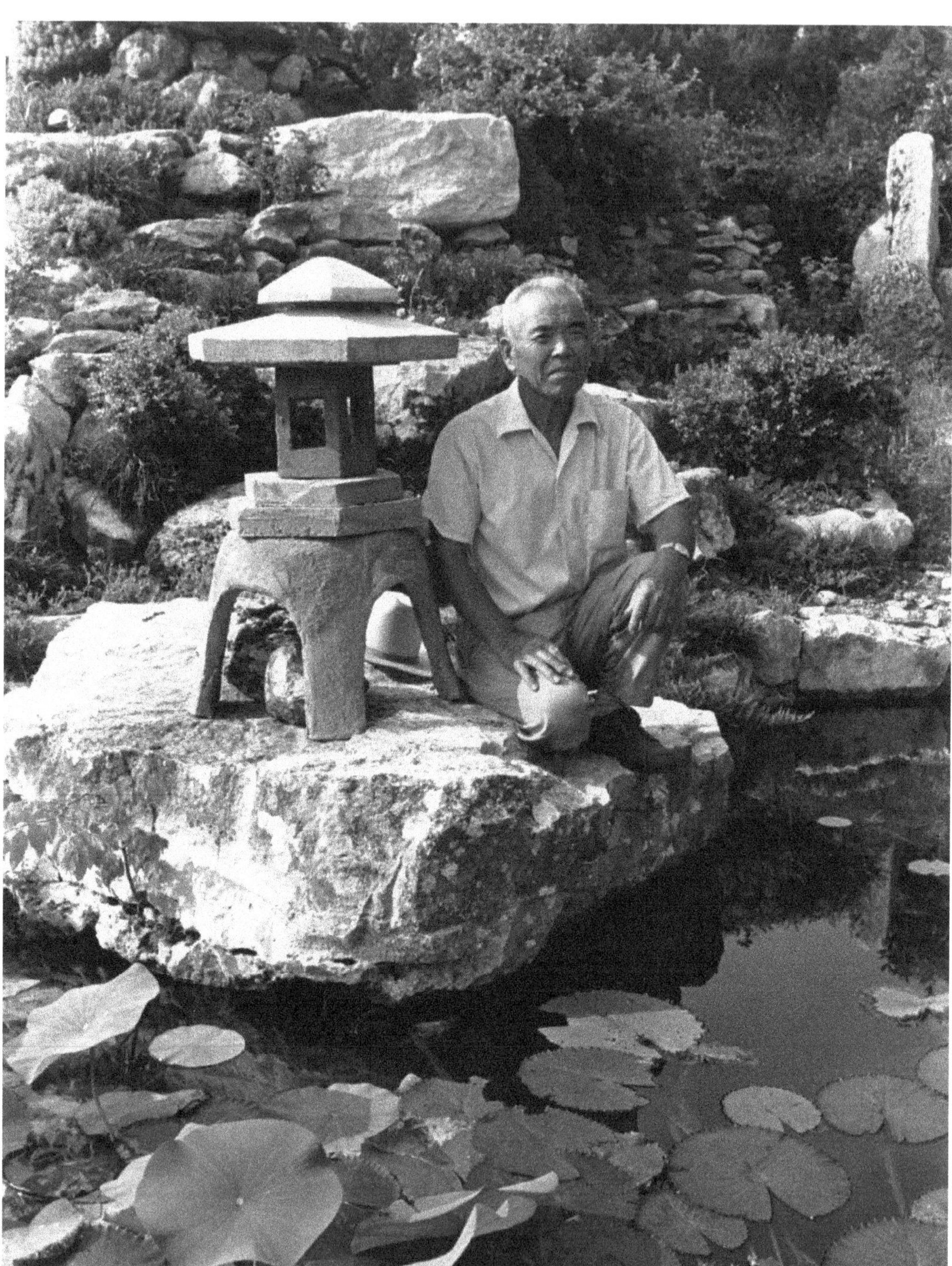

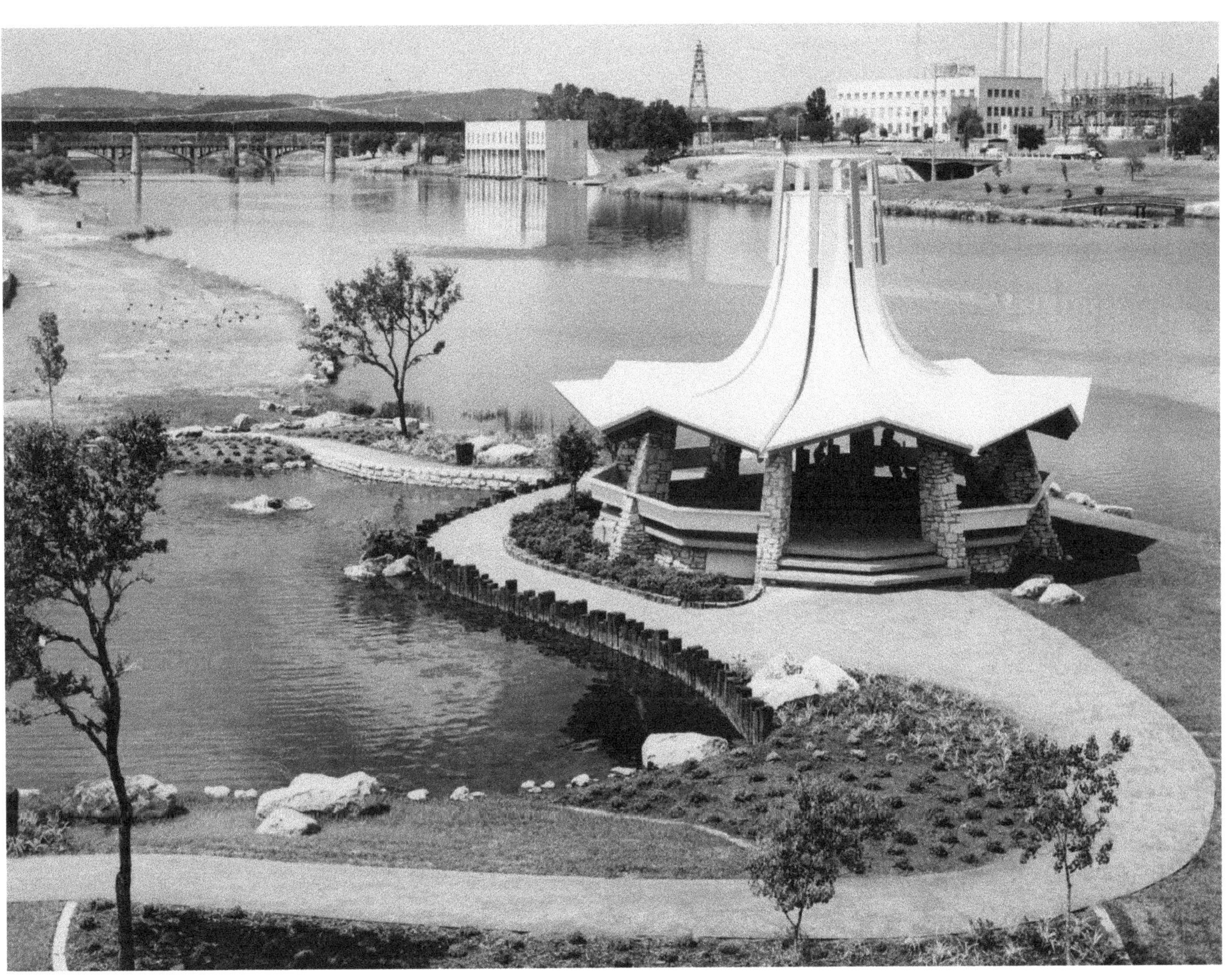

An artificial lake on the Colorado River, Austin's Town Lake was created in 1960 by construction of Longhorn Dam. Civic structures such as the Municipal Auditorium and the landmark Gazebo (foreground) dot the shoreline. The Gazebo was built by the Austin chapter of Women in Construction and dedicated in 1970, intended to inspire more beautification projects along Town Lake's shore.

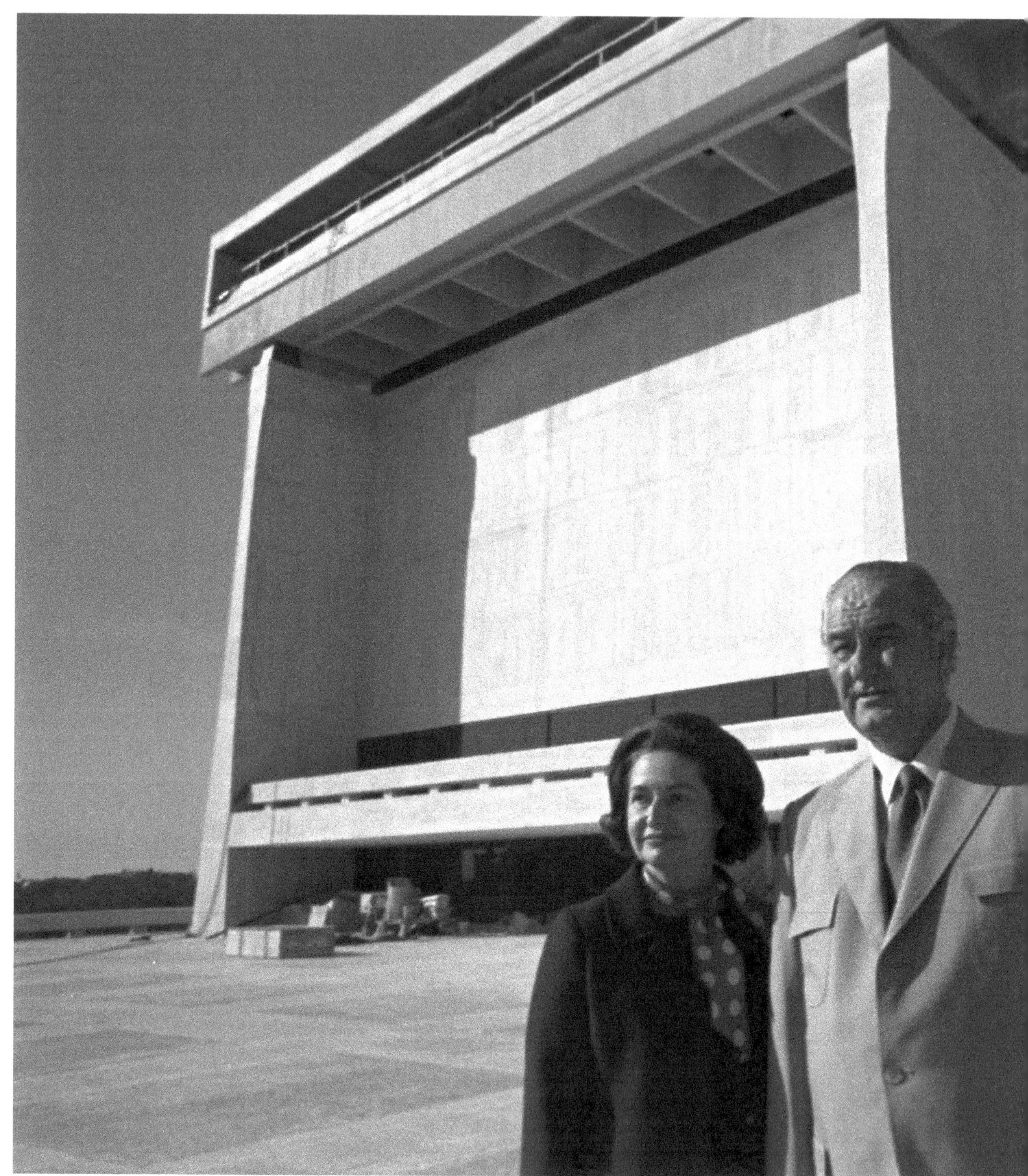

Lady Bird Johnson and Lyndon Johnson stand before the new Lyndon Baines Johnson Library and Museum, dedicated on May 22, 1971 at the University of Texas. It was the nation's fifth presidential library and the first located on a university campus. A center for scholarly research, it contains the most comprehensive single collection of material on a U.S. president, encompassing LBJ's entire political career.

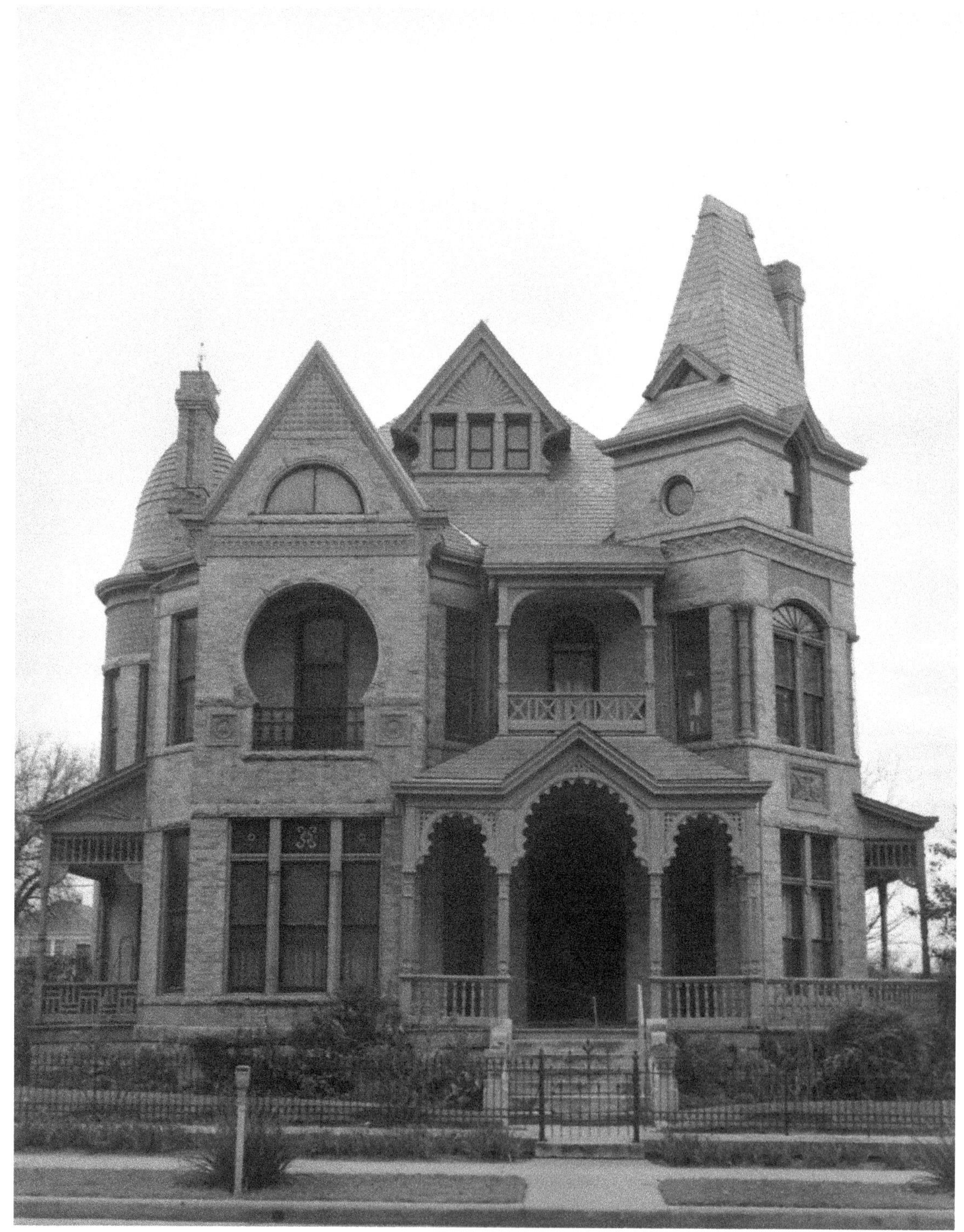

The Butler House, 309 West Eleventh Street, was built in 1887 by Michael Butler, founder of the Butler Brick Company. To construct the Gothic Revival mansion, said to be Austin's first electrified home, Butler used his own bricks and pink granite like that on the Capitol. With its keyhole arch, turrets, and gargoyles, it reflected the ebullience of the Victorian era—until it was demolished in 1971 to make way for a parking lot.

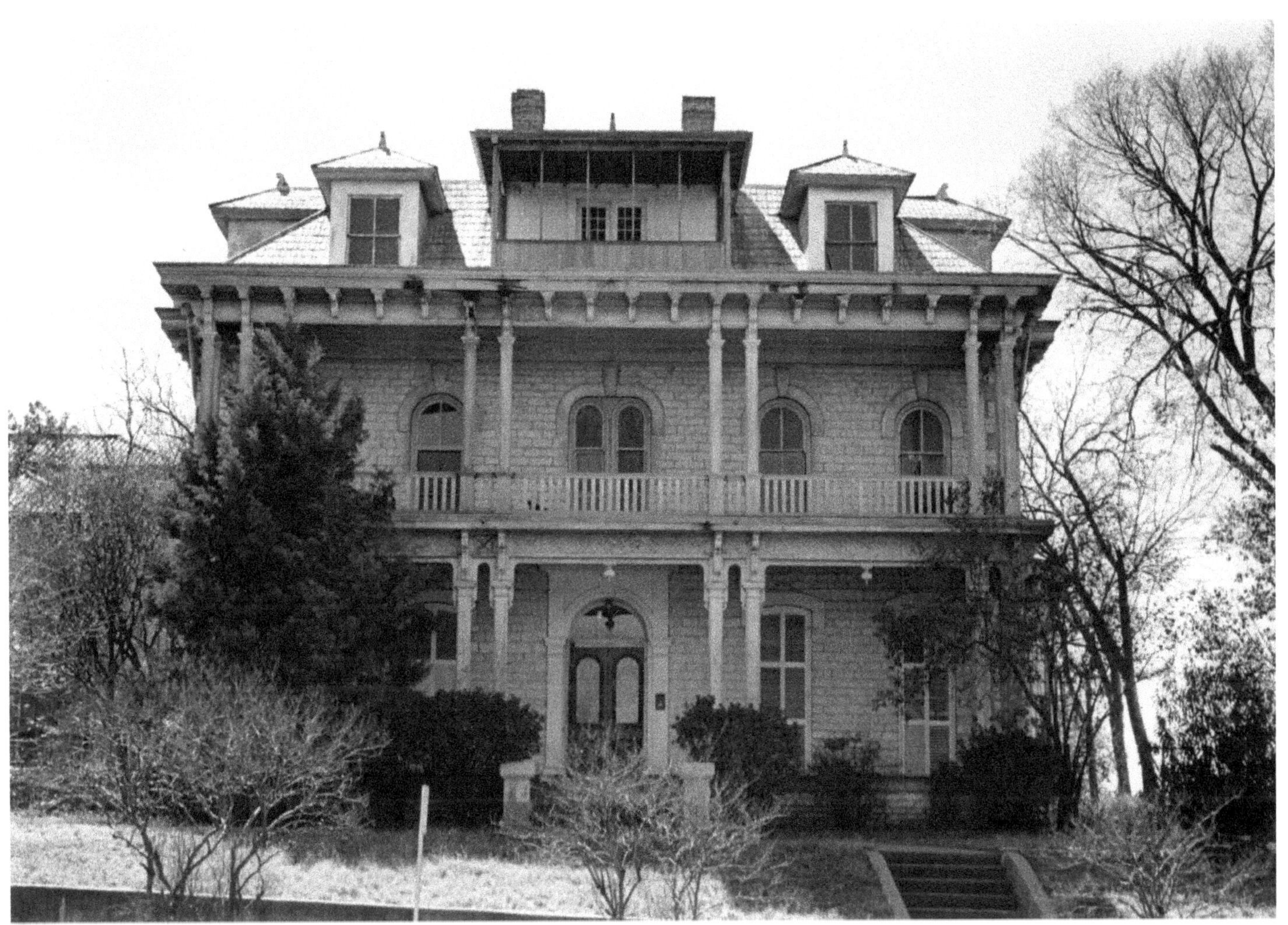

Hunnicutt House, 405 West Twelfth Street, was built in 1872 by Dr. M. A. Taylor. It boasted 22-inch-thick limestone walls and a dramatic interior staircase. Originally facing Guadalupe Street, in 1925 it was moved around the corner, after Taylor's widow deeded it to the Christian Church. It was demolished in 1974 and replaced by the church's parking lot, despite valiant efforts to save it by local preservation groups.

The John Bremond House, in the Bremond Block Historic District, was built in 1887 for Eugene Bremond's brother, John Bremond, Jr., a merchant. Like most homes on the block, this Victorian structure with lacy ironwork was designed by George Fiegel. Saved from demolition and restored by the Texas Classroom Teachers Association as its headquarters, it was the first Austin home to have indoor bathrooms.

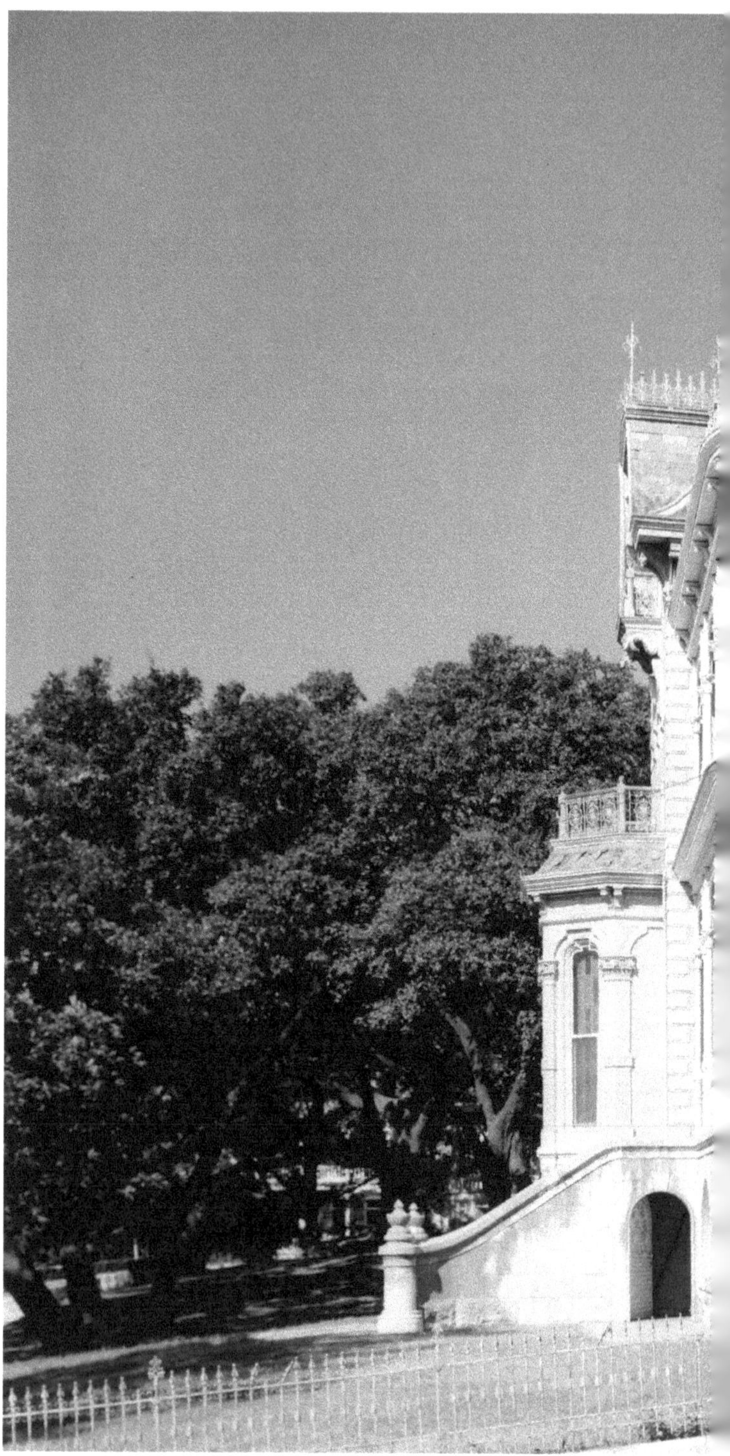

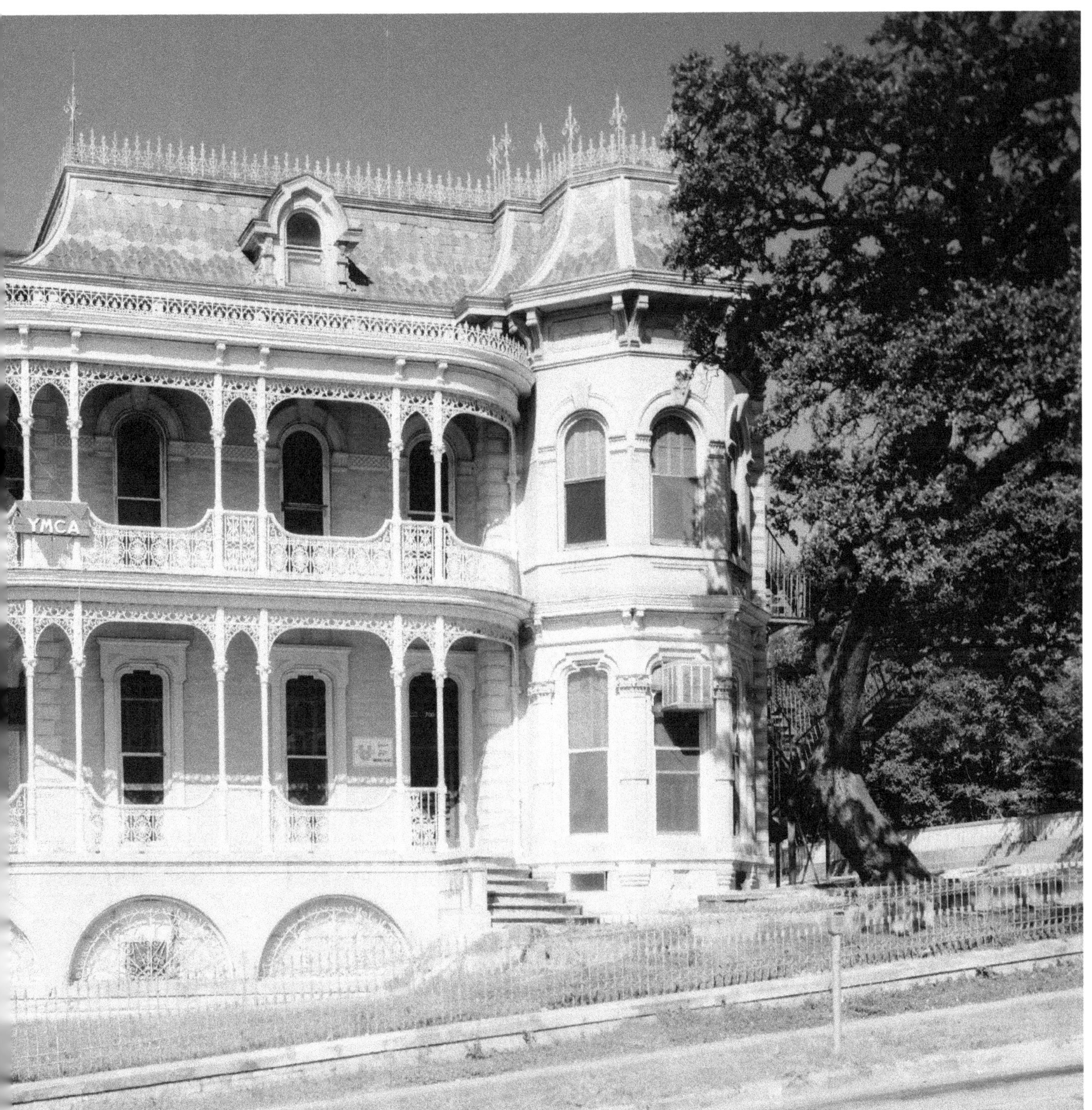
YMCA

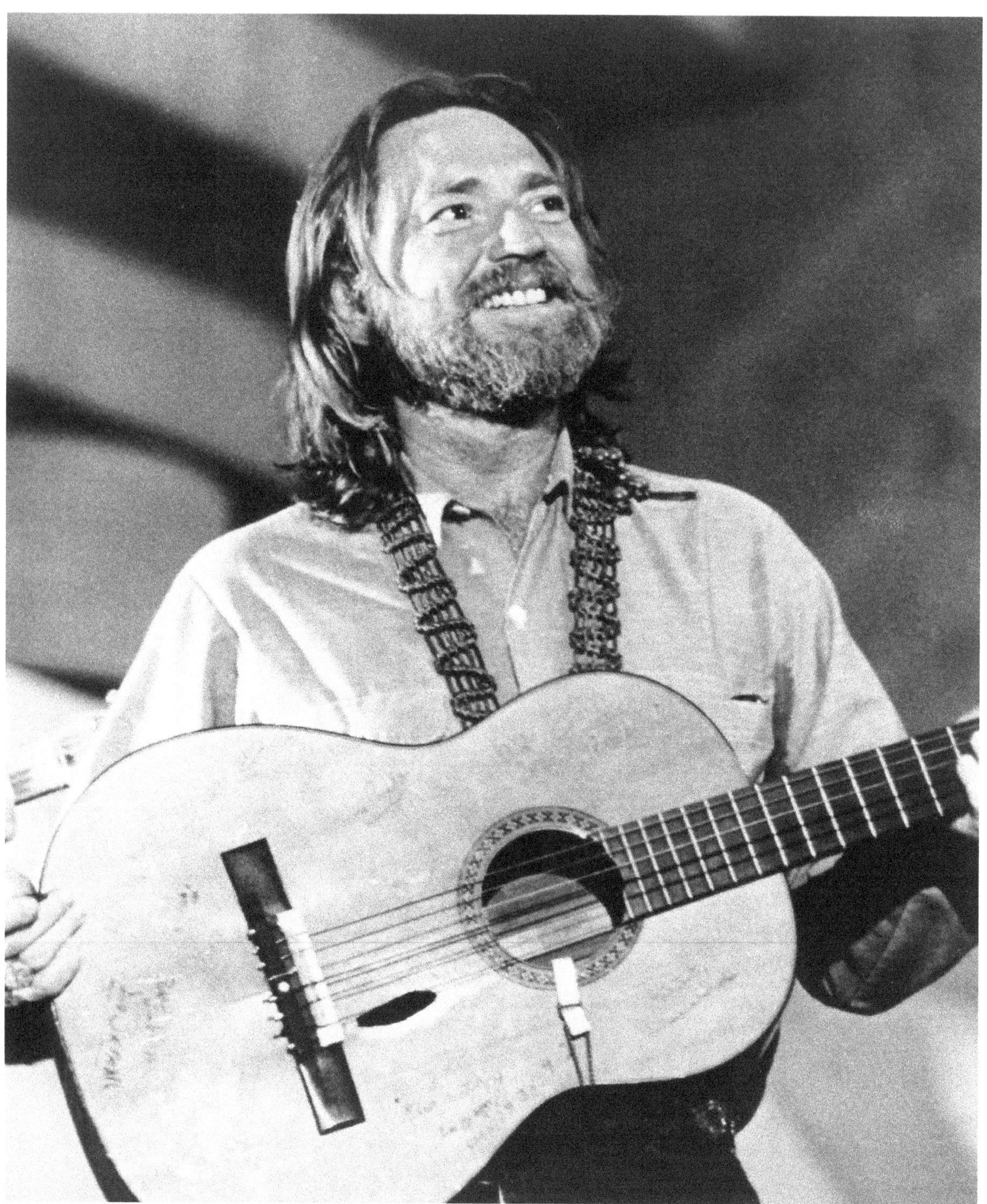

In the 1970s, Austin was the birthplace of "progressive country" music, which had a major influence on the nation's music industry. One of Austin's favorite resident performers, then and now, Willie Nelson is shown performing at his annual Fourth of July Picnic, a live-music extravaganza that has been known to attract as many as 100,000 fans. Besides singing and songwriting, Willie has starred in several films.

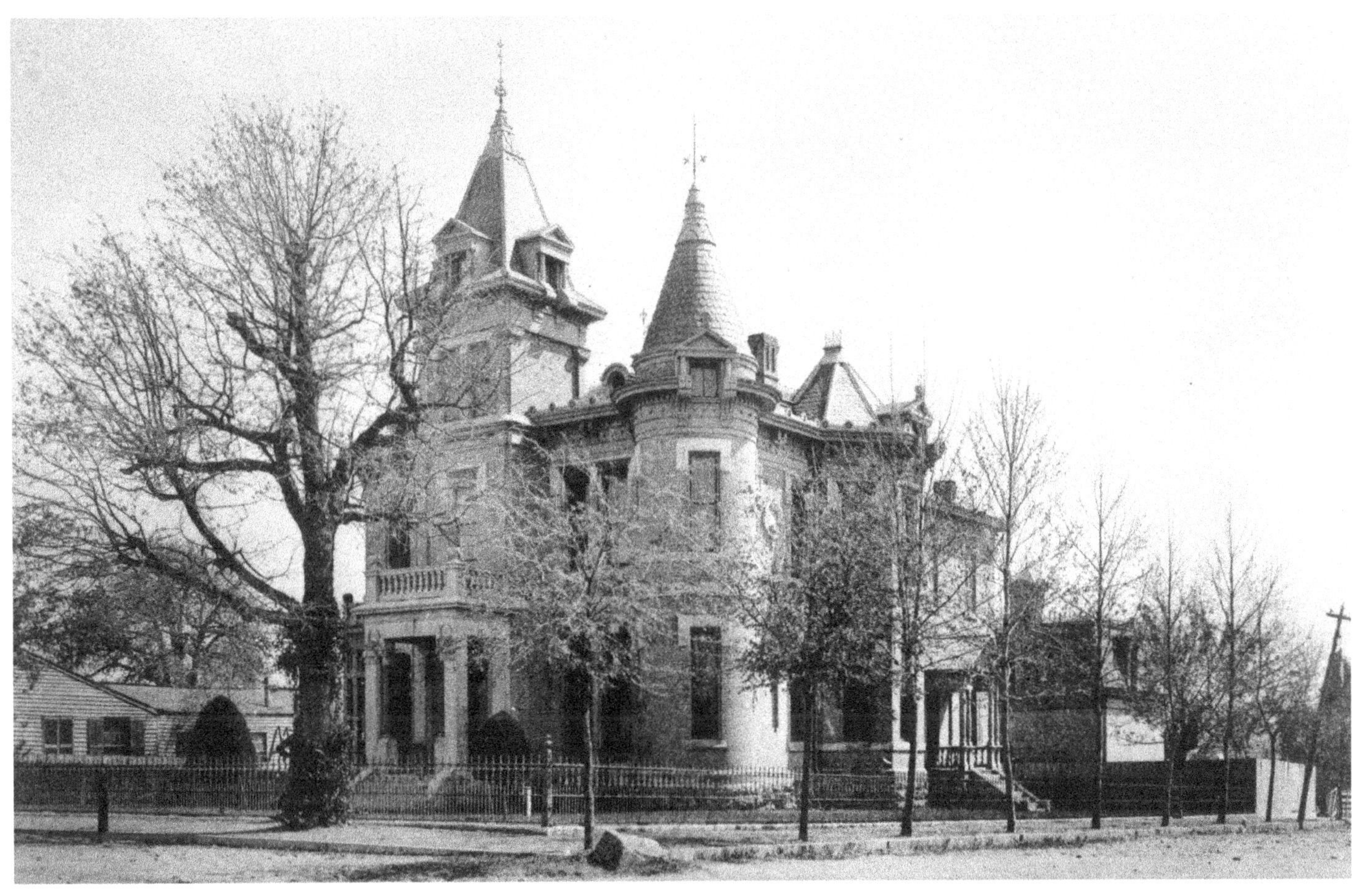

The John H. Houghton House, 307 West Twelfth Street, was built circa 1886, designed by architect James Wahrenberger. Besides artful stained glass and woodwork, its interior boasted an octagonal dining room and a large ballroom. It fell to the wrecking ball in 1973, supplanted by an eight-story parking garage. The loss of this landmark, and others, motivated Austin to legislate against further loss of its architectural history.

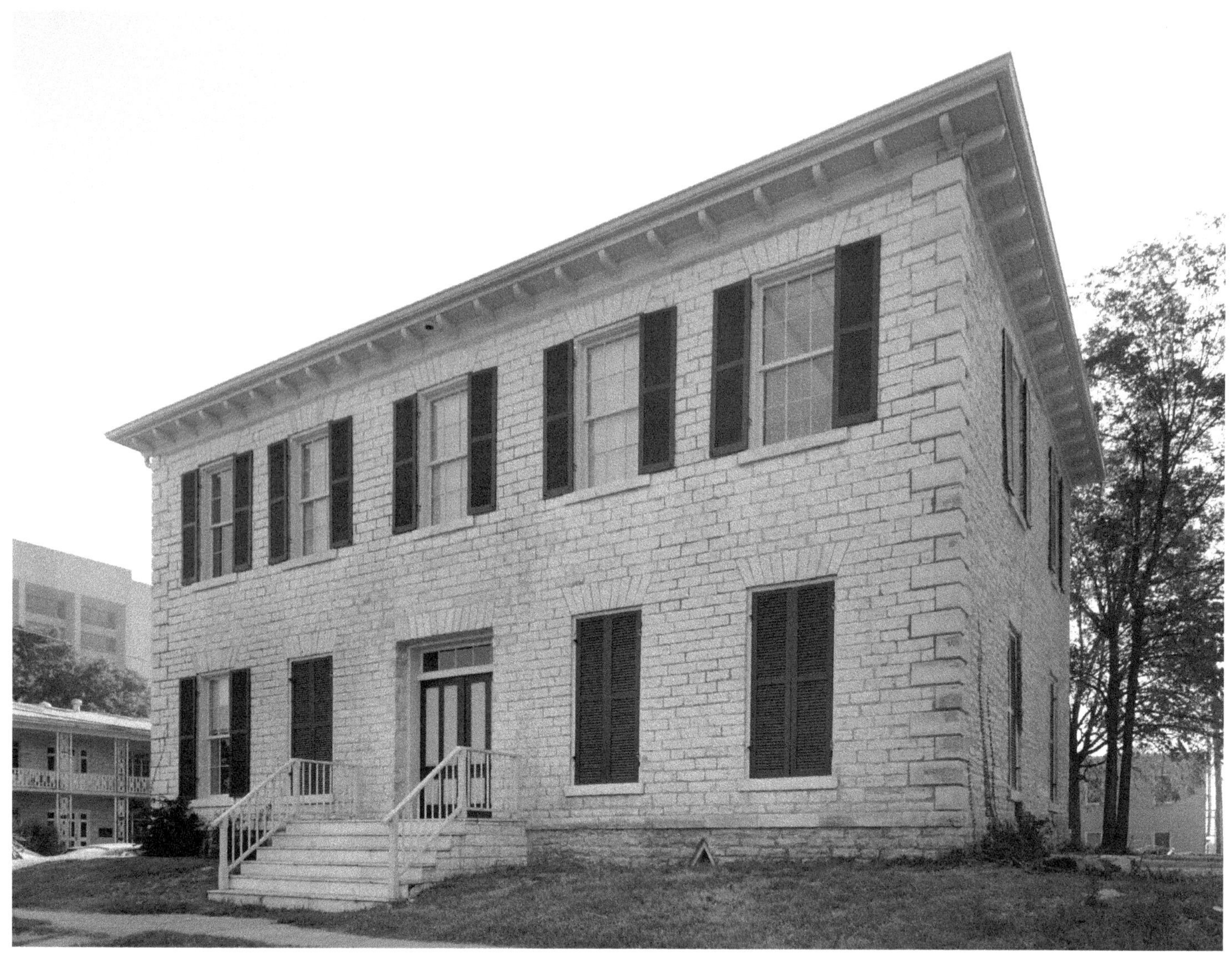

At 1511 Colorado Street, the Carrington-Covert House is one of the last remaining 1850s residential buildings in the State Capitol area. The limestone structure was built by Leonidas Davis Carrington, a local merchant and land speculator. Restored in 1973 by the Texas State Historical Survey Committee, it became the committee's headquarters and offices and is listed on the National Register of Historic Places.

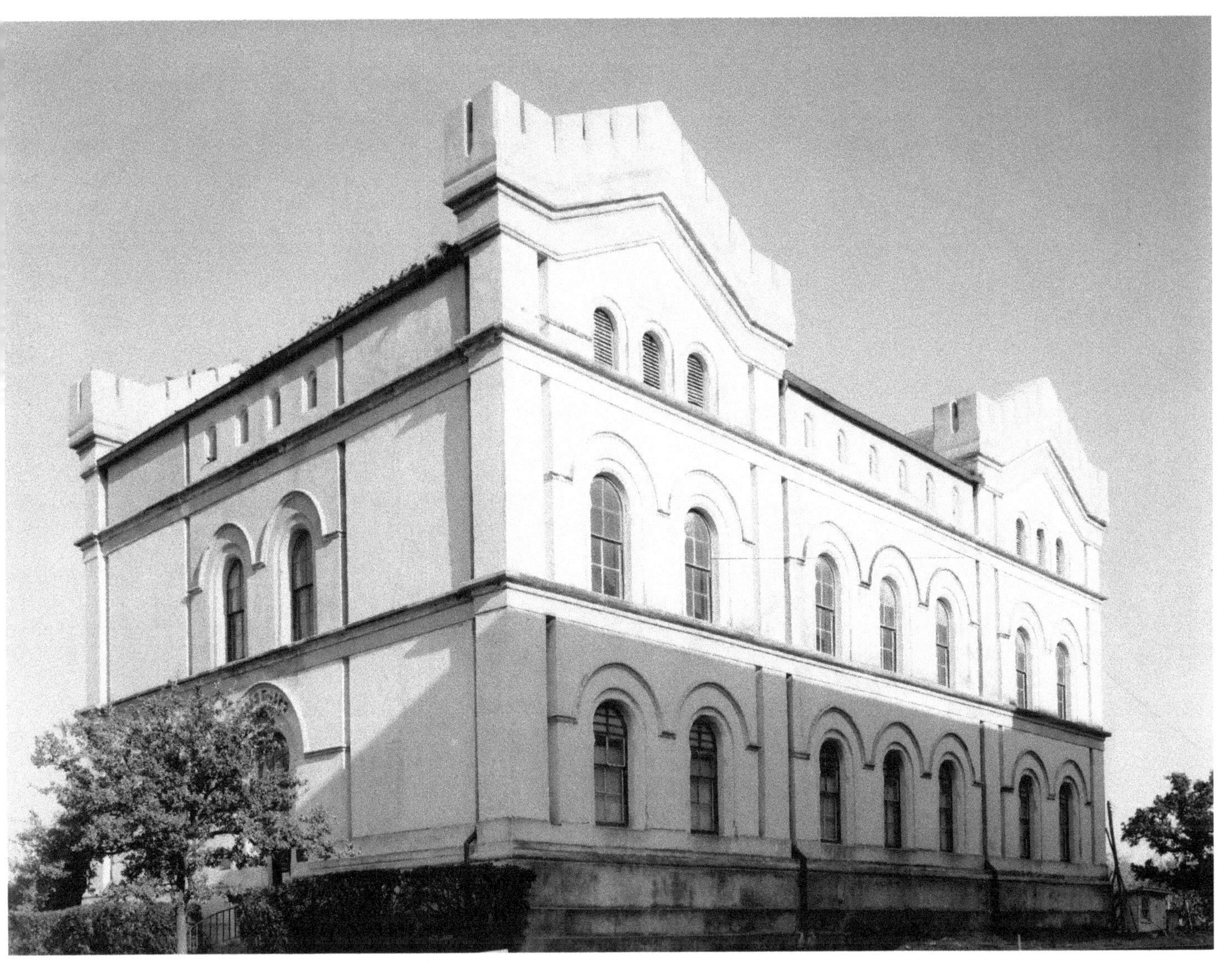

The General Land Office, completed in 1857, stands on the Capitol grounds at 108 East Eleventh Street. Designed by Conrad C. Stremme in the German Romanesque style, it is the oldest state office building still in use. William Sidney Porter (O. Henry) worked here as a draftsman. In 1918 it became a museum run by the Daughters of the Republic of Texas and the United Daughters of the Confederacy, Texas Division.

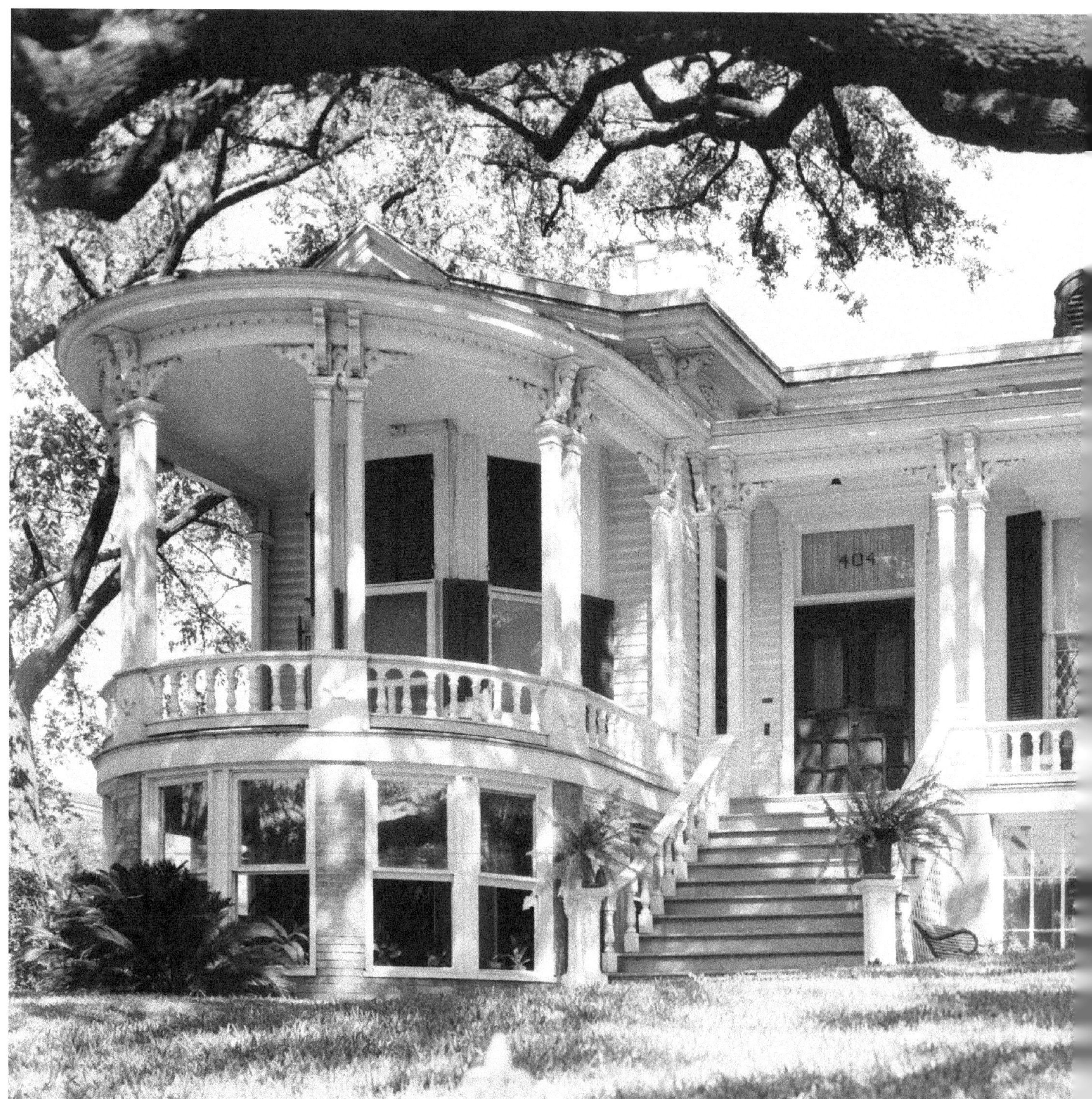
404

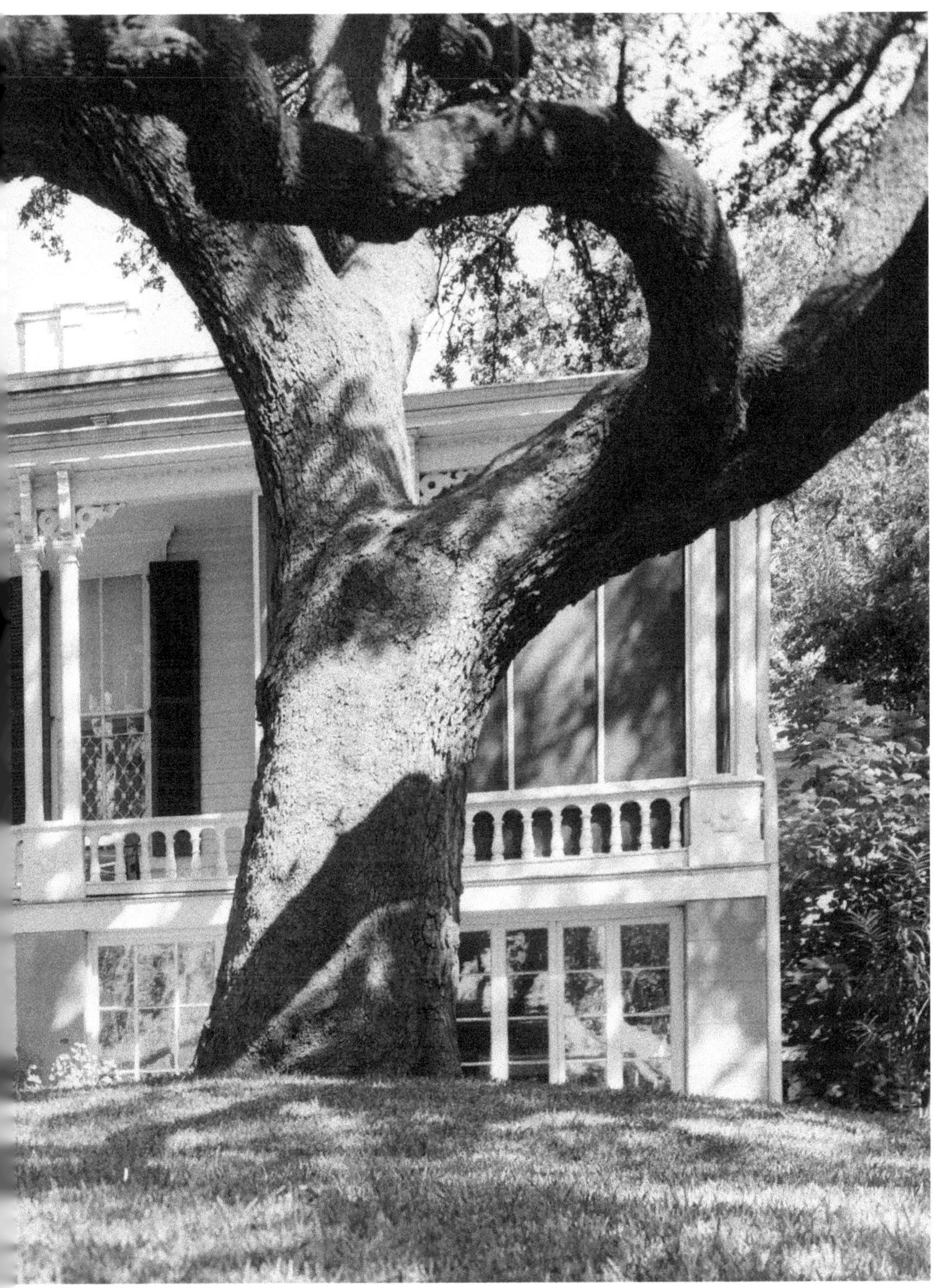

The Eugene Bremond House, 404 West Seventh Street, was the first home built in what is now the Bremond Block Historic District, developed by the Bremond and Robinson families from the 1860s through the 1890s. Designed by local contractor George Fiegel, the Victorian house with a raised basement features surrounding porches ornamented with pairs of slender square columns. Eugene Bremond was a prominent Austin banker.

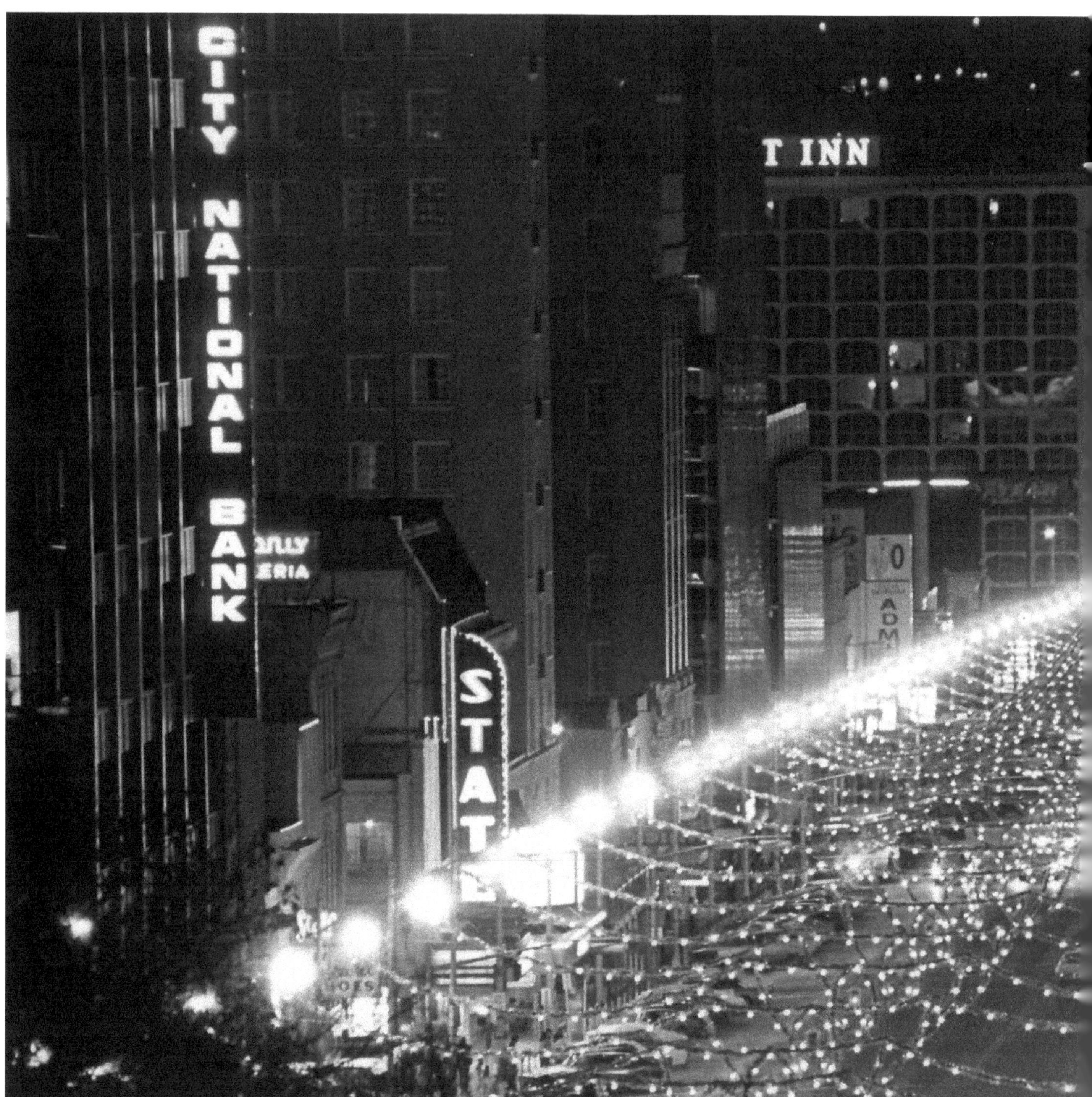
CITY NATIONAL BANK
T INN
STAT

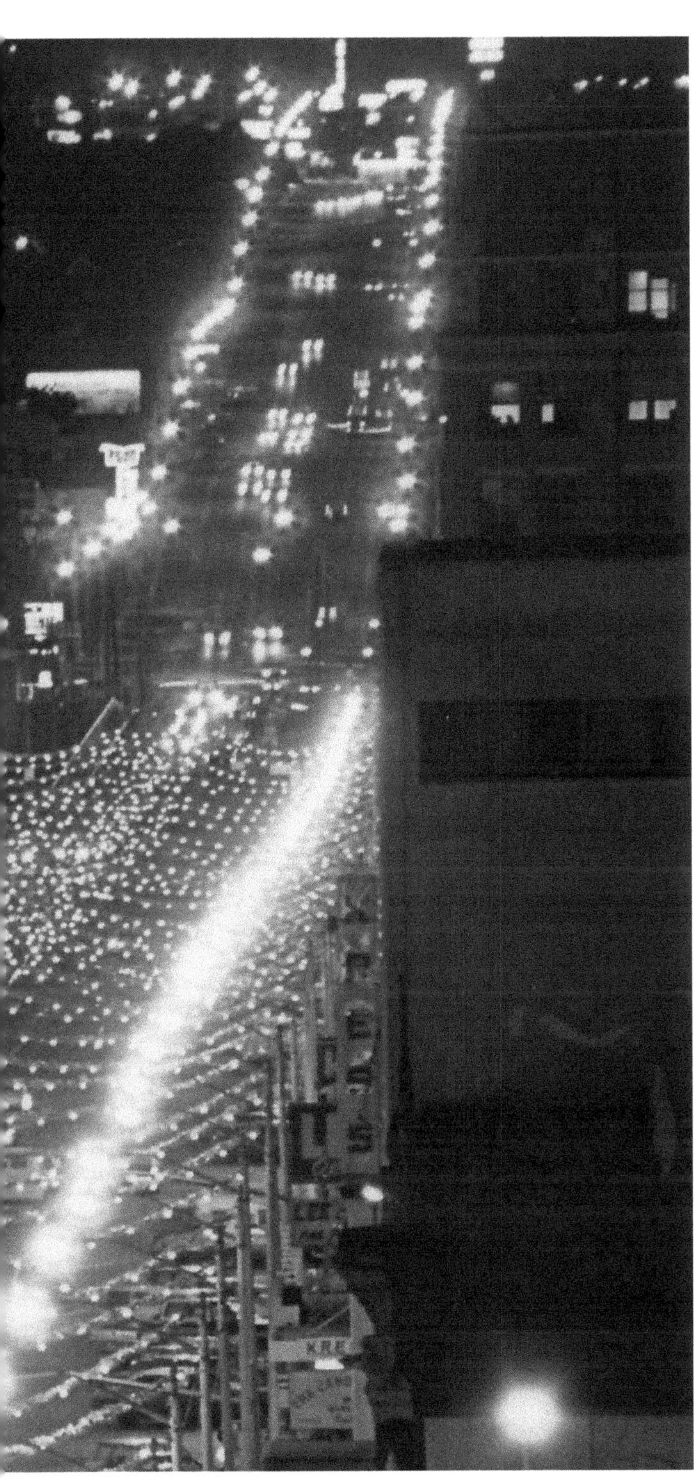

Congress Avenue is always decorated for the holidays. This nighttime photograph looking south toward the river shows the avenue covered in a blaze of lights in the 1960s.

Notes on the Photographs

These notes, listed by page number, attempt to include all aspects known of the photographs. Each of the photographs is identified by the page number, photograph's title or description, photographer and collection, archive, and call or box number when applicable. Although every attempt was made to collect all available data, in some cases complete data was unavailable due to the age and condition of some of the photographs and records.

II **Post office**
1932/5-191
Texas State Library & Archives Commission

VI **The Ben Hur**
PICA 13016
Austin History Center

X **Judge Edwin Waller**
PICA 10960
Austin History Center

2 **First Permanent Capitol**
PICA 20630
Austin History Center

3 **Congress Avenue**
PICA 02442
Austin History Center

4 **Hook and Ladder Company**
1932/5-163
Texas State Library & Archives Commission

5 **State Lunatic Asylum**
PICA 04382
Austin History Center

6 **Corner of Pecan and Brazos**
1932/5-29
Texas State Library & Archives Commission

7 **Wesley Chapel Methodist Episcopal Church**
1932/5-189
Texas State Library & Archives Commission

8 **Tightrope Walker Across Congress Avenue**
1932/5-28
Texas State Library & Archives Commission

9 **Frame Buildings on Pecan Street**
PICA 26344
Austin History Center

10 **Democratic Statesman**
C 00125
Austin History Center

12 **Pontoon Bridge**
C 01694
Austin History Center

13 **First Bale of Cotton Shipped by Rail**
PICA 04660
Austin History Center

14 Austin Graded School
PICA 07111
Austin History Center

15 Travis County Courthouse
1932/5-195
Texas State Library & Archives Commission

16 Kluge's Saloon
1932/5-44
Texas State Library & Archives Commission

17 Pecan Street in 1879
PICA 01977
Austin History Center

18 Public Hospital
C 00053
Austin History Center

19 Workers with Statue of Goddess
1989/90-1
Texas State Library & Archives Commission

20 Jessie Andrews
PICB 07908
Austin History Center

21 Old Main
CO 6713
Austin History Center

22 Temple Beth Israel
C 01281
Austin History Center

23 Market Center of Pecan Street
1932/5-117
Texas State Library & Archives Commission

24 Swante Palm House
1932/5-33
Texas State Library & Archives Commission

25 Corporation Bridge
1932/5-186
Texas State Library & Archives Commission

26 Capitol Dedication
PICA 03075
Austin History Center

27 View on Congress Avenue
PICA 18625
Austin History Center

28 Texas Capitol
PICA 27295
Austin History Center

29 View Looking South from Capitol Dome
PICA 19498
Austin History Center

30 Southwest View from Capitol Dome
PICA 01092
Austin History Center

31 Looking East from Capitol Dome
PICA 01096
Austin History Center

32 Looking West from Capitol Dome
PICA 01100
Austin History Center

33 Congress Avenue in Early 1890s
CO 0027
Austin History Center

34 Archway Across Congress Avenue
1932/5-80
Texas State Library & Archives Commission

35 Hyde Park
PICA 14480
Austin History Center

36 Racetrack at Hyde Park
1932/5-3
Texas State Library & Archives Commission

38 Gem Lake
PICA 02642
Austin History Center

39 Porcelain Tubs Arrive
PICA 02909
Austin History Center

40 Early Racecar
PICA 25622
Austin History Center

41 Austin National Bank
PICA 02864
Austin History Center

42 First National Bank
1932/5-190
Texas State Library & Archives Commission

43 Men Laying Streetcar Tracks
PICA 02460
Austin History Center

44 Hyde Park Transit Pavilion
CO 1092
Austin History Center

45 O. Henry's Home
CO 1717
Austin History Center

46 Construction of Austin Dam
PICA 13076
Austin History Center

47 University of Texas Football
PICA 19720
Austin History Center

48 Streetcar Number 15
PICA 10571
Austin History Center

49 Fulton's Ice Cream Parlor
CO 01086
Austin History Center

50 Circus parade
PICA 03009
Austin History Center

51 Excursion Car
CO 0732
Austin History Center

52 Governor's Guard
PICA 06602
Austin History Center

53 Texas Volunteer Guard Troops
PICA 06993
Austin History Center

54 Golfing
PICA 06789
Austin History Center

55 Barbershop in East Austin
PICA 13518
Austin History Center

56 Union Depot
PICA 02530
Austin History Center

57 Silver King Saloon
PICA 20951
Austin History Center

58 Zilker Park
PICA 20150
Austin History Center

60 Thorp House
PICB 13479
Austin History Center

61 The Crescent
PICA 25953
Austin History Center

62 Congress Avenue
CO 0285
Austin History Center

64 Emancipation Day
PICA 05476
Austin History Center

65 Meeting the train
PICA 18446
Austin History Center

66 Dam collapse Flooding
PICA 03994
Austin History Center

67 1900 Flood
PICA 01979
Austin History Center

68 Transportation on Sixth Street
CO 0625
Austin History Center

69 Paving Congress Avenue
C 00606
Austin History Center

70 University of Texas Women's Basketball Team
PICA 19187
Austin History Center

71 President McKinley's Visit
1932/5-4, 5, 6, and 7
Texas State Library & Archives Commission

72 President Theodore Roosevelt Speaking to Austinites
PICA 17440
Austin History Center

73 Eleventh Street
PICA 04776
Austin History Center

74 Guadalupe School
PICA 25921
Austin History Center

75 Reasonover's Central Barber Shop
PICA 18518
Austin History Center

76 Construction of Austin Depot
PICA 17083
Austin History Center

77 Elisabet Ney's Studio
PICA 17540
Austin History Center

78 Wooldridge Park
C 06049
Austin History Center

80 Construction of Concrete Bridge Across Colorado River
PICA 13968
Austin History Center

81 Majestic Theater
CO 2068
Austin History Center

82 Horse-drawn Hearse
PICA 08882
Austin History Center

83 Travis County Jail
CO 0610
Austin History Center

84 Lawmen on Horseback
PICA 18342
Austin History Center

85 Police Group Photo
PICA 01425
Austin History Center

86 Policemen on motorbike
PICA 01403
Austin History Center

88 Aerial view of Statehouse
CO 0616
Austin History Center

89 Governor Oscar Branch Colquitt
CO 0311
Austin History Center

90 Millinery Shop
PICA 15505
Austin History Center

91 Speedway Saloon
PICB 12557
Austin History Center

92 Young Men's Business League
CO 0014
Austin History Center

93 Pressmen at Statesman Office
1932/5 -17
Texas State Library & Archives Commission

94 Newsie
Library of Congress photo

95 Officer Kelley
C 00650
Austin History Center

96 Laguna Gloria
C 01564
Austin History Center

97 Deep Eddy
C 01786
Austin History Center

98 Telephone Operators
CO 3142
Austin History Center

99 World War I Doughboys
PICA 03334
Austin History Center

100 Penn Field Under Construction
PICA 18500
Austin History Center

101 Penn Field
PICA 19213
Austin History Center

102 War Signs
C11060
Austin History Center

103 Labor Day Float
PICA 10984
Austin History Center

104 Victory Parade
CO 0261
Austin History Center

105 Austin Women Register to Vote
PICA 11669
Austin History Center

106 Bryan's Boys
PICA 07048
Austin History Center

107 Tobin's Book Store
CO 5670
Austin History Center

108 Eustacio Cepeda
PICB 19452
Austin History Center

110 Paramount Theater
PICA 18224
Austin History Center

111 Projectionists at Paramount Theater
CO 6825
Austin History Center

112 Exterior of Paramount Theater
CO 1138
Austin History Center

113 Terry's Texas Rangers
CO 4897
Austin History Center

114 Texas Confederate Home
CO 3676
Austin History Center

115 Crockett Produce Company
CO 6333
Austin History Center

116 Will Rogers
CO 9944
Austin History Center

117 Tornado over Capitol
PICA 00406
Austin History Center

118 O. O. Norwood Estate
PICA 06754
Austin History Center

119 Street Railway Company Dinner
PICA 24857
Austin History Center

120 Baker School Students
PICA 25404
Austin History Center

121 Austin Fire Department
PICA 02859
Austin History Center

122 Battle Hall
PICA 20492
Austin History Center

123 Prohibition Seizure
PICA 29216
Austin History Center

124 Stephen F. Austin Hotel
CO 8993
Austin History Center

125 Memorial Stadium
C09993b
Austin History Center

126 Streetcar Derailment
CO 0598
Austin History Center

127 Grocery Store on East Forty-third
PICA 25623
Austin History Center

128 President Calvin Coolidge
PICA 07057
Austin History Center

129 South Austin Drugstore
PICA 15160
Austin History Center

130 World's Largest Tire
CO 6616
Austin History Center

131 Ladies' Auxiliary to the Carpenters
CO8678
Austin History Center

132 Norwood Building
PICA 00344
Austin History Center

133 Congress Avenue in the Late 1920s
CO 0645
Austin History Center

134 Travis County 4H Club Parade
CO 8690
Austin History Center

135 Municipal Airport
PICA 03771
Austin History Center

136 Fire Station Number Nine
CO 3254
Austin History Center

138 Eleanor Roosevelt
PICA 07070
Austin History Center

139 Hirsh's Drug
CO 0666
Austin History Center

140 Inauguration Parade
CO 0620
Austin History Center

141 Party at Austin Country Club
CO 7796
Austin History Center

142 **Austin National Bank**
PICA 02726
Austin History Center

143 **Night Hawk Restaurant**
PICA 28695
Austin History Center

144 **Texaco Station**
C11292
Austin History Center

145 **Eastwoods Park**
CO 1779
Austin History Center

146 **Sally Rand**
CO 2862
Austin History Center

147 **Varsity Theater**
PICA 06734
Austin History Center

148 **Parade Truck**
PICA 33279
Austin History Center

149 **Flood of 1935**
CO 8484-A
Austin History Center

150 **President Franklin D. Roosevelt**
PICA 25665
Austin History Center

151 **Sallie Wroe**
LOT 13262-7, no.184 (P&P)]
Library of Congress

152 **University of Texas Administration Building**
PICA 07782
Austin History Center

153 **Golden Gloves Match**
PICA 23531
Austin History Center

154 **Santa Rita Apartments**
PICA 02722
Austin History Center

155 **Last Streetcar Ride**
CO 0056 Austin History Center

156 **Littlefield Building**
PICA 01993 Austin History Center

157 **City Book Store**
1932/5-19 Texas State Library & Archives Commission

158 **Governor's Mansion**
HABS No. TEX-3304
Library of Congress

159 **Sneed House**
HABS No. TEX-399
Library of Congress

160 **French Legation**
HABS No. TEX-227-AUST-1
Library of Congress

161 **Townsend House**
HABS No. TEX-3141
Library of Congress

162 **Pease Mansion**
ABS No. TEX-330
Library of Congress

163 **Lundberg Bakery**
HABS No.TEX-3267-1
Library of Congress

164 **Scarbrough's Department Store**
CO 3182
Austin History Center

166 **WAC Members at Camp Mabry**
PICA 28622
Austin History Center

167 **Merrill Lynch, Pierce, Fenner & Smith**
CO 5823
Austin History Center

168 **Victory Celebration**
CO 1597
Austin History Center

169 **Senate Candidate Lyndon B. Johnson**
Lyndon Baines Johnson Library and Museum

170 **Police Department Picnic**
CA 30625
Austin History Center

171 **Chief Drive-In Theater**
PICA 27706
Austin History Center

172 **President Harry Truman**
AS 60-29087-1
Austin History Center

173 **Gulf Station**
CO 6348
Austin History Center

174 **Congress Avenue in Postwar Years**
CO 0581
Austin History Center

175 **University of Texas Football**
C10110
Austin History Center

176 **President John F. Kennedy**
AS 60-2876
Austin History Center

177 **Gregory Peck**
PICA 16276
Austin History Center

178 **House House**
PICA 03293
Austin History Center

179 **Oriental Gardens**
AAS 74038B
Austin History Center

180 **Isamu Taniguchi**
AAS75208A
Austin History Center

181 **Town Lake**
PICA 09283
Austin History Center

182 **Lyndon Baines Johnson Library and Museum**
Lyndon Baines Johnson Library and Museum

184 **Butler House**
PICA 00630
Austin History Center

185 **Hunnicutt House**
PICA 06614
Austin History Center

186 **John Bremond House**
HABS No. TEX-3140
Library of Congress

188 **Willie Nelson**
PICA 14619
Austin History Center

189 **Houghton House**
HABS No. TEX-3264
Library of Congress

190 **Carrington-Covert House**
HABS No. TEX-3228-2
Library of Congress

191 **General Land Office**
HABS No. TEX-397
Library of Congress

192 **Eugene Bremond House**
HABS No. TEX-3143
Library of Congress

194 **Congress Avenue at Christmas**
PICA 10595
Austin History Center

204 **Treaty Oak**
PICA 06970
Austin History Center

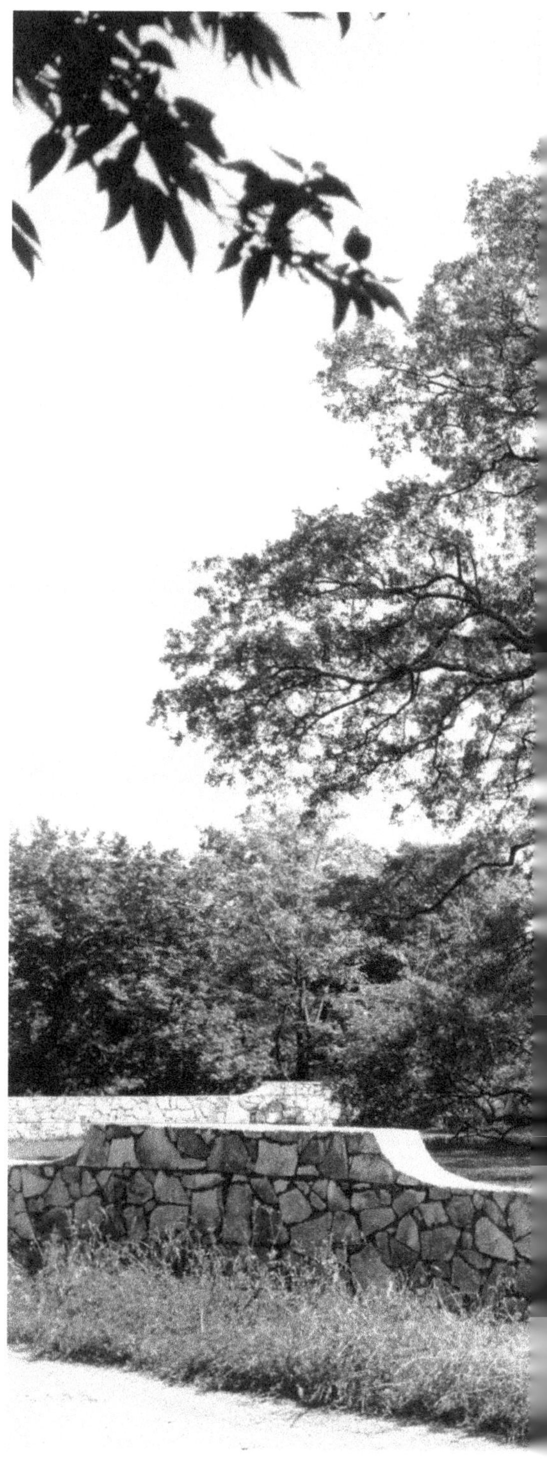

Treaty Oak—so named because Stephen F. Austin reputedly signed a treaty with Native Americans beneath it—is about 500 years old. It graced land owned by the W.H. Caldwells until 1937, when the city purchased it. Today the once-mighty live-oak tree stands in a tiny city park. Its branches once spanned 128 feet, but because it was maliciously poisoned in 1989, Treaty Oak is now only about a quarter of its former size.

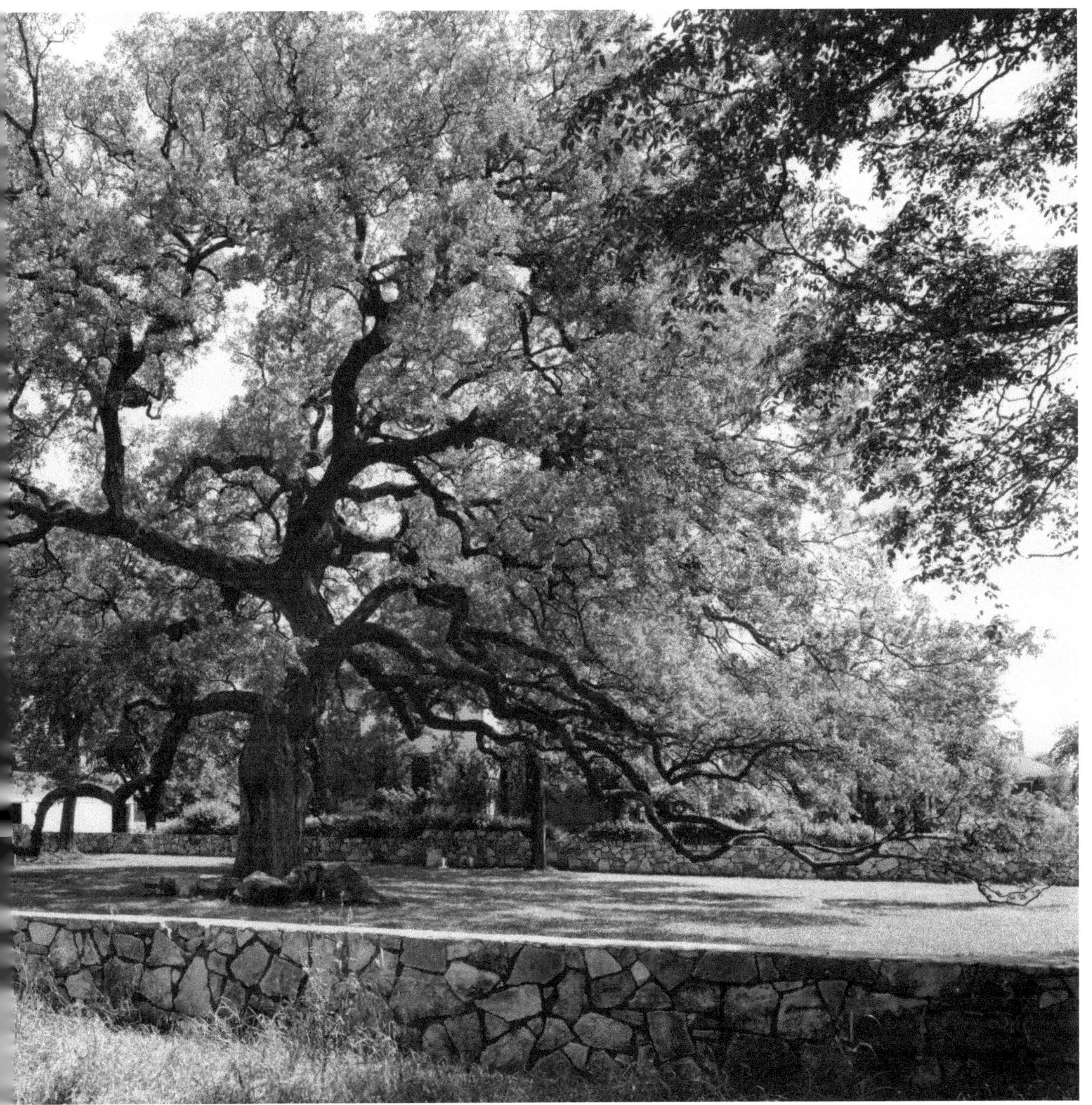

HISTORIC PHOTOS OF
AUSTIN

Nestled among the slopes of Central Texas Hill Country, Austin has grown from its frontier beginning to earn nationwide renown as a leader in arts, business, and government. Four wars and urban redevelopment have repeatedly altered the city's landscape and culture. Through its changes, Austin has endured and prospered through the persistence and innovation of its civic leaders.

This volume, *Historic Photos of Austin,* captures the journey in still photography collected from the finest archives. The book follows life, government, education, and events spanning two centuries of Austin's history. It captures unique and rare scenes as depicted in nearly 200 historic photographs. Published in striking black and white, the images portray the events and people important to Austin's history.

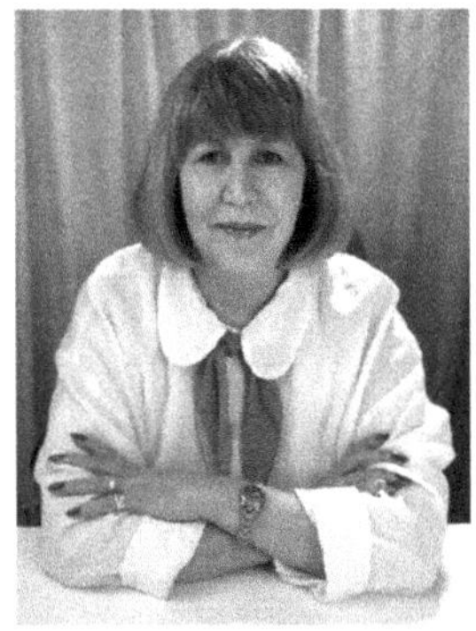

A native Texan and descendant of Sam Houston, MARSIA HART REESE became an Austinite in 1979. Having graduated from Southern Methodist University with a bachelor's degree in English, she began professional writing and editing in 1980, when she joined the staff of the monthly magazine *Austin Homes & Gardens.* As its editor and a major feature writer, Ms. Reese was introduced to Austin's history while covering many of its historic landmarks, being welcomed into some of its finest homes, and profiling many of its talented and admired citizens. In 1987 she received the annual Press Award from the Austin Chapter of the National Society of Interior Designers. In the late 1980s and early 1990s, she edited textbooks on American and Texas history for Holt, Rinehart & Winston, where her appreciation for the past further deepened. As a freelance writer and editor since 1995, she has enjoyed opportunities to explore diverse subjects, including modern dance, herpetology, and antiques. She also tutors Asian students in English and makes her home near Austin's thriving downtown.

WWW.TURNERPUBLISHING.COM

www.ingramcontent.com/pod-product-compliance
Lightning Source LLC
LaVergne TN
LVHW060603110826
845154LV00003B/32

* 9 7 8 1 6 8 3 3 6 9 2 1 9 *